A Russian Psyche

A RUSSIAN PSYCHE

The Poetic Mind of Marina Tsvetaeva

Alyssa W. Dinega

THE UNIVERSITY OF WISCONSIN PRESS

The University of Wisconsin Press
1930 Monroe Street
Madison, Wisconsin 53711

www.wisc.edu/wisconsinpress/

3 Henrietta Street
London WC2E 8LU, England

Copyright © 2001
The Board of Regents of the University of Wisconsin System
All rights reserved

5   4   3   2   1

Printed in the United States of America

Library of Congress Cataloging-in-Publication Data
Dinega, Alyssa W.
  A Russian psyche : the poetic mind of Marina =EBT=ECSvetaeva / Alyssa W. Dinega.
     304 pp.   cm.
  Includes bibliographical references and index.
  ISBN 0-299-17330-5 (cloth: alk. paper)
  ISBN 0-299-17334-8 (pbk.)
  1. =EBT=ECSvetaeva, Marina, 1892–1941—Criticism and interpretation.
  2. Cupid and Psyche (Tale) in literature.   I. Title.
  PG3476.T75 Z636   2001
  891.71'42—dc21   2001001945

This book is made possible in part by a subsidy from the Institute
for Scholarship in the Liberal Arts, College of Arts and Letters,
University of Notre Dame.

For my own two tiny male muses,
Anton and Kirill

And for Evan, who is real at last

Can a unity (any whatsoever) really give a sum? A foreign essence. A different division of atoms. A transcendent truth cannot be broken up into particles able merely to exist.
—Marina Tsvetaeva, letter to Boris Pasternak, 10 July 1926

In another human being only the forehead and some of the chest cavity belong to me. I relinquish the heart easily, I won't relinquish the chest. I need an echo chamber. The heart rings hollow.
—Marina Tsvetaeva, letter to Rainer Maria Rilke, 14 August 1926

> I fear me this—is Loneliness—
> The Maker of the soul
> —Emily Dickinson, "The Loneliness One dare not sound . . ."

Contents

Preface	xi
Acknowledgments	xv
Introduction: Walking the Poetic Tightrope	3
1. Battling Blok and Akhmatova: In Pursuit of a Muse	35
2. Conjuring Pasternak: A Divided Psyche	90
3. Losing Rilke: The Dark Lure of Mra	129
4. Ruing Young Orphans: The End of the Line	177
Postscript	226
Notes	233
Index	277

Preface

When I first encountered Marina Tsvetaeva a decade ago, I was a new college graduate studying for a semester in Soviet Moscow, entirely unsure what I wanted to "become" once I departed that magical, compelling never-never land. I remember my meeting with Tsvetaeva clearly: sitting in a friend's dingy dormitory room at Moscow State University, I looked down at the open book he proffered. No matter that the room was drenched in chilly winter darkness, lit only by a feeble lamp; no matter that my Russian was still halting, or that Cyrillic characters clustered densely on a page still had a tendency to jump and dance before my eyes instead of resolving themselves smoothly into meaningful words and thoughts. Tsvetaeva's poem "Gypsy passion for parting" ["Tsyganskaia strast' razluki"] went unfalteringly straight to my heart with its boldness, its courage, its exactitude, and its music. Sparks flew; a blinding stroke of lightning seemed to illuminate that dim mousehole of a room; and, to borrow an image from Tsvetaeva herself (who had borrowed it from Maiakovskii), a fire began to smolder in my soul.

Or perhaps it was not quite like this; perhaps it is this way only in memory. In any case, Tsvetaeva has been with me from that point on like an incurable fever. The first poem of hers that I read that evening proved to be oddly fateful:

> Цыганская страсть разлуки!
> Чуть встретишь — уж рвешься прочь!
> Я лоб уронила в руки,
> И думаю, глядя в ночь:
>
> Никто, в наших письмах роясь,
> Не понял до глубины,
> Как мы вероломны, то есть —
> Как сами себе верны.

[Gypsy passion for parting! You've just met — already you tear yourself away! I cup my forehead in my hands and think, gazing into the night: No one who riffled through our letters could understand to the core how treacherous we are, meaning — how faithful to ourselves.]

In this poem of 1915 is contained, as it were, the kernel of my book. Here is the essence of Tsvetaeva's poetic myth, which, though it modulates over time, never loses its basic features: namely, her oxymoronic "passion for parting," and the epistolary renunciation of love that passion occasions, through which the mysterious self of the poet comes into being like a phoenix rising from the ash of incinerated dreams. These mythopoetic patterns, as I will argue, form the basis for Tsvetaeva's creative imagination throughout her life. In "Gypsy passion," too, is the quintessence of Tsvetaeva's craft: her exquisitely wrought stanzaic forms, telegraphic style, unorthodox rhymes, and, permeating it all, her powerfully syncopated rhythms. Such craft balances out her paradoxical passion and belies interpretations of Tsvetaeva as an undisciplined Romantic. She herself claimed the eighteenth-century poet Derzhavin as one of her most important influences; indeed, there is a classical rigor to Tsvetaeva's poetic forms, even as her myth making is informed by a remarkably complex and consistent—albeit idiosyncratic—rigor of thought.

This book is an investigation into these rigorous patterns of thought and form that both held Tsvetaeva in their thrall and liberated her creative imagination. Truly, Tsvetaeva's poetic activity—which, especially during the years of her emigration (1922–39), she experienced as a release from the drudgery of housework and daily life—appears strangely like a kind of spiritual servitude. Her work ethic is awesome and inspiring. Living at times in the most appalling conditions of poverty, with two small children and an ailing and unreliable husband to care for, she nevertheless rose before dawn each day to write for several hours before the rest of her household began stirring. In this way, she managed to churn out with astonishing rapidity masterpiece after poetic masterpiece through the years. Counterintuitive as it seems, Tsvetaeva thrived in conditions of adversity. Her temperament was such that she enjoyed the challenge; as she herself once wrote, her constitution was one of "monstrous endurance" (6:153).[1] This phrase is fantastically apt as an expression of Tsvetaeva's unique blend of courage and chutzpah. Just as the key to her poetic genesis is the coexistence of two contradictory stimuli—passion and renunciation—so, too, the key to her poetic energy is this seemingly unrealizable confluence of ferocity and forbearance.

In writing this book, I have often envied Tsvetaeva's remarkable creative vitality. The image of her stationed at her desk—elbows as though implanted in the wooden surface, forehead in hands, fingers drumming, pen scratching, her total immersion in the music and patterns of her words—has often been in my mind as I have struggled at times to sustain a state of concentration and inspiration resembling Tsvetaeva's own tenacity of artistic purpose. The fact is that such a feat is impossible; Tsvetaeva's poetic generosity, her full absorption in her poetic world no matter what events were transpiring in the world around her, is inimitable. Nor do I pretend to exhaust the richness of Tsvetaeva's

Preface

poetic thought which, like the product of all truly brilliant minds, is inexhaustible. Nevertheless, I hope I succeed in this book in illuminating the contours of Tsvetaeva's complex — and, I will admit it, sometimes dauntingly difficult — poetry in new ways, independent of preconceived notions or theories. If Tsvetaeva comes alive again in all her perplexing paradoxicality in the pages of this book, then my purpose is accomplished.

Acknowledgments

This is an exciting time in Tsvetaeva scholarship; nearly 110 years since the poet's birth, the study of her works, long delayed by official disfavor and prejudices of various kinds, is belatedly coming of age at last. I am thrilled and honored that my own book is a participant in this explosion of serious Tsvetaeva scholarship; at the same time, my study is deeply indebted to the perceptive and provocative insights into Tsvetaeva's poetry on the part of earlier scholars too numerous to name.

This book has profited from the financial support of a number of different organizations. My research was assisted by a grant from the Eurasia Program of the Social Science Research Council with funds provided by the State Department under the Program for Research and Training on Eastern Europe and the Independent States of the Former Soviet Union (Title VIII), as well as by a Foreign Language and Area Studies Graduate Fellowship and a Detling Fellowship from the University of Wisconsin–Madison during earlier stages of the project. I am also grateful to the Institute for Scholarship in the Liberal Arts at the University of Notre Dame for a generous subvention grant to the University of Wisconsin Press, which helped to underwrite the cost of this book's publication.

My literature professors during my undergraduate years at Brandeis University helped to shape my thinking about writing and inspired me to follow in their academic footsteps; Allen Grossman, Karen Klein, Alan Levitan, Paul Morrison, and Robert Szulkin each left a particularly vivid imprint on my mind. My tireless college Russian teacher, Inna Broude, first introduced me to the beauties of Russian as a poetic language. What knowledge I have of Russian literature is thanks, first and foremost, to the generously shared expertise of my graduate professors at the University of Wisconsin–Madison; their excellence has been an inspiration to me, and their encouragement of my work has been a stimulus over the years. In particular, I am thankful to the members of my dissertation committee—David Bethea, Yuri Shcheglov, Judith Kornblatt, Gary Rosenshield, and Cyrena Pondrom—whose thoughtful comments have guided me during the process of transforming my dissertation into this book.

In this book, all translations from the original German or Russian are my own unless noted otherwise. Citations from prose are given only in English translation (with occasional interpolations of fragments from the original text given in brackets whenever necessary); citations from poetry are given both in the original language and with accompanying English translation. I make no attempt to reproduce the poetic qualities of the original (rhythm, rhyme, soundplay, etc.); rather, my translations are straight prose renderings of the texts' meanings on the most fundamental level and, as such, are best used as a comprehension aid in tandem with a careful reading of the original. Although I take full responsibility for any inaccuracies in my translations, their quality has been enhanced by two careful proofreaders: Yuri Shcheglov read the translations from Russian of Tsvetaeva's poetry, while Jan Lüder Hagens read the translations from German of Tsvetaeva's and Rilke's writings cited in chapter 3. I was fortunate to have the benefit of these scholars' meticulous attention to detail and nuance.

A number of people have read and commented helpfully on parts of my manuscript or, more generally, on my approach to Tsvetaeva at various stages; these include David Bethea, Clare Cavanagh, Catherine Ciepiela, Caryl Emerson, Sibelan Forrester, Olga Peters Hasty, Stephanie Sandler, David Sloane, Alexandra Smith, Susan St. Ville, and David Woodruff. In particular, Stephanie Sandler and Caryl Emerson, manuscript readers for the University of Wisconsin Press, far exceeded the call of duty and responded eloquently to my manuscript with pages and pages of clear-sighted reaction, queries, and suggestions for revision. It is largely thanks to their efforts that I have managed during the past months to tug and coax my unkempt dissertation into what I hope is a fully groomed and polished book. I also thank Catherine Ciepiela for sharing with me a chapter of her work in progress, which helped me greatly in formulating my own discussion of Tsvetaeva's "On a Red Steed" in chapter 1. Throughout the final stages of work on this manuscript, my colleagues at the University of Notre Dame have provided companionship and an environment conducive to concentrated work and writing. My student aide, Andrea Shatzel, has assisted with last-minute editing tasks.

This study could not have been written without the continuing wise counsel, moral support, and unstinting scholarly generosity of David Bethea, my Ph.D. dissertation advisor and former interim director of the University of Wisconsin Press, whose rare blend of intellectual probity and poetic enthusiasm has been a beacon to me from the earliest stages of this project. I thank him with all my heart for his passion for literature, his ability to energize and provoke me, his good humor under fire, and his faith in me during the darkest times.

Finally, I am grateful to my family for helping me to become the person that I am today. My parents' confidence in me throughout the years has allowed me to persevere in this and other pursuits. My twin sons are the guiding light behind this book; in their four short years, they have taught me more than I could ever have anticipated about self-discipline, commitment, and unconditional love. My beloved husband is for me a source of ceaseless wonder, warmth, and inspiration; he is, too, the facilitator par excellence who has made this adventure in life and poetry possible.

A Russian Psyche

Introduction
Walking the Poetic Tightrope

Что, голубчик, дрожат поджилки?
Все как надо: канат — носилки.
Разлетается в ладан сизый
Материнская антреприза.

[What, my little dove, do your knees tremble? Everything is as it should be: the tightrope — the stretcher. The maternal enterprise scatters into the gray mist of incense.]
— "Ni krovinki v tebe zdorovoi . . ." (1919)

Там, на тугом канате,
Между картонных скал,
Ты ль это как лунатик
Приступом небо брал? . . .
Помню сухой и жуткий
Смех — из последних жил!
Только тогда — как будто —
Юбочку ты носил.

[There, on the taut tightrope, between the cardboard cliffs, was it you who like a sleepwalker took the sky by storm? . . . I remember dry and terrible laughter — on the brink of exhaustion! Only then — it was as if — you wore a skirt.]
— "Tam, na tugom kanate . . ." (1920)

Если б Орфей не сошел в Аид
Сам, а послал бы голос
Свой . . .
Эвридика бы по нему
Как по канату вышла . . .

[If Orpheus had not gone down to Hades himself, but had sent his own voice . . . Eurydice would have walked out along it as along a tightrope . . .]
— "Est′ schastlivtsy i schastlivitsy . . ." (1934)

What does it mean for a woman to be a great poet, an inspired poet, a tragic poet, a poet of genius? This is a deceptively simple query, and one whose conceivable multifarious answers go far beyond issues of gender to have implications for language, imagery, form, genre, aesthetics, mythopoetics, metaphysics, ethics, and so on. Indeed, feminist criticism has often found the category of "genius" to be inherently problematic, insofar as it derives from a Romantic mythology of the (implicitly) male poet and therefore prevents the inclusion of women in the literary canon.[1] Clearly, what is at issue is not the possibility in itself that a woman writer can exhibit brilliance; rather, the inspirational myths that attach to the male genius, visited by his female muse or what Robert Graves has called the "White Goddess," simply do not allow for the instance when "he" is a *girl*.[2]

Yet the apparent illogicality of the question of female genius has not prevented women writers from continuing to ask it, whether implicitly or explicitly, both in their poetry and in the enigmatic biographical "texts" of their lives. In the Russian tradition, I believe it is Marina Tsvetaeva who poses this question most daringly and compellingly. For, in contrast to the more docile Akhmatova — who is largely complicit in poetic voice and projected self-image with the cultural code of the "poetess,"[3] despite the unusual strength of her talent and tragedy of her life — Tsvetaeva leaves the confines of the persona of poetess far behind. Instead, she devotes her entire life and creative opus to a ceaseless hunt for some viable resolution to the riddle of how a woman can attain the status of pure, ungendered, human greatness.

Gender is for Tsvetaeva a fundamentally negative concept. Much as she celebrates women's particular strengths and abilities, at base femininity for her is simply incommensurate with poetry. There is an axiomatic disjunction between the two essences — feminine and poetic — that define her identity that she seems to have felt intuitively from the earliest age. It is precisely her gender that forges a wedge between the demands of poetry and the demands of life. Her gender is the prime factor in the equation of her being, the irreducible "x" that ordains that, however life and poetry are divided up, their domains can never coincide.[4] Yet, at the same time, she can never bring herself to embrace either to the exclusion of the other — for life (even frustrated attempts at "life") is the fodder of poetry; whereas without poetry, life would be suffocating.

This powerful split forms the basis of my present inquiry. My project is to trace Tsvetaeva's various solutions to this feminine poetic impasse. The reasons (political, sociological, cultural, psychological, literary-historical, biological, anatomical) for the split are not my primary interest here; I do not intend to argue it into or out of existence — it is simply there, informing everything Tsvetaeva ever thought, felt, or wrote. I ask why only in poetic terms, for this is the aspect of the question that interested Tsvetaeva. It might be said that all of her explorations of the gender question in her work are simultaneous attempts to qualify the "why" of this split perspective on reality and to try to provide a set of strategies to cope with it. That her dilemma is primarily a poetic rather than a social one can be seen from her tendency to work and rework a given aspect of the problem in a whole series or "cluster" of poems, which may or may not be grouped into a formal poetic cycle or collection. This creative method motivates my own interpretive approach: I analyze groups of texts centered on a common theme or problem and illustrate the progression of her thought as she broaches more or less satisfactory solutions in each successive piece of writing.

Tsvetaeva believes fully in a spiritual realm—accessible through the transcendence of artistic endeavor—in which gender difference disappears entirely along with the body itself. Furthermore, she adamantly rejects the essentialist view that women are fundamentally excluded from the realm of meaningful human discourse, including poetic craft and tradition. Yet, conversely, she never forgets that the material of artistic production is gleaned from the experiences of real life, in which sexual (physiological) and gender (psychosocial) differences are an indubitable reality. Thus, in the immediate, physical world, real women, herself included, must struggle to overcome the internalized limitations that threaten to deny them access to the transcendent, human beyond. We find that her divided loyalties lead, in the extreme case, to an irreparable disjunction between the sphere of human interaction on the one hand (in which the "default position" must be some form of morality or ethics) and the fantastical world of poetry on the other hand (in which the analogous "default position" tends toward the aesthetic dominant and in which the dangerous possibility of making words mean more than one thing at once, or even making them mean their opposite, is on the ascendant).

Tsvetaeva's stance on the gender question thus necessitates her execution of a perilous dance over the abyss. The recurrent motif in her work of the tightrope—always explicitly in connection with the female poetic predicament—vividly illustrates this impossibly acrobatic poetic posture. Her life is a daring, sometimes foolhardy and sometimes awe-inspiring walk across the tightrope of her poetry, a metaphysical balancing act with potentially grave costs and consequences. She treads a fine line in her verse between transgression and transcendence, between a feminine subversion and renovation of human and poetic norms and the ungendered attainment of the sublime that is, in the final analysis, indistinguishable from nonbeing. Indeed, she stakes out in her poetry an exhilarating and disturbing marginal position that has elicited no dearth of critical reaction equaling in the degree of its vehemence (whether laudatory or condemnatory) anything that she herself ever wrote.[5]

In my view, Tsvetaeva's writing has been received with such palpable enthusiasm or disapprobation precisely because it brings into relief the underlying assumptions of the literary tradition and, by extrapolation, of all human norms; it "poses the question of the partiality, that is, the sexualization of all knowledges. It entails an acknowledgment of the sexually particular positions from which knowledges emanate and by which they are interpreted and used."[6] However, for all Tsvetaeva's recent modishness in high theoretical circles,[7] this potent aspect of her poetics has largely gone unrecognized, overshadowed as it is by the allure of her dramatic and provocative biography.

After Tsvetaeva's death in 1941, her works were not published at all in the Soviet Union for fifteen years, and her poetic voice was all but forgotten, both in her own country and abroad. In the wake of her comparatively recent rediscovery in the 1960s and 1970s, it was natural that the first critical studies to emerge were devoted primarily to an establishment of the biographical and literary facts.[8] Yet the fascination with her life and personality has not subsided with time; rather, even in studies ostensibly devoted to her poetry, Tsvetaeva continues to be viewed primarily as a woman, and only secondarily as a writer. Certain preconceived notions about women's writing in general have often shaped critical discussions of her work, including the idea that her poetry "inscribes" images of the female body; the interpretation of her writing as a poetic journal, an unmediated expression of her true self and experiences; and the focus on her suicide as the unavoidable consequence of male sociolinguistic norms.[9]

In my own inquiry, on the contrary, I view Tsvetaeva consistently as a writer who is a woman, rather than as a woman who transparently writes her female experience.[10] Rather than imposing any external criteria on the study of her texts, I set out to examine the intrinsic significance of her gender within the world of her poetry. I investigate the role that gender plays in her poetic grappling with the fundamental questions of human existence, as well as in her continual testing of poetry's foundations, possibilities, and limitations. Thus, although in this book my central concern is the way in which Tsvetaeva's female gender "leaves its traces in literary texts and on literary history,"[11] my primary object is neither politics nor the formation of or adherence to a particular theoretical conviction. Instead, I am interested first and foremost in understanding the specifics of the poetic text that is not only female, but human.

Tsvetaeva chafed at being treated as a diminutively female poet [zhenskii poet], most notoriously in her account of an "Evening of Poetesses" organized by fellow poet Valerii Briusov; in her memoir of the evening, she writes: "There is no women's question in art: there are women's answers to the human question" (4:38). Clearly, the human body, and the female body in particular, provides a rich source of poetic metaphor in Tsvetaeva's work. Yet her body serves her as a writer, rather than the other way around; indeed, her poetry causes her body to metamorphose into a musical instrument: "The heart: more a musical organ than an anatomical one" [Serdtse: skoree orgán, chem órgan] (4:476).[12] Truly, for Tsvetaeva poetic language is "inherently fictive."[13] Through the transformative action of such poetic language, she strives to neutralize her female gender, as it were—and it is paradoxically for the purpose of this neutralization that she keeps her gender constantly in view.

Here, then, is the central thesis of this study, which explores how gender is manifested in Tsvetaeva's writing as this theme evolves dynamically, and often unpredictably, throughout her creative lifetime. Her poetic project, as I understand it, is to inject herself into the literary tradition that excludes her, through a poetic transformation of its mythological forms and structures. She does not simply reinscribe male writing; but nor does she remain on its frontier. Rather, she transforms poetic discourse, not imitatively but originally. She revamps tired and restrictive poetic conventions by means of a manipulation of sounds, images, and etymologies. Such a revision of poetic idiom is possible precisely because, for her, language—including poetic language—is not inherently sexist or phallic or patriarchal.[14] Instead, the forms that poetry has taken have historically been male centered, simply because men have, for the most part, been its authors. In other words, the mythological structures that situate poetry in the context of other human intellectual and artistic endeavors conventionally dictate the poet as a male. This dictate, however, may be modified. When Tsvetaeva appropriates traditional poetic forms and themes for her own poetic needs, she self-consciously illuminates, and subsequently forcibly erases, their hidden gender specificity.

The overt tragedy of Tsvetaeva's life notwithstanding, failure in her undertaking is not by any means a foregone conclusion; the sheer brilliance and abundance of her literary output denies any easy claim that she does, in fact, fail. Nor does she ever settle into the comfortable morass of victimhood, for she insists everywhere on her complete freedom, which implies her complete responsibility for the events of her life (thus, she never casts her poetic and personal struggles as the fault of men, society, poverty, history, Fascism, Stalinism, etc., even when the objective facts might seem to argue otherwise). She is almost obsessed with presenting herself as the sole creator of her own destiny; her compelling sense of personal responsibility bears testimony to her immense character and artistic stature. Truly, the tensions in her work are its strength rather than its weakness, because she always prefers potentiality over perfection or completion.[15] Therefore, when we speak of her search for a "resolution" to her feminine dilemma, the emphasis should be placed squarely on the verb rather than the noun. Were she really to find all the answers she needs, her poetry would lose its impetus. Even Tsvetaeva's suicide is not unambiguously tragic. Rather, when viewed as her final poetic act, her suicide seems in itself a fittingly brilliant, albeit deeply disturbing, culmination of her poetic path—her final statement in the dialectic between ethics and aesthetics that has engrossed her throughout her creative lifetime. Although it may represent her final exclusion from the masculine poetic domain, at the same time it also enacts her final entry into a unified poetic space where the soul floats freely, unimpeded by gender difference.

Tsvetaeva loved reading poets' lives forward into their deaths, discerning in the death a symbolic continuation of the poetic personality. Rather than the death's casting a long shadow backward over the poet's creative legacy, in a sense the opposite effect occurred: the poetry wrote the biography. Similarly, I advocate here an approach in which the events of Tsvetaeva's biography—often debatable and ultimately unknowable—are never primary epistemes, but are viewed rather as the raw material and by-products of her creativity. Her love affairs and infatuations, her experience of motherhood, her boisterous personality, her domestic drudgery, and yes, even her suicide are important to this inquiry only to the extent that they shape and, in turn, are shaped by her writing. Admittedly, it remains unclear what finally serves what: the poetry the life or the life the poetry. But this is unimportant, for it is the deep and satisfying poetic logic that Tsvetaeva applies to the events of her life that interests me, rather than the events in and of themselves. Her poetry, not her biography, is her true legacy, and so I read the events of her life through her poetry as if her poetic telling of them is the truth, the whole truth, and nothing but.

Whether or not we are to interpret Tsvetaeva's life in the final analysis as a tragedy or a triumph must remain a matter of individual inclination. In one sense, my readings of her work suggest that she was doomed by her female gender to inhabit a dangerously subversive role that could not but end in frustration and self-destruction. By contrast, however, it is the very limitations of her position that consistently constrain—and thereby structure, direct, generate—her poetry. Her attempts to find poetic strategies to resist the imagined consequences of her gender indeed constitute the whole substance of her life's work, and Tsvetaeva, in contemplating her situation, frequently shifts between buoyant optimism and darkest pessimism. Metaphorically speaking, the tightrope of the poetic line on which she balances so precariously is sometimes a deathtrap, although at other times it is the launching wire for a magical and virtuoso performance of flight into the beyond. What remains constant throughout is the fact that she, acrobat-like, shows herself to be tough, resourceful, absolutely self-aware, and always and entirely responsible for her own fate: a true hero, who seeks trials so as to be transfigured by working through them.

First Steps: Tsvetaeva as Drummer Boy

> Высоко несу свой высокий стан,
> Высоко несу свой высокий сан—
> Собеседницы и Наследницы!
>
> [I carry high my tall figure, I carry high my tall honors—of Interlocutress and Inheritress!]
> — "Chto drugim ne nuzhno—nesite mne . . ." (1918)

> Барабанщиком, видно, рожден!
>
> [Truly, he was born a drummer!]
> — "Moloko na gubakh ne obsokhlo . . ." (1918)

Walking the Poetic Tightrope

Amid the nostalgic cameos of early childhood memories that constitute the majority of poems in Tsvetaeva's first two published collections, *Evening Album* [*Vechernii al'bom,* 1910] and *The Magic Lantern* [*Volshebnyi fonar'*, 1912], can be found a surprising number of pieces that prefigure the themes and concerns of her mature work, albeit still in chrysalid form. In particular, the young Tsvetaeva already demonstrates a clear apprehension of the magnitude of her poetic calling and an intimation of the personal demands and sacrifices it will require. Coupled with these realizations is her consciousness of the "unfitness" of her gender to the life's work ahead of her, expressed in terms of her singular disjunction with expected norms—both poetic and human. In numerous poems, she explores from various standpoints different possibilities for structuring her life around these disjunctions and tests out each possible solution: what would be lost, what would be gained. These are adolescent poems, poems of searching for an identity that will satisfy her dreams and desires, vindicate her talents, and accomplish her fated destiny. Yet the fervor with which the young poet endorses conflicting, mutually irreconcilable life strategies in separate poems presages the strengths and the struggles of the mature poet. The "identity crisis" of which these poems tell is far more than simply a youthful rite of passage; its underlying causes and the various themes to which it gives rise in the early poetry will remain pertinent to her thinking about her identity as poet and as human being throughout her life.

In this section, I discuss five of Tsvetaeva's early poems that are concerned with the issue of her female gender and its implications for the future of her personal life and her poetry. From this analysis I derive the basic organizing ideas of my study as a whole: the fundamentally dichotomous world-view necessitated by Tsvetaeva's gender, her consequent inability to establish valid poetic subjectivity and her concomitant inability to forge a mutual relationship with any human other, and her search for some relief from the isolation to which this impasse gives rise through intertextual dialogue with another, imposing poetic presence.[16] Each of these ideas become clearer in the course of discussion.

I begin by observing that Tsvetaeva's earliest poems that address the relationship of her gender to her poetic and human destinies can be superficially divided into two categories. On the one hand are poems ("In the Luxembourg Garden" ["V Liuksemburgskom sadu"] [1:53]; "Only a Girl" ["Tol'ko devochka"] [1:143]) in which the poet appears to swallow her unorthodox, unfeminine aspirations and ambitions, swear off poetry, and embrace the usual female role that society has prepared for her (which she, in turn, claims to find fulfilling). On the other hand are poems ("A Prayer" ["Molitva"] [1:32]; "A Savage Will" ["Dikaia volia"] [1:136]) in which the poet transgresses the limitations of her gender in both the personal and metaphysical domains and embraces poetry to the very exclusion of life itself. I argue that a third option that she develops in her poem "The Drum" ["Baraban"] (1:146–47) is one of her first attempts to chart a realistic poetic role for herself in life. Thus, I show that her apparent self-contradictions are only superficial; in all the poems discussed here, whatever her stance, she is marked indelibly by her poetic destiny, although she also never fully relinquishes her appetite for life.

THE FEMALE ROLE CONFLICTED

"In the Luxembourg Garden," for all its seeming simplicity, gives a poignant expression of Tsvetaeva's divided loyalties—the result of her heightened awareness of language. The poem describes the idyllic scene of mothers walking in a public garden with their children. There is something pleasurable here for all the senses: the beauty and fragrance of flowering trees, the babbling of a fountain, the soothing cool of shadowy alleys:

> Склоняются низко цветущие ветки,
> Фонтана в бассейне лепечут струи,
> В тенистых аллеях всё детки, всё детки . . .
> О детки в траве, почему не мои?...
>
> Как будто на каждой головке коронка
> От взоров, детей стерегущих, любя.
> И матери каждой, что гладит ребенка,
> Мне хочется крикнуть: «Весь мир у тебя!»
>
> Как бабочки девочек платьица пестры,
> Здесь ссора, там хохот, там сборы домой...
> И шепчутся мамы, как нежные сестры:
> —«Подумайте, сын мой»...—«Да что вы! А мой»...
>
> Я женщин люблю, что в бою не робели,
> Умевших и шпагу держать, и копье,—
> Но знаю, что только в плену колыбели
> Обычное—женское—счастье мое!

[The blossoming branches bend down low, the streams of the fountain in the pool babble, in the shadowy alleys are children, and more children... O children in the grass, why are you not mine? As if each little head is a little crown made of gazes, which lovingly guard the children. And to each mother who is caressing a child, I would like to yell: "You have the whole world!" Like butterflies are the girls' bright dresses; here an argument, there giggles, there preparations for home... And the mothers whisper, like tender sisters: "Can you imagine, my son—"... "You don't say! And mine—"... I love women who were not afraid in battle, who were able to hold both the sword and the spear—But I know that only in the captivity of the cradle lies my—ordinary—female—happiness!]

From the beginning of this poem it is clear that the speaker, though she is an observer of the idyll, views it from a distance and is, in fact, a stranger to it,

Walking the Poetic Tightrope 11

in the most literal sense, as indicated by the poem's title: for this is not Russia but Paris, and Tsvetaeva is a foreign tourist. The speaker's visual perspective likewise bespeaks distance; the low-bending branches and the children in the grass (not "*frolicking* in the grass" but simply *in* it, as if an attribute of it) seem to indicate that the scene is observed from above, while the abundance of plural nouns (*branches, streams, alleys*) further emphasized by the trifold repetition of the word *children,* the generalizing phrase "children, and more children," and the ellipsis at the end of the third line serve to deconcretize both the speaker and the scene she describes.

This poem was written when Tsvetaeva was only seventeen—almost a child herself and presumably still far from real aspirations to motherhood. Heard in the context of all these distancing factors, the rhetorical query that ends the first stanza ("O children in the grass, why are you not mine?") conveys the utter impossibility of her ever partaking tranquilly of the sweet, simple joys of motherhood. The anguished intonation of this cry, as of the poem as a whole, supports this reading—for if the distance the poet had to traverse in order to join the mothers in the garden were simply a temporal one, then the answer to her question would be self-evident and the question itself would not have to be asked at all. Rather, the young Tsvetaeva perceives a qualitative difference between the familial bliss observed here and whatever fate her own future holds.

The remainder of "In the Luxembourg Garden" is shaped by a similar strategy, in which poetic context and personal subtext continue to undermine the semantics of the poem's overt content. In the second stanza, Tsvetaeva's essential difference from the mothers in the garden is defined: she is distinct from them, ultimately, not by virtue of age or nationality (these are just accidents, variable conditions) but by virtue of her poetic sensibility. Precisely because of this sensibility, she is unable, as they do, to live in the singular, the concrete, the personal, the momentary. As the opening words of the second stanza ("As if") signal, in her mode of perception the literal relentlessly becomes metaphorized, even as the singular becomes pluralized and the concrete abstracted: "As if on each little head is a little crown made of gazes, which lovingly guard the children." She sees clairvoyantly, poetically, metaphorically; in this way, poetic agency fundamentally separates her from the young women she describes and envies. Her adolescent anguish at being no longer a child, and not yet a mother, is removed from the sphere of the temporal and temporary by the poetic mark that she bears and is transformed into an unavoidable existential condition.

Tsvetaeva's poetic sensibility is doubly damning: it endows her with the wholeness of vision to conceptualize through metaphor the binding blisses of ordinary human life and love that perhaps go unnoticed by those who are absorbed in simply living, while causing her to realize her own irreparable distance from this simple, unfragmented human world that she observes from the poetic beyond: "To each mother who is caressing a child, I would like to yell: 'You have the whole world!' " She intimates that the mothers do not fully realize the miracle of their own lives and children in taking them so much for granted; what is normal, usual, and instinctive for them, the young Tsvetaeva already suspects, is unattainable for her. Thus, her muffled scorn—she is superior by virtue of her poetic vision and talent—is really a mask for deep hurt and longing. Her scorn is her attempt to settle accounts with a way of existence that excludes her, but as such it would seem to provide little solace. Her cry across the garden has become a cry across the abyss between universes.

In the poem's third stanza, the level of generalization and abstraction of descriptions continues to intensify, thereby increasing the speaker's distance from the scene she portrays. The comparison of the little girls' dresses to butterflies, given the poem's preponderance of plural forms (in this metaphor alone there are four in quick succession, three nouns and an adjective), conjures not just the brightness of fluttering butterflies but their overwhelming number—a breathtaking, dazzling swarm. The sense of ceaseless, dizzying activity continues: "Here an argument, there giggles, there preparations for home..." Here as in the poem's first stanza, the ellipsis serves as a multiplier and distancer and thus as a further tool for generalization. In this line, the terms *here* [zdes'] and *there* [tam], if heard in the context of the Symbolist poetics in which they played such a pivotal role, come to sound ironically.[17] For the earthbound mothers described, these words have a purely geographical significance, and a most inexact one at that; there is no inkling whatsoever of a higher plane of reference in these women's existence.

For all that the women are lacking in metaphysical imagination, however, they do possess another kind of riches to which Tsvetaeva is not privy: an easy, conspiratorial sisterhood, as their senseless whispering indicates: "And the mothers whisper, like tender sisters: 'Can you imagine, my son—'... 'You don't say! And mine—'..." She captures the mothers' doting intonations in an impressionistic shorthand; by this means, she indicates simultaneously the mothers' communion with one another—they speak in a kind of code—and the repetitive, profligate emptiness of their conversations (their words are, in fact, pure intonation, pure emotion and possess neither form nor content), further emphasized, once again, by the two ellipses. As previously, she locates her essential difference from these women not in mere circumstance, but in her linguistic gift, which sets her fate irreparably apart: they babble sweet-nothings, whereas she is engaged in the serious art of poetry. The price she will pay for her difference, she intimates, is loneliness: exclusion from the sisterhood.

The final stanza of this poem is a puzzle in many ways—and intentionally so. Despite the accumulation of distance and difference Tsvetaeva has achieved in the poem's first three stanzas, she seemingly turns her argument upside down at the last moment to realign her hopes and dreams with the world of the young mothers in the garden, wholeheartedly embracing what she imagines to be her female destiny. However, the previous three stanzas have not merely described her vacillation between conflicting desires, but rather have enacted her sober awareness of the impact that her poetic thought process is destined to have on her future—and this impact is not so patly to be undone by a simple logical twist. Surely, the message of the poem remains unchanged: she is marked by poetry, and her fate will be marked by poetry. She knows she will not share in the fulfilling feminine "whole world" she has described with such jealous yearning and gentle scorn.

When read in light of this self-awareness, the poem's final stanza sounds hauntingly. In it, Tsvetaeva penetratingly intuits ("But I know" [No znaiu]) her peculiar isolation from her own sex and her fated abdication of her personal dreams. For, she does not write that motherhood is her destiny; rather, that it is her potential happiness. Just as the query in the poem's first stanza must be read in context as an awareness of the very impossibility of the possibility of which she speaks, here, too, context requires that this apparent embrace of "ordinary female happiness" be understood as the poet's expression of an unrealizable, though desperate, desire. Years later, she would provide a sad recapitulation of this poem's prophetic message in her unfinished *poema* "The Bus" ["Avtobus"], in which the aging poet realizes that all the other passengers on a crowded bus are bound for the land of happiness, but she will ride past.

The long dashes of the poem's final line ("Ordinary—female—happiness") transform the poet's last thought into a desperate sob. At the same time, these dashes give weight to each of the three separate components of the poet's desire. Thus, ordinariness, femininity, and happiness are all shown to be incommensurate with Tsvetaeva's poetic calling. The alternatives to the first and the third items in this formula are clear: she is destined to be extraordinary, and to be unhappy. The middle item, however, is not so easily resolved; what can possibly be the antidote to femininity's incompatibility with poetry, given that she is, after all, female? The easy answer—adherence to the Amazonian ideal—is apparently insufficient, for the poet's admission of love for protofeminist "women warriors" is conditioned by the negating conjunction "but" that leads into the poem's anguished final couplet. Her search for other answers will carry her far outside the confines of this poem.

"Only a Girl," like "In the Luxembourg Garden," contains a camouflaged rejection of feminine destiny. This poem begins in a vein of acidic sarcasm, although it later modulates into a softer, contemplative key. At the poem's outset, the speaker adopts a mock-didactic tone and appears to direct her message against her own natural inclinations. She parrots what she has been taught is the duty of a young girl like herself: to guard her virginity (in preparation for marriage), dream romantic dreams (in preparation for material riches, as the "golden castle" hints), and play with dolls (in preparation for child rearing):

> Я только девочка. Мой долг
> До брачного венца
> Не забывать, что всюду — волк
> И помнить: я — овца.
>
> Мечтать о замке золотом,
> Качать, кружить, трясти
> Сначала куклу, а потом
> Не куклу, а почти.
>
> [I am only a girl. My duty until the marriage crown is not to forget that wolves are everywhere, and remember: I am a sheep. To dream about a golden castle, to rock, spin, shake — at first a doll, and then later not a doll, but almost.]

However, Tsvetaeva's rhyming of *ventsa* (the marital crown) and *ovtsa* (sheep) in the first stanza makes clear from the start her refusal to obey the herd instincts of which marriage is a prime symptom. Likewise, the fact that in the second stanza she refrains from actually using the noun *child* — she conveys her meaning by the derogatory phrase "Not a doll, but almost," which serves to dehumanize and objectivize its referent — signals not only her rejection of motherhood, but (ominously, perhaps) her total lack of comprehension of its attraction, in marked contrast to her attitude in "In the Luxembourg Garden." In this way, certain poetic and linguistic tactics operate in the poem to undo its ostensible message of compliance.

These tactics continue in the poem's third stanza, where Tsvetaeva complements the preceding two stanzas' catalogue of a young girl's duties with the deftly executed limitation of her sphere of activity: "In my hand there is to be no sword, sound no string" [V moei ruke ne byt′ mechu, / Ne zazvenet′ strune]. In these lines the speaking subject has no agency; the metonymic isolation of her hand, combined with the hand's merely oblique grammatical relationship to any tools it might potentially hold, amounts to a symbolic amputation of the aspirations emblematized by the sword and the musical string. It is significant that the sword is paired with the string, instrument of lyricism; the juxtaposition of poetic and military endeavors indicates that, for Tsvetaeva, the female poet is equally as transgressive of her gender as the female soldier. In this third stanza, as in the first two, there is the sense of an internal split of allegiances within the speaking voice of the poem: the sheep seems to have swallowed the wolf, and the resulting strange creature, fully neither subject nor object of her own address, both argues and obeys to spite herself; for hardly has she begun to articulate her protest than she bites her tongue: "I am only a girl — I am silent" [Ia tol′ko devochka, — molchu].

This ambiguity of the speaking voice is encoded in the poem's verbal structure. Throughout both the catalogue of female virtues in stanzas 1 and 2 and

Walking the Poetic Tightrope 15

the definition of female limitation in stanza 3, there is not a single conjugated verb; rather, the infinitive forms alone are used: *not to forget* [ne zabyt'], *to remember* [pomnit'], *to dream* [mechtat'], *to rock* [kachat'], *to spin* [kruzhit'], *to shake* [triasti], *not to be* [ne byt'], *not to sound* [ne zazvenet']. The infinitive in these constructions is profoundly ambiguous. In the first two stanzas, it is noncommittal; it conveys a prescription for ideal behavior, but it does not reveal whether or not this prescription is to be heeded. Saying "My duty . . . is not to forget, to remember, to dream" is not at all the same as saying "I will/do not forget, remember, dream." The impersonal construction of the third stanza is even more expressive of ambiguity. In this construction, the infinitive forms of the verbs can have two directly contradictory meanings. On the one hand, they imply impossibility: "In my hand the sword *cannot* be, / The string *cannot* sound." On the other hand, however, they imply proscription, prohibition — which may very well be disregarded: "In my hand the sword *should not* be, / The string *should not* sound." The ambiguity of these verbal forms thus illustrates the ambiguity of the poem's lyrical voice, as the poet acquiesces with mock obedience to limitations that she herself proclaims and simultaneously — through irony and linguistic play — conveys the possibility and the verbal means of transgressing these limitations.

The third line of the third stanza marks the end of the poem's catalogue of proper female behavior and an ironic turning point of sorts: "I am only a girl — I am silent." Each of the two parts of this line can be read in two different ways — the first giving a superficial impression of the speaker's compliance with social codes; the second refuting this compliance. Thus, "I am only a girl" can be understood as self-deprecation, a belittlement of the poet's gender and of girls' innate capabilities; if, however, the primary emphasis is placed not on the word *girl* but on the word *only,* then the same phrase becomes a subversive promise of emergent possibility: "I am *as yet* only a girl, but just you wait!" Likewise, the verb *molchu* [I am silent] — notably, the only conjugated verb in the entire poem — is double edged, for even as the poet seems to acquiesce to silence, her capitulation is ironic, coming as it does in the context of this wryly outspoken poem: evidently, she is not silent after all. The very fact that she turns her apparent silence into the only verbal action in the entire poem implies that this silence is, in fact, a great feat; she knows far more than she says, but she is keeping her counsel. At the same time, her ambiguous *molchu* indicates the duplicity of her young existence: she is dutifully compliant with the norms of the social world in which she exists from day to day — but, unseen to the grown-up, prosaic nay-sayers of the mundane, she is a rebel in the realm of poetry.[18] Tsvetaeva totters precariously on the cusp of adolescence, and the rift in understanding between grown-ups and children is a pervasive presence in her other poems of this period as well.

In the final stanza of "Only a Girl," the verbs are all, once again, in the infinitive form—but here this form conveys possibility rather than prohibition, for the verbs are contextualized in a subjunctive clause, indicating the poet's secret desire:

> Ах, если бы и мне
>
> Взглянув на звезды знать, что там
> И мне звезда зажглась
> И улыбаться всем глазам,
> Не опуская глаз!
>
> [Oh, if only I could also, having glanced at the stars, know that there a star has kindled for me, too, and smile into everyone's eyes without lowering my own!]

These two whimsical dreams with which Tsvetaeva counters the myriad of repressive codes enumerated earlier in the poem seem at first to bear only the most tenuous relationship to her predicament. In fact, however, the two dreams emerge as correctives to the two aspects of her female gender that the speaker finds intolerable. On the one hand, her wistful dream that a star will kindle for her—symbolizing the realization of her poetic destiny—implies her awareness of the inherent disjunction of female gender and poetic talent, as we saw, too, in "In the Luxembourg Garden." This disjunction, it is important to note, emerges from the poet's own deep intuition, rather than from the social strictures imposed upon her. ("To know" [znat'] here echoes "But I know" [No znaiu] in the previous poem and refers to the same kind of profound, almost prophetic self-knowledge of poetic destiny).[19] Her dream that she is able to smile directly into people's eyes, on the other hand, relates to the discomfort her gender causes her not in the poetic realm, but in the realm of human and bodily existence (represented metonymically by the eyes). Although her lowered gaze might be interpreted as a portrayal of false modesty required by the social code, there is also the sense that the speaker lowers her eyes spontaneously, prompted perhaps by a feeling of shame or unease at her difference from other young women. It is interesting that the lowered eyes of "Only a Girl" become, in her later poetry, a symbol of the clairvoyant poetic gaze, and thus an image of superiority rather than inferiority.[20]

Thus we see that this poem is emphatically not what it appears to be: namely, the poet's indictment of society for her own predicament. Instead, Tsvetaeva unexpectedly shifts the terms of the discussion—for, although society expects such and such behavior of its female members, these expectations can be transgressed, given time and the will. The true challenge of her gender is to find a way to transcend her own conviction that a woman poet is an oxymoron, her own feeling of unease in the world of humans (hence, her dreams of the kindled star

Walking the Poetic Tightrope 17

and the unflinching gaze). With the articulation of these dreams, she implicitly takes full responsibility for her dilemma, which as a result is transformed from a merely social problem into an existential one, even as her situation, as a result, is transformed from an ordinary—female—problem into an extraordinary one. Paradoxically, therefore, the young Tsvetaeva shows herself to be a potentially great poet even as she voices extreme doubts about this possibility. Moreover, it is important to note that the subjunctive clause ("Oh, if only I could also...") that ends the third stanza is never delimited by the definiteness of any answering clause ("Then I would..."). This lack of grammatical closure leaves enormous space (the whole cosmos of the night sky sparkling with stars, and the whole cosmos of the earth sparkling with eyes) for the poet's future search for solutions to her difficulties. For all her perplexed sense of self, the possibilities are clearly endless.

THE FEMALE ROLE TRANSGRESSED

I turn now to the second category of Tsvetaeva's early poems about the relationship of gender to poetry—those in which she seemingly accomplishes a complete transcendence of the limitations of her gender and embraces poetry to the exclusion of all else. "A Prayer," written on her seventeenth birthday, is an impassioned farewell to childhood. The poet's superabundance of overwhelming desire for a poetic, literary existence antithetical to the mundane leads to the fervent prayer for a swift, premature death that frames the poem—shaping both its first stanza

> О, дай мне умереть, покуда
> Вся жизнь как книга для меня.
>
> [Oh, let me die, while all of life is still like a book for me.]

and its last.

> Ты дал мне детство—лучше сказки
> И дай мне смерть—в семнадцать лет!
>
> [You gave me a childhood better than a fairytale; so give me death—at seventeen!]

The fact that it is, specifically, Tsvetaeva's gender that prevents her extraordinary poetic desire from being realizable within the bounds of life is not stated explicitly in this poem, as it was in the two poems discussed earlier.

Rather, here the conflict between poetry and femininity is expressed indirectly, when the speaker dons a whole slew of female literary masks almost simultaneously in a frantic attempt to find an adequate model for her own heroic aspirations:

> Всего хочу: с душой цыгана
> Идти под песни на разбой,
> За всех страдать под звук органа
> И амазонкой мчаться в бой;
>
> Гадать по звездам в черной башне,
> Вести детей вперед, сквозь тень...
>
> [I want it all: to set out with a gypsy's soul on a robbery to the sound of singing, to suffer for all humanity to the drone of an organ, to race into battle like an Amazon. To tell fortunes by the stars in a black tower, to lead children forward, through the shadows...]

The incompatibility of these various escapist personae indicates their insufficiency; their clash is, in turn, echoed and abbreviated in the aesthetic clash that follows: "I love both the cross and silk, and the helmet" [Liubliu i krest i shelk, i kaski]. The placement of commas in this line is highly important; Tsvetaeva does not give a list of three items, in which the conjunction *and* [i] is all-inclusive: "Liubliu i krest, i shelk, i kaski." Rather, by eliminating the first comma, she transforms the meaning of the conjunction into disjunctiveness: "krest i shelk" [cross and silk] are grouped as a contrastive pair (piety vs. materialism, the spiritual vs. the physical, suffering vs. hedonism, etc.) complete in themselves, already mutually irreconcilable, when she unexpectedly ups the ante, adding a third impossible element: "I love both the cross and silk—and, moreover, I love helmets too!" Early death is the only conceivable resolution to this conundrum.

Yet despite the overt Romanticism of this poem, a sober recognition of realities underlies it, so that Tsvetaeva's fervent adolescent prayer for death comes to sound as an elaborate, self-consciously ironic bluff. The very fact that a dramatic death is the only possibility of which the young poet can conceive for the continuation of her participation in poetry is in itself telling: after reviewing all the literary female roles available to her, she finds that not a one allows for female poetic agency. In other words, in all the roles she explores, the women, whether nuns or Amazons, are female objects of male representation and desire as opposed to writing, creating subjects. All that the girl poet can do in the way of transgressing her gender is to appropriate this male representation and desire to herself; but she discovers that she cannot go so far as to conceptualize an ideal of female subjectivity. Death is the only available solution to this dilemma, for a tragic early death would satisfy simultaneously the demands of both literature (she would become a striking aesthetic object)[21] and her own poetic aspirations toward transcendence (death is undergone in supreme isolation, and thus is "poetic" in the sense that it is a triumph of subjective experience unavailable to mere mortals)—in other words, death would grant her both objective and subjective status.[22] Here it is important to avoid the temptation to read backwards from Tsvetaeva's suicide; during the composition of "A Prayer," the poet surely had no inkling of the tribulations that awaited her nor of how her life was actually to end over thirty years later. The impassioned plea for death here expresses no more a natural gravitation toward suicide than it does the poet's oft-imputed Romantic naïveté; rather, the idea of death serves a conscious poetic purpose: it is a metaphoric shorthand that encodes the irreconcilability of femininity and poetic calling that she feels so deeply and tormentingly.[23]

Thus, "A Prayer" as a whole is not, as it seems, a pure soaring into Romantic fantasy heedless of the quotidian demands of reality. In fact, this poem emanates from the poet's full (perhaps even prophetic) awareness of the burden and impact of those demands, which are destined to compete with the demands of her poetic calling throughout her life; indeed, there are lacunae in Tsvetaeva's Romanticism where a staunch realism quietly hides. True, when the poet exclaims enigmatically, "Oh, let me die, while all of life is still like a book for me," she does admit her allegiance to books over life, to the literary over reality. At the same time, though, she acknowledges that this triumph of pure imagination is now about to end—as a book is apt to end—with her entry into adult responsibility and the encroachment of the mundane into her attentions. The poetic "death" she calls for at the end of the poem is thus an antidote to the figurative death of maturation that is already upon her. Her new understanding of the relativity of literature, situated as she is now upon the threshold of adulthood, is incapsulated in the contrast between the physically contained, finite image of the ending book in the poem's first stanza and, at the poem's conclusion, the enchanted kingdom of the fairy tale, temporally and spatially infinite, that was her childhood ("You gave me a childhood better than a fairytale"). The ending book also expresses metaphorically the complicated idea of Tsvetaeva's intended passage from the status of literary objectivity to literary subjectivity that this poem as a whole represents: in finishing the book of her youth, she passes from being a *reader* into the uncharted no-woman's-land of being a *writer* (symbolic death).

Further evidence of Tsvetaeva's awareness of the conflict between poetic and daily existence in "A Prayer" can be found in the line "My soul is the trace of moments..." [Moia dusha mgnovenii sled...]. Here, in extremely condensed form, she contrasts two temporal principles: the relentless *linear* principle that governs real life and accomplishes a gradual accumulation of lived time undifferentiated into units of greater or lesser worth; versus the *discontinuous* "trace of moments" that comprises her soul—moments, presumably, of intense poetic emotion, whether gleaned from the reading of literature or from her own feeling of inspiration. The placement of this line immediately after the maximally irreconcilable conflict of cross, silk, and helmet makes it clear that a soul organized according to such a temporal principle has no place within the bounds of real possibility. Tsvetaeva's repeated pleas for death in this poem, then, are not simply an impassioned literary trope but, in fact, result from her own perspicacious understanding that she will find herself forever ill at ease in life—to whose conditions and obligations she must now, nevertheless, learn to adapt herself.

Tsvetaeva's sober appreciation in "A Prayer" for the incompatibility of her poetic talent with the demands of a real, adult female existence is voiced even more unflinchingly in the formulaic poem "A Savage Will," which consists of a series of ardently Romantic proclamations of the poet's defiant solitary stance. What saves this poem from being simply a collection of clichés is the sheer starkness of its constituent contrasts—or, to put it another way, the extremity to which Tsvetaeva extends old tropes. The concluding lines of the poem tell all: "If only in the world there were just two: I and the world!" [Chtoby v mire bylo dvoe: / Ia i mir!].[24] In arranging this mortal combat between herself and the world, Tsvetaeva trims her metaphysical inquiry down to the absolute essentials. She challenges her readers to leave aside their first, obvious impression of her impotence in the battle and to reassess the powers of poetry to which she hereby lays claim. In terms of life, certainly, she loses miserably; but she implies that in some other, unfathomable, as yet inexpressible way, if not she, then at least poetry, wins. Here again, then, her Romantic stance is a conscious, considered choice—the outcome of poetic logic as much as of emotional inclination.

Tsvetaeva sets herself up as a poetic martyr, whose allegiance is formulated—in anticipation of enmity—offensively: against the symbolic dangers of tigers, eagles, night, hurricanes:

> Я люблю такие игры,
> Где надменны все и злы.
> Чтоб врагами были тигры
> И орлы!
>
> . . . .
>
> Чтобы ночь со мной боролась,
> Ночь сама!
>
> Я несусь, — за мною пасти,
> Я смеюсь, — в руках аркан...
>
> Чтобы рвал меня на части
> Ураган!
>
> [I love such games, when everyone is haughty and mean. If only tigers and eagles were my enemies! . . . If only the night would fight with me, the night herself! I soar—jaws are in pursuit, I laugh—a lasso in my hands... If only a hurricane would tear me into shreds!]

Tsvetaeva's choice of such imposing enemies indicates her ambition to participate in struggles of what is rawly, essentially human—to emerge from the parenthesis of her gender and her resultant "female" poetic quandary into the unconstrained, unmarked space of the elemental contest between existence and nonexistence that is poetry's ultimate subject. The very fact that she does not make her gender an explicit element of "A Savage Will" is evidence of this aim. Alternatively, Tsvetaeva's choice of enemies can be read as an allegory of her desire to engage her equals in poetic talent—the (primarily male) tigers and eagles of great poetry, not the tame lace and frills of feminine craft—in her fight to establish her own unique poetic voice. In this reading, the poem becomes a hymn to the overcoming of anxiety of influence, an undertaking made all the more strenuous by the complication of gender difference.[25]

Whether or not Tsvetaeva can realize her aspirations to poetic genius is a question that is not resolved within this poem, whose phrasing remains unswervingly hypothetical to the last (the words "if only" [chtob; chtoby] are used seven times in sixteen lines). What is clear, though, is the state of complete isolation that is the logical outcome of her poetics. In claiming a powerful poetic voice, Tsvetaeva creates a subjectivity that excludes anything human, meanwhile alienating and objectifying ("enemifying") the rest of humanity through the power of metaphor, and so allowing no room for any other subjectivity that could provide her with companionship. This pattern of isolation in her own poetic subjectivity is already familiar: in "In the Luxembourg Garden" she finds herself isolated from the sisterhood of mothers and their "whole world" by her poetic gift; in "Only a Girl" she cannot bring herself to look her fellow humans in the eye; and in "A Prayer" the impossibility of establishing a feminine poetic "I" affords the young poet no other option but the death wish. In "A Savage Will," too, she is an exile from life itself when she dares to enter the poetic arena, having doffed her gender at the threshold. For all the exhilaration of the fray, it is clear that she recognizes the vulnerability of her position.

A FEMALE DRUMMER BOY

In the poems discussed earlier, no matter what the poet's ostensible allegiance—to feminine destiny over poetic ("In the Luxembourg Garden," "Only a Girl"), or to poetic destiny over feminine ("A Prayer," "A Savage Will")—we have seen that everywhere the reality is far more complex, for she is separated from complete commitment to either one of these mutually conflicting destinies by the other's competing pull. Tsvetaeva cannot meet others eye to eye, but gazes into the abyss and from the abyss to see that which is invisible to mere mortals. As a result, we observe a split within her self; she is isolated by her poetic clairvoyance from prosaic humanity and even from her own human urges. In other words, both her subjectivity and her relationship to alterity are problematic. Despite the young poet's attempts at passionate maximalism, her poems provide ample evidence that she is minutely aware of the paradox of her predicament and its possibly grave implications for her future. Her poetic task, as she implicitly defines it in these seminal poems, is to create a personal mythos that will be adequate to the expression of her talent and yet will satisfactorily incorporate her female gender into the "narrative."

Tsvetaeva's earliest success at these efforts is found in her poem "The Drum," which can be read as a poetic manifesto of sorts. Here the poet adopts a defiant, self-assured, even joyful tone to profess her true calling—poetry—which she figures metaphorically as the beating of a military drum. In this poem, Tsvetaeva's gender is made explicit, as is her transgression of the expectations of that gender: "The female lot does not entice me: I fear boredom, not wounds!" [Zhenskaia dolia menia ne vlechet: / Skuki boius′, a ne ran!]. These two lines could well serve as Tsvetaeva's motto throughout her life. The military ethos that colors this poem has been marginally present in each of the four poems already discussed. In "In the Luxembourg Garden," Tsvetaeva admitted her love for women "who were not afraid in battle, who were able to hold both the sword and the spear." In "Only a Girl," she equated the sword with the lyre's string, both of which are forbidden to her as a female. In "A Prayer," she confessed her love of the military helmet and dreamed of "racing into battle like an Amazon." And in "A Savage Will," she transformed her battle for poetic voice into an elemental struggle with the night in an open declaration of war ("If only the feast would end in war!" [Chtob voinoi konchalsia pir!]).

In "The Drum," then, Tsvetaeva articulates explicitly what she only hints at in the other poems: she conceives her poetic project metaphorically as an offensive military campaign against her own internalization of societal and poetic conventions that impede her path to poetry. Although here, as in the other poems, the poet's isolation results from the inherent conflict she perceives between life and art, she is able now for the first time to find a way out of the binds of female limitation and into a third possibility that promises to bridge the two other mutually exclusive realms and thereby alleviate her loneliness. This third possibility is her communion with the army of other poets, her male contemporaries and predecessors, at whose head, by the poem's end, she marches proudly:

> Быть барабанщиком! Всех впереди!
> Все остальное—обман!
>
> [To be a drummer! Ahead of everyone! Everything else—is deception!]

With this new vision, Tsvetaeva is able for the first time triumphantly to bear the pain ("wounds" [rany]) of her exclusion from the sisterhood and of the dichotomy she experiences between life (the deceptive "everything else") and art—to which she gives her full allegiance. Moreover, in envisioning herself as the energetic, degendered herald of poetry, she not only finds a way to surpass her femininity and enter the ranks of the great poets, but she ingeniously repositions herself at the very forefront of creative endeavor.

From the poem's first lines, Tsvetaeva rejects unambiguously, even caustically, the very core of "female happiness" (motherhood: rocking the cradle) that in earlier poems filled her with torments of longing and jealousy:

> В майское утро качать колыбель?
> Гордую шею в аркан?
> Пленнице — прялка, пастушке — свирель,
> Мне — барабан.
>
> [Rock a cradle on a May morning? Put my proud neck into a noose? The spindle for the (female) captive, the reed pipe for the shepherdess, for me — the drum.]

The tripartite formula that ends this first stanza begins Tsvetaeva's transformation. The first two elements of the formula correspond to two conflicting, equally unfulfilling options traditionally available to the female: namely, captivity to domestic, nonsignifying, cyclical labor, as figured in the image of the spindle; versus the merely feminine self-expression of the poetess (a.k.a. piping shepherdess, a stock character from the clichéd genre of the poetic idyll)[26] — who is herself more aesthetic object than speaking subject, and whose significance to matters of real poetic importance is as circumscribed as that of her wool-spinning sister. To both of these entrapping feminine circles Tsvetaeva opposes a third option, a forward-marching vector: the craft of the marching drummer that is hers alone. In contrast to the "female captive" and "shepherdess," she is fulfilling not a type or a role but herself, her own promise — hence, the personal pronoun "me," rather than any third typological noun. Indeed, the drum is a perfect metaphor for her unique poetic talent that is so driven by syncopated, transgressive, unorthodox rhythms.[27] Whereas the poetess's/shepherdess's instrument is sounded by disembodied sighs (breath), hers demands the vigorous physical engagement of both hands (beating the drum) and feet (marching).[28]

Thus, the image of herself as a military drummer effects some level of reconciliation in the various conflicts involved for Tsvetaeva in the poetic endeavor. It sublimates physical urges, replacing them with the poetic exertion of pure sound and rhythm. It channels life's inexorable forward movement of time and events into the vector of poetic progress. It frees her from female limitation to create a completely new, unique identity for herself, even as it makes accessible such traditional male privileges as physical exercise, military activity (metaphorically, of course: the campaign is waged for poetry!), power and honor: "My drum gives me everything, both power and honor" [Vse mne daruet, — i vlast' i pochet / Moi baraban]. Tsvetaeva's career as a drummer smoothes the rift between the poetic and the earthly, promising to carry her into "unseen countries" that are for once both literal and figurative: "The sun has risen, the trees are in bloom... How many unseen countries!" [Solnyshko vstalo, derev'ia v tsvetu... / Skol'ko nevidannykh stran!]. These flowering trees, so full of promise and possibility, mend the sorrow of her exclusion from the sweetness of feminine fulfillment represented by the flowering trees of "In the Luxembourg Garden."

In contrast to the desperate isolation that results from the offensive battle Tsvetaeva wages against the limitations of her gender and consequently against all of existence in the poem "A Savage Will," here, by admitting and transforming rather than denying her femininity, she manages also to transform the battle from *one against all* to a battle *for all,* and thereby to counteract the isolation of the serious female poet: she is marching to conquer hearts: "What wins hearts en route as a drum does?" [Chto pokoriaet serdtsa na puti, / Kak baraban?]. Hence her unaccustomed tone of levitating joy: "Kill every sorrow in flight, beat, drum!" [Vsiakuiu grust' ubivai na letu, / Bei, baraban!]. The double meanings of the word *beat* also serve to join the physical to the poetic in the metaphor of the drum, while lending a slightly darker coloration to this otherwise lighthearted lyric; the implication of violence is present, too, in the injunction to the drum to "kill." For all her joy in the poetic undertaking, the poet hints at its potentially high stakes.[29]

The question remains as to how, specifically, Tsvetaeva envisions the realization of the third female option she has plotted out for herself. How is the metaphor of herself as a paradoxically female drummer boy to be written into her poetry and her life? Although the poem does not provide a definitive answer to this question, there are several hints of what is to come. Firstly, the poem introduces the idea of a path (a march); indeed, in Tsvetaeva's poetic journey, chronology will continue to bear great significance by virtue of the ordered accumulation of poetic logic that chronology facilitates.[30] Secondly, the poem emphasizes the fact that Tsvetaeva, despite her feminine difference, nevertheless marches in the company of her male compatriots/soldiers, her brothers in poetry—for a drummer boy does not march alone, but leads an entire army, to which he is bound in servitude. Tsvetaeva's cry "ahead of everyone!" [vsekh vperedi!] thus succeeds in expressing simultaneously both her pride in uniqueness, and her humility to the greater cause; both isolation and companionship; both rebelliousness toward and reverence for her poetic brothers and "elders." This delicate balance is in marked contrast to the speaker's undiscriminating, unyielding, universally addressed belligerence in "A Savage Will." The difference—and thence the joy (vs. the other poem's frenzied exhilaration)—emanates from the poet's realization in "The Drum" that despite her loneliness, her cause is shared. Her ideal readers, whose hearts she sets out to conquer, and her fellow poets, whom she leads into battle—these are the intermediate

Walking the Poetic Tightrope 25

creatures who make possible a partial mending of the rift in Tsvetaeva between human and poet, and whose very existence promises her some measure of true companionship.

Yet "The Drum" presages Tsvetaeva's future poetic development not just metaphorically, thematically, and allegorically, but methodologically as well. In other words, she achieves the hopeful resolution of her poetic and personal quandary in "The Drum" not merely through contemplation, but through poetic action. Specifically, her own female participation in the male poetic fray—suggested here by the metaphor of the drummer boy—is at the same time embedded and enacted within the poem itself, via a fabric of particular intertextual echoes that refer back to the work of an imposing male poetic rival/predecessor/companion: the eighteenth-century poet Gavriil Derzhavin. Tsvetaeva's affinity with Derzhavin in her mature poetry has been well established, although scholars usually assume that her emulation of eighteenth-century Russian poetry did not begin in earnest until the year 1916 (the centennial of Derzhavin's death), with the composition of her collection *Milestones* [*Versty*], in which Russian motifs and archaic language make an obvious appearance.[31] However, given Tsvetaeva's insatiable appetite for poetry at a very early age, it is not improbable that several years earlier she would have known a frequently anthologized poem by Pushkin's admired forebear: to wit, "The Bullfinch" ["Snigir'"].[32]

The parallels between Tsvetaeva's "The Drum" and Derzhavin's "The Bullfinch" are subtle, and arguably none of these similarities taken in isolation would be sufficient to prove a connection between the two works. However, when all the parallels are considered at once, they urge in sum a recognition of the intertextual negotiation in which Tsvetaeva engages here. Derzhavin's poem was written on the occasion of the death of the great general of the Russo-Turkish and French Revolutionary Wars, Aleksandr Suvorov; in it, the lyric poet beseeches a chirping bullfinch to cease its military song, now that Suvorov is gone and humanity has been robbed of the quintessential manliness which he represented: "Who now is our leader? Who is our hero? . . . Now there is no man so worthy in the world" [Kto teper' vozhd' nash? Kto bogatyr'? . . . Net teper' muzha v svete stol' slavna]. The speaker goes on to suggest that war (symbolized by the finch's ceaseless, senseless tune) has now become pointless ("Why fight?" [Chto voevat'?]), and that the lyric poet's mournful songs are its appropriate replacement.

Thus, a military ethos shapes Derzhavin's poem, as it does Tsvetaeva's; the two central themes of Derzhavin's poem, which intersect in the event of Suvorov's death, are the relationship of poetic exploits to military ones, and the loss of a masculine ideal. Tsvetaeva borrows these two themes in "The Drum" and gives them each a creative twist. Derzhavin's literal war against the French revolutionaries (who are symbolized by the hyena in "The Bullfinch"), in service to which Suvorov spent his last years as commander of the Russo-Austrian army, is transformed into Tsvetaeva's figurative battle "for hearts"—that is, the battle for her own poetic efficacy. Whereas Derzhavin devalues the fight, replacing the military with the lyrical impulse, Tsvetaeva moves in the opposite direction, metaphorizing lyricism as a positive struggle and thereby shifting the sign of the battle within the symbolic economy of the poem from minus to plus. At the same time, the literal demise of Suvorov's manhood in Derzhavin's elegiac poem takes the ironic form, in Tsvetaeva's poetic manifesto, of her own brazen assumption of a masculine role and her concomitant rejection of stereotypical femininity. Her challenge to the reader—and, indeed, her own poetic challenge to herself—is to change the sign of this feminine lack, too, from minus to plus.

A number of other parallels between "The Drum" and "The Bullfinch" can be cited as well. Both poems employ syncopated metrical schemes based upon the dactylic foot that simulate a military march; moreover, the rhyme schemes in both poems reach beyond the borders of isolated stanzas to weave together all the separate segments of the poem. There is also a similarity in intonation: Derzhavin's poem is almost entirely composed of questions, with which it begins ("Why are you singing a military song like a flute, dear finch?") and ends ("Why fight?"). Tsvetaeva is generally far more inclined toward the exclamatory than the interrogative mood, yet she, too, frames her poem with questions.[33] Tsvetaeva's poem, like Derzhavin's, takes place in May, and her disparaging image of the poetess's trivial reed pipe [svirel'] resonates with Derzhavin's comparison of the inappropriately carefree finch's song to the voice of a flute. (In fact, the word *svirel'* [reed pipe] itself bears a vague phonetic resemblance to *snigir'* [bullfinch] that Tsvetaeva, with her paronomastic flair, might not have overlooked.) In "The Drum" as in "The Bullfinch," lyric poetry is privileged to bridge the distance between life's conflicting emotions of sadness and joy and thus holds forth the promise of healing life's very real losses, rifts, and limitations. Finally, in "The Drum," Tsvetaeva's relationship to Derzhavin is analogous to Derzhavin's relationship to Suvorov in "The Bullfinch"; in both poems, the poet stakes out his or her poetic territory on the grave of an admired forebear.

When read in the light of "The Bullfinch," Tsvetaeva's poem sounds as a pert answer to Derzhavin's repeated queries to the much-maligned finch: "Why do you sing, how can you sing, in the face of such lack?" (The actual lines are "Enough of singing military songs, finch! Martial music is not pleasing today, from everywhere is heard the lyre's languid moan" [Polno pet' pesniu voennu, snigir'! / Branna muzyka dnes' ne zabavna, / Slyshen otsiudu tomnyi voi lir].) Tsvetaeva counters the insignificance of the droning finch's/reed pipe's song with her own unique drumbeat. She sings in spite of and because of her feminine lack; it is, in fact, that lack which fires her poetic drive and propels her to the furthermost edge of poetic conquest. In opposing Suvorov's lost masculinity ("everywhere first in his austere manliness" [vezde pervym v muzhestve strogom]) with her own defiantly Romantic, androgynous preeminence ("To be a drummer! Ahead of everyone!"), she draws Derzhavin into a direct dialogue with herself—a dialogue of equals. It is not accidental that the traces of "The Bullfinch" in Tsvetaeva's poem are camouflaged, not immediately evident, and not unequivocally demonstrable; for Tsvetaeva is engaged here not in rote copying, but in the autonomous creation—through the stimulating medium of shared poetic dialogue—of her own manifesto and her own unique poetics.

This is why Tsvetaeva does not simply model "The Drum" on Derzhavin's poem but modifies, varies, corrects, and answers him. She needs Derzhavin's presence to situate her own poem within the poetic tradition and to give it aim, validity, and relational meaning; at the same time, she needs to modify Derzhavin's message to fit her own differently gendered poetic needs. The presence of "The Bullfinch" in the background of "The Drum," like the presence of Derzhavin (and other poets) at the back of the poem's female "drummer" [barabanshchik], is in itself the cure to Tsvetaeva's potential isolation. Thus we see, interestingly, that other poets are granted in Tsvetaeva's poetics the same claim to autonomous subjectivity that the young poet is staking out for herself—in eternal contest with the merely objectified "world" at large—and so it is they who can potentially provide her only companionship. Thus, in her efforts to develop a personal poetic myth, she will delve deeply into other poets' alternative mythologies and world-views. At the same time, as Tsvetaeva's treatment of "The Bullfinch" in "The Drum" demonstrates, these poetic others will be transfigured by the agency of her own poetic thought, thoroughly reimagined and reconfigured.[34]

Time and again during the course of Tsvetaeva's creative development, she will return to the axiomatic conflict she perceives between her gender and her poetry; she will attempt to overcome the isolating all-or-nothing of the poetic "I" to which her female gender subjects her through creative, dialogic, sometimes manipulative negotiations with other large poetic presences. Because in most cases her poetic interlocutors, unlike Derzhavin, will be her contemporaries, she will invest most of these creative encounters with erotic, as well as poetic, significance—thereby incorporating insatiable bodily desires as a metaphor for the inaccessibility to her of unmediated, actual, lived experience. Tsvetaeva's relationships with other poets, both real and imagined, will thus be played out according to a complex dialectic of loneliness (necessary for artistic integrity) and her yearning for love (unattainable by virtue of the oxymoron of her gender cum genius), a yearning that will be repeatedly sublimated in her sense of poetic companionship. Through her orchestrated dialogues with her fellow poets—in a simultaneously artistic and emotional arena—she will establish her entitlement to her own place in the poetic brotherhood, while forging ever newer versions of the myth of her own poetic genius. Tsvetaeva's mythopoetic negotiations with other poets of her time provide the focus for the remainder of my study.

The Problem of Alterity and Tsvetaeva's Mythopoetics: Preliminary Remarks

Tsvetaeva requires participation in an archetype, in which the participants are no longer fully independent actors, indifferent to one another, but are bonded by certain mythical relations that bring about a paradoxical freedom and a possibility of new meaning, new speech. In other words, in her poetry she searches for a way to sublimate her need to define herself against some true, human other (lover) through participation in the subtle variation of a mythological framework. Myth provides a different perspective on the self than the formlessness of interpersonal discourse that is, for Tsvetaeva, so hostile to the poetic impulse — a different exit from the self, a different entrance into externality. This is a radical intellectual departure from the usual destiny of the feminine and a daring solution to her problem of establishing viable poetic subjectivity.

Tsvetaeva's mythopoetic bent has often been remarked in the criticism; one of her correspondents, the émigré writer Roman Goul, even went so far as to term her a "mythomaniac." Yet as my earlier discussion of "The Drum" suggests, she does not merely adopt or "appropriate" her poetic myths from foreign sources, but fully inhabits them, going far beyond her own willful reinterpretations to the point of no return at which the myth begins, as it were, to "read" her.[35] Olga Hasty, in her book *Tsvetaeva's Orphic Journeys in the Worlds of the Word,* has shown convincingly and at great depth the extent to which Tsvetaeva's poetic thought is organized by mythological patterns:

> In Tsvetaeva's writings myth assumes a paradigmatic function specifically within the process of ordering the signs of the surrounding world. Apparently random and chaotic details of the quotidian crystallize around mythic plots into coherent, well-integrated structures. Myth, in other words, serves for Tsvetaeva not as a source of specific allegorization, but rather as an incentive for typological thinking. It provides the creative framework, the pattern, and the formulae by means of which various facets of existence are interrelated into a comprehensible whole.[36]

Hasty's erudite and sensitive study of the Orphic myth in Tsvetaeva's work has lent much to my own thinking about Tsvetaeva's poetics; yet, despite allusions to gender issues in the cases of Eurydice, Ophelia, and the Cumaean Sibyl, Hasty never explicitly addresses the troubling matter of how Tsvetaeva manages eventually to launch her own Orphic undertaking, female difference notwithstanding. Another, different myth, I believe, is key to understanding Tsvetaeva's struggles with this "gender issue." Specifically, Tsvetaeva's problematic relationship to alterity that emerges from her contemplation of her female gender is closely related to her attempts to find entry into the fundamental myth of poetic inspiration: the myth of the poet and *his* (female) muse.

Thus, my starting point, and the topic for my first chapter, is Tsvetaeva's explicit quest for a muse through her composition of the 1916 lyrical cycles addressed to Aleksandr Blok and Anna Akhmatova—both cycles, ultimately, unsatisfactory to her in their revelations—followed, in January 1921, by the *poema* "On a Red Steed" ["Na krasnom kone"], which provides an imaginative mythological resolution to the earlier works. I argue in this chapter that Tsvetaeva, somewhat threatened by the independent poetic stature of her two beloved poetic rivals, and intent upon accomplishing different solutions than theirs to her own inspirational dilemma, turns away from true dialogue into the realm of fantasy. There, the austere male muse she conjures is both chosen and fated, and the irresolvable psychological divisions of real life (self vs. other, active vs. passive, sexual vs. spiritual, etc.) are portrayed disturbingly and powerfully as capable of being dissolved in the potent wake of poetry incarnate. Not only language, but bodily existence and indeed all of reality are regarded as systems of free-floating signs that can be manipulated by the poet. In the course of this perilous but exhilarating activity, the fine line Tsvetaeva walks between abysses becomes her characteristically vertical inspirational "vector," launching her into poetic flight.

In my second chapter, I turn from Tsvetaeva's search for a generic muse and a workable inspirational myth to a more specific narrative—that of Psyche's courageously disobedient rebellion against her divine mate Eros in the interests of passing from a state of dark physicality, sexuality, and female sensuality into a superior state of enlightened consciousness that leads, ultimately, to her attainment of immortality. This myth, which encapsulates the fundamental paradoxes of Tsvetaeva's talent, becomes the organizing text for her passionate epistolary relationship with Boris Pasternak and lies behind the correspondence and numerous poetic works she addresses to him, most notably the 1923 cycle "Wires" ["Provoda"]. Not only does the Psyche myth provide Tsvetaeva with a way of expressing the deep psychological and emotional anguish she feels with regard to her unrealizable passion for Pasternak, but it presents her with a narrative mandate to preserve her essential loneliness—linked, through the myth, with her poetic greatness. In other words, her future poetic immortality comes at the price of her present renunciation of desire, because for the woman poet, a sexual union with her beloved, which threatens to return her to purely objective status, is tantamount to creative death. Ultimately, Tsvetaeva's relationship with Pasternak—certainly the most mutual of all her relationships with fellow poets, and moreover the one which seems to be potentially most capable of mending the chasms in her own selfhood—remains unconsummated and so deepens even further the very rifts it might have healed.

My third chapter is a consideration of Tsvetaeva's epistolary relationship with the German poet Rainer Maria Rilke. Rilke starts out in Tsvetaeva's regard and correspondence as a kind of senior alter ego for Pasternak, but, with his death from leukemia several months later, he soon metamorphoses into something entirely different and takes his place in her poetics as the hero of an entirely new myth. This myth is distinguished from the others discussed in this book by the fact that it does not have its source in any outside literary or mythological tradition but is Tsvetaeva's own creation, growing organically out of her own poetics. In some sense, this myth encompasses a partial return to the imaginary universe of "On a Red Steed," but now there is no longer an illusion that Tsvetaeva's poetic fantasies can be reconciled in any way with living human experience. In this compelling and troubling allegory of female poetic inspiration, the deceased male beloved stands in for death as the muse—representative of the realm of the eternal that is the poet's true home, beyond all human divisiveness and divisions. This equation of the woman poet's inspiration with a poetic, theatrical death is the natural consequence of the dissolution of her selfhood that the poetic enterprise entails. In contrast to the union of body and spirit with divine other metaphorized in the traditional, male conception of poetic inspiration (i.e., the triangulated union of male poet—female beloved—divine muse), Tsvetaeva's poetry becomes a metaphor for transmigration of the spirit or soul into the world beyond. In this process, "death" is redefined as "life" and vice versa, and the poet is alienated more profoundly than ever from the categories of nonpoetic realia that she strives to leave behind.

In each of the former versions of Tsvetaeva's inspirational myth, the "holistic" experience of poetic flight is accomplished at the expense of a fragmentary relationship to the experiences vouchsafed by real life. By theoretically positing an alternate world in which the body is no more than a metaphor for passion and real deeds bear no consequences other than symbolic ones, Tsvetaeva at the same time unwittingly transgresses the limits of essential human morality. As is the case in Shakespearean tragedy, what goes around, comes around. The previously straight vector of her poetic inspiration is curved into a vicious circle from which there is to be no escape. Thus, Tsvetaeva in her late lyric poetry comes to recognize the actual consequences of her previous attempts at transcendence via a division of language's literal from its figurative meanings, of language's spiritual aims from its sensual origins. Her short-lived infatuations with the young poets Nikolai Gronskii and Anatolii Shteiger that inform my fourth and final chapter are no longer attempts on Tsvetaeva's part to find some exit into true male otherness, but simply proof of her utter inability ever to do so. The central myth of Tsvetaeva's final years, appropriately, is that of the Last Judgment. Truly heroic in stature, tragically faithful to her chosen path until the bitter end, she claims full responsibility for the consequences of her poetic actions in real life—yet, even awaiting retribution, she continues to champion the poetic rightness of her dangerous words and works. Indeed, as the logic of my analysis, I hope, demonstrates, once having chosen the path of poetry and defined what, for her, that path had to mean, Tsvetaeva seems to have had precious little choice as to what route to travel—her bold "owning" of her fate thus only intensifies the tragic dignity of her stature.

As the preceding discussion has already hinted, an important goal of this study is to demonstrate that Tsvetaeva is not simply an inveterate Romantic, as she has so often been portrayed, but a serious, consistent, and intense thinker —albeit a thinker by unconventional, poetic rules and logic. In other words, through an extended examination of Tsvetaeva's poetic thought on the issue of gender, I reveal the lacunae in her maximalism. Yes, she is a Romantic, but she is a Romantic not just by nature but by choice—one who realizes the options of roads not taken and who, moreover, recognizes and admits the consequences of the road taken.

It has often been observed that Tsvetaeva is the consummate poet of the antithesis: life versus death, body versus soul, human versus poet, ephemerality versus eternity. These, among a whole host of other dichotomies inherited from German Romanticism and Russian Symbolism, inform her world-view and shape her poetic universe. The psychologically and poetically complex dialectic of love versus loneliness that lies at the basis of my inquiry is yet one more such antithesis. Through her relationships with her various poetic contemporaries, Tsvetaeva struggles to reconcile singularity with mutuality, poetic inspiration with human companionship. In other words, in her ongoing search for her own, legitimate muse, she is engaged simultaneously in the development of her poetic voice and unique metaphysics, and, on a more mundane level, in the pursuit of real emotional intimacy with another human being. This dialectic between loneliness and love quite possibly lies at the root of all the others, insomuch as it provides the impetus throughout Tsvetaeva's life for her constant reevaluation of her stance as a poet with respect both to humanity and to Poetry as a whole—and, therefore, continual inspiration for and obligation toward her poems.

It is important to emphasize that the problem of alterity that is central to this study is not simply an arbitrarily selected theoretical tool, but is, periodically, the subject of Tsvetaeva's own explicit scrutiny. A passage from her letter to Konstantin Rodzevich (with whom she had a short but intense liaison that resulted in the composition of the two great *poemy* of her Prague years, "Poem of a Mountain" ["Poema gory"] and "Poem of the End" ["Poema kontsa"], 1924) illustrates the unflinching clear-sightedness of Tsvetaeva's self-analysis on this matter:

You performed a miracle upon me, and for the first time I experienced the unity of heaven and earth. Oh, I have loved the earth even before you: trees! I loved everything, was able to love everything, except another, live person. The other was always an obstacle to me [drugoi mne vsegda meshal], a wall that I would beat myself against; I *could not be* with the living! Hence my realization: not—a woman—a spirit [dukh]! The aim not to live— but to die. Dead-end. (6:660)

In this short paragraph, the entire logic of my argument is succinctly laid out. Here we have the antithesis between sexuality and spirituality, life and poetry, earth and heaven that results from Tsvetaeva's impossible gender ("not—a woman—a spirit!"); her inability to penetrate the reality of any subjectivity discrete from her own; and, hence, her inability to love truly and, ultimately, to live at all. To the extent that it is possible for Tsvetaeva to maintain even a semblance of equilibrium in the world, such a feat can be achieved only through poetic language and the fluid mythological archetypes upon which that language draws.[37]

Tsvetaeva's acrobatic metaphor with which I began this introduction thus captures well the profound ambiguity of her life and works. The recklessness with which she tempts the elements, natural forces, and fate itself lends a perplexingly theatrical or satirical quality to events that otherwise would seem to belong squarely to the domain of high tragedy. By means of this desperate ploy, Tsvetaeva is able to create the appearance of reclaiming a large measure of freedom from the various immutable parameters of the concrete reality into which she was born and, thereby, shaping herself into a truly great poet, unencumbered by gender, history, misfortune, or any number of other inimical powers-that-be. Of course, she is never truly unencumbered, and her greatness as a poet comes in part from her responses to these very forces; her fleet-footed dance across the abyss is a feat of poetic deception skillfully and theatrically executed. The stakes in this deception are high, but so is the cost she pays—and this unsettling aspect of Tsvetaeva's poetic gamble has tended to color critical responses to her work.

However, the carefree playfulness with which Tsvetaeva engages in the perilous game of life has mostly gone unnoticed, although this gaiety, too, is an important element of her poetics. Thus, in "A Savage Will" the poet is consumed with laughter even as she implores a hurricane to tear her to shreds; thus, too, in the second epigraph to this introduction, she links laughter and impending death. Similarly, in a poem that describes an uncanny meeting between the souls of a living man and a dead girl, she insists on laughter, rather than the reactions of fear or sorrow that would normally be expected, proclaiming jocularly: "I myself always loved too much to laugh when one shouldn't!" [Ia slishkom sama liubila / Smeiat'sia, kogda nel'zia!] (1:177). Often, indeed, the instrument of Tsvetaeva's brilliant poetic unorthodoxy is no more nor less than mischievous, giggly, girlish laughter. It is precisely her transgressive playfulness—a consequence of her unseemly gender—that allows her to cross the most impenetrable boundaries of human sensibility and existence, at once shaming her and freeing her.[38]

Tsvetaeva's strong mythological bent is one source of the theatricality of her writing; the Symbolist creed of *zhiznetvorchestvo* (literally, *life-creation*), which she never references explicitly but evidently upholds, is another. She casts herself and those she is close to in the roles of mythological heroes and heroines and attempts to execute these roles in such a way that their traditional integrity is maintained at the same time as modern, individual and idiosyncratic nuances are brought out by the new context in which the parts are performed. In most cases, the different roles Tsvetaeva casts are, at the fundamental level, simply (or not so simply) projections of competing and conflicting aspects of her own selfhood—feminine and masculine, mortal and immortal, human and poetic, and so forth.[39] Ultimately, the goal of her creative work is to produce a poetic whole in which the irreconcilable fragments of her subjective being are brought into proximity and made to serve the higher interests of artistic form. Incongruous laughter is necessary for the achievement of this daring goal. Yet, for all her iconoclasm, Tsvetaeva is not alone in her approach; rather, she takes the usual poetic paradigm to its logical extreme. On this matter, Genrikh Gorchakov has written with great perceptiveness:

> *Play with reality*—this is not a subversion of the traditional image of the poet. Let us recall the masquerade quality of Arzamas, the mystical play of the Symbolists, the Futurists' yellow cardigans. Even such a serious philosopher and poet as Vladimir Solov'ev loved mischievous parodies. For some this carefree theatricality became a posture for life, a unique mask behind which to present the self, as, for example, in the cases of Bal'mont and Remizov, or a defensive mask, as, say, for Esenin. . .
>
> For the exhibition of their "oddities" many poets had a public arena: literary salons, clubs, cafes, group almanacs. Tsvetaeva's maturation into a poet knew no such public arena. She was outside of all groups. The only arena for her remained her notebook and her personal relationships . . . Maybe this is why her "oddities," which, in essence, are characteristic of poets in general, created such a shocking impression.
>
> Tsvetaeva's mystifications lost their frankly playful character. Her mystifications became manifestations and were not simply a defensive mask, but served as the confirmation of her existential and poetic principles. Marina Tsvetaeva played in earnest [igrala vser'ez]. And this for some reason offended some people, provoked animosity.[40]

Although Gorchakov does not make explicit the gender relatedness of Tsvetaeva's exile from the "public arena," the point he makes here is basically the same as my own: that Tsvetaeva's poetry, for all its seriousness and even tragedy, is essentially theatrical play in the isolated amphitheater of her soul.[41] As Tsvetaeva writes in one penetrating fragment: "It is decided—we are both playing, and moreover: we play differently: you—honestly, I—cheating. But, for all my dishonest play, I will be the one who plays to the death" [Resheno—igraem oba, / I pritom: igraem razno: / Ty—po chesti, ia—plutuia. / No, pri vsei igre nechistoi, / Nasmert′ zaigraius′—ia] (1:500). Tsvetaeva breaks all the rules of innocent play in order to move it into another sphere and achieve the metaphysical "rush" she needs for her poetry: she cheats in order not to win, but to die.

1

Battling Blok and Akhmatova
In Pursuit of a Muse

> Ох, огонь мой конь — несытый едок!
> Ох, огонь на нем — несытый ездок!
>
> [Ah, my horse is fire — an insatiable eater! Ah, the fire upon him — an insatiable rider!]
> — "Pozhiraiushchii ogon' — moi kon'! . . ." (1918)

> With a poet I always would forget that I myself — am a poet.
> — Letter to Boris Pasternak, 10 February 1923

> At age sixteen I already understood that inspiring poems is greater than writing poems . . . If you don't want to feel jealousy, offense, diminution, loss — don't vie — surrender, dissolve everything soluble within yourself, and out of what remains create a vision, something immortal. This is my behest to some distant inheritress of mine, a poet who will arise in female form.
> — "Plennyi dukh" (1934)

Tsvetaeva never met the great Symbolist poet Aleksandr Blok in person, although she was present at two of his readings in Moscow during May 1920. Her seven-year-old daughter Alia (Ariadna Efron) described in her diary her mother's appearance during Blok's reading: "She had . . . a stern [groznoe] expression on her face, compressed lips, like when she was angry . . . And in general in her face there was no joy, but there was ecstasy."[1] After each of these evenings of poetry, Tsvetaeva sent Alia backstage to convey to Blok an envelope of poems she had dedicated to him — five poems on the first occasion, one on the second — but she pointedly refrained from meeting Blok herself. One scholar records, without acknowledging her source, that Blok's reaction to Tsvetaeva's poems was to "read them — silently, read them — for a long time — and then such a lo-ong smile."[2] However, Blok never attempted to contact Tsvetaeva after this event and made no answer to her, either in person or in his poetry; he was to pass away the following summer.

Tsvetaeva's nonmeeting with Blok continued to torment her several years later; here, she reminisces about it in a letter of 1923:

In life—by the will of poetry—I missed a great meeting with Blok (if we had met—he wouldn't have died), myself a twenty-year-old, I carelessly conjured: "I rukami ne potianus'" [And I will not stretch my arms out to you]. And there was a second... when I stood *near* him, in the crowd, shoulder to shoulder (seven years ago!), I gazed at his hollow temples, at his slightly reddish, unattractive (he was sick; he had been sheared) thin hair, at the dusty collar of his shabby jacket.—My poems were in my pocket—all I had to do was reach out my hand—I didn't budge. (I sent them to him by Alia, without an address, on the eve of his departure.) . . . [This is] my experience of dangerous—almost fatal—games.[3] (6:236)

This passage subtly diverges from the facts: although Tsvetaeva's cycle to Blok was, indeed, written seven years before, the evening she is recollecting occurred only three years earlier; Tsvetaeva at the time was not twenty years old, but twenty-eight; and Alia did not seek Blok out "without an address" on the "eve of his departure," but rather, as already stated, went backstage to him after his reading. This manipulation of the facts joins with Tsvetaeva's own assessment here of her avoidance of Blok (in hopes that he will magically come in pursuit of her) as a "dangerous—almost fatal—game" to indicate her theatrical bent in operation.

Indeed, Tsvetaeva's decision not to seek Blok out is a risky gamble. She painfully decides against thrusting forward that stranger—her physical body, her nonself, her embarrassingly round-faced, rosy-cheeked female hypostasis—before Blok, whom she describes as almost disembodied (she writes elsewhere that on this evening, he was "no longer among the living" [6:228]). Instead, she chooses to come to Blok as disembodied poet and pure voice, much as she would advise Orpheus, the quintessential poet, to go in search of Eurydice in a later poem: "If Orpheus had not gone down to Hades himself, but had sent his own voice, had sent just the voice into the darkness, himself standing, *superfluous,* at the threshold—Eurydice would have walked out along it as along a tightrope..." [Esli b Orfei ne soshel v Aid / Sam, a poslal by golos / Svoi, tol'ko golos poslal vo t'mu, / Sam u poroga *lishnim* / Vstav,—Evridika by po nemu / Kak po kanatu vyshla...] (2:323–24). In real life, however, Blok did not come walking out over the tightrope of Tsvetaeva's conjuring poetic voice. Perhaps the ironic gender reversals in this real-life repetition of the mythic scenario—Tsvetaeva inappropriately plays Orpheus to Blok's Eurydice, when clearly Blok himself is the true Orpheus[4]—can explain the lapse. In any case, whatever Blok's honest reaction was to the adoring, insistent tug of Tsvetaeva's "Poems to Blok" ["Stikhi k Bloku"] (1:288–93), he never let her know.

In Pursuit of a Muse 37

Tsvetaeva's peculiar staging of her nonmeeting with Blok—first in her 1916 "Poems to Blok"; then in her conveyance of those poems through her daughter and her composition of the second Blok cycle (1920–21), more purely adulatory and hence more formulaic and less interesting than the former; and finally in the just-cited theatrical, fictionalized retelling of the episode (1923)—was to be only the first of her many excursions into the treacherous and thrilling territory of poetic flirtation with her contemporaries. In fact, this poetic adventure went hand in hand with another one, for soon after Tsvetaeva completed "Poems to Blok" in the spring of 1916, she began work on her cycle "Poems to Akhmatova" ["Stikhi k Akhmatovoi"] (1:303–9), which was finished the following summer. In 1920–21, at the same time that Tsvetaeva was renewing her interest in Blok, she was also making overtures to Akhmatova in the form of wildly adoring letters from both herself and her young emissary—that is, her precocious daughter Alia—that jar strangely with the cool ironies of her 1916 cycle.[5] These similarities in Tsvetaeva's plot-laying suggest that Blok and Akhmatova are somehow linked in her mind and that they play parallel roles in the development of her poetics. How and why this is the case, and why she feels compelled to return to a contemplation of these two poets some years after she first addressed them in verse, can be gleaned from her January 1921 *poema* "On a Red Steed" ["Na krasnom kone"] (3:16–23), which is saturated with references to Blok and Akhmatova.

The years 1916 to 1921 were a crucial period for Tsvetaeva, spanning as they did the Russian Civil War, along with a number of dramatic and painful events in her personal life. It was during this period that Tsvetaeva truly came into her own as a poet, composing the poems that make up her collections *Milestones I* [*Versty I*] (Moscow, 1922), *Milestones II* [*Versty II*] (Moscow, 1921), *Psyche* [*Psikheia*] (Berlin, 1923), and *Swans' Encampment* [*Lebedinyi stan*] (unpublished until 1957). The *poema* "On a Red Steed," the first of her great works in this genre, can fairly be seen as marking the culmination of this process of poetic maturation and thus as a turning point of sorts. In this chapter, I argue that Tsvetaeva's renewed interest in Blok and Akhmatova at the time she was composing "On a Red Steed" indicates not just an extratextual but a deep poetic, metaphysical, and emotional connection between this *poema* and the 1916 cycles to both poets. "On a Red Steed" can help to explain her seemingly odd avoidance of Blok, as well as the way she narratively recasts this behavior in retrospect; similarly, the *poema* can help to bridge the striking difference in tone between her poems and letters addressed to Akhmatova.

This introduction to the present chapter reflects my view that Tsvetaeva's lyrical cycles dedicated to Blok and Akhmatova are not at all what they appear to be: adoringly eulogistic tributes. In these works, rather, Tsvetaeva is concerned primarily with developing a solution to her own inspirational impasse (i.e., her lack of a valid entry into the muse myth); she uses the poetics of Blok and Akhmatova as a litmus test for the reliability and viability of her own poetic inclinations. This interpretation of the Blok and Akhmatova cycles recalls Tsvetaeva's intuition in "The Drum" that her entry into the poetic tradition will be legitimated through the mediating action of personal dialogue with other poets—a kind of intimacy that promises a curative, synthesizing metamorphosis. "Poems to Blok" and "Poems to Akhmatova" are, at base, experiments in just such poetic metamorphosis, interlocutionary minibattles: Tsvetaeva fills the "male" role of poetic speaker, while her addressee functions as the incarnation of her own personal inspiration (i.e., her muse) and, simultaneously (impossibly), as a competing poetic voice—practitioner of an exemplary inspirational strategy that Tsvetaeva ultimately finds to be unavailable or undesirable for herself.

As a result, her attitude toward Blok and Akhmatova is far more ambivalent, in my view, than most of the cycles' previous commentators have recognized,[6] for Tsvetaeva in these poems is engaged in a contest of competing mythologies—a subtle battle to stake out her own poetic domain. She is caught in the paradoxes of her own crossfire: she does, genuinely, love and admire the poets she addresses, yet at the same time she must overcome the psychological barrier of their greatness that threatens to silence her own gift. This ambivalence is deeper and more complex than the usual "anxiety of influence," because the poets she invokes are not merely her poetic competitors but also her potential muses and (imaginary) lovers.

Such a convoluted state of affairs recalls Tsvetaeva's intuition in her juvenilia that her poetic calling will deprive her of the pleasures and joys of a conventional feminine existence. By identifying her muse with her beloved—in the person of an imposing poetic presence who must inevitably be vanquished for the sake of her own independent poetic survival—she effectively removes any possibility of equating happiness in love with poetic success. This stance springs from an eminently Romantic faith in the poetic possibilities rampant in life's impossibilities—in the beauty of orchestrated tragedy, as it were. The unrealizability or nonrequital of love becomes a code for poetic fate. Thus, Blok's and Akhmatova's factual absence in Tsvetaeva's real life is the correlative to the imaginariness of the horseman-muse of "On a Red Steed" to whom they will eventually yield place in her evolving poetic mythology. Indeed, for all Tsvetaeva's passionately ambivalent regard for Blok and Akhmatova, both remained essentially defined for her throughout her life by the maddening grandeur of their absence.

An Angelic Muse: "Poems to Blok"

It has become commonplace to observe that Tsvetaeva revered Blok as a poetic demiurge. Ariadna Efron was the first to remark that her mother's feeling for Blok took the unique form of quasi-religious worship: "Blok was the single

In Pursuit of a Muse

poet in Tsvetaeva's life whom she respected not as a brother in the 'stringed craft,' but as a poetic deity, and before whom, as to a deity, she bowed down." [7] It is true that in Tsvetaeva's "Poems to Blok," her apotheosis of Blok as poet-martyr, poet-Christ, and broken angel provides the organizing principle. Yet these images emanate originally from Blok's own poetry; thus, their presence in Tsvetaeva's cycle is insufficient to prove her deification of her poetic addressee. Instead, when the constellation of meanings into which she draws these angelic images is considered, it becomes apparent that her primary purpose in the cycle is not Blok's eulogization but her own poetic self-definition in the shadow of his towering, shining presence. Specifically, it is the iconic unity of Blok's poetry and his life that is most threatening to Tsvetaeva's nascent self-confidence. She conceives of Blok's poetics as enacting that very transcendence of body (i.e., gender) and sublimation of erotic desire that she herself longs to achieve.

"Your name" ["Imia tvoe—ptitsa v ruke . . ."], the opening poem of "Poems to Blok," is an elaborate meditation on the sound of Blok's surname and the many associations that sound evokes.[8] Tsvetaeva weaves the themes of Blok's poetry into these acoustic associations and thereby derives his poetic genius and his entire poetic path from the primary cocoon of sound that first contained and gave rise to him: Б—Л—О—К—Ъ.[9]

> Имя твое—птица в руке,
> Имя твое—льдинка на языке,
> Одно единственное движенье губ,
> Имя твое—пять букв.
>
> [Your name—is a bird in the hand, your name—is an icicle on the tongue, one single motion of the lips, your name—is five letters.]

In drawing attention to the spelling of Blok's name, Tsvetaeva also draws attention to the presence of the silent hard sign—a pre-Revolutionary orthographic convention—at the end of his name. This sign, present but inaudible, is like the poet's spirit—the invisible aura of his visible being—and thus becomes, in this context, a mark of Blok's ineffable genius. Significantly, what the hard sign is to Blok's name, Blok's name is to Tsvetaeva's poem: the name *Blok,* itself never directly articulated anywhere in the poem, shimmers instead through abundant echoes and half-rhymes and thus serves as a kind of silent sign attesting to her own poetic election.

At the same time, though, Tsvetaeva's ebullient paronomastic play with the name masks the semantic implications of the name itself. For *blok,* in Russian as in English, conveys the sense of blockage, obstruction, impassability. It is the first syllable of the words *blokirovat'* [to obstruct], *blokada* [blockade], and *blokar'* [block-maker]. Surely these semantic nuances did not go unnoticed by

Tsvetaeva, with her intense flair for uncovering similar sound etymologies—especially given the fact that the acoustico-semantic revelation of Blok's name forms the entire substance of her poem. Rather, these nuances are obsessively present by their absence: the poet Blok is designated by his name as an insurmountable obstacle in Tsvetaeva's own efforts toward poetic voice, an obstacle that she attempts to deny and transform. Through a playful exercise of her poetic wit, she will muffle Blok's threat by conjuring a whole complex of alternative images and meanings from the name's echoing permutations.

The imagery of "Your name" seems at first to comprise a random collection of unrelated objects, generated by the intersection of, on the one hand, purely acoustic reminiscences of Blok's name—*gub, bukv, visok, kurok, zvonko, gromkoe, vek, sneg, glotok, glubok* [lips, letters, brow, shot, resonantly, loud, eyelids, snow, gulp, deep]—and, on the other hand, imagistic reminiscences of Blok's poetry—a bird, an icicle, snow, a harness bell, and so on. However, a closer examination reveals that the poem's imagery is in fact tightly organized around a single theme: the stoic tolerance of pain. Moreover, this pain is of a very particular kind: the bird fluttering (and perhaps clawing and pecking) in the hand, the icicle on the tongue, the impact of the caught ball in the palm of the hand, the silver bell in the mouth, the stone breaking the pond's surface (as felt by the pond), the pounding of the horse's hooves (as felt by the pavement, or by the listening ear), the gun's trigger striking the brow, the kiss upon the snow, the icy gulp—all these images convey a unique moment of transition at which an otherwise pleasurable, anticipated sensation is momentarily intensified and thus crosses the threshold into discomfort, violence, or torment. Tsvetaeva's tolerance of this pain is therefore ambiguous; there is a continuing savoring of pleasure that spans the transition into discomfort. The impact of Blok's poetic word on her receptive hearing and heart is implicitly likened to this ambiguous sensation of pleasure in pain.

The intensity of this sensation goes beyond the usual expectations of poetic transport. Upon further consideration it becomes clear that the physical sensation that lies at the base of each of the poem's images is only a secondary contributor to its painful impact. What is more important is that each of these images captures an instant of otherwise unarrestable motion in space and time: the bird will fly away, the icicle will melt, the ball will be thrown, the stone will sink, the horse will gallop onward out of earshot, the bullet will be irrevocable, the snow will melt, the liquid will be swallowed (and thirst will return). Blok's name—as a stand-in for Blok's poetry—is in perpetual flight: it cannot be fully grasped, slowed, possessed. Yet the attempt to grasp, slow, and possess is precisely the impulse that underlies Tsvetaeva's poem and the cycle as a whole, as she well realizes; hence, the painful paradoxes of her imagery. "Poems to Blok" records her poetic attempt to touch and catch the untouchable and uncatchable Blok and her awareness of the futility of this enterprise. Her anguished exclama-

In Pursuit of a Muse 41

tion in the poem's final stanza ("ah, impossible!" [akh, nel'zia!]) makes use of the double meaning of *nel'zia* to express in condensed form both the transgressive nature of her poetic project to "capture" Blok, and the utter impossibility of this project's fulfillment. The result is the subtle but insistent vibration of tension and frustration throughout the cycle's first poem. For all that Tsvetaeva attempts to circumlocute the creative blockage represented by Blok's name, she is left contemplating it squarely.

In "Your name" Tsvetaeva desires Blok blatantly, embarrassingly, as she should not: not as a poet desires his muse, but as a woman desires her lover. Blok's eroticism in Tsvetaeva's understanding is metaphoric, abstract, transcendent, purificatory, harnessed to poetic flight; whereas her own desire is insistently physical, possessive, desperate, tainting, enchaining. Although this distinction could well be rooted in the clash between Tsvetaeva's and Blok's poetics — the Symbolists' mysticism and exclusive orientation toward the otherworldly are foreign to Tsvetaeva, with her emphasis on concrete phenomena as a springboard for poetry — she herself chooses to interpret her difference with Blok as the sole result of gender difference. Indeed, this choice is in keeping with Tsvetaeva's usual conflation of sexuality and gender, so that she always construes her illicit passions as the natural consequence of her unseemly gender. Her aspiration to transcend her gender thus is reconceived as a striving to neutralize her erotic desire for Blok, which marks her as female:

> Имя твое — ах, нельзя! —
> Имя твое — поцелуй в глаза,
> В нежную стужу недвижных век,
> Имя твое — поцелуй в снег.
>
> [Your name — ah, impossible! — Your name — is a kiss into the eyes, into the sweet chill of motionless lids, Your name — is a kiss into the snow.]

Tsvetaeva's juxtaposition of the passionate kiss into the snow and the chaste kiss into a corpse's eyelids encodes what she believes is poetry's mandate for the sublimation of sensual passion. Here we see an eroticism that is paradoxically divested of the erotic; she wants to use the evocative power of eroticism in her poetry, while neutralizing its human meanings. Hence, in "Your name," she experiments with replacing the sensation of a kiss in the mouth with the sensation of a name, and replacing an actual bed partner with a poetic dream: "With your name — sleep is deep" [S imenem tvoim — son glubok].[10]

The "dream" that Blok's name evokes is a poetic irreality that is more real than reality itself; and this is the key to understanding Tsvetaeva's peculiar brand of poetic sublimation, and hence her cunning poetic triumph. For her, sublimation of desire is not sublimation at all in the usual sense, but a redefinition of realities: in the very act of articulating her beloved's (here, Blok's) inaccessibility, she possesses him fully by the genius of her poetic talent, and thus she draws him into a dream that she ordains as mutual (after all, the name of the dream is his name). Through her precise enunciation of his "uncapturability," she captures him completely. In fact, not only Blok's distilled essence is present in Tsvetaeva's poem; his voice is too—in the form of pirated echoes of his own poetry. David Sloane's description of the "Poems to Blok" as "a dialogue carried on by a single articulatory apparatus"[11] is apt as a definition of the ontological maneuver performed by Tsvetaeva in "Your name" as well as in the cycle as a whole. Yet this supposed "dialogue" remains avowedly imaginary. Just as Blok is accessible to Tsvetaeva only through her full appreciation of his inaccessibility, so, too, it is only within the magical space of poetry that she can come close to him. The very thrill of the dialogue emanates from its impossibility.

The imaginariness of Tsvetaeva's relationship to Blok in "Your name" indicates that this is the archetypical relationship of poet to muse, with an obvious twist on the traditional gender roles.[12] This twist bears consequences. Whereas in Aleksandr Pushkin's poem "What is in my name for you?" ["Chto v imeni tebe moem? . . ."] poetry is incarnated in the poet's own name while his muse remains an anonymous pronoun, in Tsvetaeva's poem, on the contrary, it is the name of her male muse that confers legitimacy.[13] Indeed, Blok's name serves as a convenient shorthand for the complex of relationships that configure poetic inspiration; his name is the black hat out of which Tsvetaeva, magician-like, draws the tangled colored streamers that together make up the foundation of her poetry: love, eroticism, longing, pleasure, pain, impossibility, inaccessibility, inexpressibility, transcendence, and so on. When she co-opts Blok as her muse, she transforms the genre of panegyric obeisance into an "unfeminine" attempt at self-assertion and even dominance. In my view, this strategy is not an indication of any megalomania or wounded narcissism on Tsvetaeva's part.[14] Rather, she uncovers the hidden relationship of poetic power to gender in the traditional conception of inspiration and thereby consciously reveals through the very structure of her thought the narcissism inherent in the poetic enterprise. This narcissism is essential to her daring, as a young poet and especially as a female poet, to eulogize the great Blok—whose name for her is, in the final analysis, synonymous with poetry itself.

Nevertheless, Tsvetaeva knows ahead of time that her reversals of gender and genre expectations are insufficient to bring relief from her inspirational impasse; in "Your name," the element of tension and the frustration of unattainability are omnipresent and inescapable. This outcome is to be expected, because Blok is not, in fact, a muse to her in either sense of the word—he is neither the purely abstract force of poetic inspiration, nor that force's physical, human incarnation in pure body. A true muse is, after all, an emanation of the true poet's fate: she exists only to serve him and has no independent needs or hypostases; even when she abandons him, she does so because her abandonment is fated, for the sake of his poetry. The poet's nostalgic connection with her is not broken by their separation, but is even strengthened, as in Pushkin's lyric: "There is a memory of me, there is in the world a heart in which I live..." [Est' pamiat' obo mne, / Est' v mire serdtse, gde zhivu ia...]. The muse's whole fate is contained in the poem that preserves her memory; her own name, voice, and whatever independent identity she once possessed become irrelevant. In "Your name," this configuration of poetic power is reversed. It is Tsvetaeva, the lyric speaker, who is anonymous. Blok, her would-be muse, is simply indifferent to her, wholly unaware of her existence. Blok is emphatically not Tsvetaeva's fate. Blok is a poet; Blok is his own fate.

For Tsvetaeva in "Your name," then, there can be no poetic apotheosis of the kind that Blok himself undergoes in his own poetry. His transcendence is made possible by the mediation of his "Beautiful Lady" [Prekrasnaia Dama], arguably the most famous muse of Russian literature, whereas Tsvetaeva is left without a true muse at all. She is not an angel (as she believes Blok to be), but a woman. Her genius as a poet is to be revealed not through transcendence, but through her embrace of unassuageable desire, her transgressive sensuality—the result, as she believes, of her gender.[15] Ariadna Efron's comments on Tsvetaeva's recognition of this dilemma are deeply insightful:

> Tsvetaeva experienced Blok's poetry as such an ethereal height—by virtue not of its remoteness [otreshennost'] from life, but of its *purification* [*ochishchennost'*] by life (fire purifies thus!)—that she, in her "sinfulness" [grekhovnost'] could never even dare to conceive of the possibility of sharing in this creative zenith—but could only go down on bended knee before him.[16]

Here we must surmise that the immutable "sinfulness" to which Efron refers is none other than Tsvetaeva's female gender. The impossibility for Tsvetaeva of undergoing Blokian purification from life is inherent in her femininity, which she equates with body even as she rages against the equation. Femininity is the "original sin" of her birth—a conviction apparently instilled in her since early childhood, for her mother had hoped for a son.[17]

Tsvetaeva's recognition in "Your name" of the distance between Blok and herself and her projection of her own talent as a subversive one that will prompt her to capture what is not hers to take, desire what is not hers to crave, is an important discovery in the course of her poetic maturation. A digression at this point to several important ideas from Tsvetaeva's retrospective prose essays of the 1930s will help to put the painful inspirational experiment of "Your name" into this larger context of her poetic and personal coming of age; the poem is not an isolated incident but the archetype for certain profound convictions about hopeless love and misplaced desire that originate in her earliest memory and continue to shape her writing throughout her life. In these examples, Tsvetaeva's inappropriate passion is not for the poet himself, as in "Your name," but for the poet's muse.

The three muses I have in mind appear in three separate essays: Asia Turgeneva in "A Captive Spirit" ["Plennyi dukh"], Tsvetaeva's memoir about poet Andrei Belyi; Tat′iana Larina from "My Pushkin" ["Moi Pushkin"]; and Nadia Ilovaiskaia from "The House at Old Pimen" ["Dom u starogo Pimena"]. Each of these three women takes on mythical proportions in Tsvetaeva's perception,[18] and each prompts her to recognize with renewed poignancy the double bind of her gender and her talent. In her mythopoetic descriptions of all three encounters, Tsvetaeva views her beloved—through the instrument of poetry— with a male gaze. She is female, but she is not beautiful as the female should be and therefore is not herself beloved. Moreover, she is robbed by poetry of the possibility of happy, mutual love but is given clairvoyance in recompense. She sees these three beautiful women—Asia, Tat′iana, and Nadia—as muses incarnate (even the fictional Tat′iana she first encounters in the flesh, at a school play), and, true to her identity as a poet, she is smitten by love for them. Yet this love is clearly impossible: Tsvetaeva is a young, ungainly girl—in other words, she is not a man who could love them, nor yet a true woman (who would be loved: for her beauty). Her timing, her gender, and her physical appearance are all "wrong."

However, her love is not just a young girl's frivolous crush or shallow sister love. Tsvetaeva is tormented by the passionate love of the born poet, the poet who does not yet even know she is a poet—the true poetic love inspired by loss and utter hopelessness, as she defines it in "My Pushkin":

Pushkin infected me with love. With the *word*—love . . . When the maid, in passing, picked up an orange cat from someone's windowsill where it sat and yawned, and it lived with us for three days in the room with the palms, and then ran away and never returned— that was love. When Avgusta Ivanovna said that she would leave us to go to Riga and never return—that was love. When the drummer boy left for the war and then never returned—that was love. When in springtime the pink-gossamer, moth-balled Parisian dolls are put away again in their trunk after an airing out, and I stand and watch and know that I'll never see them ever again—that is love. Which is to say that *this thing*—from the orange cat, Avgusta Ivanovna, the drummer boy, and the doll—burns the same way and in the same place as from Zemfira, and Aleko, and Mariula, and the Grave.[19] (5:68)

Indeed, Tsvetaeva's encounters with Asia, Tat′iana, and Nadia all inspire this particular kind of hopeless yearning born of loss. Beautiful Nadia dies from tuberculosis at the age of twenty-two, and only after her death does the young Marina's true passion for her begin. The imminent defection of Asia to the "other shore" [tot bereg] of marriage is the source of Tsvetaeva's love for her, love that is indistinguishable from physical pain: "And, strangely . . . already the beginning of some kind of jealousy, already the clear hint of pain, already the

In Pursuit of a Muse

first prick of *Zahnschmerzen im Herzen* [toothache in the heart], that soon—she'll go away, she'll stop—loving me" (4:230). The pain of Pushkin's fatal stomach wound is a token of this same love, as is the bench on which Tat'iana and Onegin do not sit: "The bench on which they did *not* sit turned out to be fortuitous [predopredeliaiushchei]. Neither then, nor later, did I ever love when *kissing,* always—when parting [kogda rasstavalis']. Never—when we sat down together, always—when we went our separate ways [kogda raskhodilis']" (5:71).

Tat'iana, not a poet but a literary character who learns her lessons from the Romantic novels she reads, becomes a model for Tsvetaeva: "A lesson in courage. A lesson in pride. A lesson in faithfulness. A lesson in fate. A lesson in loneliness" (5:71). Olga Peters Hasty has shown convincingly that "through the reading Tat'iana, Tsvetaeva aligns herself with the writing Pushkin."[20] Pushkin thus teaches Tsvetaeva that imagination and aloneness are inextricably linked:

A *dream* and *alone* are one and the same . . . The dream is already a substantial proof of aloneness, as well as its source and its only recompense, even as aloneness is the dream's Draconian law and only field of activity. (5:86)

Tat'iana, through Pushkin, gives Tsvetaeva the courage to choose this aloneness of the imagination over the possible togetherness of real life: "Tat'iana and the women who model themselves on her choose consciously to provoke loss and thereby to sustain the creative energy of their desire."[21] Yet Pushkin's tutelage notwithstanding, Tsvetaeva's predilection for the torment of unrealizable desire is innate, just as is her poetic talent: "Between the fullness of desire and the fulfillment of desire, between the fullness of suffering and the emptiness of happiness my choice was made from birth—and before birth" (5:72). Poetry represents for Tsvetaeva a way of rectifying the breaches of real life, rectifying accidents such as her plain face, her young age, her wrong gender—all of which forbid her from realizing her love for Asia and Nadia, and all of which only intensify her passion.

When the young Tsvetaeva glimpses her destiny as a poet, she glimpses, too, the possibility of escape from these and all limitations, the possibility of a new, self-willed, yet fated becoming. This is the sense of the German lines she quotes from Goethe in two of the essays in question: "O lasst mich scheinen, bis ich werde!" [O let me seem, until I become!] (4:231; 5:131). In her silent address to Asia, she elaborates on this sentiment: "Asia, of course I have square, completely unartistic fingers, and all of me is not worth your little pinkie and Belyi's thumbnail [i.e., she is worthy of being neither a muse nor a poet—A. D.], but, Asia, all the same I write poems and don't know myself, what I will still become—but I do know I *will become* [sama ne znaiu, chem eshche budu—znaiu, chto *budu*]!" (4:231). With respect to Nadia, Tsvetaeva is even more explicit: it is not just her own plainness that is a barrier in the real world, but her gender, which poetry (and death) will remove:

> I will become [werde], I will *realize myself* [sbudus′] there according to the shape of my soul, so I will be as beautiful as Nadia and even if *not,* even if the old shell remains . . .
>
> > Und diese himmlischen Gestalten
> > Sie fragen nicht nach Mann und Weib
>
> > [And these heavenly forms, they do not care if one is man or woman]
>
> That means that they will not look at beauty and nonbeauty... There — I will win back my losses [tam — otygraius′] . . . And I knew that in *this* love I would have no rivals. (5:131)

What is lost here in this life is Tsvetaeva's naked soul, which is canceled out by the binary relations of *Mann und Weib.* As she laments in "My Pushkin": "My God! How a person loses with the attainment of a sex!" [Kak chelovek teriaet s obreteniem pola!] (5.85). Tsvetaeva in this world is fit neither to be the muse of a true poet, nor the poet of a true muse. However, her dream of being elected by her inaccessible beloved in the next world, where she will be freed from the constraints of gender, she plots not only in her reminiscence of the dead Nadia, but in her prescience in the second poem of "Poems to Blok" of the dead Blok as well.

This poem, "Tender ghost" ["Nezhnyi prizrak . . ."], continues the dream with which "Your name" concludes. Now, however, Tsvetaeva imagines that Blok is no longer insensible to her existence. On the contrary, like the dead Nadia who sends her ghost to seek out the young Tsvetaeva in boarding school, here the "ghost" of the still-living Blok appears before her in a dream, bearing a cryptic message regarding the dangers and sacrifices her poetic destiny will entail. She welcomes him wonderingly, with feigned innocence:

> Нежный призрак,
> Рыцарь без укоризны,
> Кем ты призван
> В мою молодую жизнь?
>
> Во мгле сизой
> Стоишь, ризой
> Снеговой одет.
>
> [Tender ghost/phantom, knight without reproach, by whom are you summoned into my young life? In the gray haze you stand, draped in a raiment of snow.]

Tsvetaeva's opening question in "Tender ghost" prefigures her question to Nadia in "The House at Old Pimen": "Why did you choose to follow after *me* specifi-

In Pursuit of a Muse

cally, arise before *me?*" (5:133). In both cases the answer is, of course, Tsvetaeva's future poetic greatness. Thus, by fantasizing Blok's special mission, she implicitly transforms her frustrated erotic desire for him into a conviction of her poetic election—in the realm of dream, beyond the verifiability of fact or fiction. Later, the Blokian rider on a red steed will serve a similar fatidic function.

All the imagery of "Tender ghost" contributes to the dream scenario. Blok appears standing in mist, dressed in snow; the danger or "enmity" he represents to Tsvetaeva is experienced as a wind, the impact of his poetry as a dangerous spell. Even her own enchanted footsteps toward him are disembodied, more like floating than walking, as he continues his seductive poetic conjuring:

> Голубоглазый
> Меня сглазил
> Снеговой певец.
>
> Снежный лебедь
> Мне под ноги перья стелет.
> Перья реют
> И медленно никнут в снег.
>
> Так по перьям,
> Иду к двери,
> За которой—смерть.
>
> [The blue-eyed snow-bard has laid the Evil Eye on me. The snowy swan spreads its down beneath my feet. The feathers soar and slowly drift down into the snow. Thus I walk over feathers toward the door, behind which—is death.]

The voice in which Blok calls Tsvetaeva is inhuman, the voice of pure sound or pure music, described alternately as "distant jingle bells" [bubentsy dalekie] and "a long cry, a swan's call" [dlinnyi krik, lebedinyi klik].[22] The whole aim of this unearthly call is to propel her, zombielike, toward the threshold to the other world ("the door, behind which—is death"), to which his poetry—and, potentially, her own—give access. This terrifying doorway, like the symbolic "blue windows" beyond which Blok sings ("He sings to me from beyond the blue windows" [On poet mne / Za sinimi oknami]), is not an obstacle for him, for he is pure spirit. Tsvetaeva, however, in order to pass through to the beyond, must sever body from soul.

Until the poem's last line, it seems that Tsvetaeva senses, through Blok's example, the danger of the poetic enterprise, although she is manipulated by the irrefutable coercion of dream logic and cannot refuse poetry's summons. Yet, here as elsewhere, she plays with this appearance of coercion, hinting subtly in the poem's final line that in fact this existential predicament is of her own choosing and making—precisely *linguistic* making, for she answers Blok's threatening verbal conjuring with her own:

> Милый призрак!
> Я знаю, что все мне снится.
> Сделай милость:
> Аминь, аминь, рассыпься!
> Аминь.
>
> [Dear ghost/phantom! I know that this is all a dream. Do me a favor: amen, amen, disappear! Amen.]

The term *prizrak*—Tsvetaeva's appellative for Blok in the first and last stanzas of "Tender ghost"—shimmers ambiguously between the word's two meanings, *ghost* and *phantom,* throughout the poem, drawing attention to the ambiguous location of Tsvetaeva's vision between the realms of death and dream to which each of the two meanings, respectively, belongs. With the return of this word in the final stanza, the poem seems to come full circle, suggesting that the vision was, indeed, only a dream. If this is the case, then the dream obediently dissolves as Tsvetaeva shirks her frightening poetic destiny and renews her commitment to waking reality at the poem's close.

In keeping with this interpretation, Tsvetaeva's first two *amens* seem to tame the threat that Blok represents, suggesting her rejection of poetic sorcery in favor of traditional Christian piety and a tidy and safe awakening from nightmare. However, her apparent move toward retreat is canceled by the poem's final line and word, which in a single breath breaks through the almost-closed circle she has created, adding a magical third and final *amen.* There is no exclamation point here, but a full stop; no hysteria, no fear, no intonation of prayer or incantation. This final *amen,* in fact, is ambiguous. It may be read as an intensification of the preceding two *amens*—urging the futility of attempts to exorcise Blok's "ghost," and hence Tsvetaeva's sober acceptance of the nightmare of poetic destiny. On the other hand, the final *amen* may be read as a reversal of the preceding two, for the line break that separates it from its fellows suggests that it sanctions not the injunction to Blok's phantom to "disperse," but the poem (the "dream") as a whole. In this case it signifies not rejection, but acceptance: "so be it."

Ultimately, the only clear point is that this culminating *amen* indicates Tsvetaeva's own linguistic power and the autonomy of her poetic will—as signaled by the fact that the word creates an extra, fifth line to the poem's final stanza, which, according to the pattern previously established (alternating quartets and tercets), should contain four lines in all.[23] By this final, ambiguous twist of meaning, Tsvetaeva succeeds in establishing the verity of both meanings of *prizrak* simultaneously. For she acknowledges that this realm of poetry is only a dream;

yet at the same time, she claims poetry's irreality and impossibility as her own—her fate. We thus see here a deepening of Tsvetaeva's recognition of the stakes involved in her pursuit of her poetic calling. Whereas a dreamlike transcendence of body by spirit is possible for Blok, for her the same urge leads not to transcendence, but to an inescapable nightmare, to death. His poetic power, his poetic dream, his poetic transport are her danger.

In the wake of this chilling realization, the third poem of "Poems to Blok," "You pass by" ["Ty prokhodish' na Zapad Solntsa . . ."], recapitulates the themes, imagery, and motifs of the cycle's first poem, but in a very different key. Now Tsvetaeva no longer struggles, either against her own destiny as she apprehends it, or against Blok's inaccessibility. Rather, a quiet confidence in her own future poetic stardom pervades the poem, as she accepts the trial of "non-love"—the result of her "wrong-genderedness"—as an integral part of her own poetic self-definition. Some commentators [24] have read Tsvetaeva's refusal to pronounce Blok's name and her exclamation "Ah, impossible!" in "Your name" as an indication that Tsvetaeva in that poem stops just short of blasphemy. The liltingly beautiful "You pass by," on the contrary, seems at first to be much "tamer"; it is cast in the form of a prayer and in fact takes its first two lines and its refrain—"quiet light" [svete tikhii]—from the imagery and archaic diction of a prayer from the Orthodox liturgy.[25] David Sloane, in part on the basis of this tonal shift, discerns a generous, self-effacing trajectory motivating Tsvetaeva's entire Blok cycle: "[The heroine's] erotic, possessive love, which is strongest in poem I, ultimately yields to a different kind of love, which is akin to religious piety and imbued with the spirit of community." [26]

Despite appearances, however, Tsvetaeva's embrace of transgression in the third poem to Blok is even more blatant than in the first. Now, Blok awakens in her pure spiritual ecstasy, and she reveres him unabashedly, supplying his image, if not his name, in place of Christ's in the traditional liturgy. Indeed, Tsvetaeva's reluctance in this poem to pronounce Blok's name aloud reinforces her decision to term it a "holy name" [sviatoe imia]; she will not take Blok's name in vain, for he is fully deified: "And I will not call you by your name, and I will not stretch my arms out to you" [I po imeni ne okliknu, / I rukami ne potianus']. Indeed, Tsvetaeva's humility here is only feigned, for if Blok has become a deity, then it is the force of her own poetry that has made him so. Hence, the abstract power of his name in "You pass by" is far greater than was its erotic power in "Your name," for now Tsvetaeva is no longer in pursuit, but claims the right to speak and act in his name in the realm of poetry (though her wish to do so in the realm of real life has proved unrealizable): "And in your holy name I will kiss the evening snow" [I vo imia tvoe sviatoe, / Potseluiu vechernii sneg]. Surely this is not "religious piety" in any traditional sense; perhaps "quiet blasphemy" would be a more accurate description.[27]

Unlike Christ, Blok is martyred by his own internal lyric drive rather than by the forces of evil, and for the sake of poetry and of fulfilling his own unique poetic fate, rather than for the sake of the masses. As Tsvetaeva would later write in her 1933 essay "Poets with a History and Poets without a History" ["Poety s istoriei i poety bez istorii"]: "If we see Blok as a poet with a history, then this history is his own, Blok's, the history of a lyric poet, a history that is just the lyricism of suffering" (5:409). Blok's transcendence represents for Tsvetaeva an alternative to traditional Christian faith: her faith, her choice—she chooses to worship the poet.[28] Yet this transgressive worship is, at the same time, a restatement of her belief that poetry opens the possibility of the only true companionship: a companionship of souls stripped of gender, of the human with the human, that bypasses mediation by any legislating divinity. Her aspiration to such companionship is stated more explicitly in a poem written only several months after the 1916 "Poems to Blok": "Toward the bright and singing door, through the cloud of incense I hurry, just as a person eternally hurries away past God—to another person" [K dveri svetloi i pevuchei / Cherez ladannuiu tuchu / Toroplius', // Kak toropitsia ot veka / Mimo Boga—k cheloveku / Chelovek] (1:317). Here is the same bright, singing doorway that appears in "Tender ghost," behind which is the antithesis to mundane, proscriptive reality—the universe of poetry, be it called death or otherwise. Ultimately, as Tsvetaeva comes to accept in "Poems to Blok," her attainment of the promised meeting is not important; what is important is the constant desire, striving, hurrying toward that other realm.

Consequently, in "You pass by" there is no longer any sense of Blok as an enemy, nor is there mention of the torment Tsvetaeva's speaker feels in loving him; the only hint of her individual pain is muffled by the generalizing power of strong subtextual echoes: "Into the hand, pale from kisses, I will not pound my own nail" [V ruku, blednuiu ot lobzanii, / Ne vob'iu svoego gvozdia].[29] Tsvetaeva in this poem accepts both her poetic calling (of which her unrealizable love for Blok is a sign) and her gender difference from Blok (of which his immense distance from her is the result). She relinquishes her doubts, her desires, and her protests; she recognizes Blok's lack of passion [besstrastie] for her and, as is typical of her in such situations, she is stricken by paralysis:[30]

> Мимо окон моих—бесстрастный—
> Ты пройдёшь в снеговой тиши . . .
>
> [Past my windows—passionless—you will pass by in the snowy quiet . . .]

Hence the basic contrast that structures this poem: the speaker's stunned, stationary position (behind the windows, through which she no longer tries to climb), versus Blok in motion, in the process of transformation. The erasure of his tracks in the snow symbolizes his gradual disembodiment: "You pass by to

In Pursuit of a Muse

the West of the Sun, and the blizzard sweeps up your tracks" [Ty prokhodish′ na Zapad Solntsa, / I metel′ zametaet sled]. The poem's speaker, by contrast, leaves not only her tracks but her whole physical self buried in that same snow: "And, standing beneath the slow snow, I will bend down upon my knees in the snow" [I, pod medlennym snegom stoia, / Opushchus′ na koleni v sneg]. Blok has passed through the frightening threshold of the previous poem unharmed and purified, while Tsvetaeva, transfixed, remains behind in body but follows his every motion with her soul. There is no outward striving in this poem, either toward (as in "Your name") or away from (as in "Tender ghost") all that Blok represents; this is a peaceful interlude in Tsvetaeva's contemplation of her beloved, in which the weight of renunciation is a thing of beauty in itself, though bittersweet.

Tsvetaeva's quiet chagrin shows through, however, in the poem's middle two stanzas, which state her renunciation explicitly and qualify her professions of selfless worship of Blok:

> Я на душу твою — не зарюсь!
> Нерушима твоя стезя.
>
> [I do not lust for your soul! Your path is inviolable.]

These lines are tinged by bitterness, not only in their tone, but in their surprising shift toward figurative, spiritual lust—which, even in the denial, is just as possessive as the speaker's physical lust in "Your name." Tsvetaeva's admission of lust reminds us that her contemplation of her relationship to Blok throughout the cycle is an allegory of the process of her own inspiration, her own poetic becoming. "Soul" no less than "body," then, is a metaphor for the unnamable magnetic force that galvanizes poetic flight. The verb *zarit′sia* [to lust] at the same time suggests the ambiguous noun *zaria* [dawn/dusk], whose etymology it shares (both words are related to *zarevo* [a conflagration][31]). Although this word does not actually occur in "You pass by," it is semantically present in the poem's pervasive evening imagery: "to the West of the Sun," "evening light," "evening snow"; furthermore, the prayer that echoes in this poem is part of the Orthodox Vespers. The threshold between day and night indicated by *zaria* is that same dividing horizon "to the West of the Sun" that Blok crosses in the poem and which thus marks the moment of his attainment of poetic transcendence.

Tsvetaeva's evocation of Blok's poetic path [put′] by the word *stezia* extends this cosmic metaphor; for the word *stezia,* in addition to its biblical resonance,[32] also refers to the fiery tail of a falling star or a comet. In a poem of 1923 from the cycle "Poets" (2:184–86), Tsvetaeva would use a similar image to describe the poet's cometlike trajectory through life, subject to the gravitational pull of mysterious celestial forces that are not sensible by earthbound mortals: "By way of planets, omens, the ruts of roundabout parables... Between yes and no, even having swung his arm around from the bell tower, he will conjure a detour... For the path of comets—is the path of poets . . . Your path, maned curve, is not foreseen by any calendar!" [Planetami, primetami, okol′nykh / Pritch rytvinami... Mezhdu da i net / On dazhe razmakhnuvshis′s kolokol′ni / Kriuk vymorochit... Ibo put′ komet—// Poetov put′ . . . / Tvoia stezia, grivastaia krivaia, / Ne predugadana kalendarem!]. By using the comet's orbit to represent Blok's path, Tsvetaeva asserts his independence of earth and earthlings, and indeed of the whole solar system.

However, Tsvetaeva's promise that Blok's orbit will remain undisturbed is not the humble self-abnegation that it seems, for her very statement implies that she is his heavenly kin: another lonely planet, a cosmic force capable of luring him from his path, were she so to decide. This force is even hinted at in the poem—although its name, like Blok's, is suppressed: *star* [zvezda]. We recall that the star is the emblem of the poetic destiny Tsvetaeva dreams of attaining in her early poem "Only a Girl." The word *zvezda* does not actually occur in "You pass by," but it is present in the repetition of the letter *z* in the third stanza's rhymes (*zarius′/stezia/lobzanii/gvozdia* [lust/path/kisses/nail]), and, in particular, it echoes unmistakably in the background of the rhyme *stezia/gvozdia*. As a result, although the contrast between the speaker's stasis and humility on the one hand, and Blok's motion and grandeur on the other, seems to argue that Tsvetaeva is abandoned, left behind in the mundane world by an otherworldly poetic deity unresponsive to her prayers, her poem's purposeful omissions hint that this state of affairs is only temporary.

Tsvetaeva's refusal to utter Blok's name aloud in "You pass by" thus becomes evidence of a secret knowledge, encoded in the poem's two other unuttered words: *zvezda* portends her own poetic stardom, while her refusal to lust ("ne zarius′") contains her refusal to reveal as yet her own poetic horizons (*zaria*). Tsvetaeva's suppression of *star* [zvezda] and *dawn* [zaria] in the context of her adulation of Blok serves to take these words away from Blok, to make them her own. By the same logic, then, her suppression of Blok's name in this poem raises the suspicion that she has already taken full possession of it—that is, that she has complete confidence in his and her eventual poetic equality; later in the cycle, she will use similar cosmic symbolism and linguistic play to make this statement explicitly:

> Но моя река—да с твоей рекой,
> Но моя рука—да с твоей рукой
> Не сойдутся, Радость моя, доколь
> Не догонит заря—зари.
>
> [But my river—with your river, but my hand—with your hand will not merge, my Joy, until dawn overtakes dusk.]

In Pursuit of a Muse 53

Blok may be the dusk; but Tsvetaeva is the dawn. If he is a falling star, then she is a rising star. She may never overtake him; yet she is his other half and will chase him into eternity. Her thought has come a long way already from the frantic, insatiable, misdirected desiring of the cycle's opening poem.

The implied equality of Tsvetaeva's and Blok's separate paths, staggered in time and parallel in space, complementary yet never intersecting, is an idea that she explores in many different forms in many different works. This potential for great passion—the two paths' hypothetical meeting—that goes unrealized is another way of understanding her counterintuitive definition of true love as "nonlove" in "My Pushkin" and elsewhere: love is strongest when the imaginative potential is greatest (i.e., when the distance is farthest). This fateful Euclidean geometry of love likewise shapes Belyi's exclamation in Tsvetaeva's essay "A Captive Spirit" when she tells him of an unknown young girl's passion for him more than a decade before: "If that was she—then she was my fate. My non-fate. Because I never had a fate. And only now do I know why I perished. How deeply I perished [Do chego ia pogib]!" (4:226).

Two poems written in close succession in August 1919 also explore the idea of a fateful attraction between parallel lives (lines) that are fated never to meet and thus demonstrate the progression of Tsvetaeva's thought after "Poems to Blok." In "To You—One Hundred Years Later" ["Tebe—cherez sto let"] (1:481-82), Tsvetaeva addresses her ideal reader and lover, a man who (as the poem's title indicates) lives one hundred years after her own death, when she has been forgotten by everyone else on earth.[33] The promise of his future existence accounts for the impossibility of her living a full life during her life, while his life is destined to be similarly affected by the inaccessibility of her past: "Nonbeing—is mere convention. You are now for me—the most passionate of guests, and you will refuse the very pearl of all mistresses in the name of *this* woman made of bones" [Nebytie—uslovnost'. / Ty mne seichas—strastneishii iz gostei, / I ty otkazhesh' perlu vsekh liubovnits / Vo imia toi—kostei]. This poem clarifies the identity for Tsvetaeva of unrealizable romantic passion and poetic intimacy, of sexual frustration and creative inspiration—an identity that, as we have seen, shapes "Poems to Blok" as well. Moreover, in "To You" Tsvetaeva's name has become a receptacle of full poetic power, on a par with the names of Pushkin and Blok, for her future lover will renounce his own life in her name ("in the name of *this* woman made of bones").

In Tsvetaeva's second poem on hopeless attraction, "Two trees want" ["Dva dereva khotiat drug k drugu . . ."] (1:483-84), the role that gender plays in her unyielding poetic geometry is made explicit. In this poem, the two trees are vectored beings that express in their physical form the ideal of upward striving that for Tsvetaeva is the essential function of poetry and of the poetic soul. Their "paths"—that is, their trunks—are a simultaneously synchronic (the trunks' height) and diachronic (the trunks' concentric rings) illustration of the trees' entire destiny, congealed, as it were, in time. The two trees' paths will never cross (i.e., their trunks will never touch); yet one tree grows at an angle, ever leaning toward the other, in a palpable illustration of unrequited passion. Although *derevo,* the word for *tree,* is neuter in the grammar of Russian, the smaller, leaning tree explicitly plays the role of the female in this arboreal diagram of poetic dialogue:

> То, что поменьше, тянет руки,
> Как женщина: из жил последних
> Вытянулось, — смотреть жестоко,
> Как тянется — к тому, другому.
>
> [The one that is smaller stretches out its arms, like a woman: with its last ounce of strength — it's terrible to see how it stretches toward that one, the other one.]

Tsvetaeva here suggests that femininity is an ineradicable condition (the tree grows at an angle and cannot change the pattern of its growth, cannot tear out its own roots), but nevertheless a superficial one — a relational category rather than a category of essence. Femininity for Tsvetaeva is synonymous with unrealizable desire.

This understanding of femininity is not tied in any way to biology; we might say that Andrei Belyi in "A Captive Spirit" is, in this sense, every bit as feminine as Tsvetaeva. To this "vector" of femininity Tsvetaeva, in fact, opposes the nonvectored category of the biological female. This opposition lies at the core of the brief fourth poem of "Poems to Blok," the last poem of the cycle that I discuss:

> Зверю — берлога,
> Страннику — дорога,
> Мертвому — дроги.
> Каждому — свое.
>
> Женщине — лукавить,
> Царю — править,
> Мне — славить
> Имя твое.
>
> [For the beast — the lair, for the wanderer — the road, for the corpse — the hearse. To each — his own. A woman — must be sly, a tsar — must rule, and I — must glorify your name.]

The nouns that end the first three lines of "For the beast" (*berloga, doroga, drogi* [lair, road, hearse]) do not merely rhyme; they share many of the same sounds beyond the minimal requirements of the rhyme, so that their widely differing meanings are drawn into close proximity by the phonetic context. This similarity in sound suggests that these nouns name different aspects of one and the same thing: the special place of belonging, the home that every creature has (except, by implication, the speaker). The lair, the road, the hearse—none of these can be hers. The lair is a home for the animal who is pure body, without the soul's strivings to contend with. The road is an aim in itself for the wanderer, but Tsvetaeva's poetic journeys are vertical rather than horizontal, spiritual rather than topographical, and they are, moreover, never devoid of yearning. The hearse brings peace to the corpse, but she, despite her orientation toward the other world, is nevertheless alive and driven by the ambitions and desires of the flesh; even in death, her spirit will find no peace. Clearly, no noun can capture her essence; for nouns are static, while she is ever changing.

The creatures of the poem's second stanza, however, find their destiny in verbs rather than nouns—and here, in the process of verbal creation, Tsvetaeva proves able to find her own niche. The tripartite structure of this stanza is reminiscent of the tripartite formula that opens "The Drum." However, although Tsvetaeva's concern in that poem was to distinguish her extraordinary female destiny from the usual female lot, here she opposes her poetic calling not just to biological femininity, but to biology in toto, with all it represents. The lines "A woman—must be sly, a tsar—must rule" [Zhenshchine—lukavit', / Tsariu—pravit'] convey this totality in shorthand: with these four glib, sardonic words, Tsvetaeva dismisses not only gender per se, but all its earthly ambitions (the woman's ambition toward love; the man's—toward power). The activity she chooses for the expression of her own essence—glorification of Blok's name—indicates that for her, self-assertion is ultimately subordinated to fate. This return to the holy name no longer emanates from eulogistic convention; rather, it indicates the centrality for her creative drive of the inspiring poet's presence, of her imagined intimacy with him. She cannot write in a vacuum; in order for the vector of inspiration to propel her across the threshold, into the dangerous beyond of poetic creation, she needs the vector of desperate, hopeless feminine desire, coupled with the genderlessness of the world beyond. Therefore, the "glorification of a name" is actually an apt description of the entire mechanism of Tsvetaeva's particular poetic "factory." Given that her beloved—whoever he or she may be—is inaccessible to her by definition, yet is absolutely necessary as her muse, the beloved's earthly name becomes the physical stand-in for the absent lover, an object of erotic passion and sensation.

We see that although, as "Poems to Blok" progresses, the overt eroticism of "Your name" is gradually relinquished, what takes its place is an equally fervent spiritual possessiveness, a paradoxical declaration of fate in the two poets' nonconnection, nonmeeting. Tsvetaeva behaves here much as does Pushkin's Tat′iana in Tsvetaeva's interpretation: "And only because he did not love her, did she love him—*so much,* and only because she secretly *knew* [*znala*] that he would be unable to love her did she choose *him,* and not another, to love" (5:71). This knowledge, which we have seen before in "Only a Girl," is a fated knowing, the simultaneous knowing and choosing of destiny (i.e., the Pushkinian paradox of *dolia/volia* [fate vs. free will]) that Tsvetaeva consistently orchestrates. She owns Blok's nonlove for her more than she could ever own his love, for it is expressive of her poetic essence and encodes her poetic fate. The poems of "Poems to Blok" record her first glimpses of signs of this fate, followed by her gradual decoding of the signs. In this way, what appears at first to be a loss—Blok's indifference and inaccessibility to her in the face of her passionate yearning for him—she transforms into an ironic mark of her poetic election, even as she replaces the traditional triangle of poetic inspiration with a pair of parallel lines.

As a result of these transformations and substitutions, Tsvetaeva gradually distances herself from Blok and the inspirational experiment he initially prompted. The later poems of "Poems to Blok" thus tend to be more conventionally eulogistic, more transparent, and less interesting than the earlier poems. Tsvetaeva no longer needs to strategize, because mentally she has moved beyond the Blok blockade—not by realizing her original aim of capturing Blok's attention, but rather by denying that she ever had such an aim. Indeed, the final two poems of the cycle are personal lyrics, not fully decipherable by the outside reader. The cycle culminates with Blok's name sounding most unlike itself, reduced now from its primal acoustic power to a faint symbol: "And your name, sounding like: *angel*" [I imia tvoe, zvuchashchee slovno: *angel*]. The name, whose power Tsvetaeva could not harness, has been neutralized.[34]

A Demonic Muse: "Poems to Akhmatova"

In her essay "An Otherworldly Evening" ["Nezdeshnii vecher"], Tsvetaeva reminisces about her January 1916 trip to Petrograd, where she attended a literary evening and gave a reading of her own poetry. Although she made the acquaintance of a number of outstanding poets that evening, including Mikhail Kuzmin and Osip Mandel'shtam, Anna Akhmatova was disappointingly absent. Nevertheless, Tsvetaeva writes that she was conscious of doing battle with the absent Akhmatova as she recited her poems: "With my entire being I sense the tense—unavoidable—comparison [sravnivanie] (and, for some, staged competition [stravlivanie]) between us as I read each line" (4:286). Tsvetaeva is well aware that Akhmatova holds the reputation of *the* Russian woman poet—and that Akhmatova therefore retains ascendancy over her no matter what. She ironically expresses Akhmatova's unalterable singularity through the transformation of Akhmatova's name into an adjective: "to an akhmatovan level" [na

In Pursuit of a Muse 57

uroven' litsa—akhmatovskogo]; "akhmatovan zealots" [akhmatovskie revniteli]. Just a few months after this occurrence, in the summer of 1916, Tsvetaeva would ironically canonize Akhmatova in her cycle "Poems to Akhmatova" as the female poet of all Russia: "You! Nameless one! Carry my love to goldenlipped Anna—of all Rus!" [Ty!—Bezymiannyi! / Donesi liubov' moiu / Zlatoustoi Anne—vseia Rusi!]. Clearly, the genuflecting Tsvetaeva does not feel there is much room for her to straighten her back and draw a deep breath before Akhmatova's poetic majesty, let alone carve out her own poetic niche in the hearts of the Russian people.

As was the case with Blok, Tsvetaeva admired Akhmatova from a distance; the two women did not actually meet until 1941, after Tsvetaeva's return from emigration.[35] Despite occasional correspondence and Mandel'shtam's testimony that Akhmatova carried Tsvetaeva's poems around in her handbag until the manuscript disintegrated,[36] whatever reciprocal feeling Akhmatova may have experienced toward Tsvetaeva went unexpressed during Tsvetaeva's lifetime in poetic or any other form.[37] Even Akhmatova's answers to Tsvetaeva's warm, gushing letters were reluctant and laconic, for instance: "Your letter caught me at a moment of tremendous exhaustion, so it's difficult to collect my thoughts in order to answer you in any detail" (6:205); and later: "It's been a long time since I was so troubled by writer's block [agrafiia] . . . as I am today . . . I never write to anyone, but your kindness is infinitely precious to me" (6:206). Perhaps in part as a consequence of Tsvetaeva's personal nonacquaintance with Akhmatova, the latter appears in "Poems to Akhmatova"—as Blok does in "Poems to Blok"—as an abstract figure of superhuman dimensions. Like Blok, too, Akhmatova functions in Tsvetaeva's poems as the symbol of a certain brand of poetic power—simultaneously attractive and threatening to Tsvetaeva's nascent poetics.

Tsvetaeva claimed, puzzlingly, that, in the summer of 1916 when her cycle "Poems to Akhmatova" was composed, she was reading Akhmatova "for the first time" (4:140).[38] Although this was not literally the case, what Tsvetaeva must have meant was that, in the composition of her cycle of poems to Akhmatova, she was indeed engaged, in a deep sense, in the "discovery" (i.e., fathoming, uncovering, maneuvering, overcoming) of Akhmatova. This process provides her both with an antidote to Akhmatova's intimidating female poetic power, and with an alternative to Blok's imposing, breathtaking presence that threatens to overwhelm her own will to poetic voice. As she does in her Blok cycle too, Tsvetaeva in "Poems to Akhmatova" makes the poet-addressee's name the center of her attention—because a poet's name for her is the locus of his or her poetic essence, the acoustic stamp of his or her particular poetic genius. When Tsvetaeva manipulates another poet's name, therefore, she gains imagined access to that poet's being; the name, in a sense, functions as a wax model of the threatening but inaccessible original, whose threat she nevertheless deflates through the voodoolike pin-sticking action of her own poetic barbs.

Unlike Blok's name, Akhmatova's is a pseudonym. Joseph Brodsky once wrote that this name was Akhmatova's first successful poetic line, intimating further that her assumption of the name betokened both poetic excellence and ruthless poetic ambition: "The five open *a*'s of Anna Akhmatova had a hypnotic effect and put this name's carrier firmly at the top of the alphabet of Russian poetry."[39] In the case of Blok, the unbearable truth and authenticity of his name troubles Tsvetaeva. In the opening poem of her Blok cycle, therefore, her aim is to conceal and thereby transform the primary sound inference of Blok's name — that of creative blockage, paralysis — by the accumulation of echoes from an entirely different semantic field implying motion, flight, change. In the case of Akhmatova, on the contrary, the pretense of the name disturbs. Therefore, in the first poem of her Akhmatova cycle, "O, Muse of lament" ["O, Muza placha, prekrasneishaia iz muz! . . ."], Tsvetaeva sets for herself the inverse task: the discovery and revelation of latent meaning in Akhmatova's name (and destiny) that Akhmatova herself conceals.

The overwhelming frequency of the usually rare *kh* sound in the poem's second stanza is the key to this revelation:

> И мы шарахаемся и глухое: ох! —
> Стотысячное — тебе присягает: Анна
> Ахматова! Это имя — огромный вздох,
> И в глубь он падает, которая безымянна.
>
> [And we shy away and a hollow: oh! — a hundred-thousand voices — swear an oath to you: Anna Akhmatova! That name — is a vast sigh, and it drops into the abyss, which is nameless.]

Other velars (*k* and *g*) intensify the guttural sound of the exotic Akhmatovan *kh* in these lines; sibilants (*sh, s, ch, z*) provide a hissing complement to the velars, while the predominant open vowels *a* and *o* also originate in the vocalic melody of Akhmatova's name. Thus, Tsvetaeva derives through phonetic logic the hidden essence of the name and of the poet Anna Akhmatova: wild, elemental terror (evoked by the verb *sharakhat'sia* [to shy away, to bolt]); primordial, preverbal passion (the "hollow" [glukhoe] exclamation *oh!* [okh!] conveys this idea); and infinite, crushing melancholy (the "vast sigh" [ogromnyi vzdokh]). The stanza's final line, which grows out of (and rhymes with) the name *Anna* rather than the poet's surname, combines all three of these implications in the image of the name's falling away into a "nameless abyss" (*glub'*, incidentally, is grammatically feminine) that is rendered, through analogy, an image of Akhmatova. Furthermore, the rhyme *Anna/bezymianna* [Anna/nameless] draws attention to the fact that "Akhmatova" is indeed a forgery, an assumed name, a mask—evidence of the poet's attempts to shirk the implications of her true name, "Gorenko," which she has renounced.

In this way, Tsvetaeva discovers through the agency of sound a very different Anna Akhmatova than Akhmatova herself sets out to portray in her poems, with their refined, reticent, almost classical simplicity of phrase and image. Critics such as Viktoria Schweitzer are probably correct in suggesting that Tsvetaeva is attracted to Akhmatova by that poet's possession of "qualities which she lacked herself—above all, restraint and harmony," yet I would not agree that the "Poems to Akhmatova" are "poems of rapturous, adoring eulogy." [40] Alexander Zholkovsky's appraisal of Akhmatova comes much closer to Tsvetaeva's own, when he writes wryly of the "wise and detached . . . role-playing," "self-centered play-acting," and "powerful faking" of this woman "whose poetry, personality, and life form a consummate cultural artifact." [41] Indeed, Tsvetaeva's appraisal of Akhmatova's poetic tactics is highly ambivalent, for she sees the harmony of Akhmatova's poetic self not as an expression of her true nature, but rather as artificial posturing that barely manages to contain the stormy essence within. Just as Tsvetaeva expresses dissatisfaction with Blok's exclusive gravitation toward the otherworldly, away from the painful yet generative tensions of real, physical, bodily existence, so too in "Poems to Akhmatova" she deconstructs the refined self-image Akhmatova simulates, intimating that Akhmatova's true poetic power arises from the turbulent conflict between that poised, articulate image and the mute, seething, terrifying inner reality it tries to tame.

From this tension emanates imagery of Akhmatova's powerful effect of pleasure in pain on her readers that is reminiscent of similar imagery in "Your name." The juxtaposition of epithets in the first line of Tsvetaeva's poem ("O, Muse of lament, most beautiful of muses!") neatly summarizes this effect; Akhmatova is at once the muse of sorrow and of beauty. The proximity of these two descriptions even suggests that the second is a consequence of the first: that Akhmatova's beauty is derived from her pain (and, implicitly, her ability to cause pain). The poem's second line further intensifies this relationship, while reversing the order of ascendancy: "Oh you, mischievous spawn of the white night!" [O ty, shal'noe ischadie nochi beloi!]. The exotic, incomparable beauty of a Petersburg white night has given birth to a creature with demonic allegiance (the word *ischadie* is usually used in the phrases "Satanic spawn" [sataninskoe ischadie] and "spawn of hell" [ischadie ada]) who is at the same time as lightheartedly mischievous [shal'noe] as a thoughtless, wayward child.[42] This contradictory creature of the white nights sends a black blizzard (presumably a metaphor for Akhmatova's poetry) down upon all of Russia. Just as Akhmatova's name is a bluff for namelessness, so too the elegant, articulate beauty of her poetry is transformed into the speechless "wails" [vopli] of raw emotion as her lines reach their target (the hearts of her audience): "And your wails pierce into us, like arrows" [I vopli tvoi vonzaiutsia v nas, kak strely].

The poem's third stanza continues Tsvetaeva's exposition of the paradoxical tension between pleasure and pain:

> Мы коронованы тем, что одну с тобой
> Мы землю топчем, что небо над нами — то же!
> И тот, кто ранен смертельной твоей судьбой,
> Уже бессмертным на смертное сходит ложе.
>
> [We are crowned, because we tread the same earth you do, because the sky above us — is your same sky! And whoever is wounded by your fatal fate lies down in his deathbed already immortal.]

Akhmatova's bequest to her reader is simultaneous elevation ("we are crowned"; "already immortal") and devastation ("wounded by your fatal fate"; "lies down in his deathbed"). Tsvetaeva's expressions of pride at sharing the earth and the sky—symbolic, respectively, of the mundane and the otherworldly realms, to which she bears mixed allegiance—with Akhmatova's majesty convey more than a slight intonation of irony. This is especially true because it seems to be Akhmatova's very existence, rather than her poetry per se, which is so uplifting to humanity. There is, therefore, the suggestion in these lines that Akhmatova is a self-styled martyr, and that her suffering and beauty are orchestrated for effect. Once again, Zholkovsky's interpretation is close to Tsvetaeva's when he writes of Akhmatova's "favorite lying-down position, which makes her the center of attention, pity, service—and her bed, the seat of power."[43] We feel strongly Tsvetaeva's ambivalence toward Akhmatova's saintly-demonic posturing, which she finds both exhilarating and immodest.

In accordance with this feeling, the final stanza of "O, Muse of lament" is a seemingly sincere, straightforward tribute to Tsvetaeva's sister poet that thinly veils a profound challenge:

> В певучем граде моем купола горят,
> И Спаса светлого славит слепец бродячий...
> И я дарю тебе свой колокольный град,
> — Ахматова! — и сердце свое в придачу.
>
> [In my singing city the cupolas burn, and the wandering blind man praises the bright Savior... And I give you my belled city as a gift, Akhmatova!—and my heart as a bonus.]

Tsvetaeva's challenge to Akhmatova is contained in three elements. The first two are relatively transparent: the image of the "singing/belled city," Moscow, which Tsvetaeva bestows on Akhmatova in exchange for Petersburg's treacherous white nights; and the "bright Savior," who counteracts Akhmatova's own dark promise of tragic martyrdom. The meaning of the third image in the trio, the "wandering blind man," however, is not immediately obvious. In my reading, this figure is Tsvetaeva's answer to Akhmatova's dark threat and personifies the inspirational ideal for which Tsvetaeva yearns. In contrast to Akhmatova's femininity, the figure is male; in contrast to Akhmatova's nobility, he is of the common people; in contrast to Akhmatova's youth and beauty, he is (presumably) old and weathered. This is a true other—one whom Tsvetaeva can love and respect without having to contend with either the threat of elemental overpowerment represented by Akhmatova, or the frustrating inaccessibility of transcendence represented by Blok. At the same time, the blind man is Tsvetaeva's spiritual kin, her male double, for he possesses the basic attributes of her quintessential poet: blindness and wanderlust. Blindness—and its variants, downcast and sunken eyes—in her poems is consistently a symbol of poetic clairvoyance. The unselfconsciousness of this simple man's clairvoyance is pointedly opposed to Akhmatova's self-consciously dramatic prophetic posturing. The fact that the blind man is also a wanderer further identifies him as an emblem of Tsvetaeva's poetic ideal, for she is a wanderer by nature and avocation; the restlessness that motivates her is synonymous with the outward vector of her poetic quest.[44]

Tsvetaeva's tacit challenge to Akhmatova in the concluding stanza of "O, Muse of lament" makes it clear that her apparently generous "gift" to Akhmatova (i.e., the poems of this cycle) really amounts to a staking out of her own poetic territory, claiming the sources of her own poetic power against the bewitching spell Akhmatova casts.[45] She thus summons all the force of old Moscow, embodied in its various aspects—religious (the "bright Savior" of Russian Orthodoxy), folk (the blind wanderer), historical and architectural (the belled city), and linguistic (the Old Slavonic word for "city," *grad,* versus the modern *gorod*). All these facets of Tsvetaeva's Muscovite heritage merge through her poetic perception to create a new entity that is truly her own, a space at once real and mystical: the singing city with burning cupolas.[46] Her use of the first-person plural throughout the first three stanzas of the poem similarly serves to bolster her defensive poetic stance through the power of numbers. That Tsvetaeva's priority, however, is not communal but individual is indicated by her shift to the singular in the last stanza, where she claims all of Moscow as exclusively her own: "In *my* singing city . . . And *I* give you *my* belled city . . ." The Russian people are just another weapon in her repertoire of poetic strategies in her battle to define her own self, her own voice.[47]

Tsvetaeva recognizes that Akhmatova is of a radically different poetic breed than herself—because she is of a radically different female breed. Indeed, Akhmatova is a strange hybrid: a beauty like the unpoetic Asia and Nadia and a poet like the unbeautiful Marina. Just as Blok is able to transcend the boundary between body and spirit, Akhmatova manages to achieve a delicate, unstable equilibrium of perfection in both aspects; she inhabits an infinite loop where she is simultaneously both poet and muse.[48] This strategy potentially has great relevance to Tsvetaeva's quest, given that Akhmatova is, like herself, female, and thus would seem to be caught in the same inspirational quandary. Yet Akhmatova suffices for Tsvetaeva neither as a muse, nor as a teacher of inspirational myth. Akhmatova as the lamenting muse coerces Tsvetaeva into a state of delirium and creative paralysis not unlike that which Blok also threatens; the repeated prelinguistic utterances in "O, Muse of lament" (e.g., "wails" [vopli], "a hollow: oh!" [glukhoe: okh!], "a sigh" [vzdokh]) and the reference to a frightening aphasic space ("nameless abyss" [glub' bezymianna]) are evidence of this danger. On the other hand, Tsvetaeva cannot mimic Akhmatova's inspirational strategies and take herself as her own muse, for Akhmatova's self-reflexive posturing before her own mirror image is an option that is neither available to Tsvetaeva (Akhmatova is a beauty; her reflection is a legitimate, if egotistical, inspirational force) nor consistent with Tsvetaeva's most basic inspirational need—an outlet into otherness, a motivating goal for the poetic vector of her inborn passion.

Akhmatova, however, is a dangerous and unsuitable outlet. In the second lyric of "Poems to Akhmatova," she inhibits Tsvetaeva's elemental creative drive by, quite literally, inhabiting her voice. In "I clasped my head" ["Okhvatila golovu i stoiu . . ."], the invasion of Tsvetaeva's poetic realm by the violent force of Akhmatova's talent is first expressed through onomastic echoing:

> Охватила голову и стою,
> — Что людские козни! —
> Охватила голову и пою
> На заре на поздней.
>
> [I clasped my head and stand—what are human schemes!
> —I clasped my head and sing at dusk, late dusk.]

The opening past-tense verb here is ambiguous; its ellided, feminine subject could conceivably be either *I* [ia] (Tsvetaeva) or *she* [ona] (Akhmatova). This confusion is resolved only with the second, present-tense verb *stoiu* [I stand], whose conjugation makes clear that this is first-person speech. A hint of the initial ambiguity remains, however, for although the subject of this sentence is implicitly Tsvetaeva, the echo of Akhmatova's name in the poem's opening verb (*okhvatila* [clasped]) resists this grammatical separation. In fact, Akhmatova's ominous presence invades this verb and hence the sentence's grammatical integrity, so that Tsvetaeva's act of clasping her head in shock at the power of Akhmatova's poetic presence modulates imperceptibly into Akhmatova's repressive act of embracing/girding round Tsvetaeva's head ("*she* clasped my head") with the binds of her own competing and compelling lyrical force. In other words, the initially (incorrectly) suspected subject "she" overpowers the implicit (actual)

In Pursuit of a Muse 63

subject "I" in the poem's first sentence; what is described, as a result, is an experience not of isolated amazement but of violated selfhood. For, Akhmatova intrudes not only upon Tsvetaeva's body and personal space but upon the internal coherence of her speech, her grammar; this Akhmatovan constriction specifically of Tsvetaeva's head is an apt shorthand for the simultaneous violation of both her physical and her mental integrity.

Akhmatova's threat against Tsvetaeva is also felt in the acoustic patterns of the poem as a whole, which is repeatedly punctuated by variations on the first syllable of Akhmatova's name (***okhvatila, akh, oblaka, dykhan'e*** [clasped, ah, cloud, breath]). In addition, the stressed vowel *a* that repeats in Akhmatova's first and last names forms the poem's vocalic basis, occurring in such various contexts as the repeated prepositions of folk song ("***Na*** zare na pozdnei" [At dusk, late dusk]), stressed noun endings (*luna, oblaka, zaria, mgla* [moon, cloud, dusk, haze]), pronouns (*odna* [singular]), gerunds (*daria* [giving]), and feminine past-tense verbs with ending stress (*podniala, nazvala* [raised, named]). This predominance of final-syllable stressed *a,* unusual in Russian (three of the poem's twelve rhyming pairs are open syllables ending on precisely this vowel), draws attention to the fact that the poem's acoustic fabric is woven with the respun weft of Akhmatova's name, where the stressed vowels *a* occur instead in initial or internal syllables. This reversal of the vocalic patterns of Akhmatova's name alerts the ear to the power her name conceals and contains; it is as if Tsvetaeva has uncovered the hidden key to this power (stressed *a*) and thrust it to the outside for all to witness.

Thus we see that, even as Akhmatova infects Tsvetaeva's poetic voice, Tsvetaeva at the same time retaliates by revealing Akhmatova's poetic violence for what it is. This muted poetic battle between Tsvetaeva and Akhmatova in "I clasped my head" takes place on the level not just of sounds and grammar, but of imagery as well. Throughout the poem, Akhmatova's encroaching threat against Tsvetaeva's exercise of poetic voice alternates with Tsvetaeva's re-creative sallies against Akhmatova, intended to achieve an insulating, distancing effect. These occur most often in the form of threatening natural imagery: Akhmatova is compared to a furious wave ("neistovaia volna"), the moon, a raven piercing the clouds, and night itself. The moon perhaps implies the risk of insanity, but its more immediate threat to Tsvetaeva is stated outright: it is unique, single, unrepeatable: "I sing you, who are singular among us, like the moon in the sky!" [Ia tebia poiu, chto u nas—odna, / Kak luna na nebe!]. Uniqueness is indeed the crux of Akhmatova's threat to Tsvetaeva; for Akhmatova's poetic invasion of Tsvetaeva's Muscovite demesne in this poem ("above my crimson Kremlin you spread your night" [nad cervonnym moim Kremlem / Svoiu noch' prosterla])—is the logical result of her uniqueness: all of Russia has room for only one serious female poet, and prefers, if given the choice, a beautiful one. As a result, Akhmatova's song strangles Tsvetaeva ("with a singing bliss, like a belt, you tied my throat" [pevuchei negoiu, kak remnem, / Mne stianula gorlo]) and stops her from breathing ("your voice—O depths, O haze!—constricted my breath" [golos—o glub', o mgla!—/ Mne dykhan'e suzil]). Elsewhere in the cycle, Akhmatova's dark, constraining presence takes the form of a stone column that blocks the sunlight and hoards the stars: "You block from me the sun on high; all the stars are in your fist!" [Ty solntse v vysi mne zastish', / Vse zvezdy v tvoei gorsti!].

In revealing, and thereby remaking Akhmatova in "I clasped my head," Tsvetaeva gains ascendency over Akhmatova's powers. She achieves this aim first through a grammatical ploy: she transforms an initially intransitive verb into a transitive one, and in so doing shifts its meaning from aimless adoration to a pointedly aggressive, possessive strike-back. The verb in question is *poiu* [I sing]. In the third line of the first stanza, in Akhmatova's grip, Tsvetaeva meekly sings her praises ("I clasped my head and sing [poiu]"); the parallelism and rhyme with the poem's first line ("I clasped my head and stand [stoiu]") serve to equate this laudatory song with stoic nonresistance. In the poem's second stanza, however, Tsvetaeva amends this stance by the subtle addition of an object to the action of her song: "I sing *you*" [Ia *tebia* poiu] (my emphasis). In singing Akhmatova (a fit description, incidentally, of Tsvetaeva's primary activity not only in this poem, but in the cycle as a whole), Tsvetaeva takes back the upper hand from her powerful sister poet. Her project is completed with the poem's culminating riposte—a posthumous word from beyond the grave, as it were—the explicit renaming of Akhmatova:

> Ах, я счастлива, что тебя даря
> Удаляюсь — нищей,
>
> Что тебя, чей голос — о глубь, о мгла! —
> Мне дыханье сузил,
> Я впервые именем назвала
> Царскосельской Музы.

[Ah, I am happy that, giving you as a gift, I leave—a pauper; that it was you (whose voice—O depths, O haze!—constricted my breath) whom I was the first to name the Muse of Tsarskoe Selo.]

Akhmatova in the final appellative phrase ("the Muse of Tsarskoe Selo") is circumscribed, localized, characterized. Her unassailable elemental power, though undiminished, is at least tamed by the finiteness of geographic specificity. Tsvetaeva, despite her losses, emerges from the poetic fray defiant as ever. She has ultimately achieved what she needed to: the naming of Akhmatova as enormously different from herself; the creation of difference and distance from Akhmatova and from her own love for Akhmatova.

In the latter lyrics of "Poems to Akhmatova," Tsvetaeva, now at a safe re-

In Pursuit of a Muse

move, retaliates against Akhmatova's prior incursions into her poetic voice by reversing the situation: she apes Akhmatova's poetic style, using characteristically Akhmatovan images and even Akhmatovan meters and rhymes in order to create a slight satirical edge that urges a reevaluation of the effects of Akhmatova's stylized verbal posturing.[49] In "How many companions" ["Skol'ko sputnikov i druzei! . . ."], the fifth poem of her cycle, Tsvetaeva once again uses an onomastic revelation to make her point. From the beginning of the poem it is clear that *Gorenko,* Akhmatova's birth name that she conceals and shuns, phonetically encodes her true nature:[50]

> Сколько спутников и друзей!
> Ты никому не вторишь.
> Правят юностью нежной сей —
> Гордость и горечь.

> [How many companions and friends! You are second to none.
> This tender youth is driven by — pride and bitterness.]

Here, the unpleasant secret of Akhmatova's strength, unexpected in light of her apparent "tender youth" [iunost' nezhnaia] — a description that implies fragility, sweetness, and malleability — is located in her acoustic inheritance: "gordost'" [pride] and "gorech'" [bitterness]. In these two characteristics is the origin of Akhmatova's darkness; in concealing her heritage, she commits an act of symbolic self-destruction from which emanates the seductive danger of her poetics. The image later in the poem of a "rose's wing/petal in [Akhmatova's] mouth" [i vo rtu / Krylyshko rozy] expresses this idea as well, for wings in Tsvetaeva's poetic lexicon are symbolic of the poetic gift and calling. Whereas Blok's wings are broken through the immense effort of his flight into the beyond ("Oh, see how his wings are broken!" [O, pogliadite, kak / Kryl'ia ego polomany!]) — the breakage is even encoded in the enjambement of this line — the autovorous Akhmatova is insulated from such pain by her own erotically suggestive invention: she eats her own wings.

The mysterious "stone in an engraved frame" [kamen' v reznoi oprave] of the following stanza can be viewed as a talisman of Akhmatova's poetics: round, self-enclosed, and self-referential, its aesthetic appeal lies in the illusion it presents of inner depths and magical powers. The distant young man whom Akhmatova, apparently, ignores may be associated with her first husband, the poet Nikolai Gumilev, through his proximity to the sails of the ships in port and the poem's earlier reference to "southern winds" (later, in the fourth poem of the cycle, "The child's name is Lev" ["Imia rebenka — Lev . . ."], Gumilev is clearly associated with the "southern ocean"); this youth is at the same time an echo of Tsvetaeva's wandering blind man, an inspirational other whom Akhmatova shuns:

> И — высоко у парусов —
> Отрока в синей блузе.
> Гром моря и грозный зов
> Раненой Музы.
>
> [And — high up near the sails — a boy in a blue blouse. The thunder of the sea and the threatening call of the wounded Muse.]

Akhmatova-Gorenko is focused on her own self-referential symbols, her own seeming. Her love for others (whether the "companions and friends" of the poem's first line, or her own husband) merely furnishes her with a foil, a mirror, in which she can further define her own independent, flagellant self (in another poem of the cycle Tsvetaeva terms her "bogoroditsa khlystovskaia" [madonna of the Flagellants]). The "wounded muse" [ranenaia muza] of the poem's final line is an emblem of this masochistic self-absorption. The menacing chaos of elements Akhmatova evokes (*grom/groznyi* [thunder/threatening]), which Tsvetaeva at first found so frightening, is now seen through the logic of sound similarities to emanate not from the exotic abyss of "O, Muse of lament" (*Akh!/glukhoe okh!/vzdokh* [Ah!/hollow oh!/sigh]) but from the vulgar secret of bitter pride (*Gorenko/gorech'/gordost'* [Gorenko/bitterness/pride]).⁵¹ Akhmatova feigns turmoil to achieve maximal poetic effect. In other words, Tsvetaeva now portrays Akhmatova's poetry as not after all spurred by the elemental or indeed any other external force, but as indulgently self-referential in both origin and concerns.

The portrait of Akhmatova first as a corpse, and then as a statue in "Yet another vast sweep" ["Eshche odin ogromnyi vzmakh . . ."], the third poem in Tsvetaeva's Akhmatova cycle, urges the danger of such poetic self-referentiality. The implication is that Akhmatova consciously makes herself into an object of veneration, even worship:

> Еще один огромный взмах —
> И спят ресницы.
> О, тело милое! О, прах
> Легчайшей птицы!
>
> [Yet another vast sweep — and the lashes sleep. O, dear body! O, dust of the lightest bird!]

In Tsvetaeva's visionary portrait of the dying Akhmatova, there is no sense of an inner life, of pain, of true physicality; her body is nothing but "dust of the lightest bird" that has now fluttered away. This image provides a striking contrast to Blok's "broken wings" [Kryl'ia ego polomany!] in the sixth lyric of "Poems to Blok," titled "They thought he was a person!" ["Dumali — chelovek! . . ."], where Tsvetaeva likewise portrays Blok on his deathbed. Indeed, there is an implicit comparison to the Blok lyric throughout "Yet another vast sweep." In Tsvetaeva's vision of the dead Blok, Christian imagery and references to his resurrection convey an image of innocent self-sacrifice on the altar of poetry. In the case of the dead beauty that is Akhmatova, however, Tsvetaeva is ambivalent, detecting traces of an angel, eagle, and demon. (Elsewhere in the cycle, too, Akhmatova is characterized as possessing "a sad and demonic beauty" [krasa / Grustnaia i besovskaia].) Akhmatova's entry into the realm of the spirit is far easier and smoother than Blok's torturous progress toward death; this divergence is captured in Tsvetaeva's different descriptions of their corpses' two pairs of eyes: Blok's lids are sunken ("The dark lids sank inwards!" [Veki vvalilis' temnye!]), while Akhmatova's eyelashes are stilled mid-sweep ("Yet another vast sweep—and the lashes sleep" [Eshche odin ogromnyi vzmakh— / I spiat resnitsy]). Blok undergoes a painful transition into incorporeality (the dark, sunken lids seem to suggest empty sockets underneath); whereas Akhmatova's death is as superficial a pose as her life has been (then, the eyelashes batted flirtatiously; now, they are pathetically still). Akhmatova's eyelashes themselves are an image of superficiality and invulnerability (they are barely a bodily attribute and do not sense pain; nor do they directly aid or inhibit vision of any kind), whereas Blok's eyelids are the "gates" to vision and the doorway to the mind and soul.

There are two primary subtexts in "Yet another vast sweep": Pushkin's famous "I erected a monument" ["Ia pamiatnik sebe vozdvig nerukotvornyi..."], the poet's ambivalent assessment of his own creative legacy, and Akhmatova's 1911 cycle "In Tsarskoe Selo" ["V Tsarskom Sele"], in which she concretizes and appropriates Pushkin's figurative "monument" while roaming disconsolately through Pushkinland (i.e., Tsarskoe Selo, the site of Pushkin's happy lyceum days).[52] In her cycle, Akhmatova admits "now I have become a puppet" [teper' ia igrushechnoi stala] and goes on with feigned humility to twin herself with Pushkin's statue ("But there is my marble twin" [A tam moi mramornyi dvoinik]) and then to prophesy her eventual transformation into just such a monument: "Cold, white, just wait, I also will turn to marble" [Kholodnyi, belyi, podozhdi, / Ia tozhe mramornoiu stanu]. In "Yet another vast sweep," the temporal distance between Tsvetaeva's poetic vantage and the Akhmatova-adoring present moment results in an ambiguous corrective to Akhmatova's appropriation of Pushkin's legacy:

> Часы, года, века. — Ни нас,
> Ни наших комнат.
> И памятник, накоренясь,
> Уже не помнит.
>
> Давно бездействует метла,
> И никнут льстиво

> Над Музой Царского Села
> Кресты крапивы.
>
> [Hours, years, centuries. — Neither us, nor our rooms. And the monument, rooting itself firmly, already does not remember. The broom has long been idle, and the nettle crosses droop in adulation above the Muse of Tsarskoe Selo.]

In these lines, Akhmatova's aspirations to Pushkin's poetic status are deflated when Tsvetaeva reverses both the situation and the agency of Pushkin's original. Whereas Pushkin's metaphorical monument is remembered gratefully by the people ("I will long be dear to the common folk" [Dolgo budu . . . liubezen ia narodu]), Akhmatova's actual, physical monument in Tsvetaeva's poem has itself forgotten the inhabitants of the present moment. Whereas the "people's path [to Pushkin's monument] is never overgrown" [K nemu ne zarastet narodnaia tropa], Akhmatova's monument has itself put down roots and is venerated by nettles. These divergences from Pushkin's poem seem to argue for the comparative insignificance of Akhmatova's poetry; in Tsvetaeva's portrayal, Akhmatova is rendered, ultimately, as a mere object — statue, muse — and her poetry is not remembered. The meaningful echoes of Akhmatova's name in "Yet another vast sweep" (*vzmakh, prakh, vzdokh* [sweep, dust, sigh]) likewise disperse the threat implicit previously in both her name and her presence. Akhmatova is rendered incorporeal and incoherent.

On the other hand, it is Akhmatova (or rather, her statue) who does the forgetting in Tsvetaeva's lyric, not the people who forget her, suggesting that she is superior to them and thus indifferent, a phenomenon outside the realm of the merely human; the "nettle crosses," a variant on the crown of thorns, mark her as a symbol of superhuman endurance. Indeed, Akhmatova from the very beginning of "Yet another vast sweep" practices a technique of paradoxically proactive waiting; hence, Tsvetaeva asks: "What did she do in the fog of days? She *waited* and sang..." [Chto delala v tumane dnei? / *Zhdala* i pela...] (my emphasis). This idea perhaps emerges from Akhmatova's own lines: "Cold, white, just wait . . ." In her very act of composing "Poems to Akhmatova," Tsvetaeva implicitly challenges Akhmatova's power with her own brand of endurance: strength and longevity of voice. If Akhmatova's longevity consists in her statuesqueness (the lifelessness of a statue, the frozenness of a pose), then Tsvetaeva answers with all the power of the unpredictable future growth of her own unkillable, unfreezable, rebellious poetic voice.[53]

Nevertheless, for all Tsvetaeva's resistance, Akhmatova's self-objectification continues to hold strong sway over her. In the cycle's tenth poem, she turns to yet another artistic medium to convey this magical force: namely, the medium of

In Pursuit of a Muse

the icon, whose evocative power emerges paradoxically from its flat stylization, its coded colors and features:[54]

> Для всех, в томленьи славящих твой подъезд, —
> Земная женщина, мне же — небесный крест!
>
> Тебе одной ночами кладу поклоны,
> И все *твоими* очами глядят иконы!
>
> [For everyone who languidly blesses your approach you are a mortal woman, but for me — a heavenly cross to bear! To you alone by night do I bow down, and all the icons gaze with *your* eyes!]

This peculiar icon, which is reminiscent of the demonic portrait in Gogol''s tale "The Portrait," is infested with Akhmatova's living gaze. The entrapment of living eyes in an icon frame is inconsistent with the icon's symbolic inertness and can lead to heresy or insanity, or both. In Tsvetaeva's view, Akhmatova's self-styled martyrology leads her to toy irresponsibly with the necessary boundaries between the sacred and the profane; the blasphemy here is overt, no longer implicit as in "Poems to Blok." Yet even as Akhmatova spurs her readers to this verbal sin, her own poetics remains a theatrical pose, as different as possible both from Tsvetaeva's playing to the death and from Blok's unwilled, unresisting, torturous path toward the transcendent. Akhmatova does not suffer so much as bring suffering down upon others.[55]

In concluding my discussion of "Poems to Akhmatova," I would like to touch upon the seventh poem of the cycle, "You, tearing off the shroud" ["Ty, sryvaiushchaia pokrov . . ."], which summarizes what Tsvetaeva has learned in her inspirational experiment thus far. Here the shift that has occurred in her attitude toward Akhmatova in the course of the cycle is marked by a subtle grammatical change. We have seen that, in the cycle's first two lyrics ("O, Muse of lament" and "I clasped my head"), Akhmatova's storminess is expressed through verbs: "you . . . *unleash* a blizzard" [ty . . . *nasylaesh'* metel'], "your wails *pierce*" [vopli *vonzaiutsia*], "that name . . . *falls*" [eto imia . . . *padaet*], "a wave *raised* me up" [menia volna *podniala*], "having swooped like a raven" [voronom *naletev*], "*pierced* the clouds" [v oblaka *vonzilas'*], "*spread* night" [noch' *prosterla*], "*tied* my throat" [*stianula* gorlo], "*constricted* my breath" [dykhan'e *suzil*]). In "You, tearing off the shroud," Akhmatova's actions are characterized instead primarily by nouns (the nominal verbal form *tearing off* [sryvaiushchaia] in the poem's first line provides a transition between these two parts of speech). The difference between verb and noun — between "you unleash a blizzard" [ty nasylaesh' metel'] (from "O, Muse of lament") and "unleasher of blizzards" [nasylatel'nitsa metelei] (from "You, tearing off the shroud") — is subtle but real. While the verb leaves the question of intentionality ambiguous (it expresses what happens, not why or how), the noun conveys two root qualities of the verb's executor: gender and intention. Gender, by virtue of the obligatory feminine suffix *-itsa;* intention, because an avocation like "unleasher" cannot but be intentional. No longer are Akhmatova's storms and winds uncontrollable, unpredictable, and potentially overpowering, beholden to no human law ("What are human schemes!" [Chto liudskie kozni!]). On the contrary, Tsvetaeva now sees this turbulence as a result of conscious witchery on Akhmatova's part. In other words, the chaos Tsvetaeva intuits lurking behind the tranquility of Akhmatova's careful pose she now views as a simulated nuance of the pose itself.

Thus, Akhmatova is not only an "unleasher of blizzards" but also a "maddener of winds" [raz″iaritel′nitsa vetrov], a "wizardess" [chernoknizhnitsa], and a "feudalist" [krepostnitsa]. This last epithet makes explicit what the others hint: that Akhmatova's relationship to the external world is a systematic exercise of control that paradoxically takes the form of unleashing chaos; she stands unscathed in the eye of the hurricane as it envelopes her admirers (her "serfs"). Akhmatova is immune to her own threat; unlike Blok, who is inseparable from his melting icicles and chilling snows, she stands outside the natural world. Blok's achievement of the beyond in "You pass by" is the culmination of his long and difficult "path" [stezia], which consists in the slow annihilation of the pull of the earthly within himself and thus is something to be justly celebrated: "The bard lies dead and celebrates resurrection" [Mertvyi lezhit pevets / I voskresen′e prazdnuet]. Akhmatova's "beyond" is a matter of definition, a ploy, a spell, a flirtatious game of hints and symbols (the enigmatic red-and-black sails, roaring lions, and chariot in "You, tearing off the shroud," for example; or the gypsy's inscrutable prophesying in "How many companions") from which Akhmatova herself escapes unharmed.

This discussion reveals how differently Tsvetaeva regards the suffering Blok and the insufferable Akhmatova. In "You, tearing off the shroud," Tsvetaeva implicitly juxtaposes her two poet-addressees by means of strong intertextual echoes. In describing the dead Blok in "They thought he was a person!" she had prayerfully intoned:

> Три восковых свечи —
> Солнцу-то! Светоносному!
>
> [Three wax candles — for the sun itself! The light-bearer!]

In "You, tearing off the shroud," she now produces a variation of the same lines — the same sun, the same adjectival compounds, the same dative case — yet these similarities only draw attention to the enormous difference between the meek, pitiful, Christ-like Blok, and the pitiless Akhmatova, who functions here rather in the role of the Old Testament deity:

In Pursuit of a Muse 71

> Жду, как солнцу, подставив грудь
> Смертоносному правосудью.
>
> [I wait, having exposed my breast to the death-bearing force of justice, as if to the sun.]

The direct echo between these two passages emphasizes the dubious moral origins of Akhmatova's poetry, which brings death rather than light to the beholder. Blok is a source of spiritual illumination; Akhmatova is a source of terror and darkness. Tsvetaeva overcomes her awe of both poets, and her hurt at their independence from and indifference to herself, by ascribing to their poetry superhuman and supernatural origins; but Akhmatova's menace is ultimately greater—hence Tsvetaeva's treatment of her is harsher.

In the course of Tsvetaeva's composition of "Poems to Blok" and "Poems to Akhmatova," a clear pattern has been established. Twice now, Tsvetaeva's strong attraction to and love for another poet—who, as poet, possesses an irrefutably independent subjectivity—has proven dangerous to the integrity of her own voice. In the poems to Blok, Tsvetaeva negates this threat by repossessing Blok's name as a symbol of her own poetic destiny; in the poems to Akhmatova, she undoes the threat by stripping Akhmatova of her pseudonym (her aesthetic incognito).[56] Neither Blok's incorporeal transcendence, nor Akhmatova's explosive inspirational autonomy, are options for Tsvetaeva, who craves an external inspirational source for her inseparably erotic/poetic passions. Caught repeatedly in the impossible dilemma of an inspirational love that risks paralyzing her own will to poetic voice, Tsvetaeva soon transforms her eulogies into exercises in exorcism.

The Insatiable Rider: "On a Red Steed"

In the years following the composition of her poetic cycles to Blok and Akhmatova, Tsvetaeva extrapolates from these poets' suspected indifference to her—a mask for her own resistance to them—the belief that her love for other poets is fated to be forever linked with renunciation. It is important to note that, in 1916 when the cycles were composed, this was a pure conjecture born of the internal logic of Tsvetaeva's own poetics, unbolstered by empirical data. To reiterate, the logic runs thus: other poets must be overcome, as love must be overcome; the mechanism for this process is the appropriation and transformation of the "foreign" poet's essence: his or her inspirational myth. In other words, Tsvetaeva's infatuations with other poets result in far more than mere "dialogues" and occur on a much deeper level than that of the singular word or text. Tsvetaeva is perhaps unique in the extent to which she enters the alternative poetic universe of her "rivals" and attempts to comprehend and transform their alien visions from within. That these experiments are risky in the extreme, given the other party's lack of participation and failure to give permission for such intimate trespassing, should come as no surprise.

Fast forward now to the peculiar episodes of 1920 and 1921, with which I began this chapter. Contrary to what one might expect, Tsvetaeva espies in Blok's May 1920 appearance in Moscow not an opportunity to meet her revered poetic elder face to face, but rather a chance to test her mythopoetic hypothesis. She summons Blok from a distance, and, via the complicated logic of the "Poems to Blok," her own poetic destiny is vindicated by the painful veracity of his presumed indifference. Tsvetaeva, in fact, orchestrates this nonmeeting with Blok; much as she desires a meeting, she needs the laden symbolism of the nonmeeting more—and Blok himself perhaps senses as much from her poems. She transposes poetic truths into her actions in real life.

The situation vis-à-vis Akhmatova is equally as complex. In the aftermath of the poetic frictions of "Poems to Akhmatova," in a letter written to Akhmatova in April 1921, Tsvetaeva unexpectedly declares her adoration for Akhmatova exuberantly, histrionically, fanatically:

You are my most beloved poet, at one time I—a long, long time ago—about six years ago—saw you in a dream, saw your future book: covered in dark green morocco, with silver—*Golden Words*—some kind of ancient witchcraft, like a prayer (rather, the opposite!)—and—upon awakening—I knew that you would write it.

I am so sorry that all of this is just words—*love*—I can't stand it this way, I would like to have a real bonfire, on which I would be burnt. (6:201)

Just as Tsvetaeva's apparent invitation to Blok (the deliverance to him of her poems through Alia) is the opposite of what it seems, so too in this letter to Akhmatova, Tsvetaeva doth protest too much: the lavishness of her love hints at the ambivalence that lies beneath. Here, again, she exhibits genius in her orchestration of the situation; she seems to venerate Akhmatova, while the very enthusiasm of her words communicates a covert message of antagonism. Akhmatova, like Blok, is able to read the covert message beneath the overt one, for she refrains from responding to Tsvetaeva in kind, thus once again setting Tsvetaeva free to pursue her own lonely poetic destiny.

It is my sense that, at the time Tsvetaeva composed her cycles to Blok and Akhmatova, she did not fully recognize the terrifyingly systematic workings of this mechanism, nor did she realize that her primary concern in the poems was not, in fact, glorification of her poetic "beloved," but clarification of her own poetic tendencies and inspirational needs. In my opinion, these realizations came to her gradually, with the passage of time. Tsvetaeva often insists on the importance of chronology; in her autobiographical essay "My Pushkin," she explains how, as she matures, she becomes able to articulate consciously what previously she had only intuited. Most often, such intuitive knowledge relates to

In Pursuit of a Muse

her own poetic calling: "I say this now but I knew [znala] already then; then—I knew, but now I have learned how to say it" (5:71). This formula can be applied equally well to explain Tsvetaeva's gradual recognition of the basic meaning of her cycles to Blok and Akhmatova—that is, the role these cycles play in her poetic coming-of-age.

The sign of Tsvetaeva's reappraisal of the significance of these cycles is her reorganization and renaming of them for their republication in a new collection, *Psyche* (Berlin, 1923). The cycles' original dedicatory titles, "Poems to Blok" and "Poems to Akhmatova," are no more than the name of their source in life; the initial impetus for the poems is emotional. From this inspirational kernel of feeling, sensuality, fear, desire—the kiss Tsvetaeva offers Blok and the heart she offers Akhmatova, at the end of the first poem of each cycle, respectively—grows a complex investigation of a poetic, spiritual problem. Several years later, Tsvetaeva realizes in hindsight the inner coherence of her earlier cycles, their philosophical unity. By this time she has learned to give this unity—this problem through which she had begun fumbling and stumbling five years previously, a name: *inspiration*. In the revised versions of the cycles, consequently, Tsvetaeva mutes the real names of Blok and Akhmatova, replacing these with her reconceptualization of the inspirational roles the two poets have played in her own poetry. Thus, the Blok cycle becomes known as "Quiet Light" ["Svete tikhii"], while the Akhmatova cycle is dubbed "The Muse" ["Muza"]. Typically of Tsvetaeva's strategy, these new titles diminish their objects even as they glorify them.

The collection *Psyche* is not organized chronologically, as are most of Tsvetaeva's other books, but symmetrically. It is therefore significant that "The Muse" appears as the third cycle of poems in the book, followed immediately by "Quiet Light," whereas the third-to-last work in the volume is the 1921 *poema* "On a Red Steed," Tsvetaeva's most explicit and most extended work on the theme of the muse.[57] Clearly, the latter work is intended as a counterbalance to the former two; both the 1916 cycles and the 1921 *poema* explore the inspirational possibilities which, in Tsvetaeva's view, are open to the woman poet. The fact that "On a Red Steed" was later revised and was, in the process, subjected to a whole series of dedications (first to the minor poet Evgenii Lann,[58] one of Tsvetaeva's numerous short-lived unrequited loves, then to Akhmatova; subsequently, all dedications were removed) suggests that this work too, like the poems of the earlier cycles, underwent a gradual transformation from intimately personal to general, philosophical relevance in Tsvetaeva's regard.

"On a Red Steed" is Tsvetaeva's private inspirational allegory. In it, she traces her poetic genesis through her repeated assignations with her muse, who is now rendered as male and imaginary. This austere horseman is her true beloved; he gallops on his iconic (and Pegasan) red steed through three symbolic episodes that encode the feminine destiny that Tsvetaeva, in choosing poetry, must renounce. Thus, she first meets the horseman as a young girl, when he saves her doll from a fire only to command her to shatter it; later, a similar fate befalls the speaker's lover, whom the horseman has saved from drowning, as well as her firstborn child, whom the horseman has saved from falling off a cliff. At each stage of her female existence—as a tender girl [devochka], a romantic young woman [devushka], and a mature woman and mother [zhenshchina]—Tsvetaeva must prove her total dedication to poetry and poetry alone by renouncing and even destroying all her earthly loves; the triangular structure of this formula has the effect of a magical spell. Finally, at the end of the *poema,* she renounces Christ in the midst of a cataclysmic snowstorm and plots her troth, instead, to the mighty horseman; in the final scene, she incites him to an unequal battle in which she is vanquished and thus united with him forever, becoming immortal in the process. Her exclamation in the preamble to the original version of the *poema* that she was "not born a mortal woman/wife" [Ne smertnoi zhenoi—Rozhdennoi!] therefore has a poignant double meaning. It is highly significant that in "On a Red Steed," the military ethos and its trappings continue, as they did in Tsvetaeva's juvenilia, to function as a convenient shorthand for the transgressive nature of her will toward the poetic act.

In each episode of this haunting work, the terrible choice between life and poetry entails the poet's election of a state of complete isolation. Precisely at the moment when she is closest to realizing her impossible desire (for the doll, the lover, the child, the deity, all of whom seemed to have been lost beyond recall), she must acknowledge that it is her muse who has brought her to this point and so, maddeningly but inescapably, her muse who must be served. This situation is reminiscent of Tsvetaeva's anguishing exorcism of Akhmatova and Blok; it is her poetry that brings her into their orbits in the first place, and so it is her poetry that ordains that she keep her distance from them. In each of these potential encounters, Tsvetaeva has maximal existential freedom, though she imagines the parameters of her choice to be inflexible. If she meets Blok or Akhmatova, she will realize her desire, but she will not be a poet. If she does not pledge herself entirely and irreversibly to her muse, if she allows one earthly tug on her feminine affections, then her unique poetic myth—in which solitude and renunciation play so great a part—cannot take shape.

Akhmatova's and Blok's relevance to "On a Red Steed" is visible throughout the *poema* in a number of ways. Despite Tsvetaeva's removal of the dedication to Akhmatova for the work's republication, Akhmatova's challenging presence obviously remains lurking in Tsvetaeva's negative invocation to the traditional, feminine muse in the preface:

> Не Муза, не Муза
> Над бедною люлькой
> Мне пела, за ручку водила.

In Pursuit of a Muse

> Не Муза холодные руки мне грела,
> Горячие веки студила . . .
>
> Не Муза, не черные косы, не бусы,
> Не басни, — всего два крыла светлорусых
> — Коротких — над бровью крылатой.
> Стан в латах.
> Султан.
>
> [Not the Muse, not the Muse above my poor cradle sang to me, led me by the hand. Not the Muse warmed my cold hands, cooled my hot eyelids . . . Not the Muse, not black braids, not beads, not fables — but just two reddish-blond wings — short ones — above a winged brow. A figure in armor. A plume.]

Here the negated "black braids," "beads," and "fables" all evoke Akhmatova. Indeed, Tsvetaeva explicitly replaces Akhmatova-the-muse with her own masculine inspirational fantasy in these lines. The shade of Blok in "On a Red Steed" is perhaps less evident but has likewise been remarked by several scholars, prompted by Ariadna Efron's claim in her memoirs that Blok is, in fact, the model for the poem's central figure, the rider on a red horse who lends the poem its title: "The *poema* 'On a Red Steed' . . . presents us with a complex image, dynamic in its iconicity, of Tsvetaeva's 'deified' Blok — creator of 'The Twelve,' the Revolution's St. George the Avenger, purest and most dispassionate Spirit of poetry." [59] Simon Karlinsky rightly finds this assertion to be politically motivated;[60] other scholars have seen Blok's presence in the *poema* in less concrete terms. Thus, for example, David Bethea compares Blok's Sophism and worship of the "eternal feminine" to Tsvetaeva's religious transgression in the poem and her corresponding search for a male ideal.[61] Catherine Ciepiela similarly discusses connections between Tsvetaeva's concept of poetic inspiration in "On a Red Steed" and Blok's own inspirational myths.[62] Furthermore, the wintry Blokian imagery in "On a Red Steed" has been remarked by practically all its commentators.[63] Clearly, the figures of Blok and Akhmatova are irrefutably linked in the genesis of "On a Red Steed"; their shades hover constantly at the *poema*'s fringes and infiltrate its winds and snows. However, to reiterate, in my interpretation this work does not encode Tsvetaeva's emulation or deification of Blok and Akhmatova, but rather enacts her conclusive overcoming of their powers over her.[64]

We have seen that the 1916 cycles "Poems to Blok" and "Poems to Akhmatova" are inspirational experiments, interlocutionary competitions in which each of the other poets functions both as a competing poetic voice and as Tsvetaeva's own personal inspiration or "muse." However, the inspiration afforded by both Blok and Akhmatova — because of the different, thus challenging power of their own poetry — amounts to anti-inspiration (in the most literal sense: expiration, suffocation, loss of breath, creative death). Tsvetaeva turns to these other poets seeking validation of her own soul, but she finds only a foreign essence; it comes to pass that the fulfilling dialogue between poets that she has imagined theoretically (and naïvely) as a passionate, mutually adoring companionship of echoing souls is not yet destined to be. In summary, her intimate encounter with the poetics of Blok and Akhmatova has left her with several unsolved problems: Blok's transcendence (versus her own conflicting ties to both the worldly and the beyond); Akhmatova's self-referentiality and resultant destructive posturing (versus Tsvetaeva's insistence on an outward-looking, brutally honest trajectory into the heights and depths of consciousness); and both Blok's and Akhmatova's indifference to, even unawareness of, her own existence and poetic gift. The problem can be restated in simpler terms: Blok's poetic curve points only upward and directs its desires exclusively into the beyond; Akhmatova's poetic curve points only inward and satisfies all its own desires (Akhmatova acquiesces to her feminine objective status: she is desire's object personified, and so has no desires of her own). Tsvetaeva must find both a myth potent enough to explain her own poetic curve that points in all directions at once—inward and outward, upward and downward—and a beloved that can satisfy her need, for every arrow in the quiver of her poetic urge is tipped with the barb of desire (for body and soul, earth and sky, life and death) that is doubly insatiable: by virtue of its strength and its logical impossibility.

Both the myth and the beloved are found—or, rather, find her—in "On a Red Steed." This simultaneity of the passive and active verbs is essential. Whereas Tsvetaeva's relationship to Blok and Akhmatova is one of pursuit and possessiveness, the hero of "On a Red Steed" repeatedly goes in pursuit of *her*. This is how poetic inspiration *should* work, how the muse *should* behave. This is also how ideal love should arise—unbidden, unorchestrated, of its own accord. In reality, Tsvetaeva's own immense need has generally overridden any answering emotion in her companion and driven him or her away: "With my own insatiability I overfeed everyone!" [Nenasytnost'iu svoeiu / Perekarmlivaiu vsekh!] (1:567). This is the insatiable, self-defensive, unbalanced hunger of pure subjectivity—the "myself against the world" [ia i mir] syndrome of "A Savage Will," as it were. Tsvetaeva longs to find an exit from this predicament: to be able to play the role of object to someone else's subject, without risking the loss of her own subjectivity as she does in the Blok and Akhmatova cycles. The rider in "On a Red Steed" allows her this resolution, for he is at once a true other (as his maleness indicates) and an emanation of her own consciousness (he appears to her in dreams).

A brief consideration of the role played by natural forces in "On a Red Steed," in contrast with the Blok and Akhmatova cycles, will serve to clarify my argument. Cosmic imagery is common to all three works; in the *poema*, the rider is addressed as "light" [svet] and his weapon is a ray of light, reminiscent of the

In Pursuit of a Muse 77

description of Blok ("Rays emanated from him—hot strings along the snow!" [Shli ot nego luchi—/ Zharkie struny po snegu!]). Just as Blok's poetic path is the orbit of a heavenly body in "You pass by," so too the branches in "On a Red Steed" that resist the impact of the blizzard and its winds ("Raise up, raise up the branches!" [Vzdymaite, vzdymaite metly!]) are at the same time comets (*metla* can mean "a comet's tail"). Whereas Akhmatova blocks the sun from Tsvetaeva's vision, the horseman is the sun personified ("The armor on him is like the sun... A steep upward flight" [Dospekhi na nem—kak solntse... / Polet krutoi]) who promises to elevate the speaker into the empyrean heights or "azure" [lazur'].

In fact, all three works are set in motion by the exhilarating force of the elements: snowstorms, winds, fires, storms. In "Poems to Blok" these elements emphasize the irreconcilable conflict between Blok's otherworldliness and Tsvetaeva's "sinful" desire, isolating her from him and thus from her inspiration; in "Poems to Akhmatova," the elements are stirred up by Akhmatova's play-acting "wizardry" and similarly threaten to silence Tsvetaeva's poetic gift. In "On a Red Steed," on the contrary, the elements act on behalf of the rider and Tsvetaeva simultaneously—although she does not immediately recognize their summons. Thus, for example, the phrase "my soul is burning" [dusha gorit] at first seems to imply her soul's demolition by external flames, but actually conveys its own fiery renascence; similarly, the frightening, almost demonic image of "two conflagrations—in place of eyes" [zamesto glaz—/ Dva zareva] at the same time refers to poetic clairvoyance.[65] In psychoanalytic terms, one might say that the elements in this *poema* symbolize a transgressive, subconscious, poetic urge that breaks through the conservative, antipoetic barrier of the speaker's controlling ego. The elements here achieve that very purification that is unavailable to Tsvetaeva in relationship to Blok: for they purify her, paradoxically, not of desire but of desire's earthly limitations—the limitations of gender roles (girl, lover, mother) and, ultimately, of gender itself. In "On a Red Steed," in other words, she fantasizes that earthly sensuality is "undone" by a paradoxical (and, arguably, ultimately untenable) sensuality of the otherworldly.

Thus, in "On a Red Steed," Tsvetaeva overcomes the logical impasse created by the mythological non sequitur of her female gender by forging an original inspirational myth—a myth that allows her legitimate participation in the Russian poetic tradition and facilitates the realization of her own unique, deepest talents and the satisfaction of her most cherished desires. The horseman's actions in this *poema* amount to a paradigm for ideal love (which is synonymous, in this context, with true poetic inspiration), in which the infiltration of self by other is experienced not as a violation but as a liberating synthesis. A passage from a recent theoretical work on poetic inspiration provides a concise summary of this mechanism:

[The space of composition] is potentially transgressive: it skews distinctions of inner and outer, conception and reception. It is a place of unlocatable agencies with their effects of surprise or disappointment, agencies that skew seeming boundaries between self and other, act and passivity, paralysis and gift.[66]

This transcendent interpenetration of opposites, in which questions of agency become irrelevant, is precisely the state of inspiration that Tsvetaeva succeeds in entering through her union with the imaginary horseman.

The unique genius and terror of Tsvetaeva's invention in "On a Red Steed" lies in her recognition that, for her, the achievement of this paradoxical inspirational state requires that the real and the metaphorical change places: the solution to her "gender problem" necessitates the erasure of all literal meanings. She can escape from the confines of her body only if language itself mimes the possibility of a similar escape from the impossible; thus, the dubious "liberation" the horseman promises is a freedom from gender, sex, physicality — ultimately, from life itself. Fervently devoted to her endeavor, Tsvetaeva does not limit herself to the use of traditional symbolic tropes and language to express her liberation; instead, she purges the literal of its literalness, refuses the referent its reference. Her poetic striving urges her relentlessly toward an attitude to sign and meaning so unanchored, so symbolic, as to verge upon and then, indeed, cross over into the territory of the inhuman. Yet the human, the sensual, the erotic continue as the metaphors for this transcendence; they erase themselves, but in the process they are ironically reinforced. With Blok's pure spirituality and Akhmatova's enraptured self-imaging unavailable to her, Tsvetaeva discovers in this counterintuitive strategy her only possibility of poetic greatness.

This process of undoing is by no means without its costs and consequences. In the preface to "On a Red Steed," the horseman's liberation of Tsvetaeva's caged birds can be read as symbolic of her false dreams' dissolution, a preview of what is to come: "He released all my birds — into freedom" [Vsekh ptits moikh — na svobodu / Puskal]. The disturbing irony, of course, is that Tsvetaeva's supposed "delusions" (love, marriage, motherhood, etc.) are phenomena that belong to the real world, while the "salvation" the rider offers her is a figment of her poetic imagination. The question thus arises as to what she means by her annihilation of such seemingly positive values; can she really be advocating destruction, murder, eternal damnation? The answer she would have us accept is really an evasion of the question, for in this *poema,* poetic language points relentlessly outside of itself — that is, it is allegorical, typological, metaphorical, metonymic, or symbolic, but never purely literal. In other words, the "murders" that the rider on a red steed advocates must be understood in figurative terms; the reader's difficulty in achieving this twist of mind results from the fact that literal meanings are readily available in everyone's personal experience of childhood, love, parenthood, and faith. Furthermore, it is tempting to associate the traumatic events of Tsvetaeva's *poema* with the biographical facts of her own life (her failed love affairs, her daughter Irina's death from starvation, etc.).

Figurative meanings, on the contrary, are hidden from view by the complexity of Tsvetaeva's own private, associative poetics and are thus nearly inscrutable; perhaps the only viable route to them is via the poetic logic of intertextuality. Therefore, the interpreter of this *poema* is obliged to resist the emotions evoked by a literal appraisal of the scenes described and go in search of the work's figurative significance. "On a Red Steed" demands that its reader engage in its co-creation.[67] Just as the *poema*'s heroine complies with the destruction of her various beloveds of her own free will, so too the *poema*'s reader is implicated in these acts. The reader, too, is engaged in "liberating Love": by crossing the gulf between literal and poetic speech through the interpretive quest, the reader denies the *poema*'s human implications while affirming its symbolic meaning. The very act of interpretation, indeed, replicates the *poema*'s most disturbing claims. It is very likely that it is precisely this consequence of the co-creative interpretive endeavor that has been responsible for many critics' extreme discomfort with this work.

Indeed, it will be instructive to consider a recent example of such critical discomfort in light of the new interpretation of the *poema* I propose. David Bethea has suggested that the symbolic murder of a child in "On a Red Steed" constitutes a direct reference to the tragedy of Tsvetaeva's daughter Irina's death eleven months previously. It is plausible that in Tsvetaeva's mind (possibly subconsciously) there is a link between fact and fiction here; however, it seems to me unfair to suggest that poetic hindsight (which, in this case, may create a bearable narrative out of an unbearable fact) is at all the same thing as malice aforethought (apropos of Bethea's reference to Lady Macbeth). Instead, the fact that the child in the *poema* is not a daughter but a son argues for a symbolic reading of this disturbing episode. There is also a biblical, Old Testament resonance to Tsvetaeva's imagined sacrifice of her child (we recall Abraham's willingness to sacrifice Isaac to prove his faith; Job may be present here as well) that challenges Bethea's judgment that Tsvetaeva in this episode proves herself "the ultimate monster." [68]

This is not to say, however, that there is no danger inherent in Tsvetaeva's project of purifying the poetic word. She herself is maximally aware of the risks she takes: "Life is dirty, my notebook is clean" (5:288). She knows that too often (if not always), her attempts at symbolic meaning are inexorably forced back into the realm of the physical, the personal, the biographical when life ("life as it really is" [zhizn', kak ona est'], as Tsvetaeva phrases it wryly in "Poem of a Mountain" [3:30]) intrudes. As she writes to Pasternak: "How I understand you in your fear of words already deformed [iskazhaemye] by life, already made ambiguous" (6:251). Poetic language is "infected" by life, and

Tsvetaeva is trying desperately, impossibly, to "cure" it. This is not simple immorality, I think, but lyricism taken to its logical extreme.

The remainder of this chapter is devoted to a discussion of precisely how it is that Tsvetaeva accomplishes the transformation of literal/physical meanings into symbolic/spiritual ones in "On a Red Steed." I focus on three key moments: the destruction of the doll in the *poema*'s opening episode, the cathedral scene in which the speaker renounces Christ, and the losing battle Tsvetaeva fights against her muse in the work's finale. The doll scene is chilling, and prepares the reader for what is to come. This is the horseman's first appearance in the *poema*:

> Как Царь меж огненных зыбей
> Встает, сдвигает бровь.
> — Я спас ее тебе, — разбей!
> Освободи любовь!
> ———————
> Что это вдруг — рухнуло? — Нет,
> Это не мир — рухнул!
> То две руки — конному — вслед
> Девочка — без куклы.

[Like a Tsar among tongues of fire he rises, furrows his brow. "I saved her for you — shatter her! Liberate love!" What was it that suddenly — shattered? — No, it wasn't the world — that shattered! Those are two hands stretched out after the horseman — a girl — without a doll.]

A folkloric parallelism between the meter, phrasing, and imagery of this scene and the two that follow (describing the deaths of the heroine's lover and of her first-born child) creates a formula of symbolic destruction that clearly ties together these three episodes. One of the most perplexing aspects of the *poema* — namely, the question of agency and responsibility — is present from the very beginning, and from the beginning, this question is irresolvable. This is why the break between stanzas, marked by a horizontal line, functions as a kind of cinematic fast forward: we never actually see the doll being destroyed, and the speaker herself seems confused at what has happened. She is even psychologically dissociated from her own actions (though she never tries to shrug off responsibility for them) and so pictures herself in the third person ("Those are two hands stretched out . . . a girl without a doll").

On the other hand, just as the young Tsvetaeva in her earliest lyrics never shirks responsibility for her poetic alienation from life, so here too, less subtly and much more emphatically, she proclaims her antagonism toward the gendered limitations (symbolized, in part, by the doll) of life and poetic tradition and her own purposeful agency in refusing these constraints. The key to her

In Pursuit of a Muse

freedom of choice is the fact that the doll is not destroyed in the fire that threatens it, nor does the rider destroy it himself; rather, he miraculously saves the doll in order to proffer it to Tsvetaeva's heroine with the command to destroy, a command that she can decide to obey or not at her own discretion. Her own considered compliance signifies her unflinching embrace of poetic destiny—her rejection of fate [dolia] (at least in fantasy!) in favor of risky but exhilarating Pushkinian free will [volia]. In Tsvetaeva's poetics, this metaphysical choice is deemed essential to the identity of a true poet; for her, poetry is never just words on a page (that is dilettantism), but a whole system of being.

Two closely related Tsvetaevan texts can make clearer the doll's negative symbolism in Tsvetaeva's poetics—a symbolism that flies in the face of expectation (a doll usually connotes sweetness, tenderness, nurture, etc.). The first subtext is one I have already discussed at length: the early poem "Only a Girl," in which the doll is an emblem of the suffocating limitations of female destiny as it is preordained by social custom—and thus of the unavailability to the female "nonself" of a poetic, speaking self. Similar examples may be found in other of Tsvetaeva's early poems, as, for example, in "Boring Games" ["Skuchnye igry"]: "I picked up the stupid doll from the chair and dressed her. I hurled the doll onto the floor: I'm sick of playing mommy!" [Glupuiu kuklu so stula / Ia podniala i odela. / Kuklu ia na pol shvyrnula: / V mamu igrat'—nadoelo!] (1:113).

The second related text likewise emerges from Tsvetaeva's childhood experience with dolls, but here she imagines herself with respect to the doll not in the female role of future mother to the doll/child, but in the male role of future (male) lover/poet of the doll/muse. The passage I have in mind is the reminiscence of a Parisian doll in Tsvetaeva's 1937 essay "My Pushkin," already quoted earlier. We recall that this exotic doll is connected with Tsvetaeva's first knowledge of the pain of lost love and with her first enchantment by the word *love* itself, signifying that her initiations into both love and poetry are inseparably linked. Further on in the essay, she expands upon the doll's symbolic significance: it is an emblem of the lover's/poet's self-delusion, a mere empty vessel for the containment of poetic passion: "It is not the eyes that are passionate, but *I* feel passion, evoked in me by those eyes (and by the pink gauze, and the scent of moth balls, and the word *Paris,* and the business of the trunk, and the inaccessibility to me of the doll), and I attribute it—to the eyes. Not I alone. *All* poets. (And then they shoot themselves—because the doll *is not* passionate!) All poets, and Pushkin first" (5:69). The doll here reveals the unbearable inadequacy for the poet of real-life love.

Clearly, the doll for Tsvetaeva is a negative symbol through and through: it represents female limitation, unrequited (misguided) love, delusional passion, and creative bankruptcy.[69] The doll as a metaphor for the male poet's traditional muse (empty vessel, pure object) draws attention to the ambivalent unavailability to Tsvetaeva of such an arrangement (her beloved doll is locked up in a trunk, and Motherhood—in the figure of her own, uncomprehending parent—keeps the keys). The horseman's command to the little girl in "On a Red Steed" to "liberate Love" demands to be interpreted in light of these symbolic meanings. When read in this context, Tsvetaeva's destruction of the doll is transformed from a callous and cruel act into a courageous deviation from the limitations of society and custom—the beginning of a brave quest for a new myth that will be deserving of her talent and her passion, and for an inspirational relationship that will allow her both subjectivity and companionship. The "freedom" she gains is synonymous not with anarchy but with a new compulsion (symbolized by the horseman's cold austerity). This compulsion, just like Tsvetaeva's destruction of the doll, must be read symbolically rather than literally: as the compulsion of poetic form understood in its broadest sense, ranging from the constraints of meter and rhyme to the contours of myth.

The next two episodes of "On a Red Steed," in which the poet forfeits both her lover and her child, could be subjected to the very same kind of intertextual symbolic "unveiling" as I have already undertaken with respect to the doll scene. The central themes of these episodes—respectively, the isolation required of a woman "marked" by the poetic calling ("A young woman—without—a friend!" [Devushka—bez—druga!]), and the female poet's refusal of purely uterine destiny ("A woman—without—a womb!" [Zhenshchina—bez—chreva!])—both have huge symbolic significance for Tsvetaeva's poetics.[70] The latter theme, for example, recalls Tsvetaeva's visceral definition of the poet in terms of a fatal stomach wound in both "My Pushkin" ("D'Anthès hated Pushkin because he could not write poetry himself, and so he summoned the poet to a duel, i.e. lured him out into the snow and there killed him with a pistol shot in the stomach" [5:57]) and "Poem of the End" ("I am no more than an animal someone wounded in the stomach. It burns..." [Ia ne bolee chem zhivotnoe, / Kem-to ranennoe v zhivot. // Zhzhet...] [3:42]). In the interests of brevity, I will not elaborate further on the meanings of these various themes of "On a Red Steed." It is clear, however, that the scenes in which Tsvetaeva forswears romance and motherhood, like the opening doll scene, urge an appreciation of the symbolic and the transcendent, and a simultaneous erasure of real, physical, human meanings—even as these meanings are the very currency by which the transcendent is purchased. Such philosophical acrobatics as Tsvetaeva advocates is morally distressing, even as it is poetically exhilarating.

Nevertheless, for all that Tsvetaeva claims to have renounced all human allegiances and to be faithful only to Poetry, this is not, in reality, the case. Despite her seeming single-mindedness, she is loath to follow all the way down the path where her ear and poetic logic lead. The human in her does confront the poet—although, naturally, outside the framework of the poetic text that is the poet's exclusive domain: in the extratextual fact of the work's revision. Hence, in the revised version of "On a Red Steed," the two murderous episodes that follow the destruction of the doll have been cut. Evidently, Tsvetaeva realized with time that the literal implications of the acts described in these scenes are so shocking as to overpower the reader's ability to discern the symbolic meanings that were her intention. The original version of the *poema* reads dangerously like a murder ballad; the revised text is pure allegory. In the original version, however, the powerful emotional crescendo achieved by the rhythmic accumulation of near echoes between successive scenes, each more haunting than the preceding, creates a masterful piece of musical orchestration. In eliminating the two scenes, Tsvetaeva loses this effect; the original version of "On a Red Steed" is, poetically speaking, far stronger than the revised text—though humanly far more revolting. Here, then, is an example of Tsvetaeva's choosing life over poetry, even in the midst of her poetic trumpeting, ostensibly, of precisely the opposite choice in her poem itself. Such moments are hard to discern, since they are by definition extratextual; but, in my view, they were the rule of Tsvetaeva's life rather than the exception.

    I turn now to the two episodes that conclude the *poema:* the cathedral scene and the final battle. Two of the work's recent commentators, David Bethea and Catherine Ciepiela, have taken each of these scenes, respectively, as the basis for their readings of "On a Red Steed" as a Tsvetaevan rape fantasy. Bethea situates his interpretation in the context of Toril Moi's claim that a rape fantasy functions as a kind of magical "open-sesame" for the female creative psyche, allowing the fantasizer guilt-free entry into the forbidden realm of poetic language. Ciepiela comes to a similar conclusion by a different route, seeing in the *poema*'s climax a humiliating reworking of Symbolism's inspirational fantasy of the muse/prostitute. I would like to offer an alternative to both interpretations.

    As I have argued already, Tsvetaeva does not sense any inherent linguistic barrier to her poetic endeavors by virtue of her femininity per se; poetic language is, on the contrary, her natural element, her inborn entitlement, her mode of cognition from earliest childhood (her discussion of her attainment of language in later autobiographical essays such as "Mother and Music" ["Mat' i muzyka"] [1934] and "My Pushkin" [1937] make this position very clear). If this is the case, then it does not make sense to view her transgressions in "On a Red Steed" in terms of her presumed lack of access to poetic idiom. Furthermore, in my view, Tsvetaeva's revisionary poetic project is an undertaking fraught not with guilt, but with logical and psychological complication—something which the reading of this *poema* as a rape fantasy is not equipped to explain, relying as this interpretation does upon binary oppositions. Moreover, Bethea's intimation that the horseman provides an excuse for Tsvetaeva to shirk her own responsibility (he italicizes Moi's comment that in a rape fantasy "the woman is blameless") fails to take note of the free choice that she pointedly exercises throughout.

Ciepiela's corrective to Bethea rightly situates Tsvetaeva's work in the context of the very tradition that she is attempting to revise; she comments that Tsvetaeva's "rewriting of the symbolist scenario has the power of critique: 'Red Steed' exposes the gender logic of the poet's union with the muse." [71] Yet I disagree with Ciepiela's exclusively negative interpretation of the *poema*'s conclusion: "The poet lies abandoned in a ditch, now simply waiting for transcendence rather than claiming or pursuing it; she has utterly lost her agency." [72] Bethea's reading ends on a similarly grim note: "What the Rider impregnates or 'pricks' [the heroine] with is the death of her self." [73] In my reading, the *poema*'s conclusion is a triumph of inspirational potentiality—a state that is for Tsvetaeva far preferable to the stifling realization of any actual meeting. Thus, it is Tsvetaeva's union with her horseman/muse that finally enables the birth of her poetic self in all its ambivalent, compelling, and troubling glory.

I would argue further that, in "On a Red Steed," the speaker's union with her muse, violent though it be, is distinguished from a rape fantasy in two essential points. First, rape is by definition unexpected and unplanned. In a rape fantasy, the "victim" imagines herself as a passive participant in a forced encounter that actually encapsulates her hidden, inarticulable desire. But Tsvetaeva's heroine, on the contrary, exercises her free will at every step in her systematic destruction of each false object of her previous, misguided passion. She desires and orchestrates the climactic encounter with the rider—whose reciprocal desire for her she contrasts with her earthly lover's indifference ("He loves me not!—So I will leap onto the steed! He loves me not!—I'll leap up—to the sky!" [Ne liubit!—Tak ia na konia vzdymus'! / Ne liubit!—Vzdymus'—do neba!])—by taking the initiative against him in battle: "We'll see, we'll see—what kind of a man is the prideful one on the red steed when it comes to a battle!" [Posmotrim, posmotrim—v boiu kakov / Gordets na kone na krasnom!]. When the rider inevitably vanquishes her, she welcomes him with tender ecstasy ("I, raising my hands: 'My Light!'" [Ia, ruki vozdev: Svet!]). She is an instigator and an initiator, even in fantasy.

The second point is that rape is by definition a sexual act. Bethea and Ciepiela read the Freudian implications of Tsvetaeva's impalement under the left breast in the *poema*'s concluding battle scene as a codification of sexual penetration:

> В груди холодок—жгуч.
> И входит, и входит стальным копьем
> Под левую грудь—луч.
>
> [In my breast a chill—burns. And it enters, it enters, like a steel dagger beneath my left breast—a ray of light.]

I would argue that, in the context of the *poema*'s other meanings, it becomes clear that Tsvetaeva here intends quite an opposite logic: her asexual impalement encodes not sexual penetration but the dissolution of sexuality altogether.[74] This interpretation is supported by the fact that, in the metaphorical description of the rider's weapon, the expected relationship of tenor to vehicle is reversed: the weapon is really a ray of light that is only compared to a steel dagger, not the other way around. This movement of poetic thought away from the concrete/physical/sexual and toward the abstract/elemental/spiritual serves to dissolve the former and substantiate the latter. Furthermore, it must be noticed that the line describing Tsvetaeva's wounding by the rider is preceded by the wound's prolepsis: that is, the sensation of the wound (the oxymoronically burning chill in the speaker's breast) precedes the actual wounding. This paradoxical ordering of events amounts to a maximally compressed declaration of inspirational interpenetration of opposites; the equation of extreme cold with extreme heat is but a hint to the reader to look farther and deeper. Thus, the line also implies that this pain of ambiguous heat/cold originates internally, in the speaker's own breast, and arises before the answering blow is received. Her subsequent wounding is an objective correlative for her poetic intuition, rather than its unambiguous cause.[75]

In summary, although the idea of a rape fantasy does in fact capture the three issues that are at the heart of "On a Red Steed" (relationship of self to other, questions of agency, interpenetration of opposites), I believe that this idea is an insufficient interpretive tool to describe the complexity of Tsvetaeva's project here—and, furthermore, that its general "vector" is wrong; it lends to her union with the rider on a red steed a far more negative coloration than she intends. Indeed, it might be said that Tsvetaeva writes not about a rape, but about a paradoxical antirape: a fantasy of existence—or, at the very least, of a state of mind—in which sexuality satisfies itself through its own undoing, and body and soul, self and other, activity and passivity are entirely inseparable in consequence. This is the peculiar, alogical state of inspiration that is Tsvetaeva's true aim in her *poema*—and she achieves it through the upward vector of disembodiment, not the downward vector of demeaning physical violence.

In my reading, then, what seems to be debasement in "On a Red Steed" demands to be reconstrued as elevation. The rider himself is the very image of upward striving that is synonymous, for Tsvetaeva, with the poetic impulse. His every appearance is a gesture heavenward, a rising sweep and, simultaneously, a motion away from the physical world and toward the incorporeal substance of the pure elements or even purer abstraction. This elevating effect is accomplished first and foremost through phonetic play: specifically, the acoustic elements of the prefix *vz-/vs-*, denoting upward motion, echo in a majority of verbs and nouns describing the horseman's activities throughout the *poema*. Here are several of numerous instances: "Raising the doll . . . he rises up, like Fire itself" [**Vz**dymaia kuklu . . . / **V**staet, kak sam Pozhar]; "with an upward sweep of his cloak, he threw me up into the air" [**vz**makhom plashcha / **V voz**dukh menia—

vskinul]; "A splash . . . A smooth leap . . . He rises up, like the River itself" [**Vs**plesk . . . Plavnyi **vs**kok. / . . . **Vs**taet, kak sam Potok]; "He rises up, like Battle itself" [**Vs**taet kak sam Nabeg]; "He pounded onto the altar" [**Vz**gremel v altar′]; and finally, at the work's conclusion, "The dawn is bright. O who has suspended these weightless wings from my shoulders?" [**Vos**khod **s**vetel. / O kto ne**ves**omykh moikh dva / Kryla za plechom—/ **Vzves**il?].

The prefix *vz-/vs-*, with its connotation of swift upward motion, in fact becomes the morphological twin of the rider himself, who remains anonymous throughout the *poema*—as a muse should be—and is known only as the mysterious "Rider" [vsadnik]. The actual morphological boundary in this word occurs between *v* and *s* (*v-sadnik;* one meaning of the related verb *vsadit′* is "to penetrate sexually"). Yet the connotation of inward motion, penetration, and invasion associated with the prefix *v-* [in-] is overridden by the coincidental proximity of the *s* that begins the next morpheme. This sound, in the strong acoustic/sematic context established by the repeated verbal prefix *vz-/vs-* in the rest of the *poema,* combines with the word-initial phoneme *v-* to shift the morphological boundary forward, so that the noun's etymology is falsely heard as *vs-adnik,* and the rider's inwardly invasive action upon the speaker is diverted upward and outward (the suggestion that the rider of the red steed is a denizen of hell [ad] is perhaps not insignificant).

A similar transformation occurs in the cathedral episode that is the focus of Bethea's analysis. The verb Tsvetaeva uses there to denote the rider's stamping on her breast/chest is *vstavat′:*

> Доспехи на нем—как солнце...
> —Полет крутой—
> И прямо на грудь мне—конской
> Встает пятой.
>
> [The armor on him is like the sun...—A steep flight—And right on my chest/breast—he steps with his horse's hoof.]

Here the action is ambiguously directed, for *vstavat′* means both "to step on" (downward vector) and "to stand/rise up" (upward vector). When the phonetic context (the association of the Rider with the prefix *vz-/vs-*) is taken into account, the implication is that the downward motion/debasement that is ostensibly described by the verb *vstavat′* is metaphysically "overriden" by the *vs-*cluster's elevating effect. This interpretation is further supported by the fact that, just as is the case with the poet's light-ray wound at the *poema*'s climax, so here, too, we find that the inspirational flight begun by the steed's brutal and liberating gesture is preceded by this flight's prolepsis. For, the line "A steep flight" evokes not only the downward trajectory of the horse's descending hoof,

In Pursuit of a Muse 87

but simultaneously the speaker's sudden expectation of soaring upward, prior to her contact with the offending limb.

This transformative acoustic play on the word *vsadnik* that underlies the derivation of the muse's semantic and hence symbolic function in "On a Red Steed" is extremely reminiscent of the sound play on Blok's and Akhmatova's names in their respective cycles; here, however, the "name" is, instead, an anonymous nomer that is therefore free of the threatening onomastic allure of the other two. That the rider has no name implies that he is an emanation of myth and that, however violent his effect on Tsvetaeva might seem to be, he never truly possesses—bewitches—her as the real Blok and Akhmatova are able to do. He is an image of otherness, yet he has no strangling, external reality; he is, in other words, Tsvetaeva's ideal muse.

The horseman's loving address to Tsvetaeva at the *poema*'s conclusion poignantly expresses her freedom from gender, the ultimate boundary to her genius:

> И шепот: такой я тебя желал!
> И рокот: такой я тебя избрал,
> Дитя моей страсти—сестра—брат—
> Невеста во льду—лат!
>
> Моя и ничья—до конца лет.
> Я, руки воздев: Свет!
> —Пребудешь? Не будешь ничья,—нет?
> Я, рану зажав: Нет.
>
> [And a whisper: this is the way I desired you to be! And a rumble: this is the way I chose you to be, child of my passion—sister—brother—bride in the ice of armor! Mine and no one's—until the end of time. I, raising my hands: "My Light!"—"Will you stay? You will be no one's—no?" I, pressing my wound: "No."]

The use of the neuter *child* [ditia] and the equation of the terms *sister* and *brother* reiterate the idea that poetic release for Tsvetaeva as a woman poet comes only with the effacement of all sexual difference and of the very body that defines her as female. This is the reason, too, why she must consign herself to a life of celibacy ("You will be no one's—no?") in favor of an experience of spiritual enlightenment ("My Light!").[76] Through her asexual (antisexual) union with the rider on the red steed, she manages to achieve a wholeness of being that, until now, has been unavailable to her. In her liberation from the barriers of gender, she is simultaneously freed from the inequality of desire that plagues her relationships with both Blok and Akhmatova. The horseman desires her and chooses her even as she desires and chooses him; the dangers of sexuality and the boundaries of subjectivity are dissolved in this infinite mutuality of inspiration's ambiguous agency. Yet the language in which Tsvetaeva expresses this asexual, spiritual ideal is, at the same time, saturated with erotic passion. In this realm of poetic fantasy, *love* and *poetry* are rendered synonymous through Tsvetaeva's inspirational union with the horseman, as her deepest intuition claims them to be: his choice of her as his lover is also a vindication of her poetic genius.

This union, ultimately, is one of potentiality rather than actuality, a nonunion that is in a state of perpetual becoming:

> Немой соглядатай
> Живых бурь—
> Лежу—и слежу
> Тени.
>
> Доколе меня
> Не умчит в лазурь
> На красном коне—
> Мой Гений!
>
> [Dumb spy of live storms—I lie—and guard shadows. Until he speeds me away into the azure on his red steed—my Genius!]

In my reading, this final passage conveys not creative paralysis, but quite the opposite: we find here, rather, a picture of Tsvetaeva's ideal of creative receptivity, in which the phenomena of mundane reality recede into the distance and the poet, tense with expectancy, readies herself to take flight. The seeming paradox of this fullness-in-emptiness is echoed in Tsvetaeva's repeatedly professed preference for a clean sheet of paper to a manuscript: "An empty notebook! Ode to an empty notebook! A blank page with nothing yet, with still—already—everything!" (4:133). Her imaging herself as that very sheet of empty paper, receptive to her muse's "pen," in a poem of 1918 that remained one of her favorites throughout her life, has many affinities with the conclusion of "On a Red Steed": "I am a page for your pen. I'll accept everything. I am a white page. I am the keeper of your plenty: I'll return and return it a hundredfold" [Ia—stranitsa tvoemu peru. / Vse primu. Ia belaia stranitsa. / Ia—khranitel′ tvoemu dobru: / Vozvrashchu i vozvrashchu storitsei] (1:410). In quoting this poem years later in her essay "A History of One Dedication" ["Istoriia odnogo posviashcheniia"], Tsvetaeva terms it a "prayer" ("Ved′ eto zhe molitva!" [4:135]).

"On a Red Steed," in this sense, is also a prayer, as are the cycles to Blok and Akhmatova. But while Blok and Akhmatova are dangerous deities, indifferent and inaccessible, the imagined angel of the *poema* is intimately present in his absence. We recall that Tsvetaeva responds to the poetic threat represented by

In Pursuit of a Muse

Akhmatova and Blok by renaming and thereby remaking them in her dedicatory cycles—Akhmatova is revealed as "Gorenko," whereas Blok is replaced by a faceless "angel." Likewise, Tsvetaeva renames her horseman/muse in "On a Red Steed" when she soars above the *vz-/vs-* sound play that threads through most of the work to reach a stunning climax at the *poema*'s final word: namely, the revelation that this mysterious rider is none other than her own "Genius." The term *genius* [genii] captures Tsvetaeva's paradoxical condition of simultaneous agency and passivity at this climactic moment and indeed throughout the entire *poema*—indeed, the word itself enacts the very genius of which it speaks, weaving together the numerous contradictions of the work in a magical inspirational equilibrium. For this versatile Russian word refers at once both to Tsvetaeva's own creative brilliance ("vysshii tvorcheskii um") and to an external spiritual guardian ("dukh-pokrovitel'").[77] Here, then, in the person of this equine guardian spirit, is a brilliant resolution to Tsvetaeva's subject/object problem.

This double meaning implies what has been hidden until now: the rider on the red steed is none other than the imagined phantom of Tsvetaeva's future greatness, the emblem of her duty to her calling and of the many sacrifices and revisions it will entail. Far from being a rapist who renders her selfhood a victim to his cruelty, the horseman is both the emanation of Tsvetaeva's unrelenting struggle to usher her poetic selfhood into being, and the emblem of her unyielding determination to bear all due credit and censure for this poetic becoming. Accordingly, the martyrology of the poet in "Poems to Blok" and "Poems to Akhmatova" (Blok as angel; Akhmatova as icon) is rejected in this *poema* in favor of an ideology of personal responsibility in both earthly and otherworldly realms. The horseman's stomping on the heroine's breast just at the moment when she is about to offer herself up as a sacrifice on Christ's altar is the signal that Christian faith is "overridden" by this flaming Pegasus; by now, Tsvetaeva has gone far beyond the tentative hints of blasphemy present in her earlier poetic cycles to an out-and-out alliance with the devil of poetry.[78]

2

Conjuring Pasternak
A Divided Psyche

> Давным-давно — перекричать разлуку —
> Я голос сорвала.
>
> [Long, long ago—to outyell parting—I broke in my voice]
> — "Ia knigu etu poruchaiu vetru . . ." (1920)

> Кастальскому току,
> Взаимность, заторов не ставь!
> Заочность: за оком
> Лежащая, вящая явь.
>
> [Mutuality, do not create impediments for the Castalian stream! Unity in distance: a more intense reality, lying beyond what the eye can see.]
> — "Zaochnost'" (1923)

> Она, Психеи бестелесней,
> Читает стих Экклезиаста
> И *не* читает Песни Песней.
>
> [She, more bodiless than Psyche, reads the verse of Ecclesiastes but *doesn't* read the Song of Songs.]
> — "Starinnoe blagogoven'e" (1920)

In May 1922, Tsvetaeva and her daughter Alia emigrated to Berlin, where, the following year, Tsvetaeva's collection *Psyche* was published. Tsvetaeva writes of this collection that it is "a summation, rather than a stage" [*ne* etap, a itog] (7:394); this book is distinct from all her previous ones in that it is structured not by pure chronology, but rather by poetic problems and outcomes. Although the book itself consists exclusively of works written prior to Tsvetaeva's emigration (including the cycles to Blok and Akhmatova and "On a Red Steed"), its title shows that by 1923 she has reinterpreted even the initial stages in her poetic self-definition in terms of the myth that currently consumes her attention: the tale, first recorded by Lucius Apuleius in his *Metamorphoses* or *The Golden Ass,* of Psyche and Eros.

Tsvetaeva's comment about the uniqueness of her collection *Psyche* could be applied equally to the role of the Psyche myth in her oeuvre as a whole. Although she explores other myths in her writing at various times, the Psyche myth is not a phase but a summation of her poetics. Indeed, this myth goes beyond myth to infiltrate her entire sense of her own identity and destiny, in particular during the early period of her emigration in Berlin and Prague, 1922 to 1925, while she was composing the lyrics that would make up her virtuosic collection *After Russia [Posle Rossii]*. Even where the Psyche myth is not explicitly invoked in the poems of this collection, it is the shadow text for many of Tsvetaeva's favorite poetic themes. Thus, I would like to argue that this myth is not merely an incidental subtext, but an overriding, organizing belief system—the entire mythopoetic basis of Tsvetaeva's identity and poetics during this period. Psyche becomes absolutely central to Tsvetaeva's understanding of herself, both as a poet and as a woman; indeed, the name *Psyche* and its Russian equivalent *dusha* [soul] are synonymous with Tsvetaeva's innermost self, requiring no derivation, no extraneous explanation: "Everything falls away like an old skin, and under the skin is live meat or fire: I: Psyche. I don't fit into any one mold—not even into the most spacious of my poems! I don't know how to live. I'm not like other people [Vse ne kak u liudei]" (6:607).[1]

This quotation, from a September 1923 letter Tsvetaeva wrote to the young émigré critic Aleksandr Bakhrakh, points to the reasons for her attraction to the Psyche myth: it allows her to reconceptualize her compulsion toward the barrier-breaking "inhumanity" of poetic inspiration—which, in "On a Red Steed," she mythologized through her union with the demonic horseman/muse—in terms of a more positively valenced pursuit, painful yet precious, of her own intrinsic talents. Moreover, the Psyche myth, like Tsvetaeva's earlier inspirational narratives, incorporates her own struggle between feminine, human destiny and lonely, poetic immortality. In this chapter I show that Tsvetaeva replaces the maximally Romantic myth of her winged horseman/genius with the newly ascetic myth of a Psychean renunciation of love, in order to make sense of her overwhelming passion for fellow poet Boris Pasternak—a passion that, she senses intuitively, is destined to go unconsummated. Furthermore, I demonstrate that Tsvetaeva's Psyche myth, with Pasternak and herself in the roles of hero and heroine, respectively, serves not only as a *conceptual framework* enabling her to understand, and translate into literary form, the huge emotional and inspirational force of the two poets' unconsummated epistolary romance, but also as a *narrative mandate* that determines the course of her very actions in relation to Pasternak, often against her own personal will and desires. This mandate is for a spiritual (non)meeting that is very different from Tsvetaeva's prior triumphal vanquishment by her winged genius—for Pasternak is real, not imaginary, and her union with him is sealed by faith, rather than obedience.[2]

Tsvetaeva's relationship with Pasternak began shortly after her emigration, when, in the summer of 1922, he sent her a copy of his book *My Sister—Life* [*Sestra moia—zhizn'*]. The two poets' exchange of letters and poems gained in emotional intensity during that fall and the following winter, when Pasternak, too, found himself in Europe for a time. He was in Berlin, she was newly arrived from Berlin in Prague by that time, and the question of whether they would arrange a meeting was urgently and passionately discussed. The climax and dénouement to this situation came early the next spring, when Pasternak departed for Moscow with his new bride, not yet having met Tsvetaeva. Nevertheless, their epistolary relationship was to continue sporadically until the end of her life, reaching a second peak of intensity during the summer of 1926.[3] Here, however, I focus on the earlier stage of Tsvetaeva's involvement with Pasternak.

Thus, Tsvetaeva's letters and poems to Pasternak written during the period 1922 to 1925 (the period of *After Russia*) are the subject of this chapter. Through analysis of these texts, I explore the ramifications for Tsvetaeva's poetics of this arguably most important of her "nonrelationships," which has already received ample attention in the critical literature on both poets.[4] Tsvetaeva craves the transport of poetic transgression, of imaginary inspirational unions; yet she never relinquishes permanently the song of the flesh, the lure of human passion, human closeness. In my view, Pasternak is the unique, pivotal figure in her life who holds the promise of being able to unite the two aspects of Tsvetaeva's selfhood, since her love for him is perhaps the single instance when her raw sexual passion and her metaphysical strivings coalesce. For this very reason, paradoxically, Tsvetaeva's love for Pasternak is inexorably doomed by the harsh logic of her poetics.

It has been customary in the criticism to interpret Tsvetaeva's role in her relationship with Pasternak—through the template of her numerous other ill-fated relationships—as one of insistent desperation: she longs for him, he pulls back. A reading of her works to Pasternak in the context of the Psyche myth reveals that, much to the contrary, she is determined to maintain the physical separation between herself and Pasternak at all costs. In this way, she preserves both the possibility of an eventual spiritual union between them, and the state of unresolved emotional and sexual tension that functions for her as poetic inspiration. Psyche's dual essence as a mortal woman who, through transgression of her divine husband Eros's prohibitions, eventually herself attains divine status encapsulates Tsvetaeva's sense of inherent disjunction between her own dual essences, feminine and poetic, and her resultant belief in the necessary transgressiveness of her poetic talent.

Tsvetaeva's revisionist reading of the Psyche myth accords well in many respects with the psychoanalytic interpretation given in Erich Neumann's commentary that accompanies his own rendering of Apuleius's tale.[5] Neumann, like Tsvetaeva, understands the Psyche myth as an essential parable about woman's escape from the bondage of sexual object status and her resultant formation of a liberated feminine consciousness. Thus, I use Neumann's interpretation as a way of illuminating the myth's significance for Tsvetaeva. The gist of this interpretation is as follows.

Psyche is a mortal woman, so beautiful that men from all over the world come to admire her and abandon their worship of Aphrodite, goddess of beauty. Yet Psyche's is not the beauty of lust, sexuality, and fertility purveyed by Aphrodite, but a competing beauty of the spirit. Psyche is condemned to what Neumann terms a sacrificial "marriage of death"[6] to satisfy Aphrodite's jealous wrath; she is to be cast off from the edge of a cliff, and she goes toward her death willingly. But she does not die after all; instead, Eros, god of love, saves her by hiding her away in a magical palace. In the palace, Psyche dwells cut off from all her ties with humanity, surrounded by untold riches, served by invisible hands, serenaded by lovely music played on invisible instruments. Eros comes to her only at night and is her lover, but Psyche is forbidden to look at him. Eventually she disobeys this prohibition and lights her lamp while Eros sleeps—metaphorically shedding the burning light of consciousness upon him. In doing so, she accidentally spills a drop of hot oil on his shoulder, waking him and wounding him profoundly, and simultaneously wounding herself with his love-inducing arrow. In symbolic terms, Psyche makes the transition from passive acquiescence to her husband's desire and demands to active participation in mutual passion. Yet at this very moment, Eros flies away; Psyche has forfeited him (and her animalian, purely sexual coexistence with him) for the sake of knowledge and the hope of a different kind of love, based in equality and conscious mutuality.

Psyche is trapped in an impossibility: the same act that awakens her sense of self and thus her ability to love also necessarily deprives her of her beloved. The attainment of love is equivalent to exorcism of the beloved. Just as Tsvetaeva wields her poetry in an attempt to transform the gender-bound nature of merely mundane, erotic passion—to "see" her beloved's essence and, by this very act, to define her own poetic self vis-à-vis his radical alterity—so too Psyche's act defines "a new love principle, in which the encounter between feminine and masculine is revealed as the basis of individuation."[7] Psyche's true love, is, ultimately, akin to utter loneliness and the undoing of gender: "With the self-sacrifice of her act she gives up everything and enters into the loneliness of a love in which, at once unconsciously and consciously, she renounces the attraction of her beauty that leads to sex and fertility."[8] Eve's biblical exit from her own preconscious Eden is achieved through precisely the opposite process: she follows a path away from Platonic friendship into sexuality and fertility—into gender. This fundamental opposition between the developmental trajectories of Psyche and Eve is the basis for Tsvetaeva's claim in letters to Pasternak that she is a Psyche (soul), not an Eve (body).[9]

Psyche eventually finds herself in Aphrodite's power and undergoes a series of trials: she must sort a huge pile of grain and seeds; gather golden fleece from the rams of the sun; bring back a jug of Styx water from its source on the summit of the highest mountain; and, finally, journey into Hades and retrieve a box filled with Persephone's beauty.[10] In Neumann's interpretation, the first three of these trials represent Psyche's confrontation with the masculine essence, which threatens to overwhelm her; she must "['tame'] the hostile masculine principle, in the erotic binding of what might have been destructive in the form of the paternal uroboros."[11] Psyche is assisted in her task by helpers of the elements—earth (ants), water (reed), and air (Zeus's eagle)—which are finally emanations of her own consciousness: "It is characteristic of the 'labors of Psyche' [as opposed to the Labors of Hercules—A. D.] that . . . [the] masculine spiritual element . . . is at first unconscious but gradually develops into a conscious attitude."[12] This configuration of the problem could well be taken as a metaphor for Tsvetaeva's transgression into the masculine poetic realm and her appeal to a masculine spirit helper for safe passage.

Psyche's final trial—the descent into Hades—is reminiscent of Orpheus's descent and thus is a metaphor for poetic inspiration. Psyche is a female, however, and therefore her Orphic descent is a descent with a difference: unlike Orpheus, who leaves Eurydice behind in the underworld, Psyche returns to earth with a box containing Persephone's Hadean beauty intact. In other words, she is profoundly changed by her descent and cannot live on the earth as she did previously. Instead, she makes the conscious choice to open the box and don Persephone's beauty—which, by definition, is the beauty of death. Psyche falls into the sleep of death; in simple terms, she commits suicide.[13] Only after this act does Aphrodite relent, making Psyche's reunion with Eros possible. Death, ironically, makes her immortal; this is the tragic immortality of the poet. Psyche becomes a goddess, and Psyche and Eros are reunited in a new nonphysical, fully conscious, fully mutual otherworldly love. After entering into the divine heights of Olympus, Psyche gives birth to Eros's child, whose name, Pleasure, refers pointedly to the spiritual pleasures of the soul.

There are a number of affinities between Tsvetaeva's inspirational predicament as we have witnessed it so far and the Psyche tale. Psyche's salvation by Eros, who sends the West Wind to catch her as she falls to certain death, is reminiscent of the mounted horseman's intercession just in the nick of time in various near catastrophes in "On a Red Steed." In particular, the poet's anticipation of salvation by her long-awaited muse as she lies half-dead in a ditch at the *poema*'s conclusion suggests that she must have studied Psyche's example. When Tsvetaeva is smitten with love for Pasternak, accordingly, she breaks out of an erotic marriage to a potent male divinity (the winged genius on a red steed) who has caused her—by her own acquiesence, if not free will—to sever her ties with her family and indeed with mundane reality itself. Just as Psyche transgresses against Eros's command that she not attempt to look upon him, so too Tsvetaeva breaks her vow of faithfulness to her austere "genius," continuing to love and desire the impossible contact with real men (such as Pasternak) that her imaginary muse cannot offer.

These two transgressive acts are similar not only by virtue of their authors' disobedience to the injunctions of a beloved male deity, but also through an inherent likeness: for Tsvetaeva, as we have seen, sight and vision are attributes of the nonpoetic, the antipoetic, the world of phenomena rather than noumena. Psyche's attempt to look upon her husband's physical aspect speaks of a loss of faith, an urge toward the earthly and away from the poetic. Tsvetaeva's continuing erotic desire for real lovers is evidence of a similar vacillation in her poetic commitment. Yet the situation is more complicated; she craves real lovers not only in spite of her poetry, but for the sake of it; the fiery imagery which she often employs to express her passion conveys the ultimate inseparability for her of the erotic and poetic drives. Similarly, the instrument that Psyche uses to reveal Eros's physical aspect and with which she, unintentionally, causes him a painful and disabling burn is, precisely, a flaming lamp—that is, poetic fire, which both illuminates and wounds. Both women are prompted by the poetic urge (whose root is the urge toward knowledge) to act against poetry. The myth of Psyche perfectly incapsulates the basic paradox of female creativity as Tsvetaeva understands it.

As Tsvetaeva moves farther away from the fantasy of "On a Red Steed," Pasternak himself comes to play the role of Eros in her mythopoetics. Like Eros, Pasternak is at once pure spirit and pure body, the dizzying quintessence of sex and poetry intermingled—and Tsvetaeva's longing for him is almost unbearable. Yet, in the interests of elevating their love and perpetuating his inspirational effect upon her, she, from the very beginning of her correspondence with Pasternak, consistently heeds the three central teachings of the Psyche myth: (1) its warning against the dangerous temptation of visual verification of spiritual truth, (2) its privileging of love as the process of attaining higher consciousness rather than love as sexual intimacy, and (3) its envisioning of an otherworldly, posthumous union of equal souls made possible only through earthly isolation, torments, and trials.

Psyche Fledges Her Wings: First Poems to Pasternak

Like Psyche, Tsvetaeva first recognizes her ideal mate through the agency of a flood of light: the light of Pasternak's poetry, and the light of her own awakening consciousness brought about by her deep, instinctive understanding of that poetry. Her first ecstatic response to the poems in Pasternak's collection *My*

Sister—Life is contained in an essay she titles "A Downpour of Light: Poetry of Eternal Masculinity" ["Svetovoi liven': Poeziia vechnoi muzhestvennosti"]. (Catherine Ciepiela points out that the standard English translation of *muzhestvennost'* as *courage* is inadequate in the context of Tsvetaeva's concern with the essential role gender plays in the determination of poetic identity; this noun should be understood, also, as meaning *masculinity*.[14]) Tsvetaeva has glimpsed in Pasternak at the very outset two basic features of her Eros: his embodiment of the ideal of masculinity against and through which she seeks to redefine her own limiting femininity, and his affiliation with the illuminating principle of light/poetry which is to point her route toward a higher consciousness and ultimately to the possibility of personal reintegration.

In her transformation of the Psyche myth, Tsvetaeva amends the power imbalances in her source: for her it is important that she and Pasternak, woman and man, be equal in status, neither one of them more human or divine than the other. The light must, therefore, emanate from him, by his consent; he is not the sleeping, forbidding Eros, but the guiding light of masculinity that helps Psyche through her trials in her tortuous path toward divinity and reunion with her beloved. Yet, in Tsvetaeva's poetics, the prospect of salvation is collapsed with the moment of Psyche's original transgression; the poetic act for her as a woman necessarily implies both. Hence, Pasternak's light-giving poetry is also dangerous: "A downpour: the whole sky plummeting down onto your head: pouring straight and slanting—right through, a draft, a fight between rays of light and rain [skvoz', skvozniak, spor svetovykh luchei i dozhdevykh]—you have nothing to do with it: but if you got caught in it—grow!" (5:233). Like the burning oil of Psyche's lamp, Pasternak's poetry has the potential to scorch unbearably, as Tsvetaeva discovers in reading his collection *Themes and Variations:* "Your book is a scorch [ozhog] . . . I was in pain, but I didn't blow. (Others smear themselves with cold cream, sprinkle on potato starch! — scoundrels [pod—le—tsy]!)" (7:233).[15] For Tsvetaeva it is Psyche, and not Eros, who is burned.

Even the title of the first collection of Pasternak's poetry that Tsvetaeva reads —*My Sister—Life*—plays directly into her understanding of the Psyche myth; she gladly takes upon herself the role of Pasternak's "sister-life." In "My Pushkin," she later speaks about the genesis in her of this "sister-self": "Thus at the age of three I found out for sure that a poet has a stomach and—I'm recalling all the poets whom I've met at one time or another—I worried about this *stomach* of the poet, which is so often not-full and in which Pushkin was killed, no less than about his soul. With Pushkin's duel began the *sister* in me" (5:57).[16] Tsvetaeva's emphasis in this passage on the "sister's" relationship specifically to the physical aspect of the male poet might seem on the surface to contradict the ideal of Psyche, who is the embodiment of spirit. Yet Tsvetaeva struggles not against bodily incarnation per se, but against the limitations of gender divisions and as-

A Divided Psyche 97

sociated sexual bondage. The body—and the vulnerable "humanity" for which it stands—is an indispensible aspect of love for Tsvetaeva, as it is an ineradicable aspect of her selfhood, despite and even because of all the binds and paradoxes it creates. This fact can account for Ariadna Efron's claim that "[Tsvetaeva] loved mythology for the ability of its gods and heroes to slip up and bruise themselves like mortals [po-zemnomu]—despite their superhuman feats and deeds."[17] By calling attention to the physical vulnerability of male poets, Tsvetaeva implies that her own female predicament is not, after all, of marginal significance, but is representative of the human condition in general. When Pasternak complains about a toothache in a letter to Tsvetaeva, she responds with all the compassion of her soul; this simple, human woe, in the light of his divinity-like poetic stature, is the very collusion of opposites that paradoxically comprises Tsvetaeva's ideal beloved and allows her to take on—in letters and imagination at least— the identity of the Psychean "sister": free, conscious, and fully passionate beyond the threat of pure eroticism. This is "life" that is more than life itself— and must, therefore, be less. The ideal meeting of brother and sister, Eros and Psyche is Tsvetaeva's code for genderless love and must remain a dream if it is not to be defaced.[18]

Tsvetaeva's first poem addressed to Pasternak, "Life lies inimitably" ["Nepodrazhaemo lzhet zhizn'..."] (2:132–33), written in Berlin during the summer of 1922 under the strong impression of *My Sister—Life,* is an impassioned answer to Pasternak's poetry that already adheres to this Psychean aversion toward "real life." Pasternak's evocation of his "sister-life" celebrates the overwhelming fullness of life's poetic possibilities, the inspirational fecundity of even the most mundane and insignificant objects and occurrences; for Tsvetaeva, on the contrary, life is an ineffable lie: "Life lies inimitably: beyond expectation, beyond lies..." [Nepodrazhaemo lzhet zhizn': / Sverkh ozhidaniia, sverkh lzhi...]. Her internal rhyming of *rye* [rzhi] (a metonym for the physical, natural world; for life itself) and *lie* [lzhi] drives her point home. The magic of Pasternak's "life" might be compared to Eros's magical palace (the word *enchantable* [zavorozhimy] in the third stanza further supports this link), whose sensual pleasures Psyche rejects in favor of a higher, nonphysical truth.

Thus, the call of Tsvetaeva's soul—which resonates through Pasternak's summons—is experienced as the perversely pleasurable dissolution of her flesh, represented metaphorically by the buzzing of bees in honeysuckle blooms: "A murmuring—through honeysuckle—of a hundred bee stings... Rejoice!—he has called you forth!" [Bormot—skvoz' zhimolost'—sta zhal... / Raduisia zhe! —zval!]. The rhyme *zhal/zval* [stings/called] emphasizes the opposition of physical existence (bodily pain) to the soul's calling; at the same time, the awakening of the spirit is oddly metaphorized through this titillating experience of physical, almost sexual pain. The appearance of Pasternak in Tsvetaeva's life, as of his powerful poetry, is apprehended as a welcome torment. This torment is very different from the unrequited pain Tsvetaeva experienced in reading Blok's poetry, however. That was the pain of pursuit, but now, miraculously, the Poet (in Pasternak's incarnation) has himself come calling (as Tsvetaeva writes in a letter to Pasternak: "for the first time in my life not *spells* [chary], but knowledge [znanie]" [6:284]). This spiritual knowledge that she has awaited since she was "only a girl" is an agony of recognition, for she precociously intuits the impending necessity of renunciation. Psyche's love requires its own forfeiture in order to prove itself.

In the second half of this poem, Tsvetaeva answers Pasternak's call with a tantalizing balance of rash, precipitate passion and gentle but firm repudiation that is to serve as the pattern for her entire future response to her brother poet. She begs Pasternak not to blame her for her impetuous, headlong rush into the "dream" of intimacy he offers her, implicitly, in his "song": "And do not blame me, friend, so enchantable are the souls of us bodies—that I'm already: headfirst into the dream. Since—why else did you sing?" [I ne kori menia, drug, stol' / Zavorozhimy u nas, tel, / Dushi—chto vot uzhe: lbom v son. / Ibo—zachem pel?]. She admits her erotic arousal by Pasternak; yet, true to the winged woman she is, she tacitly rejects her body's cravings—and Pasternak's implicit sexual invitation—in favor of her soul, her forehead, and their mutual dream. These three elements feature prominently in Tsvetaeva's emergent revision of her inspirational myth: the soul represents poetic striving, the forehead is emblem of the taxing exertions of the creative process,[19] and the mutual dream replaces the imaginary muse with an inspirational force that is at once more "real"—because induced by and shared with a real human being—and more remote (that human being is inaccessible except through dream).

This new inspirational paradigm signals Tsvetaeva's movement away from starkly Romantic poetics and into the ascetic isolation of what is, paradoxically, a new faith in life's impossibilities. Romanticism annuls those impossibilities, imagines them away; her new stoic poetics of renunciation celebrates the power, the beauty, and the pain of what might have been, could have been, should have been but is not and will not be:

> В белую книгу твоих тишизн,
> В дикую глину твоих «да» —
> Тихо склоняю облом лба:
> Ибо ладонь — жизнь.
>
> [Into the white book of your quietnesses, into the wild clay of your yesses—quietly I cup the slant of my brow: since my palm—is life.]

Tsvetaeva bends her forehead into Pasternak's book, cupping it in her palm, and answers his "quietnesses" and "yesses" (like Eros's contradictory lust for

Psyche, which offers her everything but a glimpse at who he really is) with her own peculiar "no." For, she rejects Pasternak's outward-looking, all-embracing concept of "life," which she counters with her own: the palm of her hand that cradles her creative, creating brow. Real, external life is not available or attractive to her; she chooses rather the hermetic stance of the prophet, for whom life is created through the movement of poetic thought and the productive tension of unfulfilled desire.[20]

Had Tsvetaeva decided to remain in Berlin just a little while longer, she and Pasternak would have met in the fall of 1922 and, very likely, their relationship would have lost its mythopoetic potential, either by verging into the nonpoeticism of the merely physical, or by fizzling out in the burdening flood of expectations incommensurate with reality. Tsvetaeva, with her wealth of experience in similar matters, her unflinching knowledge of herself and her own weaknesses, and her keen prophetic instinct, chose the distinction of myth over the commonality of sexual liaison—she fled Berlin for Czechoslovakia. Ariadna Efron perceives her mother's decision to leave before Pasternak's arrival as a mythopoetic act in itself: "In her departure from Berlin on the eve of Pasternak's arrival, there was something of the nymph's flight from Apollo, something mythological and not of this world—for all the indubitable rationality of the decision." [21]

Tsvetaeva provides her own explanation for her actions in a letter written on 19 November 1922 to Pasternak in Berlin from her new home in a Prague suburb: "I don't like meetings in life: colliding heads [sshibaiutsia lbom]. Two walls. That's not the way to break through. A meeting must be an arc: then the meeting is—*above.*—Heads flung backwards [zakinutye lby]!" (6:226). This "arc" that describes the contour of Tsvetaeva's ideal of nonmeeting recalls the arch of Eros's bow (we recall that, in the Psyche myth, it is Psyche's accidental self-wounding by Eros's arrow that awakens both her passion and her consciousness). From this bow, the love-arrow that is the vector of Tsvetaeva's transgressive poetic passion is to be shot upward into the heavens, in the process rending lover from beloved, body from soul.[22] Elsewhere, she euphorically recognizes in the inspiring upward slope of Pasternak's handwriting an inscription of her own ruthlessly outward- and upward-striving poetic vector: "You have beautiful handwriting: you chase the miles! Miles—and horses' manes—and sleighs' runners! And suddenly—a blow of the reins [okhlest vozzhzi]! Breaking the head—and the head isn't broken! Beautiful, significant, masculine handwriting. One trusts it immediately" (6:226). Tsvetaeva trusts the vector of Pasternak's inspiring absence—whose envoy is his handwriting, her masculine guiding spirit—over the delusion of his bodily presence. She cannot, in fact, imagine his body at all and answers his protests of its existence and wants with its emphatic erasure: "*It is as if in place of yourself, you send your shadow into life, giving it full powers*" (6:226; emphasis in the original). She answers Pasternak's request for a meeting with her insistence on a nonmeeting: "My favorite means of communication is otherworldly [potustoronnii]: dreams—meeting in dreams. And my second favorite is letter writing" (6:225).[23]

Pasternak and his wife remained in Berlin until March of 1923. In February, as the time for their return to Russia drew near, Tsvetaeva was overtaken by a rush of emotion that she frantically channeled into a series of letters and poems addressed to Pasternak. At first, now that the danger of a drawn-out relationship was past, she harbored plans of making a brief trip to Berlin just to meet Pasternak, to see him off: "And so, Pasternak, let me know, I'll come. To all appearances—on business, honestly—to you: for your soul: to bid farewell . . . I ask for: what? Well, just a handshake. In general I have my doubts that you exist at all" (6:232). The only meeting Tsvetaeva can conceive of is a meeting with Pasternak's soul—a meeting that is also a farewell. At the same time, she explains less than ingenuously that her love for him is profoundly disinterested: "Read this as indifferently [otreshenno] as I write it, it isn't you or I that's important here, I'm not to blame that you didn't die one hundred years ago, this is almost impersonal [bezlichno], and you know it . . . I make confession (I don't atone, but adulate!) not to you but to the Spirit in you . . . while your greatness is such that you are not jealous" (6:229). Whether Pasternak does succumb to Tsvetaeva's powerful conjuring and refrain from the strange jealousy to which she alludes (jealousy of the real man, whom she rejects, toward his own shadow, which she reveres) is, of course, debatable; what is clear is that Tsvetaeva here is attempting to render Pasternak in the mold of her ideal reader/lover of the poem "To You—One Hundred Years Later," with whom the only possible contact is, by definition, the contact of faith—Psyche's enduring passion for the first unseen, then unattainable Eros.[24]

By such tactics, Tsvetaeva jealously guards her possession of Pasternak's nonpresence in her life, thereby allowing her imagination free rein in creating him, muselike, for herself, when and where and how she needs him to be: "I won't say that you are essential [neobkhodimy] to me, in my life you are *inescapable* [*neobkhodny*], *whatever* direction my thoughts take, the lamp arises of its own accord. I conjure the lamp into being" (6:230). This "lamp" that is Pasternak's illuminating essence is also Psyche's lamp; Tsvetaeva retains the privileges of both conjuring and banishing her lover at her own whim, because for her his interpenetrating presence and absence are the reciprocal conditions of her love for him. She describes calmly and coolly her imaginary meetings with him at the train station during the previous fall (an experience which provides the basis for her poem "Dawn on the Rails" ["Rassvet na rel'sakh"] (2:159) and her effortless refusal of his presence as soon as she is forced to abandon her soul and reenter her body, return to real life: "Leaving the station, rather: getting into the train—I would simply part with you sensibly and soberly. I never brought you with me into life" (6:230). During the time of her imaginary intimacy with him, she kept their meetings a secret: "I tell you this, because it has passed" (6:230). Sensing that Pasternak is not as eager or as able as she to make such a separation between body and soul, life and poetry, she advises him to plunge into the composition of a long work: "This will be your second life, first life, only life. You will no longer need anyone or anything. You won't notice a single person. You will be horribly free" (6:234). This project of creating an alternate life of the soul en route to a higher existence is reminiscent of Psyche's trials and is, moreover, precisely the project in which Tsvetaeva herself engages in relation to Pasternak.[25]

Although Tsvetaeva initially proclaims her intentions of coming to Pasternak, the growth of her Psyche myth gradually overtakes the strength of her desire for a meeting. Yet in her letters she continues to vacillate wildly. Indeed, her letters to Pasternak are by no means simply an expression of pure thoughts and emotions; they are in a sense the rough drafts for her poems to Pasternak and, as such, contain the traces of her developing poetic logic. This is the explanation for the unaccountable, apparently self-contradictory (and certainly aggravating to the letters' recipient) shifts in logic that occur from letter to letter and sometimes in the course of a single missive. The mythopoetic nature of Tsvetaeva's thought process is made explicit in her letter of 10 February, in a highly ambiguous passage in which she simultaneously calls her beloved to her and, in the same gesture, banishes him to the farthest reaches of the earth or beyond: "And now, Pasternak, a request: don't leave for Russia without having seen me. Russia for me is *un grand peutêtre,* almost the other world [tot-svet]. If you were leaving for Guadeloupe, going to the snakes, to the lepers, I wouldn't call you back [ia by ne oklikuula]. But: for Russia—I call you back [oklikaiu]" (6:232). Here once again, Tsvetaeva collapses the separate poles of her mythological source. Russia, according to her logic, is now equated simultaneously with Hades and with Eros's Olympian heights [tot-svet]—for Russia is both the dark, enigmatic hell that she knew during the Revolutionary years, and the lost paradise of her childhood. In the very process of uttering her plea to Pasternak not to abandon her, she recognizes anew the necessity and inevitability of their separation.

Yet, as Tsvetaeva well realizes, she would be taking an enormous metaphysical risk in executing this contemplated act of faith and renunciation. She demonstrates her recognition of the danger with which she toys by linking her ambivalence about whether to come to Pasternak to her earlier indecisiveness with respect to Blok, as we have already seen.[26] Tsvetaeva here, like Pushkin in the plague in her later essay "Art in the Light of Conscience" ["Iskusstvo pri svete sovesti"], is tempting fate by her stoic resistance to the force of her own desire; she may well lose the contest and forfeit her happiness, but she gains, in the process, something larger and more enduring—access to the reality of myth, the feeling of being on equal terms with her gods (Pushkin, Blok, et al.), and, hence, a poetic stature all her own. Thus, she implores Pasternak at the conclusion of her letter of 14 February: "Manage, finally, to be the one who *needs* to hear this, that bottomless vat, containing nothing (*read carefully!!!*), so that [I burst] through you—as through God—in a TORRENT!" (6:236; emphasis in the original).

This is simultaneously a warning to Pasternak and a dare to herself—she is prepared to lose him entirely, but not to possess him partially as she possessed Blok. Pasternak must be a consenting muse, a willing conduit for her inspiration, if he is to be her lover at all. In renouncing his own desires, he must prove that his will and stature are equal to her own. He must be her mirror image: an empty vessel for her fullness, a female-like receptacle for her male-like passion, an immaterial landscape through which her unconsummated desire can tear a poetic rift with full force. This is, of course, immense egotism on Tsvetaeva's part—although not egotism in the usual sense of the word, because what she demands of her beloved is that he agree to the dissolution of his ego in order to unite with her in the dissolution of her own. This is an elemental, life-and-death dare in the language of poetry, which she trusts Pasternak of all people to understand.[27] Outsiders cannot judge; theirs is a coded language, and a system of values and logic outside the ordinary. She gambles here not just with her happiness, but with her genius and almost with her life.

In essence, Tsvetaeva executes this bid at poetic genius by entering into the Psyche myth in such a way as to orchestrate a reversal of the traditional paradigm of the passive, abandoned woman which, as Lawrence Lipking has shown in his book *Abandoned Women and Poetic Tradition,* is a trope that recurs throughout the history of poetry. Lipking notes the ambivalence of this figure: "Those who are banished are also let loose; utter surrender resembles utter freedom ... Women who live in 'abandon' are capable of sudden dangerous turns ... Victim or outlaw, powerless or powerful, [the abandoned woman] can change in an instant from the acted-upon to the actor." [28] Tsvetaeva plays subtly with this ambiguous boundary between active abandoning and passive abandonment in her poetry and in her life; at times it even seems that she encourages Pasternak's interest for the whole purpose of being able then to refuse him, in a terrifying act of creative liberation. For if Tsvetaeva can reverse woman's traditional passivity by actively renouncing the romantic bliss that is supposed to comprise the extent of feminine fulfillment, then she can also break out of her gendered destiny as the male poet's muse to become, herself, an independently creating entity. In the process of this transformation, she struggles to render Pasternak as the peripheral figure that she herself fears to become. She openly confesses to him her insecurities: "I have been a nanny to poets, the gratifier of their lowly needs—not at all a poet! nor a Muse!—but a young nanny (sometimes a tragic one, but even so)! With a poet I always would forget that I myself—am a poet."

A Divided Psyche

In stoically rejecting Pasternak, then, Tsvetaeva in effect realizes Neumann's reinterpretation of the turning point in the Psyche myth: when Psyche looks upon her sleeping husband and so forfeits him, this "loss" must be read not as Eros's punishment of his disobedient wife, but as Psyche's conscious and intentional act of self-liberation. Psyche/Tsvetaeva is the actor here, not the acted upon.

The shifting perspective between passive and active abandonment structures Tsvetaeva's lyric "No need to call her back" ["Ne nado ee oklikat'"] (2.161). Overlaying the mythical persona of Eurydice on that of Psyche, Tsvetaeva dissociates herself from her own desire for Pasternak, instead projecting her desire onto him and scolding him for summoning her away from her chosen isolationary path. Interestingly, this is a poetic transformation of the situation that obtains in her letters to Pasternak, where the initiative for the decision whether or not the two poets should meet lies entirely with Tsvetaeva ("I wouldn't call you back [ia by ne okliknula]. But: for Russia—I call you back [oklikaiu]"):

> Не надо ее окликать:
> Ей оклик — что охлест. Ей зов
> Твой — раною по рукоять.
>
> [No need to call her back: your call to her is like a blow. Your summons is a wound up to the hilt.]

Earlier, Tsvetaeva compared Pasternak's handwriting to a "blow of the reins [okhlest vozhzhi]" (6:226); here, similarly, Pasternak's poetic summons strikes her like a blow—not only because it intrudes upon her carefully honed emotional and spiritual equilibrium, but also because it recalls the equally painful imagined call of Blok, which never materialized in reality but which left a deep scar. The word play in this poem's opening lines (oklik/okhlest [call/blow]) is a reminiscence of that long-ago wounding; for in the seventh poem of "Verses to Blok," where Tsvetaeva expresses her resignation to the unrealizability of her love for Blok, she writes: "And a *blow* [of the reins/whip] follows the [driver's] *call*, and again the sleighbells sing" [I *okriku* vsled—*okhlest*, / I vnov' bubentsy poiut] (my emphasis). The resumed singing of the bells in this line can be read as a statement of the poet's stoic commitment to her art, in spite of the wound of the muse's driving whip, which supersedes Blok's deceptive call and is the only answer to her own plea for companionship.[29]

Now, in the interests of self-protection (in order to avoid a repeat of her humiliating adoration of Blok), Tsvetaeva dissociates herself from her own desire and projects that desire onto Pasternak. She therefore absents herself from her body and speaks as if from an enormous distance with the pure voice of her soul—which is imaged as a mountain peak or a castle parapet. Yet this careful separation of body and soul is in danger of being disturbed by Pasternak's call:

> Сталь и базальт —
> Гора, но лавиной в лазурь
> На твой серафический альт
> Вспоет — полногласием бурь.

[The mountain is made of steel and basalt, but it will sing like an avalanche into the azure, with the full voice of storms.]

These threatening avalanches and storms are Pasternak's own, emanations of elemental power characteristic of the imagery in his poetry. Indeed, Tsvetaeva's poem, for all its overt declaration of independence, is steeped in Pasternakian imagery and so is itself an illustration of the explosive potential of the two poets' creative meeting. She senses the danger that Pasternak poses to her, but she also knows him to be her fated poetic equal, a seraph like herself. Her complex attitude is summed up by one of the key phrases of "No need to call her back": "the creative fear of invasion" [tvorcheskii strakh vtorzheniia] — or, in the parlance of current literary theory, "the creative anxiety of influence." Pasternak is for Tsvetaeva, from the start of their epistolary relationship, her ideal lover, reader, and mate. Her terror of their union is a terror of contact with the elemental, for such contact — like mortal Psyche's gaze upon divine Eros — is at once ecstatically electrifying, and deadly.

In a letter of 14 February, Tsvetaeva uses a characteristic play on words to express this exhilarating danger: "In my life you are *exhausting,* my head grows weary, how many times in a day I lie down, collapse on the bed, *overpowered* by this whole polyglossia [raznogolositsa] of skull and ribcage: made up of your lines, feelings, revelations — yes, and simply your noises . . . Can it really all come from a *human?!* . . . It's hard to play with an angel (demons!) [S angelom (aggelami!) igrat′ trudno]" (6:235–36).[30] The ecclesiastical term *aggel* refers to an evil spirit or demon and thus has precisely the opposite meaning from its acoustic near-twin *angel;* for Tsvetaeva, Pasternak is both. Her substitution of poetic "play" for Jacob's biblical wrestling with an angel likewise attempts to mask the danger that Pasternak represents to her and so speaks to the subversive daring of her enterprise.

Tsvetaeva at once fears the intrusion of Pasternak's poetic voice and desires the transformation which that voice promises to induce in herself. The image of the pipe organ that provides a refrain for "No need to call her back" brilliantly encapsulates this contradictory logic of her poetics of renunciation. For the organ, like her poetry, is a colossus, a fortress that protects her from the outside world, a mountain that raises her to the heights, a complex apparatus of myths and meanings heaped up stone by stone, poem by poem over the course of years. At the same time, her poetry, like the organ, is set in motion by the infusion of foreign breath — here, Pasternak's inspiring poetry. Only with

A Divided Psyche

this threat to the carefully honed integrity of Tsvetaeva's own poetics do the organ's hundreds of separate pipes begin to resonate with the finest nuances of sound:

> И сбудется! — Бойся! — Из ста
> На сотый срываются... Чу!
> На оклик гортанный певца
> Органною бурею мщу!
>
> [And this will come to pass! — Live in terror! — From a hundredfold (pipes/tries), on the hundredth they break loose... Hark! In response to the singer's guttural call, I avenge with/ like an organ's storm!]

The infusion of breath that starts the air moving through this organ's pipes is the invading voice of Pasternak that Tsvetaeva simultaneously so loves and so fears; the organ's storm with which she avenges his invasion is, at the same time, his own storm from his own poems.

The collusion of their two poetic voices is at once immensely powerful, and unbearably painful. The bodily subtext in the poem—"org*á*n" [musical organ] is uncomfortably close to "*ó*rgan" [anatomical organ], a similarity to which the noun *depths/bowels* [nizy] and the adjective *guttural* [gortannyi] draw attention—explains why this pain is so overwhelming. Figurative "inspiration" has become literalized in the form of torrents of foreign air moving agonizingly through the poet's body. Tsvetaeva has only half-heartedly obscured this bodily subtext; it is as if she renounces her sexual desire in order to experience the very torment that provides the substance of her poem. She renounces desire, in other words, in order to write passionately about the torment of this renunciation.[31]

Thus we see that the poem "No need to call her back," with its infiltration by Pasternakian imagery, itself reveals the explosive potential of the two poets' creative meeting. How much more destructive, then, an actual meeting would be! Ariadna Efron's well-tutored assessment of Pasternak's unique role in Tsvetaeva's poetic development, interestingly, emphasizes the same two principles that we see in operation in Tsvetaeva's poem: namely, her anxiety about and insistence on her own poetic autonomy, and her utilization of Pasternak as the pretext for her inspirational torment:

The influence of Tsvetaeva's correspondence with Pasternak on her writing was as significant as it was unique, for this influence was expressed, not to the extent that one personality was appropriated or swallowed by the other, nor in some degree or another of "assimilation"; no, it was evidenced in the newly resolute focus of Marina's creative self-sacrifice [tvorcheskaia samootdacha]—self-sacrifice which had now found a concrete addressee.[32]

Tsvetaeva's sense that her meeting with Pasternak would ruin them both, while their nonmeeting may transform her into a great poet, speaks of her stoic commitment to the isolation of her unique poetic path—even in the face of the temptation of true togetherness which, she recognizes, is tantamount to creative assimilation and thus surrender of her creative self: "My Pasternak, maybe some day I will truly become a great poet—thanks to you! For I have to tell you the infinite: turn away! In conversation this is done by silence. But I have at my disposal only the pen!" (6:239). Every lyric poet needs a tragic muse; the distance Tsvetaeva establishes between herself and Pasternak is all the more necessary because of the strength of her love for him and the danger that her gender poses, for—in a union with him—she would become, by default, just a physical object: she would lose her voice. They are both able to retain their separate and equal voices only in the genderless ether of epistolarity.[33]

Language assists Tsvetaeva in transforming reality and dissociating her voice from her physical self; she interprets accidents of sound as the will of Providence, and she complies with its summons with all the stubborn, austere humility of ultimate faith. However her treatment of Pasternak may look in the light of everyday, human logic, her fidelity to poetry is complete and beyond reproach. Like Psyche, she recognizes that she can only experience true love in its loss. Her dissociation from her bodily self is at the same time an achievement of a higher, spiritual self that is the instrument of her poetry; Pasternak/Eros as her muse is, as she desperately insists (and seeks to ensure), only the occasion for her own hermetic "stormy polyglossia," rather than an alien infiltration of her voice. With Blok, she yearned—unrealistically—for more; with Pasternak she could realistically have more but forestalls this possibility. With Pasternak, Tsvetaeva insulates herself from true loss—by preempting it.[34] This is not a matter of avoidance of pain; on the contrary, in protecting herself from the loss of what is most dear and most necessary to her—poetic inspiration—she is forced to sacrifice her own personal happiness. The will toward isolation becomes equated with the will toward poetry. Her desire for Pasternak is deep; but her desire for poetry is deeper.

In the poem "The Soul" ["Dusha"] (2:163–64), Tsvetaeva celebrates the flight of her soul away from her body, inspired by Pasternak's tantalizing, untouchable love. We recall that the Russian *dusha* is the equivalent of the Greek *Psyche;* here, Tsvetaeva's soul is imaged as a Psychean butterfly—an exuberant upward rush of two stormy, blazing, foamy wings.[35] Triumphant in her mastery of the delicate aerodynamics of inspiration and secure in the intimacy of her spiritual union with Pasternak, Tsvetaeva revisits several themes of her earliest poems that dealt with her struggle to create a poetic voice and identity in spite of her female gender, as if trying to gauge how far she has progressed since the start of her poetic journey. These early themes are compressed into the poem's final two stanzas:

A Divided Psyche

> Так, над вашей игрой — крупною,
> (Между трупами — и — куклами!)
> Не́ общупана, не́ куплена,
> Полыхая и пля — ша —
>
> Шестикрылая, ра — душная,
> Между мнимыми — ниц! — сущая,
> Не задушена вашими тушами
> Ду — ша!
>
> [Thus, above your high-stakes game (among corpses — and — dolls!), *not* groped, *not* bought, blazing and danc — ing — six-winged, generous, among shams — bow down! — real, unsuffocated by your carcasses — my soul!]

We see again the familiar symbolism of the doll in Tsvetaeva's poetics, representing ordinary female, maternal destiny from which the poet's soul is liberated. Here she links dolls, by means of a slant rhyme and a pair of long dashes, with corpses; both dolls and corpses, taken together, summarize the limitations of female, bodily existence. The corpses draw attention to the ephemerality of physical passions and physical pains, whereas the dolls signify the inauthenticity and secondariness for the poet — in the light of a spiritual higher reality — of maternal caretaking and, indeed, of all human sharing and caring. These two different species of lifeless bodies serve as a grotesque taxonomy of bodily being in the poet's apprehension. In the context of the line that follows, with its crude, derogatory reference to the soul's freedom from sexual and marital bonds (*"Not* groped, *not* bought"), the corpses also represent the pure objectivity of a female body deprived of a self or soul. The dolls' connotation of automatism thus characterizes the female poet's experience not only of motherhood but of sexual love as well.

In the poem's final stanza, Tsvetaeva returns implicitly to the theme of "A Savage Will" — namely, her battle against the whole world; the vague possessive pronouns *vashei/vashimi* [your] refer obliquely to the rest of humanity against whom she wages her ongoing poetic campaign. Here, with the liberation of her soul made possible by its union with her muse (in the form of Pasternak's spirit) — a maneuver of which the rest of humanity (read: the rest of womanhood) is incapable — the battle ends in victory; the supercilious "bow down!" [nits!] indicates her gloating pride at this outcome. Like the disobedient Nereid in this poem who neglects to beg permission from punishing, paternal authority before sailing forever out of his aquatic element and up into the azure,[36] Tsvetaeva celebrates her spiritual freedom from the chains of demeaning female destiny, while enacting that freedom in a virtuosic orchestration of sounds and sense. The crux of this poetic symphony is the poem's title, final word, central concern, and highest pitch: *soul* [dusha]. Out of this word (or, more accurately, into this word) grows a dizzying whirl: "danc—ing" [plia—sha] / "generous" [ra—dushnaia] / "real" [sushchaia] / "unsuffocated" [ne zadushena] / "carcasses" [tushami] / "soul" [du—sha]. This brilliant sound sequence is Tsvetaeva's tour de force—a thorough definition of that most indefinable thing of which she writes, her triumph thanks to Pasternak and her sanctuary from him: her soul.

The elements of the definition are as follows. "Plia—sha": the soul is a dancer, constantly in motion, playful and beholden to no restraining laws. "Ra—dushnaia": the soul is gladly welcoming yet uncontainable; happy to give and to take, but unwilling to be bound. "Sushchaia": the soul is the expression of a higher essence than apparent reality—which, in a reversal of the platitudes of mundane perception, is proclaimed to be merely imaginary. "Ne zadushena": the soul is everything that is not stifled by mundane reality and the demands of the body.

The soul's diametric opposite—a shocking intensification of the already shocking "corpses" [trupy] of the previous stanza—is a rotten carcass: "tusha." (The phonetic proximity of *tusha* to the French *touche* [touch], a foreignism which exists in Russian as well as in English, strengthens Tsvetaeva's association of a lover's caresses with death and ruin; the English pun caress/carcass achieves a similar effect.) Carcass [túsha] and soul [dushá] are the two aspects of the poet's divided being. The two nouns are distinguished only by the voicedness of their opening consonants—the *d* of *dusha*, appropriately, is voiced, whereas the *t* of *tusha* is voiceless—and by a difference in stress—the levitating end stress of *dushá* illustrates the soul's upward striving, whereas the anchoring initial stress of *túsha* emphasizes the body's gravitation toward the depths. "Tusha" [carcass] and "dusha" [soul] are diametrical opposites; and yet, their near phonetic identity reveals how intricately they are bound together, how insidiously they resist separation, how seductively they cling. Other phonetic echoes of the two that do not actually appear in the poem further complicate the relations of body and soul: "tush′" is the ink in which the soul writes its liberating lines, whereas "tushit′" is to extinguish (the flame of inspiration?). The body [tusha] is at once both the medium in which poetry is written (poetry's "fuel" or ink [tush′]) and poetry's sworn enemy [tushitel′]. All the more remarkable, then, is the soul's feat of leaping across the poem's final line break. With this triumphant enjambement, the Psychean soul is freed from her sexual fetters, established in the full independence of her own separate line and the full isolation of the white abyss that remains after the poem ends.

Psyche Hesitates, Then Soars: "Phaedra" vs. "Wires"

On the surface, the two-poem cycle "Phaedra" ["Fedra"] (2:172–74)—composed in early March 1923 as Pasternak's departure for Russia loomed ever closer—is an agonizingly pure, embarrassingly explicit cry of sexual frustra-

A Divided Psyche 109

tion, a veritable hymn to illicit feminine desire. As such, the cycle reveals a phase of apparent weakness in Tsvetaeva's austere resolve against a meeting with Pasternak. For it is clear that Phaedra's incestuous passion for her stepson Hippolytus must be read as a palimpsest for Tsvetaeva's forbidden sexual passion for her "brother" poet Pasternak.[37] So, if Pasternak is indeed the shadowy presence behind Tsvetaeva's Hippolytus, then why in "Phaedra" does she apparently champion illicit female sexual passion? Why the desperate embrace of pure physicality? What of the poet's ascetic commitment to Psychean solitude? The answers to these questions lie, I believe, in a recognition that Tsvetaeva is a poet who thinks by means of extremes and diametric opposites. Counter to the principles of Aristotelian logic, she often strives to extract some deep common truth from a profound exploration of seemingly antithetical phenomena or psychological attitudes.

"Phaedra" serves as just such a testing ground for Tsvetaeva's nascent convictions. Almost set in her growing resolve not to visit Pasternak, whose departure from Berlin is looming ever closer, Tsvetaeva launches recklessly into a new poetic experiment—a scathing denunciation of all her previous arguments to her potential lover. Indeed, her Phaedra scoffs at the very ideal that Tsvetaeva herself has been pursuing: a Psychean self-willed separation of body from soul (a renunciation of all claims of the former, in favor of the latter). Phaedra argues that she can assuage her soul's cravings only through sexual contact—and, lest this pointed corrective to Tsvetaeva's earlier stance go astray, she underlines the clash of ideas by her ironic mention of Psyche twice in this unlikely context:

> Утоли мою душу! (Нельзя, не коснувшись уст
> Утолить нашу душу!) Нельзя, припадя к устам,
>
> Не припасть и к Психее, порхающей гостье уст...
> Утоли мою душу: итак, утоли уста.
>
> [Succor my soul! (It's impossible to succor our souls without having touched the lips!) It's impossible, falling upon the lips, not to fall also upon Psyche, the fluttering guest of lips... Succor my soul: which means, succor my lips.]

And later:

> О прости меня, девственник! отрок! наездник! Нег
> Ненавистник!—Не похоть! Не женского лона—блажь!
> То она—обольстительница! То Психеи лесть—
> Ипполитовы лепеты слушать у самых уст.
>
> [Oh forgive me, male virgin! youth! horseman! hater of blisses!—This isn't lust! Not a caprice of the female bosom! Sometimes she's a seductress!

> Sometimes she flatters like Psyche—so as to listen to Hippolytus's babble at his very lips.]

This second passage, especially, reads almost like a wry self-parody—as if Tsvetaeva is catching herself out in her professions of spiritual love for Pasternak. Her repeated invocation of Psyche and soul, she intimates here, is nothing but a ruse to obscure her real project: to listen to Hippolytus's (Pasternak's) babble (poetry) at his very lips. In other words, her Psychean motives are not as pure as they seem, for Psyche and Phaedra are uncomfortably close—Phaedra craves contact with her lover's soul, while Psyche craves contact with his lips.

The sexually hungry Phaedra ("insatiable Phaedra" [nenasytnaia Fedra]) and the spiritually hungry Psyche are thus revealed to be not antithetical to one another, but merely two complementary aspects of the paradoxical feminine essence. In fact, Phaedra's voraciousness is reminiscent of Tsvetaeva's damning description of herself in another poem: "With my own insatiability I overfeed everyone!" [Nenasytnost′iu svoeiu / Perekarmlivaiu vsekh!] (1:567).[38] Tsvetaeva seems to have vacillated between the belief that the body is merely a "wall" hiding the soul and the contradictory belief that sexual intimacy is the necessary vehicle to spiritual closeness—and, at various times with various potential lovers, she seems to have acted upon each of these beliefs.[39] In her poetry, though, one way or another, the soul always wins out ultimately over the body. Just as Tsvetaeva did battle with her horseman/muse in "On a Red Steed," transforming sexuality—through violent sexual metaphor—into a rigorously asexual confrontation of souls, so here, too, Phaedra proclaims to her horseman/lover [naezdnik] her own campaign to plunge into the abyss of his spirit from the acme of her sexual passion: "I am a horsewoman *also!* And so, from the height of breasts, from the fateful double hillside into the abyss of your breast!" [Ia naezdnitsa *tozhe!* Itak, s vysoty grudei, / S rokovogo dvukholmiia v propast′ tvoei grudi!]. The difference in meaning between the plural *breasts* and the singular *breast* sums up the whole arbitrary but inexorable injustice of gender: one and the same word, when applied to a woman, means "body," and when applied to a man, means "soul."

This inconsistency is the ultimate reason why Phaedra's admission of a connection between sexuality and spirituality is shocking and distasteful to Tsvetaeva, who is determined to salvage the special spiritual intimacy she feels for Pasternak. A sexual relationship would necessarily align her, the female, with the category of the bodily—and she would forfeit the undifferentiated spiritual equality with Pasternak she now possesses, thanks to the physical distance between them. Thus, despite the fact that the "Phaedra" poems' embrace of sexuality apparently contradicts the chaste wisdom of her Psychean commitment to enlightened loneliness, Tsvetaeva's admission of the irrepressible force of her own sexual desire for Pasternak paradoxically has the opposite effect of what

A Divided Psyche

might be expected. Whereas earlier she toyed with the thought of traveling to Berlin for a "farewell meeting," now, after the composition of "Phaedra," her resolve to maintain at all costs the distance between herself and Pasternak is noticeably deepened. She will withstand her own longing, and in this deed of endurance will make herself (and him) anew.

And so, without further ado, over the course of several days, she writes to Pasternak one last time before his impending departure; the letter's very first, bluntly forthright words are: "I will not come . . ." (6:237). She then launches into a whole medley of logistical reasons why the trip to Berlin is impractical and impossible (ostensibly so as not to hurt Pasternak's feelings; despite her unwavering conviction of their otherworldly bond, Tsvetaeva rightly senses that in this world, he is often confused by her contradictory signals). She fobs him off with talk of visas and family responsibilities. She assures him disingenuously—and rather transparently—of her own desire to come, which has been thwarted by circumstances alone: "My dear Pasternak, I have nothing but my *yearning* for you, it will not help" (6:237). She tries to preempt all his possible assumptions about her true reasons, thus in effect admitting she is deceiving him: "Not out of coyness (you'll remember better if I don't come. *Not* better— that's a lie!), not out of calculation (I'll remember too painfully if I see you! whether or not I do it's *too much*—and more is impossible!) and not out of cowardice (to disappoint, be disappointed)" (6:238). Yet, in reiterating once more all the practical reasons why she cannot come, she slips—as if by accident— into an admission of the truth: "I will not come because it's too late, because I am helpless, because Marc Slonim for example can get a visa in an hour, because this is my fate—loss" (6:238). From now on, she is brutally honest; using the exaggerated idiom of Romantic tragedy, she illustrates in the remainder of her letter an ornate portrait of Psyche recalcitrant: "These are not unmeasured [chrezmernye] words, these are immeasurable [bezmernye] feelings: *feelings* which eliminate the very idea of measure!" (6:239).

Tsvetaeva's anticipation of Pasternak's departure is like a premonition of death: "Please excuse me for such an eruption of the truth; I write as if just before death" (6:238). She no longer mentions Russia by name, but writes of her native country, which will soon swallow her beloved into its treacherous depths, as a mythical and otherworldly "there" [tam] that invokes in her an emotion of pure terror: "How can I live with this? The problem is not that you—are there, while I—am here, the problem is that you will be *there,* that I never will know whether you exist or not. Longing [toska] and fear for you, wild fear" (6:238). At the same time, Tsvetaeva continues to reason by a peculiar logic that a meeting with Pasternak would deprive her of his constant presence in her thoughts: "A meeting with you would be for me to some extent a valid liberation from you.—Do you understand? An exhalation [vydokhom]! I would exhale you even as I breathed you in [ia by (ot Vas zhe!) vydyshalas' v Vas]"

(6:238). The alliteration in this passage and the play on the prefix *vy-* is strongly reminiscent of Tsvetaeva's particularly untranslatable 1922 poem "The Emigrant" (2:163),[40] in which Pasternak himself is the refugee from the "tatters of moneys and visas" [rvani valiut i viz] that now confound her and serve as the pretext for her insistence on a nonmeeting: "Superfluous one! Your Highness! Expatriate! A challenge! He has not grown unaccustomed to rising up..." [Lishnii! Vyshnii! Vykhodets! Vyzov! Vvys'/ Ne otvykshii...]. For Pasternak, as Tsvetaeva describes his situation in "The Emigrant," the prefix *vy-* (meaning "ex-," outward movement) signifies an exit from the limits of reality into the infinity of poetry. In her letter to Pasternak, on the other hand, the liberation that *vy-* promises is an antiliberation—a jolting, inexorable return to the reality of Pasternak as a man, no longer just a disembodied poet. Like the gender difference between *breast* and *breasts*, this different meaning of the prefix in differently gendered contexts demonstrates Tsvetaeva's faith in the wisdom of her restraint. At a distance, she and Pasternak can remain poetic siblings; a meeting would mean (at best) that he would gain a lover, while she would lose a muse. (At worst, their meeting would be a nonmeeting in the most negative sense: a fiasco of mutual nonrecognition, noncomprehension: "If we met, you would not recognize me ... In life I am *immeasurably* wild, I'd slip out of your hands" [6:240]).

A meeting in the body is a painful deception of the spirit; a nonmeeting in the spirit is a painful truth. Tsvetaeva has experienced both pains before and has usually gravitated toward the former.[41] Now, for the first time, motivated by the Psyche myth, she opts for the latter, greater pain.[42] She chooses the Platonic ideal of her perfect lover/reader over the real man: "Pasternak, I will think of you only good things, real things, big things.—As if one hundred years from now!—I won't allow a single accidental detail, not a single act of willfulness" (6:240). She chooses the torment of her all-too-human heart for the sake of austere spiritual exultation, and in so doing, she rends her being in two: "I am a live person and this is very painful to me. Somewhere in the heights of myself there is ice (*renunciation!*), in the depths, in the pith [v serdtsevine]—pain" (6:239). This image of Tsvetaeva's divided self as a tree originates in an unfinished poem of 1921 in which she describes the humanly painful inhumanity of her poetic striving by means of an arboreal metaphor: "I know: not a heart is within me—but a tree's pith, along the trunk's entire length" [Ia znaiu: ne serdtse vo mne,—serdtsevina / Na vsem protiazhen'e stvola] (2:17–18). The upward vector of the tree's "pith" is the contour of Tsvetaeva's poetic soul; at the same time, the enormous length of this substitute "heart" allows for the multiplication of heartaches' intensity. She is simultaneously both inhuman and far too human. The irreparable split within her self is a direct result of the vector of her poetic commitment: "From the dark womb, where ores are hidden, upward—is my cryptoclairvoyant path. From the earth's bowels—and up to the sky: hence my double essence" [Iz temnogo chreva, gde skrytye rudy, / Vvys'—moi tainovidcheskii put'. / Iz nedr zemnykh—i do neba: otsiuda / Moia dvuedinaia sut'].

Having made certain that Pasternak fully appreciates the chasm in her psyche and thus accepts her legislation against a barren meeting in favor of the spiritual fecundity of a nonmeeting, Tsvetaeva ends her final letter to him before his departure with a sign of their otherworldly union:

> Yesterday evening (I had not yet opened your letter, I held it in my hand), my daughter's yell: "Marina, Marina, come!" (I thought to myself: the sky or a dog?) I go out. She points with an outstretched hand. Half the sky, Pasternak, is a wing, a wing stretches across half the sky, something previously unseen [nevidannoe]! There are no words for such a color! Light become color [svet, stavshii tsvetom]! And it races onward, having wrapped across half the sky. And I, staring: "The wing of your departure!" (6:241)

This "wing" of colored clouds, the wing of Pasternak's departure, is simultaneously proof that he is Tsvetaeva's true muse—her other half, her other wing that was torn from her at birth. This sweeping arc of color that she shares with Pasternak through the intimacy of the written word recalls the otherworldly "arc of meeting" from her earlier letter. The two poets are joined by this flaming arc of insubstantial color precisely by the fact of their separate, mutual striving toward its summit—the beyond: the ultimate source of their poems, the goal of their poetic *becoming,* the promise of their posthumous meeting. In this way, the sunset serves as a symbol of the two poets' union in distance. For, their separate contemplation of a mediating transcendent essence (celestial light/color as a stand-in for poetry) gestures toward their ultimate union with one another.[43]

As Pasternak's return to Russia first looms and then becomes established fact, the wrenching psychological process that Tsvetaeva has undergone during the preceding months as she has wavered between her conflicting human and poetic desires culminates dramatically in her composition of the ten-poem cycle "Wires" ["Provoda"] (2:174–82).[44] In order to understand "Wires" fully, we must read it in the context of Tsvetaeva's letters and other poems to Pasternak—for this cycle cannot be interpreted simply as the lamentation of a woman deserted by her lover. On the contrary, Tsvetaeva's pangs in "Wires" are the pangs of loneliness freely chosen—with all the sexual torment that choice entails—in the hopes of glimpsing through poetic creation a new possibility of union with another human soul that transcends sexual difference. This work is Tsvetaeva's Psychean masterpiece, an ecstasy of transformative self-denial—and, therefore, the replacement for "On a Red Steed" in her ongoing struggle to forge a personal epic that captures the inherent logic of her creative genius.

If Tsvetaeva's earlier writings to Pasternak resonate with Psyche's break with Eros, Psyche's trials, and Psyche's descent into Hades, then "Wires" projects the final destination of Psyche's tortuous path through the lonely evolution of consciousness: her attainment of immortality and of a new, ineffable union with her lost husband. Whereas in "Phaedra" Tsvetaeva performs the final test of her conviction that she must maintain her Psychean separation from her beloved, here we see the consequences of that choice: a reenactment of her poetic genesis, in her metamorphosis from abandoned woman into abandoning woman poet and, thence, into an omnipotent, genderless abstraction. Indeed, free choice is as central to the interpretation of "Wires" as it is to that of "On a Red Steed." The torment of Tsvetaeva's unfulfilled but active sexual desire, rather than the passive feminine grief we might expect, lends the poems of "Wires" their power and their pathos. In "Wires," she opts for complete self-reliance over external sources of inspiration; as a consequence, she experiences both the freedom and the agony of the resulting fragmentation of her own selfhood.[45]

The very title of "Wires" sets out immediately the core of the cycle's relentless logic. For, like the arching sunset that augurs Tsvetaeva's ultimate bond to Pasternak precisely at the moment of his departure from her universe (the cosmos of her exile), the wires of "Wires"—via a paronomastic play on words—are a perfect image of the two poets' togetherness ("provodá" [wires/links]) in separation ("próvody" [leave-taking]). The image of the wires, in turn, develops as the cycle progresses. In its first poems, the wires are the physical wires that connect telegraph pole to telegraph pole and so weave Tsvetaeva's Czechoslovakia together with Pasternak's Russia. In the third poem, however, she already recognizes the insufficiency of this modern technological miracle of communication and shifts her hopes to a miracle far more ancient: the telegraph wires become "lyrical wires," and the communications between herself and her beloved are liberated from the limitations of space and time and, indeed, from all laws of the physical world. After her further exploration of the metaphysical significance of this newfound freedom in the fourth poem, the wires disappear from the cycle altogether, for they have become redundant: Tsvetaeva has relinquished her body and has honed her entire being into the wires' prolonging, binding essence—as she says, "I twist and lengthen" [V′ius′ i dlius′]. The remaining six poems are a triumphant celebration of her new disembodiment and the poetic power it bestows.

The first poem of "Wires," I believe, should be related to Psyche's exit from Hades and her conscious decision to commit suicide in order to be reunited with her lover. Thus, indeed, Tsvetaeva's first message sent over the telegraph wires is not just a metaphor:

> Вереницею певчих свай,
> Подпирающих Эмпиреи,
> Посылаю тебе свой пай
> Праха дольнего.

[Along a line of singing pillars that support the Empyrean,
I send to you my ration of earthly dust.]

Here, from the very outset, Tsvetaeva leaves her body behind and sends Pasternak the dust that is its remnant as a sign of her yearning soul. Her predicament with respect to Pasternak, like Psyche's with respect to Eros, is the archetypical "catch-22" of the female self: she cannot live with her lover in this world, for she would have to sacrifice her autonomy and thus her consciousness; yet she cannot go on living without him—her sorrow, passion, and loneliness are so enormous that they destroy the integrity of her being and force her soul out of her body: "I implore... (It won't all fit on the telegraph blank!)" [Umoliaiu... (pechatnyi blank / Ne vmestit!)]. Tsvetaeva expresses this paradox repeatedly throughout the first poem.

For example, Tsvetaeva's description of her farewell yell to Pasternak as the "last retch of a broken throat" [poslednii sryv / Glotki sorvannoi] is a concatenation of overlapping, mutually irreconcilable meanings. On the most obvious level, this is the poet's own voice, breaking with grief at her lover's departure; breaking in the static of long distances in the journey over telegraph wires; and breaking, too, in the grammatical chasms gouged by enjambement ("sryv / Glotki") in the sentences of this poem. At the same time, though, this "broken voice" resonates with other of Tsvetaeva's poems, where it is a symbol of her painful transition from adolescence into adulthood: "Long, long ago—to outyell parting—I broke in my voice" [Davnym-davno—perekrichat' razluku— / Ia golos sorvala] (1:507). In poems such as this, the broken voice represents Tsvetaeva's entry into poetic maturity—precisely through the agony of separation from her beloved (as is the situation in "Wires" as well). Moreover, this image of the breaking voice is suggestive of her attainment of a certain "masculine" rigor of spirit, because women's voices, after all, do not break.

In contrast, the androgynous, breaking voice is also Tsvetaeva's way of characterizing Pasternak's incomparable poetic tonality in yet another poem: "Among cathedralesque Alps an unfledged alto struggles with the rosary. Girlish and boyish: on the very borderline. Unique of a thousand—and already broken" [Mezh kafedral'nykh Al'p / To b'etsia o rozarium / Neoperennyi al't. // Devichii i mal'chisheskii: / Na samom rubezhe. / Edinstvennyi iz tysiachi—/ I sorvannyi uzhe] (2:162). The height of poetic expressiveness—the threshold, or "borderline" [rubezh] to the other world—is here equated with the painful, asexual merging of sexual essences that characterizes Tsvetaeva's sisterly relationship to Pasternak. Hence, we see that the "broken voice" in the first poem of "Wires" is simultaneously Pasternak's voice and her own; the image thus recalls both Pasternak's threat to the integrity of Tsvetaeva's poetic voice, and, at the same time, the very genesis of her voice in the pangs of her separation from Pasternak and in the shattering of boundaries this separation entails.

Later in the first poem of "Wires," the phrase "Conjuring distance" [Dal' / Zaklinaiushchee], similarly broken by enjambement, is likewise ambiguous:

> Это — про́водами стальных
> Проводо́в — голоса Аида
>
> Удаляющиеся... Даль
> Заклинающее: жа — аль...
>
> [Those are the retreating voices of Hades — like the farewells of steel wires... Conjuring distance: too ba — ad...]

Psyche returning from Hades (like Tsvetaeva reeling from the self-inflicted blow of Pasternak's departure) is conjuring the distance separating her from her ideal lover simultaneously into and out of existence. In light of this Psychean sorcery, yet another ambiguity is apt: when Tsvetaeva cries out her farewell to Pasternak ("Pro — o — stite..."), she makes at the same time a plea for forgiveness, for this Russian word conveys both meanings at once.

All of these ambiguities foreshadow the brilliant puzzle of the poem's final line: the archetypal cry of all abandoned women, in whose deafening chorus Tsvetaeva/Psyche fears her own, different voice may be lost:

> (В сем хоре — сей
> Различаешь?) В предсмертном крике
> Упирающихся страстей —
> Дуновение Эвридики:
>
> Через насыпи — и — рвы
> Эвридикино: у — у — вы,
> Не у —
>
> [(In this chorus — do you distinguish this one [voice]?) In the predeath cry of stubborn passions — is Eurydice's sigh: across hills — and — ditches is Eurydice's: a — a — las, don't l —]

In this final, abortive wail, the wires' extension of sound (time) through space effects a paradoxical etymology of grief. The "alas!" [uvy!] of regret is discovered to conceal the kernels of a seemingly inconsistent desire for escape: "u-" and "vy-," both of which can be rendered approximately by the Latinate prefix *ex*-. The fragmentary line that follows ("Ne u — " [Don't l —]) is as rich in meaning as it is sparse in sound. It is a negation of the cry that preceded it ("*not* alas" [*ne* uvy]) which only increases that cry's ambiguity. It is, at the same time, a plea to the lover to remain ("Don't leave!" [Ne ukhodi!]), a variant of Ariadne's cry "return!" [vernis'!] earlier in the poem. But this latest return summons is choked off midway; Tsvetaeva bites her tongue. As a result, its speaker is removed from the ranks of stereotypical, passively abandoned women — hence her voice's difference from the rest of the chorus.

The reasons for the call's suspension are inconclusive. Tsvetaeva's Eurydice (a.k.a. Psyche) perhaps herself stifles the call, choosing to bear her grief in dignified silence, convinced of the painful necessity of her separation from her lover. A week later, Tsvetaeva would write in "Eurydice to Orpheus" ["Evridika—Orfeiu"]: "I've already paid—remember my yells!—for this last expanse. There is no need for Orpheus to go down to Eurydice or for brothers to trouble their sisters" [Uplocheno zhe—vspomiani moi kriki!—/ Za etot poslednii prostor. / Ne nado Orfeiu skhodit′ k Evridike / I brat′iam trevozhit′ sester] (2:183). By contrast, Eurydice's call may be uttered to completion but lost in the instantaneous explosion of distance (the noise of the separating/connecting telegraph wires) that results from her plea, since her lover's backward glance (like Psyche's forbidden gaze upon her husband) causes their irrevocable separation. In either case, this final utterance (or nonutterance) of the poem is a rejection of the abandoned woman's traditional passivity—an act of conscious feminine will. Tsvetaeva intimates here that the woman poet's will to love must be inseparable from her will to lose, for the enormity of her poetic genius arises precisely in the enormity of her endurance of this equation. This is the vow "yours and no one's" [tvoia i nich′ia] (from the conclusion of "On a Red Steed") with a new vengeance.

In fact, this centrally important, endlessly ambiguous last line of the first poem of "Wires" cannot even be termed a line at all, for it is a mere heap of signs ("Ne u—"): the fragmentation of poetic voice that Tsvetaeva craved and feared in "No need to call her back" has occurred. As it turns out, her fears were, in a sense at least, in vain; fragmentation results not in the loss of poetic meaning but rather in its multiplication to the nth power ("From a hundredfold [pipes/tries], on the hundredth they break loose"). The breaking voice, the abortive final cry, the jumble of revised and only half-remembered mythological references—which function as palimpsests for Tsvetaeva's own persona—all demonstrate the genesis of her new poetic self in the very idea of disintegration. Whereas in "On a Red Steed," poetry is a powerful and commanding force—the all that annihilates the nothing of mundane, mortal, human, and especially female existence (subsistence)—in "Wires" poetry is defined, on the contrary, in a negative and diminutive sense: a poem is a mere shard of the inexpressible. As Tsvetaeva writes to Pasternak: "Lyrical poems (as they are called) are separate instants of a *single* motion: a motion in fits and starts . . . Lyric poetry is a dotted line that seems whole and dark from afar, but look closely: it's full of omissions between the dots—an airless space—death. And you die from the end of one poem to the beginning of the next" (6:234). The very form of "Wires"—a lyrical cycle that narrates a single emotional contour in fits and starts—is evidence of Tsvetaeva's developing sense of poetry as fragment, in contrast to the round, folkloric wholeness of "On a Red Steed."

In the first poem of "Wires," it is only the telegraph blank that is too small to encompass the speaker's grief; later, it is poetry itself that is a mere fragment, an inkling:[46] "If only I could express to you... but no, not pressed into lines and narrow rhymes... The heart is wider!" [Chtob vyskazat′ tebe... da net, v riady / I v rifmy sdavlennye... Serdtse—shire!]. Tsvetaeva's love of whimsical metaphysical hierarchies in the medieval style is at work here;[47] she does not mean to diminish poetry by this insistence on its fragmentariness, but rather to elevate poetry by evoking the comparative infinity of its source. The enormity of poetry is defined by the exponentially greater enormity of all that poetry strives—and fails—to attain.[48] Tsvetaeva's isolation—the singularity of her fate—measures the vast scope of her poetic gift. Poetic lines and rhymes painfully compress her heart and, in so doing, perpetuate its agony and thus ensure the continuity of her poetic impulse. This is a newly self-reliant, almost hermetic (or, rather, masturbatory) conception of poetic inspiration; Pasternak is a mere stimulus or occasion for Tsvetaeva's own auto-inducement of her inspirational delirium, rather than her poetry's immediate, active cause.

Variations on the themes of fragmentation, inexpressibility, and isolation give shape to all the remaining poems of "Wires" and constitute the basis for the new myth of poetic genius constructed in the cycle, since the inexpressibility of Tsvetaeva's grief is a sign of the heights of consciousness she attains. Thus, in the second poem of "Wires," the truth of her suffering is both greater than the greatest literature ("too little for such misfortune are *all* of Racine and *all* of Shakespeare!" [malo dlia takoi bedy / *Vsego* Rasina i *vsego* Shekspira!]) and infinitesimally, uniquely less ("But Phaedra had *one* Hippolytus! Ariadne's lament was for *one* Theseus!" [No byl *odin*—u Fedry—Ippolit! / Plach Ariadny—ob *odnom* Tezee!] [my emphasis]).[49] In another poem of the cycle, Tsvetaeva's recognition of the overwhelming self-referentiality of her passion is reflected in the image of herself as encompassing the circular infinity of her own loss: "Vanity! It is inside me! Everywhere! With closed eyes: it's bottomless! and endless!" [Tshcheta! vo mne ona! Vezde! zakryv / Glaza: bez dna ona! bez dnia!]. Bottomless and endless, Tsvetaeva's agony overcomes the physical dimensions of time and space, transforming her body into the incarnation of separation and death: "Since Naxos—is my own bone! Since my own blood beneath my skin—is Styx!" [Raz Naksosom mne—sobstvennaia kost′! / Raz sobstvennaia krov′ pod kozhei—Stiksom!].

The lover for whom Tsvetaeva longs is transformed, too. He is an invisible spirit, and she a blind bard—and in this doubly impossible bind is the painful perfection of their simultaneous union and disunion; they complement each other in such a way that they are destined never to meet in this world: "Oh, in what seas and cities should I seek you? (A blind woman—seeking an invisible man!)" [O po kakim moriam i gorodam / Tebia iskat′? (Nezrimogo—nezriachei!)]. Yet, after all, Tsvetaeva is the only one who can find him, because only she is clairvoyant; human sight does not help in the quest for the invisible. We recall the importance of the wandering blind man in Tsvetaeva's "Poems to Akhmatova"; here she has merged with him, through her longing for Pasternak, to become the poet that she earlier dreamed wistfully of becoming. Pasternak, as her muse, is—like her new conception both of poetry and of her own, capacious poetic self—defined by the immensity of all that he is not:

> Терзание! Ни берегов, ни вех!
> Да, ибо утверждаю, в счете сбившись,
> Что я в тебе утрачиваю всех
> Когда-либо и где-либо *небывших*!
>
> [Torment! Neither shores nor boundaries! Yes, for I assert, having lost count, that in you I am losing all who sometime and somewhere *never existed!*]

The pain of Tsvetaeva's loss is so vast precisely because of her unflinchingly clear knowledge that the intensity of her own passion is equaled by the irreality of her passion's object. The sexual torment of which she speaks here cannot, then, be expressed in any other way except through poetry.

Tsvetaeva highlights this cruel logic in the third poem of "Wires," in which she parses her ineffable grief by means of a simple triangle that sketches the necessary coexistence of love, pain, and poetry. This triangle, which is implicit in the Psyche myth, collapses if any of the three elements is absent. (The relationship among the three is clarified further in the poem "Words and Meanings" ["Slova i smysly"], written shortly after "Wires," where she offers the formula "prolong—distance—and pain" [dlit′—dal′—i bol′] [2:190].) Indeed, Tsvetaeva's inspirational process consists of prolonging the pain of hopeless love; the "lyrical wires" are a perfect image of this creative lengthening: "Know that as long as heaven arches above, as long as dawn moves toward the horizon—so distinctly and omnipresently and lengthily I bind you" [Znai, chto dokole svod nebesnyi, / Dokole zori k rubezhu—/ Stol′ iavstvenno i povsemestno / I dlitel′no tebia viazhu]. Tsvetaeva's lyrical wires transgress and transform even the laws of physics: all of time and space are compressed into a vertical line as she binds Pasternak to her "with the springtime of rain gutters and the wire of spatial dimensions" [vesnoiu stokov vodostochnykh / I provolokoiu prostranstv]. This image of the pointedly linear lyrical distance dividing the lovers is, at the same time, Tsvetaeva's poetic vector (Eros's arrow—in Psyche's subversive possession).

Tsvetaeva's lyrical "binding" of Pasternak implies her new understanding in "Wires" of what it means to possess a lover, an understanding which Ariadna Efron interprets thus:

> That fear of onlookers, of the evil eye ... was so characteristic of Marina with her striving and devotion to the *secret* of possessing a treasure: whether it was a book, a piece

of nature, a letter—or a human soul... For Marina was a great materialist in the world of immaterial values, in which she did not tolerate co-owners and spies [sovladel'tsev i sogliadataev].[50]

Whereas Blok was a foreign essence that, frustratingly, kept getting away from Tsvetaeva and refusing to be caught or expressed, Pasternak's/Eros's ineffable distance and secrecy are, perversely, the very proof of Tsvetaeva's mutual bond with him. The tie between them, like a blood vow, is formed by their shared endurance of the torment of their nonmeeting. Hence the poet's indifference to her bodily suffering—for it is erased as a reality in itself and exists for her only as a metaphor for the abstraction of her poetic desire. In later poems to Pasternak, Tsvetaeva would use the bizarre fantasies of a suicide pact with her lover and their shared cremation in order to further develop this principle.[51]

Tsvetaeva blasphemously equates diametric opposites, even as she shatters the integrity of what was previously whole. In forcibly separating sexual desire and its object, she takes apart body and soul and puts them back together again in a radically new, shocking configuration. This poetic chutzpah amounts to her taking over the powers and voice of the Almighty Himself, as she in fact does when she avows in the cycle's fifth poem "I am and will be" [Esm' ia i budu ia]—echoing God's perplexing, untranslatable answer to Moses' query from out of the burning bush[52] in Exodus 3:14.[53] Like God, Tsvetaeva's essence—her desire—transgresses time and space, giving her access to every niche of the universe where her lover could possibly hide: "Wherever you might be—I'll overtake you, suffer you out—and return you back" [Gde by ty ni byl—tebia nastignu, / Vystradaiu—i vernu nazad]. Her greatness is explicitly the result of her infinite suffering, which propels her ever onward and outward. This idea is emphasized by the prefix *vy-*, which begins the last lines of four of the poem's seven stanzas. In the first three instances, the action of this prefix is explicitly connected with the poet's ability to retrieve her lost lover, as in the lines cited earlier. This active returning (i.e., the use of the transitive verb *vernut'* rather than the reflexive *vernut'sia,* and of the indicative rather than the imperative mood) is evidence of the huge psychological progress Tsvetaeva/Psyche has made since Ariadne's archetypical cry of "return!" in the cycle's first poem.

In the last instance in which the prefix *vy-* appears in this poem, however, Tsvetaeva beats a sudden, bold retreat into self-reflexivity: "I will lure you out—and return alone" [Vymorochu—i vernus' odna]. The phoneme *s,* which in the previous instance gives her power even over death ("I will return you from the death bed" [vernu s odra]), here, in an ingenious shift of morphological boundaries, returns the poet to herself [vernus' odna]. Precisely at the moment when her beloved is most attainable, she will choose freely to relinquish him. This is a radical reversal of Orpheus's project with respect to his own beloved. Tsvetaeva's shocking shift toward sudden self-reliance illustrates precisely the

A Divided Psyche 121

contour of the arrow elsewhere in this poem: "An arrow, having described a circle…" [Strela, opisavshi krug…]. Tsvetaeva is the embodiment of this boomeranging arrow of her poetic vector.[54] Like Psyche, in venturing into poetry (the masculine realm of consciousness), she has turned Eros's arrow against herself. Yet this return to the reflexive verb is a triumph, rather than the defeat that it might seem. What at the opening of the cycle smacked of arbitrary Fate (for all that the persona in the first poem behaves actively rather than passively, her predicament still remains an insoluble one) has become a fully conscious choice, made in complete freedom. Eros, her muse, is essential to her, ultimately, only insofar that he exist somewhere; as Tsvetaeva ends her letter to Pasternak on the eve of his departure from Berlin: "My last words: stay alive, I don't need anything else" (6:241). If he exists, then she is a great poet; her new poetics, however, are self-referential and self-perpetuating. She is an island of consciousness in a sea of flesh.[55]

With Tsvetaeva's attainment of full consciousness of her poetic omnipotence, a new tranquility appears that sets the tone for the remainder of the cycle. Her faith in her spiritual companionship with her beloved is wafted from the beyond, as the gifts of the Magi are brought to the baby Jesus, precisely at the moment when night falls, obscuring the world of the merely visible. Furthermore, just as Tsvetaeva in her poems to Blok linked poetic transcendence with the twilit periods of dusk and dawn, here nightfall is also the moment when the poet's new, autogenerative poetic inspiration sets in:

> Умыслы сгрудились в круг.
> Судьбы сдвинулись: не выдать!
> (Час, когда не вижу рук)
>
> Души начинают видеть.
>
> [Intentions gathered into a circle. Fates shifted: so as not to reveal answers! (The hour when I don't see my own hands) souls begin to see.]

Intentions [*Umysly*] was the title Tsvetaeva originally proposed for her book *After Russia;* thus, the circularity of her intentions here relates not only to the isolation of her person and the insularity of her poetics, but also to the complex intratextuality of this verse collection as a whole. Even poems in *After Russia* that are supposedly addressed to lovers other than Pasternak (Abram Vishniak and Aleksandr Bakhrakh, primarily) reverberate with the same themes, images, sounds, and vocabulary as the Pasternak poems and are, on some level, addressed to him—for he is nothing and everything to Tsvetaeva, an archetype: the image of her muse who is, in truth, her unchanging beloved.

Thus, we see that her poems are her created, self-contained, chosen world; true clairvoyance occurs only when she transcends the limitations of physicality by means of an intentionally blind gaze. Again and again, fragmentation of both body and language is the price she pays for this transcendence:

> Точно руки — вслед — от плеч!
> Точно губы вслед — заклясть!
> Звуки растеряла речь,
> Пальцы растеряла пясть.
>
> [As if my hands — after him — strain from my shoulders! As if my lips after him — strain to swear a vow! The sounds of my speech are scattered, the fingers of my hand are scattered.]

This state of self-willed fragmentation, the brokenness of her voice, is the secret to Tsvetaeva's wrenching lyrical power. Her uncontainable desire to hold Pasternak back is banished to the parenthesis of her own private thoughts and remains unstated; her voice breaks grievously in this superhuman effort, overflows the boundary of the poetic line, and then floods away in an overpowering ellipsis:

> В час, когда мой милый гость...
> —Господи, взгляни на нас! —
> Были слезы больше глаз
> Человеческих и звезд
> Атлантических...
>
> [In the hour when my dear guest... — Oh God, look down upon us! — There were tears bigger than human eyes and Atlantic stars...]

In her search for the proper epithet for her lost beloved, Tsvetaeva has passed through "brother" and "friend" and has now lit upon the truth of his identity: he is the male guest [gost'] to her female guest [gost'ia]. In a letter to Pasternak three years later, this is how she would define her Psychean self in relation to the "housewife Eve": "To shoot oneself for the sake of Psyche! But she never existed at all (just a particular form of immortality). People shoot themselves for the sake of the mistress [khoziaika] of the house, not for a guest [gost'ia]" (6:264). Both Tsvetaeva and Pasternak are guests, pure souls — visitors on this earth from the other world.[56] Her sorrow at his absence, therefore, is otherworldly and so cannot be contained in the poetic line or the poetic stanza. This is why the enjambed final line, like the Atlantic Ocean itself, overflows its shores upward — into the heavens, reaching the stars. Tsvetaeva's choice of adjective is significant; "Atlantic" is not simply an evocation of passionate immensity, but it suggests at the same time both "Atlas" (Russian "Atlant"), the ancient Greek god who supports the world on his shoulders, and "Atlantis" (Russian "Atlantida"; "Atlant" also means a dweller of Atlantis), the mythical drowned continent.[57] With Pasternak's departure, Tsvetaeva's whole universe is ambiguously collapsing, drowning, expanding.

Although Tsvetaeva manages to escape the fragmentations and limitations of physical reality through her poetic communion with Pasternak, all the same she is subject to fragmentation of a different kind—for she exists for him not even as a memory, but as a collection of random likenesses, unrealized possibilities, unmet fates:

> С другими—в розовые груды
> Грудей... В гадательные дроби
> Недель...
>   А я тебе пребуду
> Сокровищницею подобий
>
> По случаю—в песках, на щебнях
> Подобранных,—в ветрах, на шпалах
> Подслушанных...
>
> [With others—into the pink mounds of breasts... Into the doubtful fractions of weeks... But I will remain for you a treasure hoard of likenesses—collected by chance amid sands and crushed bricks—overheard in the winds, on the rails...]

This powerful passage, beginning as it does the final poem of "Wires," strongly recalls Tsvetaeva's revelation in "Phaedra" that it is precisely the subsuming force of female sexuality—emblematized both there and here by the hill-like female breast, which appears almost gruesomely detached from its host human being—that threatens the woman poet's creative autonomy. In "Wires" Tsvetaeva succeeds, though at enormous human cost, at escaping this threat to create her own poetic masterpiece in her own, uniquely female, yet free, Psychean voice. Poetry and poetic inspiration are to be her and Pasternak's only offspring, their idealistic challenge to reality's depraved depths: "The certainest density of the depths I will overcome with fantasies!" [Nedr dostoverneishuiu gushchu / Ia mnimostiami peresiliu!]. Whereas in "The Soul," however, she haughtily claimed that her imagined self was more real than reality's semblance, here she soberly admits the pure conditionality of her poetic fantasies.

Hence, Tsvetaeva's love child with Pasternak is not a real creature of flesh and blood but poetry itself, which, provocatively, is expressed in a pointedly physiological, if not sexual, idiom: "Know that a miracle of the depths is beneath my skirt, a live child: song!" [Znai, chto chudo / Nedr—pod poloi, zhivoe chado: / Pesn'!]. In the coded language of her metaphysics, this child is termed *pervenets;* he is a tellingly masculine firstborn who indicates Tsvetaeva's allegiance to the predominantly male poetic tradition, which she enters victoriously and wearily, much as Psyche enters ultimately into the Olympian heights. Indeed, Tsvetaeva's poetic child recalls Psyche's own child, born to her only after her attainment of immortality through suicide. In Tsvetaeva's case, too, her paradoxical poetic project to undo physical realities through attaining the transcendent heights of metasexual fulfillment results in the chilling equivalency of death with poetic perfection. Thus, she speaks metaphorically of the triumph of her own death, a hope warranted by acoustic coincidences:

> Смена царства и въезд вельможе.
>
> И домой:
> В неземной —
> Да мой.
>
> [A change of kingdoms and the lord's entry. And homeward: into the unearthly realm — my own.]

Tsvetaeva's otherworldly "home" in this passage is pointedly contrasted with the mundane domestic realm, the usual province of women; while the noun *vel'mozha* [lord], which she uses in reference to herself, though grammatically feminine, yet is eminently masculine in meaning. Similarly, she compares herself to a male consort awaiting his queen, who is Pasternak's strange female double: "Fingers fisted — thus a consort awaits a Queen" [pal'tsy v zhgut — / Tak Monarkhini zhdet nalozhnik]. Such shifts in the anticipated gender categories suggest the desired erasure of gender altogether in the realm of death.[58] This erasure is key to the resolution of Tsvetaeva's Psychean dilemma with which "Wires" began: the impossibility for the female of simultaneously loving (or, rather, being loved) and knowing — the impossibility of being both a body and a self, an object and a subject, a woman and a poet.

Through this harsh logic, Pasternak, in "Wires," becomes a larger-than-life emblem of life's arbitrary cruelty and senselessness: the husband of the soul who cannot be the husband of the body. The torment of Tsvetaeva's infinite wait for a meeting with her beloved forces an ironic reversal in which life, Hades-like, is equated with senseless, mindless, manual labor and with mental and physical tortures, and the land of the living is none other than an "archive" and an "Elysium of cripples":

> . . . наняты сердца
>
> Служить — безвыездно — навек,
> И жить — пожизненно — без нег!
> О заживо — чуть встав! чем свет! —
> В архив, в Элизиум калек.

> [... hearts are hired out to serve—without exit—forever, and to live—a life sentence—without bliss! Oh buried alive—hardly having arisen! earlier than dawn!—into the archive, the Elysium of cripples.]

Accordingly, in a long enumeration of life's tortures, Tsvetaeva casts death as the object of desire (revenge—upon life!), even as she prolongs her imagination of unattainable orgasmic bliss for the pain it causes: "Patiently, as death is awaited . . . I will await you (fingers fisted) . . . I will await you (gaze to the ground, teeth sunk in lips. Frozen. Stone). Patiently, as bliss is lengthened, patiently, as beads are strung" [Terpelivo, kak smerti zhdut / . . . Budu zhdat' tebia (pal'tsy v zhgut) / . . . Budu zhdat' tebia (v zemliu—vzgliad, / Zuby v guby. Stolbniak. Bulyzhnik). / Terpelivo, kak negu dliat, / Terpelivo, kak biser nizhut]. This mantralike repetition of tortures illustrates Tsvetaeva's state of renunciatory paralysis, equivalent to a kind of inspirational trance, that is her typical response to profound love and profound loss. Poetry is the product of otherwise unexpressed sexual hunger; the liberating effect of the poetic process is therefore equivalent to self-cannibalism, as the poet figuratively gnaws her own flesh in an attempt to speed death's approach: "Patiently, as rhymes are awaited, patiently, as hands are gnawed" [Terpelivo, kak rifmy zhdut, / Terpelivo, kak ruki glozhut]. The perfection of a finished poem is like a foretaste of the perfection of death.[59]

The quiet ferocity of these passages testifies to the fact that Tsvetaeva's achievement of the heights of spiritual freedom through her otherworldly union with Pasternak does not preclude her appreciation of her actual situation in real life, but, on the contrary, emerges from her sober meditation on this very real predicament. Indeed, we catch glimpses of the real, human Tsvetaeva here and there throughout the poems of "Wires." In the final two lines of the cycle's second poem, for instance, the omnipotent voice of the self-contained and vastly powerful, passionate poet gives way to an entirely different tonality—the human voice of her discarded body, fragile, tiny, pathetic, and sad: "I entrust my leave-taking to the wires, and leaning against the telegraph pole—I weep" [Ia próvody vveriaiu provodám, / I v telegrafnyi stolb upershis'—plachu]. Here the woman without the poet, without the soul, is nothing—the very image of isolation. She has no human shoulder to cry on (this theme is repeated in the cycle's ninth poem: "Oh, sorrow of those who weep without a supporting shoulder!" [O, pechal' / Plachushchikh bez plecha!]), and her only support comes from a lifeless object—the telegraph pole, a dead tree.[60] This image of the woman embracing a dead tree trunk (phallic image, perhaps?) in place of her departed lover underlines the human cost that the woman poet pays for the necessary fissure of body and soul. "Ordinary female happiness" is sadly inaccessible to her, because she is split and dissociated from her familial, bodily self—there is always a higher goal in her consciousness, always something more important and more pressing (a poem that needs to be written), always a spiritual hunger that is forever unassuaged.

Ultimately, for all her brazen mythologizing, the real reason for Tsvetaeva's inability to unite with Pasternak is purely quotidian, a fluke of bad luck, bad timing, bad judgment: "the places are occupied . . . hearts are hired out" [zaniaty mesta . . . naniaty serdtsa]. She and he are both married, with their own families who must be "served" to the end; as she laments bitterly at the conclusion to the cycle's penultimate poem, they both are "slaves—slaves—slaves—slaves" [raby—raby—raby—raby]. Although she is often willing to overlook her marital vows, Pasternak is a unique case: the husband of her soul, whom she prefers to forfeit altogether rather than shove into some demeaningly secondary lover's "slot." No matter what poetic heights Tsvetaeva attains, she continues to be torn by the contradictory desires of the poet and the woman within her. The woman—although her voice is usually stifled—does not refuse her claim on the poet's intentions; when Tsvetaeva's son is born two years after "Wires" was written, it is all her husband can do to convince her not to name him Boris in Pasternak's honor. She relents, ultimately, only in light of her continued hopes of bearing Pasternak a real son some day: "Clearly and simply: if I were to name him Boris, I would forever bid farewell to the Future: you, Boris, and a son from you" (6:242). These obviously hopeless hopes are a remarkable admission of emotional vulnerability, bodily yearning, and maternal craving by the bodiless soul who is the supposedly omnipotent, genderless author of "Wires."

Tsvetaeva's poetic commitment to the light is a consciously self-delusional cry against the darkness which she knows all too well. Her faith in the soul is not a naïve presumption, but is born of an all-too-intimate acquaintance with the unassuageable cravings of the body and the grind of daily life. Her poetic outlawing of physicality is a considered response to the physical and psychological toll exacted by her lifelong commitment to satisfying the unrelentingly daily physical needs of herself, her family, and often her friends as well. As she writes to Pasternak in the concluding poem of *After Russia:* "Give me your hand—for that whole other world! Here—mine are both busy" [Dai mne ruku—na ves' tot svet! / Zdes'—moi obe zaniaty] (2:259). Whether or not Tsvetaeva is, ultimately, a good wife or mother is not after all the issue; in fact, she may quite plausibly have believed herself a failure in the domestic realm—thereby giving rise to others' condemnations as well. The point is that, until her death, she never broke her basic commitment to those among the living who depended on her—whatever she wrote in her poetry. Her poems are a refuge, a fiction—and it is foolish and insensitive to read them as hard fact.[61] Sadly, even Pasternak himself seems to have failed to understand this nuance, for Tsvetaeva writes to

A Divided Psyche

him reproachfully, in the last surviving letter of their correspondence (October 1935):

When I die I won't have time to think about my soul, I'll be too busy: are my future pallbearers fed, did my dear ones go broke paying for my medical consultations, and maybe in the *best* egotistical case: have my manuscripts been carted off.

I have been myself (a *soul*) in my notebooks and on solitary roads—rare, since all through life I have led a child by the hand. I have not had the luxury of "softness" in relationships, only of relationships: service: *useless* self-sacrifice. A *mother pelican* enthralled to the system she herself has created for nourishing—*evil*.—Well, there you have it. (6:277)

By the end of "Wires," it becomes clear that the Psychean fantasy that gives rise to the cycle, according to which Tsvetaeva abandons bodily desire in favor of spirit, is just that—a pure poetic fantasy.[62]

The reality is that she remains a servant to the most essential human needs of those close to her. She forgoes Persephone's alluring feast not for flight, but for plain bread. Compelled, like Psyche, by her love for her husband/muse Pasternak to separate from him in order to experience the boundless potentiality and elevating consciousness of superhuman pain, Tsvetaeva attains poetic genius precisely through her willing enactment of life's inherent impossibility. She simultaneously admits human desires, and denies herself their fulfillment; and this double perspective—when her human anguish peeks around the sharp corners of her poetic determination—constitutes the poignancy of her stance. She is not resigned to her solitude; she is split and torn. Her poetry is an exercise in exorcism, without which she would fly to her potential lover with hardly a backward glance. This tension between Tsvetaeva's real and imagined worlds is most often concealed in her poetry or is present, at best, in certain ironic nuances. All the more shocking, then, her sudden, candid exposure of the untenability of her position in real life at the conclusion of "Wires"—precisely, moreover, at her moment of greatest poetic vigor, at her highest pitch of lyrical faith. She believes—in spite of life:

I have made my soul into a home (*maison son lande*), but never my house—into a soul. I am absent from my life, I am *not* at home. A soul in a house, a soul-house, is unthinkable to me, in fact I don't think about it. (6:243)

This soberly realistic underpinning of Tsvetaeva's outspokenly Romantic poetics has gone mostly unrecognized by her friends, her enemies, and her critics alike.

In later years, the Psyche myth is no longer played out narratively in Tsvetaeva's works, but becomes rather a kind of hidden talisman of the whole complex logic of her poetic identity. In several works, the connecting/separating wires that give shape to "Wires" metamorphose into various other forms, as she pictures her split Psychean self as the incarnation of intermediacy and in-betweenness, unable ever to find peace or equilibrium. For instance, in "I wander" ["Brozhu—ne dom zhe plotnichat'..."], the sighs and vows of Tsvetaeva's abstracted "lyrical wires" are returned via yet another metaphorical twist to their abandoned physical origins: "They make rigging from my sighs! They build bridges from my vows!" [Moimi vzdokhami—snastiat! / Moimi kliatvami—mostiat!] (2:233-34). Similarly, in "Poem of the End," a bridge in Prague becomes an image of the poet's passage from love to isolation and, on the deepest mythopoetic level, from life into the Hadean underworld—from human happiness into the hell of poetic inspiration: "The good luck of hopeless lovers: bridge, you're—like passion: conditionality: complete betweenness" [Bla—gaia chast' / Liubovnikov bez nadezhdy: / Most, ty—kak strast': / Uslovnost': sploshnoe mezhdu] (3:40).

The idea of Psychean "betweenness" is also central to the *poema* "Attempt at a Room" ["Popytka komnaty"] (3:114-19) in which Tsvetaeva fantasizes a physical space where she and her poetic beloved can finally meet that she explicitly likens to Psyche's enchanted palace.[63] Yet the room never materializes. Its walls stretch instead into a series of endless corridors, the physical embodiment of nowhere—a transgression of domesticity which, paradoxically, is harbored by domestic space itself: "Corridors: the domesticity of distance" [Korridory: domashnest' dali]. These corridors ultimately give way to their poetic notation—the long dash, which simultaneously connects and separates: "The entire poet hangs on a single long dash..." [Ves' poet na odnom tire / Derzhitsia...].[64] This dash, along with all Tsvetaeva's other bridges, riggings, corridors, and lyrical wires, is yet another incarnation of the impossible tightrope the woman poet walks thrillingly between body and soul, home and nowhere, life and death. Sometimes she barely hangs on—dangling from an enjambement by her heels.

3

Losing Rilke
The Dark Lure of Mra

> Мимо свадебных карет,
> Похоронных дрог...
>
> [Past the wedding carriages, past the funeral hearses . . .]
> — "Chtob doiti do ust i lozha . . ." (1916)

> Ибо правильно толкуя слово
> *Рифма*—что—как не—целый ряд новых
> Рифм—Смерть?
>
> [Since understanding the word rhyme correctly, what else is death
> —except—a whole sequence of new rhymes?]
> — "Novogodnee" (1927)

The artist Leonid Osipovich Pasternak, father of poet Boris, enjoyed a friendship with the German poet Rainer Maria Rilke that dated back to Rilke's days in Russia at the beginning of the century.[1] Through a bizarre sequence of events, Rilke renewed his contact with the elder Pasternak in the spring of 1926, after having seen two of the son's poems published in French translation; a grateful letter from Boris Pasternak to Rilke followed this exchange. In his letter, for somewhat inscrutable reasons, Pasternak brought Tsvetaeva to Rilke's attention and requested that the German poet write to her and send her his collection *Duino Elegies*. Rilke was amenable, and on 3 May 1926, he wrote his first letter to her. This was the beginning of Tsvetaeva's short-lived but intense correspondence with Rilke, whom she had loved and revered since her youth on a par with Blok and even with Orpheus himself.[2]

Rilke was one generation Tsvetaeva's senior, yet Tsvetaeva, who in any case never consented to the tyrannical limitations of time, interpreted Rilke's age more as a sign of his spiritual superiority than as any barrier to an equal friendship. Indeed, the letters exchanged by these two great poets read, from the very beginning, as an intimate conversation between equals who, moreover, share not only an intuitive rapport with one another, but also a gratifying awareness of their poetic kinship.[3] Even in Rilke's first, gracious letter to the unsuspecting Tsvetaeva, he takes her talent on faith, writing nostalgically of his recent trip to Paris:

But why, I must now ask myself, why was it not vouchsafed me to meet you, Marina Ivanovna Tsvetaeva? After Boris Pasternak's letter I must believe that for both of us, such a meeting would have led to the deepest, innermost joy. Will it sometime be possible to make up for this?![4]

In this passage, Rilke unwittingly adopts Tsvetaeva's central thematic concern: namely, the missed or impossible meeting between two great poets. Furthermore, he inscribes his *Duino Elegies,* which he sends to her at Pasternak's request, as if with her own most cherished words and images:

> Wir rühren uns. Womit? Mit Flügelschlägen,
> mit Fernen selber rühren wir uns an.
> *Ein* Dichter einzig lebt, und dann und wann
> kommt, der ihn trägt, *dem,* der ihn trug, entgegen.
>
> [We touch each other. With what? With beating wings, with distance we touch each other. *One* poet only lives, and now and then it happens, he who bears him comes toward the one who bore him.][5]

Here are Tsvetaeva's wings, symbolic throughout her oeuvre of the poetic gift; here is her motif of the poet's spiritual elevation and consequent isolation; here is her theme of poetic kinship across space and time. In her response to Rilke, she staggers under the force of his miraculous recognition: "Rainer, Rainer, you said this to me, without knowing me, like a blind man (a seer!) by chance. (The best shots are blind!)." [6] Tsvetaeva confidently casts Rilke as the blind man who, as far back as her "Poems to Akhmatova," has been her soul mate, her double, and her muse.

Rilke, whom she would never have dared approach on her own initiative, has suddenly, magically come into her most intimate life of the soul like an apparition of her innermost self. In the process, he shatters Blok's wounding indifference and unresponsiveness to Tsvetaeva years before. Not yet having heard her poetic voice, Rilke believes in her gift—and by this single, generous gesture, he confirms the metaphysical basis for her poetic genius. Indeed, for all her humility before Rilke, Tsvetaeva is now no longer a poetic adolescent, but a fully formed poet confident of her own voice and destiny. Since her renunciation of Pasternak on the spiritual plane (in the spring of 1923), and the ruinous rupture of her passionate, though short-lived liaison with Konstantin Rodzevich on the physical plane (in the fall of 1924), she has cultivated a careful tranquility—

The Dark Lure of Mra 131

akin, at times, to barrenness—in her affections and emotions.[7] It is no wonder at all, therefore, that she reacts to Rilke's uninvited incursion into her circumscribed existence with shock akin to sheer ecstasy. Even Rilke's ensuing death, unwelcome though it is, she will paradoxically experience as a gift—his very last gift to anyone, just as his "Elegie an Marina Zwetajewa-Efron" is, at least as far as Tsvetaeva knows, the last poem he ever wrote.[8]

For, unbeknownst to Tsvetaeva at the time, Rilke, when he wrote his first letter to her, was already stricken with the leukemia that would kill him just half a year later—indeed, what he casts as his recent pleasure trip to Paris was, in reality, a visit to a sanatorium. The precise moment when Tsvetaeva realizes Rilke's illness is unclear; she tactfully refrains from bemoaning her imminent loss to him in her letters. Still, Rilke provides enough hints that it is inconceivable that the always prescient and perceptive Tsvetaeva could have remained oblivious to the gravity of his condition. This, however, is what the predominance of commentators on the Tsvetaeva–Rilke correspondence have, in fact, assumed; moreover, they have read the letters that Tsvetaeva and Rilke exchanged during the summer of 1926 as an imbalanced contest between her importunate longing and his genteel, polite, but perturbed and detached resistance to her desires. As a result, most critical focus has been on the perceived rifts between the two poets. Rilke's very willingness to engage in the correspondence at all has been viewed as a condescension to Tsvetaeva's supposed desperation, and the eventual end to the correspondence is interpreted as the logical result of this inherent emotional inequality.

On the contrary, I would argue that not only the abrupt end to the correspondence in September 1926, but also an earlier lapse in late May, were not the result of any mismatch or misunderstanding; instead, these breaks are testimony to Tsvetaeva's tacitly growing recognition of Rilke's illness. The pianist Artur Schnabel once said, "The notes I handle no better than many pianists. But the pauses between the notes—ah, that is where the art resides!"[9] Indeed, the breaks in Tsvetaeva's correspondence with Rilke speak as eloquently as do the letters, and sometimes more so, for they reveal the limits of what can be said in human language and, therefore, suggest the presence of unspoken sympathies between the two poets that are testimony to the genuineness of their bond. In my reading of the Tsvetaeva–Rilke correspondence, therefore, I emphasize the lapses, the breaches, and the silences as an intrinsic part of the communication. Furthermore, I show that this correspondence is yet another movement in the ongoing development of Tsvetaeva's symphony of poetic mythologies—a movement that begins with a recapitulation of previous themes but then varies them so greatly that, in the process, an entirely new melody is created.

Thus, Rilke first arises in Tsvetaeva's mythology, for all his imposing greatness, as Pasternak's shadow.[10] Only gradually does he separate and grow into his own complete, independent being—that is, only gradually does he attain his own myth in her mythopoetic system. In the process, Tsvetaeva shifts her creative energies from renunciation of the living (Pasternak) to a passionate embrace of the dying and, later, the dead (Rilke). There are two distinct phases to Rilke's metamorphosis in Tsvetaeva's poetics that I trace in this chapter. The poets' correspondence records the first phase, in which she at first mistakenly anticipates that Rilke will be distinguished from Pasternak by her real meeting with him, in contrast with her nonmeeting with the other poet. Her subconscious realization that such a meeting is not, after all, going to occur shapes the latter part of the correspondence and gives rise to her *poema* "Attempt at a Room" ["Popytka komnaty"] (3:114–19), composed in early June 1926.

The second and definitive stage in Tsvetaeva's poetic mythologization of Rilke occurs in the wake of his sudden death on 29 December 1926—an event that she, despite her premonitions, experiences as no less shocking than was his entry into her life in the first place. At this point, she leaves behind her previous dreams: her hopes of a future, posthumous meeting with Pasternak and of a future, real-life meeting with Rilke. In her two great *poemy* "New Year's Letter" ["Novogodnee"] (3:132–36) and "Poem of the Air" ["Poema vozdukha"] (3:137–44), she tests the outer limits of human language in her pursuit of Rilke's fleeing soul, enacting in the process a present-tense, out-of-body union with the dead poet that is paradoxically more palpable and immediate than is her connection with any member of the living. In this way, Rilke's passing acts as a "cure" to all the irreconcilable divisions and contradictions in her poetics. Through a vicarious poetic sharing of Rilke's death, Tsvetaeva imagines in her writing that she exits the constraints of body, factuality, and physical reality, which are in the process replaced by pure abstractions.[11]

She thereby achieves a new wholeness that was previously inaccessible, of which the dynamic, open, widening circle is the image. Her vertical poetic vector, with its combustive requirements for a successful launch into the beyond, is replaced by a reassuring, undulating curvaciousness; the binary oppositions that previously gave her poetry its impetus are simply erased, as death is transformed from the ultimate defeat into the ultimate idiom of spiritual liberation.[12] Tsvetaeva's communion with Rilke and her embrace of the infinite resonance of death are, truly, the high point of her poetic career. Yet this achievement of her lifelong fantasy is at the same time profoundly ambivalent from an earthbound (i.e., mortal) perspective. For, in the absoluteness of her merger with the deceased Rilke, as we shall see, all of her earthly anchors are lost.

A Rebellion against "No": Tsvetaeva's Letters to Rilke

When Tsvetaeva received Rilke's generous first letter, his death was surely the farthest thing from her mind.[13] Rilke's initial, delicate hints about the state of his health must almost surely have gone astray. Thus, for instance, although Rilke mentions his visit to Paris the previous year, he does not disclose the length of his stay (eight months), nor the fact that it was undertaken for medical reasons. In his letter of 10 May, he reveals that he has been staying in a sanatorium since December, but still gives no indication of the seriousness of his condition. Even when he returns to this topic in his letter of 17 May and admits that he is ill, he is extremely vague on the details of his disease, making it sound rather like a malady of the spirit, and suggesting that the primary purpose of his journey to the sanatorium was, after all, to visit old friends: "For the first time in my life and somehow insidiously, my own solitude, with a physical sting, turned against me, making being alone with myself suspicious and dangerous . . . That is why I am here."[14] Still, as the hints begin to accumulate, Tsvetaeva surely realizes the truth. Her metaphysical instincts are refined, and, as a result, she is often prophetic, sometimes against her own will.

Yet she persists in pointedly ignoring the specter of death that threatens to intrude momentarily in her new friendship; she continues to write to Rilke as if there is nothing that could ever divide them. This behavior is not evidence that Tsvetaeva is oblivious to Rilke's affliction (indeed, she inquires, in her letter of 13 May, how long he has been sick); instead, it speaks of a studied combination of respect and stubborn will: she both respects Rilke's reticence (indicating his intense need for privacy, a need that she shares) and rebels against the cruel reality from which he attempts to shield her. Her unwillingness to discuss Rilke's illness is evidence of a very Russian superstitiousness. That which is unspoken remains unreal; perhaps the sheer force of her desire not to lose Rilke will be enough to appease the Evil Eye.

The first rift in the two poets' correspondence came after Rilke's letter of 17 May, the very letter in which he first discusses his ailment. For two weeks afterwards, Tsvetaeva refrained from writing to him, pouring out her grief instead—in coded form, never explicitly—in letters to Pasternak: "I am not writing to Rilke. Too great a torment. Fruitless. It gets me off-track—distracts me from poetry . . . He—doesn't need it. For me—it's painful" (6:253). Apparently misled by her delicacy, critics have assumed that Tsvetaeva must have misinterpreted Rilke's comments about his illness as a subtle rebuff to her. Indeed, it has become commonplace to explain the breach in the two poets' correspondence in late May as the result of Tsvetaeva's having taken offense at Rilke's obscure comment that, even if he ceases writing to her for a time (as a result of his incapacity), she should continue her letters to him.[15] Yet she openly admits to Pasternak that she is writing in code—that is, that she is not revealing to him the true source of her grief: "Boris, I do not write true letters [ne te pis′ma pishu]. The real ones don't even touch the paper" (6:251). Mindful of Rilke's wish for privacy and wishing to spare Pasternak the grief that she herself is feeling, Tsvetaeva hides the facts that she has begun to discover in the generality of lyrical lament. Furthermore, she could not have taken offense at Rilke's plea for indulgence, for in her very first letter she had released him from all obligation to herself: "You need not answer me. I know what time is and I know what a poem is. I also know what a *letter* is. So, then." [16]

Instead, Tsvetaeva's quick reversal of this avowal is evidence not of hurt feelings, but rather of panic and of great despair. Faced with the possibility of Rilke's grave illness and encroaching death no sooner than he—the incarnation of poetry, her living muse, for whom she has been searching and waiting all her life—has finally searched her out (with a little help, of course, from Pasternak), Tsvetaeva is overcome by psychological shock, a variant of the emotional paralysis that typically strikes her when she is in the grip of passion. She prefers, for a time, to cut all ties between herself and Rilke, secluding him once again in the safe never-never land of her imagination from which he first emerged, rather than admit his mortality and the possibility that he will soon die and leave her behind. Death has always been an important theme in Tsvetaeva's poetic repertoire; now, however, the purely theoretical nature of her previous poetic musings on death is suddenly, shockingly brought into relief, and she needs some time to assimilate death's reality in relation to a poet, *the* Poet, Poetry itself (in her first letter to Rilke she terms him "Poetry embodied" [17]).

During the initial weeks of her correspondence with Rilke, Tsvetaeva neglects Pasternak; this fact in itself indicates her difficulty during this period in considering the two poets as separate beings in the context of the mythological frameworks by which she makes poetic meaning of the accidents of her life. When at the end of May she stops writing to Rilke, Pasternak at once reemerges in her consciousness. She writes him four letters during the next two weeks; yet when she resumes writing letters to Rilke in June, her correspondence with Pasternak yet again becomes infrequent and then, in July, lapses completely, not to be resumed until after Rilke's death. This time, Tsvetaeva's break with Pasternak is not just tacit. After a crushingly final response to his very real intentions of coming to live with her in France [18] (his marriage was in the process of disintegrating, and his wife and son had left for an extended stay in Germany), she writes (in a letter that has not survived) to tell him of her feeling that their correspondence should end—a decision that he supports in his reply. In a letter to Rilke, she justifies her resolve thus:

When I found out about this his second abroad, I wrote: two letters from abroad—forget it! There is no such thing as two abroads. Abroad and at home [Ausland und Innland]—yes. *I* am his abroad. [*Ich* bin Ausland.] *Am* and will not share.

Let his wife write to him, and he to her. Sleep with her and write to me—yes, write to her and write to me, two envelopes, two addresses (one France)—*sistered* by his handwriting... Him for a brother—yes, her for a sister—no.[19]

Tsvetaeva had once been willing to allow Pasternak's sexual love for his wife to coexist with the spiritual bond that she and he felt so keenly; yet she is filled with antipathy at the thought that Pasternak's wife will now share in their special epistolary relationship.

Oddly, however, Pasternak is the first person to whom Tsvetaeva will turn for comfort after Rilke's death. Indeed, she will interpret Rilke's death (to Pasternak, at least) as granting her right to be together with Pasternak in a way that, during the previous years, she has conscientiously and systematically renounced: "His death gives the right of way for you and me to exist together—more than the right of way, it is his personal order for such a union" (6:268).[20] This strange inference is less abstruse if it is recalled that Rilke himself expresses his own fear, in his letter of 19 August, that his presence in Tsvetaeva's life is squeezing out Pasternak: "Truly, it was after all my arrival that barred the path of his passionate streaming towards you?"[21] Indeed, it does seem as though Tsvetaeva's protest against Pasternak's "two abroads" masks her discomfort at her own practice of that very same romantic bifurcation of which Pasternak stands accused. For she, too, finds herself unable to balance the huge emotional and creative demands of a simultaneous correspondence with her two ideal, absent poetic lovers/muses: Rilke and Pasternak, Switzerland and Russia. Tsvetaeva's giving notice to Pasternak—although certainly her jealousy of his letters to his wife contains some amount of truth—is, at the same time, a tactful way of bowing out of a demanding correspondence.

Her rejection of Pasternak is also a kind of bargain with fate: by renouncing Pasternak, perhaps she will gain a meeting with Rilke, thereby retrieving him from the clutches of death.[22] Thus, surprisingly, when she resumes her letters to Rilke, she is not subdued and resigned to the reality of his impending death but, on the contrary, more insistently focused than before on her desire to meet him not only in the spirit, but in the flesh. On the one hand this agenda is a protest against Rilke's mortality; by proving his physical reality, Tsvetaeva might somehow defeat the possibility of its dissolution. At the same time, because of her private awareness of Rilke's illness, her plans to meet him are a kind of a game: as if she knows now that the prospect of any meeting is purely fictional and her solitude therefore is safe, she throws herself wholeheartedly into the imagining. Accordingly, the topic of a meeting forms the refrain of all her letters following the May rift in the two poets' correspondence. This theme is linked with a burgeoning intimacy of tone—a palpable intensification of her desire. This boldness of tone has been perplexing and even offensive to other commentators on the correspondence; however, as I argue, Tsvetaeva's fervency must be considered in the context of her artistic style—as an indication that Rilke has entered into the metaphysical economy of her poetics, becoming the successor both to the winged horseman and to Pasternak/Eros.[23] Similarly, the coolness of Rilke's tone in response to Tsvetaeva is a function of his own style, rather than an index of his respect or interest.

Nevertheless, the logically and emotionally complicated underpinnings of Tsvetaeva's hopes and desires with respect to Rilke often lead to confusing inconsistencies in her letters. For instance, in her first letter to him after her two-week-long silence, she begins by denying her desire for Rilke altogether, in a paradoxical, jumbled passage in which any desire of hers to be together with Rilke is superseded by her intense desire *not to be*—together with Rilke:

I get over my desires quickly. What did I want of you? Nothing. Rather—to be near you. Maybe simply—to come to you. Without a letter it began to seem I was without you. The longer I waited—the worse it got. Without a letter—without you, with a letter—without you, with you—without you. *Into* you! Not to *be*.—To die!

Such am I. Such is love—in time. Thankless and self-destructive. Love I neither respect nor love.[24]

Tsvetaeva here marks the particular nature of her desire for Rilke as something made dearer by its ephemerality.[25] It is the pain of this recognition that has kept her from writing to him for the past two weeks, she intimates. However, on 14 June, in a parenthesis which she does not quite succeed in stifling (or so her punctuation suggests), she admits to loving Rilke and to her desire to come to him—a desire that she no longer directly qualifies: "Rainer, I love you and want to come to you." [26]

Yet this desire is spiritual and metaphorical rather than explicitly sexual as it might seem. Indeed, other sections of the same letter indicate that Tsvetaeva is continuing to come to terms with the possibility of Rilke's death. She finds something fantastic in his authorship of the "Elegie" to her, saying that she had always expected such a poem to be written by her lover who would appear "after one hundred years" [nach hundert Jahren].[27] A photograph Rilke has sent her seems to record the poet's metaphysical passage from the landscape, from the terrestrial world:

The smaller [photograph] is a farewell. Someone departing on a journey, who one last time, apparently in haste—the horses are already waiting—looks over his garden, like a page covered with writing, before it goes off in the mail. Not tearing himself away—freeing himself [Nicht sich losreißend—loslösend]. One who—gently—lets fall from his hands an entire landscape. (Rainer, take me with you!)[28]

Tsvetaeva apparently intends these passages as distancing devices that will offset her hesitant overtures toward intimacy in other places in her letters. In the closing salutation of her letter of 6 July, similarly, we find the simultaneous assertion and erasure of physical desires: "May I kiss you? For a kiss is no more than an embrace, and to embrace without kissing is almost impossible!" [29] Rilke, perhaps, misunderstood such contradictory passages; or Tsvetaeva, at least, is afraid that he might misunderstand and so takes pains to provide ongoing commentaries to her own affectionate outbursts.

As we have seen, Tsvetaeva's balancing act between imagination and anticipation, between the abyss of the spirit and the abyss of the senses, originates

The Dark Lure of Mra 137

in "On a Red Steed." Here as there, she attempts to achieve a spiritual union with her beloved by imagining an encounter that neutralizes explicitly sensual, sexual language and harnesses it to her poetic purposes. Yet by the time of her friendship with Rilke, five years after her composition of the earlier *poema,* the stakes are far higher, and her sober appreciation of the stark reality of her longings' extravagance supersedes her earlier romantic thrill-seeking. Nevertheless, Tsvetaeva is heroic in her continued attempts to achieve the impossible and conquer death through the force of her own hopeless passion. Aware that her endeavor is doomed to failure in the most mundane sense, she battles to create a poetic narrative that will transform the senseless tragedy of Rilke's coming death into a resonant, consoling myth.

The climax to Tsvetaeva's efforts in this direction comes in her letter of 2 August, in which she makes a dangerously tender, alarmingly explicit proposition to Rilke:

Rainer, I want to come to you also because of the new Marina who can emerge only with you, in you. And also, Rainer (Rainer is the leitmotif of this letter)—don't be angry, this is *me,* I want to sleep with you—to fall asleep and to sleep . . . Simply—sleep. And nothing further. No, also: to burrow my head into your left shoulder, my arm on your right shoulder—and nothing further. No, also: to know even in the deepest sleep that it is you. And also: to hear how your heart resounds. And—to kiss your heart.[30]

Tsvetaeva's motivation for these dreams, as she indicates, is one of poetic self-realization: "I want to come to you also because of the new Marina who can emerge only with you, in you . . ." Earlier, in her second letter to Rilke, she has already made clear that her love for him is, indeed, a love for this inspirational "third" in the romantic union of every human twosome, whose one-dimensional bond is thereby transformed into an upward-striving triangle (she may well, at this early stage in her correspondence with Rilke, have in mind her own special connection with Pasternak)—or, to put it yet another way, her love for Rilke is the infinity that elevates every apparent end to an awareness of perpetually creative process. Rilke is not a barrier to her poetic striving, but the medium of her desire:

Priests are only an interference between me and God (gods). You, you are my friend [Freund], who *deepens* and heightens the joy [Freude] (is it joy?) of a great hour between two (the eternal pair!); without whom one cannot any longer sense any *other;* and whom one after all *loves exclusively.*[31]

In order to achieve this union with the infinity that Rilke represents, however, Tsvetaeva finds it necessary to resort to sexual language in order, paradoxically, to undo all spiritual limitations to which her gender subjects her. Her trepidation at the risks entailed by such a project moves her in her 13 May letter (after the suggestive comment that, while she was reading Rilke's poems, her bed was transformed into a cloud) to warn: "My love, I already know *everything*—from me to you—but for much it is still too early. Something in you must still become accustomed to me." [32]

By the time Tsvetaeva composed her letter of 2 August, she must have felt that Rilke had already grown sufficiently accustomed. For in this letter she inverses and thus "decodes" her epistolary attempts at sexual transcendence through her uplifting love for Rilke, when she confesses, with a strikingly painful, almost embarrassing frankness, her lifelong feeling of alienation from sensual love; the feigned automatism of her sexual responses; and other bodies' instinctive (animal-like) mistrust and dislike of her:

Bodies languish in my company. They sense something and don't believe me (mine), although I do everything like everyone else. Maybe too... unselfishly, too... benevolently. Also too trustingly! . . . Love hears and feels only itself, it is very focused and punctual, *that* I cannot fake.[33]

This passage is turgidly phrased—Tsvetaeva's verbal defense against the brutally painful honesty of her shyly proferred self-evaluation—and Rilke may well have failed to recognize that the topic of her discussion is, in fact, sex. Tsvetaeva, perhaps realizing this, makes one more attempt to offset the damaging effect she fears her admission of her yearning for Rilke may have had. Thus, later in the same letter, she explicitly plots out the nature of her poetic project, emphasizing the movement of her bodily language away from the physical toward the symbolic, the abstract, the metaphysical:

I have always felt the mouth to be a world:[34] a vault of sky, a cave, a ravine, an abyss [Untiefe].[35] Always I have translated the body into the soul (*dis*embodied!), and "physical" love—in order to love it—I have so glorified that suddenly nothing remained of it. Plunging in, I have sapped *it,* penetrating, I have squeezed *it* out. Nothing remained of it but me myself: soul . . .[36]

The mouth—instrument of the kiss that she has already confessed to desiring—is, for Tsvetaeva, the entryway into the abyss of the soul. She requires physical love only insofar as the experience allows her to overcome the body's need and, thus, to transcend the body altogether. Her sweet-talk with Rilke, she is trying to tell him, is only her way of trying to realize all the possibilities of her soul. Her sensual means of expression is simply a necessary metaphor, just as her gender is a necessary facet of her physical incarnation. These obstacles must be acknowledged and actively transgressed if they are to be overcome.

Rilke, apparently, is somewhat confused by Tsvetaeva's mixed signals. Yet he does not respond directly to her epistolary lovemaking; rather, he expresses his consternation between the lines, as it were. For example, he chides her gently for her suspicions against the battered exterior of a train that nevertheless reliably transports one of her letters. Rilke in this passage possibly intimates a metaphoric connection with himself: "The train, Marina . . . which you subsequently mistrusted, rolled toward me breathlessly; the uncanny mailbox was old, as camels and crocodiles are old, shielded since youth onward by old age: the most dependable quality." [37] Rilke also tactfully protests Tsvetaeva's shunning of Pasternak in his favor—which he may feel places a romantic obligation on himself that he is unwilling to accept—as well as what he interprets as her claim to exclusive status in his affections: "I find you to be too strict with me, in wanting me never and nowhere to know Russia, except through you! I rebel against any exclusion (which grows out of the love-root but then turns wooden): do you recognize me thus, and *also* thus?" [38]

Tsvetaeva reflects upon this charge in her last known letter to Pasternak (1935), where she writes:

All my dear ones—and they are few—turned out to be infinitely softer than I am, even Rilke wrote to me: "You are right, but you are hard"—and this upset me because I could not be otherwise. Now, taking stock of my life, I see: my seeming harshness was only a form, a contour of being, a necessary self-protective boundary—against *your* softness, Rilke, Marcel Proust and Boris Pasternak" (6:277).

Tsvetaeva finds it necessary to insist upon divisions and separations that the male writers in her life need not make. By an ironic coincidence, she answers Rilke's admonishments in what also ends up being her last full-length letter to him. She does so straightforwardly and calmly, explaining that she was merely indulging in flights of verbal inventiveness that can have, at best, only an antagonistic relationship to the reality of any encounter between the two poets. Unperturbed, she smoothes over Rilke's misinterpretation in her characteristically outspoken, authoritative manner:

Rainer, when I tell you: I am your Russia, I am only saying (once again) that I love you. Love lives by exceptions, emissions, exclusivities. Love lives by words and dies by deeds. I am too prudent really to want to be your Russia! An idiom of speech. An idiom of love [Redensart. Liebesart] . . . I want only the word, which for me is already a thing. Deeds? Consequences?

I know you, Rainer, as I know myself. The farther you go from me—the farther *into* me. I live not inside myself, but outside. I do not live in my mouth and he who kisses me passes *me* by.[39]

Meanwhile, Tsvetaeva reiterates her desire for a meeting with Rilke, but this time in a matter-of-fact tone and practical terms, explaining that she will wait for him to plan the details of the trip and that he will have to cover her part of the expenses (she is too poor to afford the journey, as she wryly admits: "a rare guest!" [40]). To this end, she gives him the dates when she might be able to travel and makes suggestions as to what the best location for their meeting would be.

Rilke had earlier proved receptive to similar explanations; although he sometimes interpreted her statements and her exuberance in ways she had not intended, she had always managed to convince him later of her rectitude, through the sheer force and exactness of her language. In fact, Rilke finds himself under the sway not only of Tsvetaeva's compelling poetic logic, but also of her unique manner of composition:

> As in your first letter, so in each successive one I marvel at your very scrupulous seeking and finding, your inexhaustible means of expressing what you intend and, always, your rightness. You are right, Marina (is that not rare for a woman?), so right in the most valid, the most innocent sense. This rightness has no aim and hardly any origin; but is so purely frugal because it emanates from wholeness, from completeness—and thence your eternal right to infinity. Whenever I write to you, I want to write as you do, *to express myself as you do,* adopting your way with words that is imperturbable, yet so sensitive.[41]

Despite their occasional misunderstandings, Tsvetaeva's and Rilke's letters to one another truly read like a dialogue of equals, in which neither is shy about expressing criticisms of the other—nor do they take offense at these criticisms, for each respects the independence of the other's views and sensibilities. Both poets are always ready to explain, to excuse, to reevaluate, and to forgive. Far from seeming "an unwilling participant [in what had begun as correspondence but had evolved into a one-sided epistolary contest],"[42] Rilke, who all his life enjoyed and actively sought out epistolary friendships with a wide range of female correspondents, appears frank, honest, and sincere in his admiration and sympathy for Tsvetaeva—although he is equally frank in expressing misgivings when such arise. His letters no less than hers are filled with immense tenderness and even passion, and he shares with her his thoughts, feelings, and accumulated wisdom with the utmost generosity.

Furthermore, when Tsvetaeva discovers that, even with her helpful marginal notes, Rilke is able to read her relatively straightforward early poems only with great difficulty, I would argue that her chagrin is caused by her unaccustomed, painful awareness of cultural distance from Rilke, as she explains to Pasternak:[43]

> Boris, what follows is vileness (on my part): Rilke reads my poems with difficulty, although just ten years ago he read *Goncharov* without a dictionary . . . What a waste! In this for a moment I saw him as a foreigner, i.e. myself as a Russian, and him as a German! Humiliating. There exists a world of firm (and base, firm in their baseness) values, about which he, Rilke, should not know in any language. Goncharov . . . loses too much when uttered by Rilke. (6:257–58)

It is Rilke's mention of the prosaic, obsolete Goncharov that offends Tsvetaeva here—signaling as it does Rilke's jarringly foreign perspective on Russian literature—more than the simple fact of his rusty Russian. Elsewhere for Tsvetaeva, Rilke is the universal, quintessential Poet of all poets, for whom no linguistic or cultural barriers should exist. Nevertheless, Rilke's inability to appreciate

The Dark Lure of Mra 141

her poetry fully does not inhibit his regard for her poetic talent, which is able to shine through the clever word plays and eloquent phrasing of her letters to him—all written in her excellent, near-native German, which Rilke describes fondly and with admiration:

> Your German, no, it's not that it "stumbles," but now and then it treads more heavily, like the footsteps of someone descending an uneven stone staircase who cannot judge as he climbs down when his foot will come to rest, now already or suddenly farther below than he expected. What strength you have, poetess, to be able to realize your intention in this language also, enough to remain yourself. *Your* gait that resounds upon the steps, your tone, *you.* Your lightness, your controlled, generous weight.[44]

Clearly, even without the ability to understand Tsvetaeva's poems well, Rilke has not the slightest doubt of her poetic genius and is even able to recognize her unique poetic stamp upon the prose she writes in another language. Indeed, the two poets understand each other remarkably well, and they never falter in their respect and consideration for one another.

Even after Tsvetaeva's extremely sexually suggestive letter of 2 August, Rilke does not shun her, as several critics, trying to locate the reason for the end to the correspondence, have surmised. On the contrary, when Rilke, in the opening of what was to be his final letter to Tsvetaeva, written 19 August, corrects her innocent enthusiasm for a meeting, his remarks must be read as a reference to the imminence of his death, rather than as a disgruntled attempt to distance himself from her boisterous presumptions of intimacy:

> Yes and Yes and Yes, Marina, all Yesses to what you want and what you are, as large, taken together, as a Yes to Life itself... : but in this there are also ten thousand unforeseeable Nos.[45]

The very structure of this statement suggests that Rilke identifies "Yes" with life's potentiality and "No" with death's unpredictability. He answers "yes" to Tsvetaeva's desires and dreams but cautions her inscrutably that there may be a "no" lurking that is outside the realm of their mutual yearnings. This absolute use Rilke makes of the interjectives "yes" and "no" is one that Tsvetaeva must comprehend, having herself repeatedly used the words in exactly this way in her own poems.[46]

Throughout Rilke's final letter, it is clear that his devotion to Tsvetaeva is unchanged; indeed, despite his veiled warnings, he still expresses his own cherished hopes that the two poets will after all manage to arrange a rendezvous. Admitting that he himself has already been searching the map for a possible meeting place even before she raised the subject—and that he has, magically, come up with the same solution as she did (*"cette petite ville en Savoye"*)—he wonders bemusedly at their almost psychic connection: "Who knows, Marina, whether my answering did not come *before* your asking?"[47] He anticipates their encounter with great impatience; indeed, he even hints that his own longing for her is stronger than hers for him:

After all, I need no less (no: more than ever) for once to rest *thus* from the greatest depths, from the well of wells. But until then, fear before the many days that must pass, with their repetitions, fear (suddenly) before the accidents which know nothing of this [i.e., his and Tsvetaeva's plans to meet — A. D.] and are unteachable.

...Don't wait until winter!...[48]

The "accidents" that Rilke fears in this passage are yet another camouflaged reference to his growing awareness of impending death. Tsvetaeva, who has assured him that she cannot make the trip to meet him until November at the earliest, recognizes the urgency of his trepidation only in retrospect; his cry "Don't wait until winter!" was to haunt her later.

Tsvetaeva is as penetrating a reader as she is a poet; undoubtedly, by this time, she understands the gravity of the situation, though she may not quite realize how little time is left. The uncharacteristic ease with which she accepts the unexpected end to her correspondence with Rilke speaks of her compassion for his physical condition; her only attempt to restore the lines of communication is her hopeless, tiny cry into the wilderness of the silence of death that has come between them: "Do you still love me?" [Ob Du mich noch liebst?].[49] This last plea indicates resignation rather than protest. Read in the light of her recognition of Rilke's impending passing, then, Tsvetaeva's reiterated plans for the two poets' meeting are an intrinsic part of her poetic rebellion against reality, death, "no," limitations of all kinds. Numerous passages in her final two letters to Rilke show that her premonitions of his death are growing ever stronger. In her letter of 14 August, she urges him to assure her that their meeting will take place: "Say yes, so that from this day forward I will have a great joy, something to look forward to (look backward upon?). The past is still ahead." [50] This confusion of tenses and times indicates the fantastic nature of their plans. Similarly, in her final letter to Rilke (of 22 August), Tsvetaeva shifts suddenly from a discussion of the practical aspects of her trip ("Train. Ticket. Hotel. [Thank God, no need of a visa!]")[51] to an avowal of doubt: "And... a slight shudder. Something prepared, won,... wheedled out [vorbereitetes, erobertes,... erbetteltes]. *You* must fall from the sky." [52]

Perhaps it was, in fact, the anguishing exactness of this prophecy that prompted Rilke to refrain from answering Tsvetaeva, if in fact he did not; his own recognition that the desired meeting between them was not, after all, to take place must have caused him to avoid the sorrow of further unrealizable hopes and to pass his final days and months in a state as closely approaching tranquility as possible. Given his poor state of health, Rilke may also simply have found the mental and physical exertion of continuing his correspondence with

Tsvetaeva too much to manage. The fact that he wrote unusually little during his last months corroborates the idea that he found creative work to be exhausting; indeed, he says so several times in his last letters to Tsvetaeva: "My life is so curiously heavy inside me, often I cannot budge it; the force of gravity, it seems, is forming a new relation to my life—since childhood I have never known such an inertness of spirit." [53] This statement is made in the context of Rilke's apology for not having responded sooner to Tsvetaeva's previous letter (which he had received nearly three weeks before); in this way, he tactfully prepares the ground for the time, soon after, when his replies to her letters will cease altogether. Still, when Rilke's letters stop coming, Tsvetaeva, insecure as she tends to be, clearly imagines (as her last forlorn postcard suggests) that she has somehow offended him; it is less painful for her to believe this than admit openly to herself that he is dying. When Rilke does pass away on 29 December—putting an abrupt end to her state of denial—the long-dreaded event comes almost as a relief. For it provides a resolution to her doubts; now she understands that Rilke did not write *not* because he did not want to, but because he could not. His death, therefore, ironically becomes for Tsvetaeva the proof of his continuing love, and, in this sense, his final gift to her.[54]

"No" Becomes Poem: "Attempt at a Room"

Death for Tsvetaeva is a poetic metaphor, expressing the magic of her potential union with Rilke. Death is a creative boon, the true identity of her muse, the culmination of all her transgressive, otherworldly strivings. Yet death is also a reality, threatening to take Rilke out of her reach forever. Death can and will destroy her poetic "I," along with all that she loves and desires. Tsvetaeva's gradual process of reconciling herself to this latter aspect of death—specifically, through an exploration of the metaphysical possibilities of the former—gives shape not only to her correspondence with Rilke, but also to her *poema* "Attempt at a Room," which was written, for the most part, during the first lapse in the two poets' correspondence (late May to early June 1926), while she was attempting to make peace with her realization that Rilke was gravely ill.

Tsvetaeva writes to Pasternak after Rilke's death regarding the psychologically convoluted compositional history of this *poema:*

> There is something very important, Boris, about which I've wanted to tell you for a long time. A poem about you and me—the beginning of "Attempt at a Room"—turned out to be a poem about him and me, *every line.* A curious substitution occurred: the poem was written during my intense concentration on him, but was directed—according to my conscious will—toward you. It turned out after all—so little about him!—to be about him—now (*after* December 29), i.e. it was a premonition, an insight. I was simply telling him, alive—whom I *did plan* to meet!—how we did not meet, how we met *otherwise.* Hence the strange nonamorousness [neliubov′nost′], indifference, *resis-*

tance [otkaznost'] of every line, which I then found so distressing. The work was called "Attempt at a Room" and I resisted every line—with every line [ot kazhdoi—kazhdoi strokoi—otkazyvalas']. (6:269)

This passage is extremely revealing of the dual philosophical processes that give rise to "Attempt at a Room." On the one hand, as we have already seen in the correspondence, Tsvetaeva is attempting to distinguish the role that Rilke plays in her poetic mythology from Pasternak's role by concocting a scenario for her actual meeting with the German poet that will counterbalance her carefully conjured nonmeeting with her Russian peer. On the other hand, she senses that Rilke's death is near and that such a meeting will not, after all, take place (perhaps her intuition of his impending death is one reason, perversely enough, that she finds herself even able to contemplate the possibility of an actual meeting).

The result is a fantastically self-generating, self-consuming attempt at an alternative reality. No sooner does the newly attired snake of Tsvetaeva's self emerge from its old skin than it bites off its own tail (tale!) in an impossibly acrobatic posture, filling the space where it previously existed with the dense, negative metaphysical matter of black holes.[55] Words in "Attempt at a Room" act not to identify the objects and concepts they represent, but to dissolve them in a flourish of antisubstantive legerdemain. What begins as a tentative dream room with floor, ceiling, and three walls—only the fourth is slightly doubtful ("I can't vouch for the fourth" [Za chetvertuiu ne vruchaius'])—is taken over entirely by abstractions by the end of the work. The entire room ultimately is nothing but a vaguely geometrical jumble of intersecting planes ("A room? Simply—planes" [Komnata? Prosto—ploskosti]) that themselves also vanish into nothingness.

This is the complex ontology that Tsvetaeva has in mind when she writes, with characteristic brevity, of the peculiar "resistance" [otkaznost'] of the *poema* in her letter to Pasternak: "I resisted every line—with every line" [ot kazhdoi—kazhdoi strokoi—otkazyvalas']. The neologism *otkaznost'* refers not only to her own emotional resistance to the sad truth that she is discovering through the writing of "Attempt at a Room," but also to the intractable, self-referential viscosity of language itself. The previously quoted passage, in fact, not only expresses, but also enacts, the process that it describes. The repetition of the definite adjective *every* [kazhdoi] is only a seeming repetition; in the first instance, the adjective is in the genitive case, whereas it is in the instrumental case in the second instance. This single word, without changing its superficial form, actually undoes its own meaning: Tsvetaeva protests *against* every line *with* every line. What is even more remarkable—because counterintuitive—is that the negating genitive case is followed by the instrumental, rather than vice versa. In other words, language, fully recognizing the impossibility of which it speaks, rebels against that impossibility. Not merely doubting (like the biblical

Thomas whom Tsvetaeva, true to her scorn for iffy "inbetweeners," repeatedly maligns [56]), but knowing the irreality of the concrete objects it describes, the language of the *poema* asserts a different, poetic, anticoncrete, purely verbal reality that is paradoxically incontestible because integrally private.

The replacement of concrete objects with poetic abstractions is carried out in part through a process of linguistic estrangement: language makes itself strange by calling attention to its own meaningless automatism and, through this process, attains new, different meaning. (The technique is similar to a game familiar to children or foreign language learners who roll a single word around on the tongue, repeating it until it begins to sound like a nonsense syllable and loses all definiteness of sense and spelling). This process begins in the poem's first lines, when Tsvetaeva expresses the unknowability of the fourth wall of the room she envisions: "Who can know, with his back to the wall? Maybe, but then again it may *not* be" [Kto zhe znaet, spinoi k stene? / Mozhet byt′, no ved′ mozhet ne / Byt′]. The expression that is deautomatized here is the common "maybe" [mozhet byt′] (in English, the degree of automatization is so great that the morphological boundary is lost and the two words are written together as one). As Tsvetaeva judiciously notes, "maybe . . . may *not* be."

Her bold insertion of the negative particle into the architecture of this sentence—which encodes her consideration of death's place in the geometry of being—startlingly enacts the transition between life and death. What was intended as a mere connective, raising expectations of some continuing clause ("maybe . . .") becomes the sentence's grammatical termination and whole substance: the expected concrete nouns, verbs, and adjectives are replaced by the abstractions of conjunctions and particles that contemplate only themselves. The enjambement "ne / Byt′" draws attention to the shift of meanings instigated by the particle *ne* and furthers the process of linguistic estrangement by fragmenting even these surviving "nonsense words" into nonsemantic shards. In this single incomplete sentence, Tsvetaeva manages to recapitulate the entire subject/object dilemma of the woman poet—through the agency of pure grammar.

Besides such linguistic play, she also carries out her project of reconstituting language and the reality it describes by replacing the nouns and verbs of concrete experience with various technical instruments of her poetic craft— enjambements, paragraphs, stanzas, lines, rhymes, dashes. In other words, she not only uses these techniques themselves, and not only names them in the process, but incarnates them, thereby subsuming the apparent realia of chair, desk, book, forehead, hand, mouth. In so doing, she ventures far beyond the merely metapoetic to craft a fantastic alternative universe consisting entirely of the abstract, indefinite richness of verbal forms and signs that are often inscrutable. Here is the *poema*'s first such example:

Для невиданной той стены
Знаю имя: стена спины

За роялем. Еще — столом
Письменным, а еще — прибором
Бритвенным (у стены — прием —
Этой — делаться коридором

В зеркале. *Перенос* — взглянул.
Пустоты переносный стул).

[For that invisible wall I know a name: the wall of someone's back at a piano. And also — at a writing desk, and also — at the razor (this wall has a habit of turning into a corridor in the mirror. An *enjambement* — glanced. The portable/metaphorical/enjambed chair of emptiness).]

The room's fourth wall first metamorphoses into a piano player's erect back, then into the erect back of a poet (presumably) sitting at a desk, then into the erect back of someone shaving at a mirror, then — and by now the accumulation of instrumental completions to the original preposition *at* [za] is so extensive as to lose the grammatical flow altogether — into an endless regression of images in a double mirror, suggested by the differently reflective surfaces of all three preceding images (piano, desk, mirror).[57] The razor edge illustrates an attribute of Euclidean geometry — a horizontal line segment with a clear ending and beginning — which Tsvetaeva is intent upon obliterating. Through the action of poetry, this edge metamorphoses into a corridor: the same line, but now transformed into a poetic vector, endlessly self-extending.

The finality and finiteness of mortal life (symbolized by the razor) is thus transformed through the agency of poetic technique [priem] into an image of infinite spiritual striving. Yet the "enjambement" [perenos] that completes this progression is not merely an element of poetic technique, but is itself an actor. While the wall is transformed into a corridor by the agency of a reflexive verb (*to be turned into* [delat'sia]) and of the reflecting double mirrors (an image of the female poet's self-referential consciousness), the inanimate, abstract enjambement suddenly, shockingly glances — that is, apparently, it peeks out of the mirrors. As the jolting stanza break that introduces this unexpected development suggests, enjambement is the poet's exit from the mirrors' double trap: a stand-in for her necessary third, her muse, her true other, empty space, death. It is enjambement that singlehandedly transforms her vector from an entrapping horizontal into an elevating, liberating, energizing vertical — for this device, so unique to poetry, operates on a synchronic grid, counteracting language's usual diachronic horizontality.

Through this logic of imagistic and acoustic free association, concrete reality is thoroughly transformed into a mêlée of nightmarish abstractions by the conclusion of "Attempt at a Room" — a dense and difficult work that requires extensive commentary. For our purposes here, it is enough to remark that the elements of poetic technique in the *poema* turn out to be, paradoxically, both the intrusive barrier to a real-life meeting between Tsvetaeva and Rilke (they usurp the reality of the meeting place),[58] and, at the same time, the instrument of a different kind of intimacy between the two poets. As Tsvetaeva expresses this paradox: "Between us there is still a whole paragraph . . . And so you are poised ten stanzas, ten lines away" [Mezhdu nami eshche abzats / Tselyi . . . Tak i ty cherez desiat' strof, / Strok]. These paragraphs, stanzas, and lines do separate the two poets; but they also point to the fluidity of time — they destroy time by collapsing it, bridging endless expectation with poetic fulfillment that sublimates the emotional fulfillment of the desired meeting. This overcoming of temporality is related to the destruction of linguistic automatism in the *poema*, as the image of the Chinese water torture makes clear. The maddening, meaningless drone of the dripping sound replicates the effects of automated language: "Do you recall, an old torture, one drop per hour?" [Pomnish', staraia kazn'—po kaple / V chas?]. Poetic inspiration is dependent upon achievement of an extratemporal state that is synonymous with death. Hence, the terror of death that had threatened to separate Tsvetaeva from Rilke forever may, after all, be the only route to their true meeting, if she can summon the courage to follow, in her poetic journey, the trajectory that he is about to trace in reality.[59]

Writing from a Star: "New Year's Letter"

In one of her first letters to Rilke, Tsvetaeva writes: "A topography of the soul — that is what you are";[60] in her last letter, she writes: "I rejoice *hugely* in you, as if you are a whole, *wholly* new realm." [61] These metaphors of Rilke as a space for spiritual exploration lay the foundation for Tsvetaeva's conception in her *poema* "New Year's Letter," where she interprets Rilke's passing as a personal invitation to her to join him in his forays — now, no longer merely metaphorical — into the beyond. The result is that her habitual dissociation from life is replaced by an intimate acquaintance with the celestial heights; the intangible and the otherworldly take on a palpable philosophical and physical, almost mundane, reality that a younger Tsvetaeva, engaged long ago in awed contemplation of the ethereal Blok, could hardly have imagined.

This grieving, ecstatic *poema* is really a posthumous poetic "letter" to Rilke whose design and themes extend those of the poets' actual correspondence. The work bears the date of the fortieth day after Rilke's death — the day on which, according to Orthodox belief, the soul of the deceased departs from this world; Tsvetaeva resourcefully catches a ride with Rilke as he flies into the beyond. Much excellent critical work has already been done on "New Year's Letter," most famously by Joseph Brodsky and, more recently, by Olga Peters Hasty.[62]

Although I have benefitted enormously from both these discussions of Tsvetaeva's *poema,* my own analysis of the work is in a somewhat different vein. I show that Tsvetaeva's adoption of the dead Rilke as her new muse in "New Year's Letter" remedies the intense feelings of dissociation and isolation that emerged from her relationship with Pasternak, replacing these with a newfound faith in the possibility of a true communion of souls. This triumphant reunification of life and death, being and nonbeing, at the same time deepens Tsvetaeva's rift with reality even further. This paradoxical outcome is suggested by the fact that the reintegrated state of all-encompassing wholeness that Tsvetaeva achieves through her poetic "participation" in Rilke's death exists entirely on the metaphysical plane. In a sense, then, the myth of poetic genius developed in "New Year's Letter" returns Tsvetaeva to the pure imaginariness of "On a Red Steed"—with the difference that here, the violence of her relationship with her horseman/muse is replaced by intimate mutuality. Hence, she no longer expectantly waits, but pursues her inspiration—her love, her death—recklessly, wholeheartedly, and at her own whim, confident that Rilke, too, is straining from the brink of the other world back toward her.[63]

It is precisely Tsvetaeva's certainty that Rilke yearns for her as much as she for him that gives rise to this *poema* in the first place. As we have seen, Rilke's silence in the months before his death, despite Tsvetaeva's intuition about his condition, caused her to doubt his continuing regard and love for her. Rilke's death transforms his retreat into a renewed approach, a summons. Suddenly Tsvetaeva is convinced that he stopped writing to her precisely because the desire to write was too strong for him in his fragile state and distracted him from concentrating on his approaching initiation into the next world. Such an act of painful renunciation is intimately familiar to Tsvetaeva, with her similar renunciatory bent; "New Year's Letter" is her improbable expression of joy at the unbreakable emotional and creative bond between herself and Rilke that she imagines his death to have revealed. The result of this revelation is Tsvetaeva's unaccustomed feeling of inner peace, of undivided happiness. Thus, the sign of her poetic genius in "New Year's Letter" is no longer the immensity of pain and grief, as she derives it in "Wires," but the rivaling immensity of her capacity for joy in the unlikeliest context.

In Tsvetaeva's previous attempts to grapple with the significance of death for her poetics, she has imagined herself speaking posthumously to the living and, in this way, she has utilized death as a thematic bridge to a discussion of her own poetic legacy.[64] In "New Year's Letter," the scenario is reversed. It is not Tsvetaeva who is dead, but Rilke—who is, posthumously, not only her ideal and most beloved poet, but also her ideal reader, for now his unpracticed Russian is no longer an obstacle to comprehension. Moreover, "death" itself does not exist in "New Year's Letter" as a separate entity at all, for Rilke, in dying, has outdone death and so has fused with it completely. As Tsvetaeva writes to

Pasternak, "For you his death is outside the natural order of things, while for me his life is outside the natural order, of a different order, it is itself a different order" (6:271); or, as she puts it in "New Year's Letter": "If you, such an eye, have darkened, it means that life is not life, death is not death. It means—a darkening, I'll finish understanding when we meet!—there is no life, no death—but a third, new thing" [Esli ty, takoe oko smerklos', / Znachit zhizn' ne zhizn' est', smert' ne smert' est'. / Znachit—tmitsia, dopoimu pri vstreche!—/ Net ni zhizni, net ni smerti,—tret'e, / Novoe].

Saying "life is not life, death is not death" is very different from saying "life wants not to live . . . death wants not to die," as Tsvetaeva had done previously, during the period of *After Russia* (in her 1923 poem "The Pedal" ["Pedal'"] [2:190–91]). In her earlier statement, the antagonism between the two existential states is maintained and even deepened; they contaminate one another and, in so doing, deepen their mutual enmity. The earlier statement, therefore, reflects the profound psychological division that emanates from the clash of Tsvetaeva's gender and poetic aspirations. On the contrary, the composite "third, new thing"—the "other order" to which Rilke's improbable death and more improbable life both belong—destroys all existential boundaries between being and nonbeing and all related psychological conflicts. This "third thing" is no less than the metaphysical home of poets toward which Tsvetaeva has been striving all her life and from which Rilke now gazes down upon her, beckoning and gesturing. This transcendent state is enacted and exists through poetry: "By the way, you *are*—so verse *is:* since you yourself are—verse!" [Vprochem *est'* ty—*est'* stikh: sam i est' ty—/ Stikh!]. She purposely leaves out the connectives in this sentence, thereby enabling the arrows of logic to travel in both directions, mimicking Tsvetaeva's and Rilke's striving toward one another through their mutual striving toward Poetry. He exists *because* his poetry exists; he exists—*therefore* his poetry continues. Premise and conclusion are interchangeable; Tsvetaeva has gone far beyond Psyche's need for pure faith, which is essentially unidirectional ("I believe; therefore . . ."), and her own correspondent poetic identification with the unswerving trajectory of Eros's arrow. She is no longer willing to wait for immortality in order to be united with her beloved; the force of her poetic genius means that, even in life, she can transcend all delimiting physical and existential categories.

Tsvetaeva in "New Year's Letter" does not only exit the boundaries of life, but obliterates them entirely. In this transgression of transgression, her geometry of genius is transformed from a vector into something resembling a sine curve with gradually increasing amplitude or a growing spiral: a circle continually opening outward. Her preposterous union with the dead Rilke removes her entirely from any reference to the world of the living, and from any need to struggle further against her own split identity. Life is no longer fuel for her poetics in this *poema;* she does not blast off from anywhere, but soars in a continual, exhilaratingly fast-paced orbit between outer space and earth, Rilke and herself, herself and herself, Rilke and himself, all of which are simply aspects of a whole. The divisions between body and soul that once structured her metaphysical thinking are now seen to be false; whereas what is truly remedied by death is far broader, and thus far more vague and inexpressible, as she explains: "Not a poet with dust, soul with body (to separate them is to offend both), but you with yourself, you with your own self... you-Castor with you-Pollux, you-marble with you-grass" [Ne poeta s prakhom, dukha s telom, / (Obosobit'—oskorbit' oboikh) / A tebia s toboi, tebia s toboiu zh / ... Kastora—tebia s toboi—Polluksom, / Mramora—tebia s toboiu, travkoi]. Tsvetaeva is liberated and thus no longer experiences the need to choose: marble and grass, the infinite and the ephemeral, the inanimate and the organic, art and nature... all are encompassed within the wholeness of Rilke's death.

Joseph Brodsky's comments on the contrast between the *poema*'s infinitely high emotional pitch and shockingly common, concrete diction—leading into numerous "take-offs from the gutters into the empyrean" [65] (and back again!)—reflects his similar sense of this work as a celebration of metaphysical integrity:

The purity (as well as the frequency, for that matter) of this voice's vibration was akin to an echo-signal which is sent into mathematical infinity and finds no reverberation, or, if it does, immediately rejects it . . . [But] Tsvetaeva was a poet very much of this world, concrete, surpassing the Acmeists in precision of detail, and in aphoristicness and sarcasm surpassing everybody. More like that of a bird than an angel, her voice always knew above *what* it was elevated, knew what was there, down below (or, more precisely, what—there below—was lacking).[66]

More like a bird than an angel: this is an apt way of characterizing the change in Tsvetaeva's poetic persona in "New Year's Letter." No longer divided between suffering soul and tattered wings,[67] she is transformed through her union with Rilke into an extraterrestrial creature whose peregrinations between earth and heaven, however, are not a supernatural occurrence, but a natural mechanism that can be frankly parsed into linguistic, poetic, and even basic physical components (this is in contrast to Psyche's ultimate ascent to Olympus, which is made possible only through Zeus's miraculous intercession with Aphrodite). Just as the concreteness of poetic technique in "Attempt at a Room" replaces the abstractness of an unrealizable meeting between poets/lovers, so too the complex design of "New Year's Letter" exhibits the integrative curvaceousness of Tsvetaeva's new poetics on every level.

The *poema* begins with a temporal circle that opens outward: "Happy new year—world/light—edge/country—shelter!" [S Novym godom—svetom—kraem—krovom!].[68] Here, the cycle of the new year coincides with the cycle of Rilke's new, posthumous existence; in this way, Tsvetaeva corrects what, in a letter to Pasternak, she calls "life's last stroke of petty vindictiveness against the poet" (6:266)—namely, the fact that Rilke's actual death occurred not on New Year's Eve, as would have been symbolically fitting, but two days earlier.[69] The temporal circle quickly modulates—through the agency of sound, as is usual for Tsvetaeva—into a series of much broader circles: the circle of a new world [svet], then the circle of that new world's farthest horizon [krai]. Surprisingly, the outer circle of the greeting [S novym krovom!] is, at the same time, the most intimate, referring as it does to the shelter Rilke finds from the otherworldly equivalent of earthly needs and wants. This oscillation of Tsvetaeva's attention between radically different perspectives—the lightning speed at which the circles of her speech expand and narrow—is typical of "New Year's Letter" as a whole and intimates a metaphysical freedom new to her poetry, a freedom made possible by her overcoming of the strictures of subjectivity through her vicarious experience of Rilke's passing. The logic of this freedom is tangled and multidirectional, for it not only enables her composition of the *poema* but emanates from the very act of composition. Similarly, Tsvetaeva's new poetics is not simply the result of her faith in Rilke's continued being but simultaneously allows her to derive the continuity of his existence out of the abysmal nothingness he has left behind. The sound patterns of the poem's opening line illustrate the complexity of these conditions: the ever-widening circles of the poet's New Year's greetings to her dead friend culminate unexpectedly in "krov" [shelter]—because the *o* of *god* [year], the *v* of *svet* [world/light], and the *kr* of *krai* [edge/country] demand it. The acoustic necessity of shelter at the same time demonstrates its inexplicable metaphysical necessity, even in the other world. If Rilke still needs shelter, that means that the next life is not so much different from this one—just one step higher.

The logic of poetry reveals the logic of essence; Tsvetaeva's shift from vector to circle triggers the unfolding of a complex metaphysics that challenges all the human preconceptions she has hitherto grudgingly accepted. Once again humble as a schoolchild discovering an exotic new geography, she unlearns all the specious information that she once digested by rote: "How many times at a school desk was I asked: What mountains are there? Which rivers?" [Skol′ko raz na shkol′nom taburete: / Chto za gory tam? Kakie reki?]. Now, captivated by the poetic rhythms of the circle, Tsvetaeva listens as the ultimate heaven of Christianity expands into a blasphemous "terraced afterlife" with an infinity of layers, while God himself loses his singularity and branches like a great tree:

    Не ошиблась, Райнер—рай—гористый,
    Грозовой? Не притязаний вдовьих—
    Не один ведь рай, над ним другой ведь
    Рай? Террасами? Сужу по Татрам—
    Рай не может не амфитеатром

Быть? (А занавес над кем-то спущен...
Не ошиблась, Райнер, Бог—*растущий*
Баобаб? Не Золотой Людовик—
Не один ведь Бог? Над ним другой ведь
Бог?

[I was not mistaken, Rainer—paradise—is mountainous, thunderous? Not the paradise of old widows' claims—there is not, after all, just one paradise, for above it there is another paradise? In terraces? I'm judging by the Tatra Mountains—paradise cannot be other than an amphitheater? (And the curtain is lowered on someone...) I was not mistaken, Rainer, God—is a *growing* baobab? Not a Louis d'Or—God is not, after all, alone? For above him there is another God?]

The metaphor of God as a "*growing* baobab" (the dynamism of the image is heightened by the italics) is at the same time a metaphor for "New Year's Letter" itself.

For the *poema,* like the endlessly branching baobab, has the structure of a fractal.[70] However unrelated they may seem, each of the poem's semantic nodes is structured by the same principles as every other and, although each mounting level of meaning may not be visible or predictable from a particular vantage point in the dense foliage, all spring from the same inner core of truth. On whatever scale we observe the *poema,* the interrelationships between its compositional elements are identical—whether we focus on the circles of individual leaves (sounds) that crown a group of stems (words), or the circles of accumulated growth (metaphors, images) that adorn a whole gathering of branches (stanzas). Guided by an architectural, topographical, or geometrical principle that determines the basic configurations and growth patterns of constituent elements, the *poema* is at the same time an unpredictable tangle of themes, implications, and digressions whose cause and effect cannot be separated any more than can life and death. This structure resolves the troubling matter of how agency operates within female poetic inspiration in a strikingly new way. In "On a Red Steed" Tsvetaeva's solution was to suspend the question, melding agency and passivity in the metaphor of a desired, sensual, but desexualizing interpenetration; in "Wires," on the contrary, her persona took all agency upon herself, so that even her inspiration was an autonomous act of will and a statement of ultimate isolation. In "New Year's Letter," for the first time, the problem of agency is dissolved entirely in the endlessly developing, cycling and recycling confluence of elements of the interrelated All. Tsvetaeva's rapturous attainment of this state of wholeness that surpasses the logic of cause and effect, self and other, loss and gain, is her new version of what poetic inspiration means.

It is not only Rilke's death that teaches Tsvetaeva the lesson of forbearance and joy (in spite of all) upon which she draws in "New Year's Letter," but Rilke's beloved poetry as well. In particular, the huge influence of his beautiful, wistful "Elegie an Marina Zwetajewa-Efron" on "New Year's Letter" can be intensely felt. Rilke sent his "Elegie" to Tsvetaeva with his letter of 8 June, the first letter he wrote to her after the May hiatus in their correspondence. The poem was his answer to her silence, from which he had clearly suffered (he writes of it in the opening of his letter as a "huge shadow" [71]), even though he seems to intuit the cause of her reticence (namely, her realization of his impending death). In his "Elegie," Rilke responds to all these variegated sadnesses with a broad meditation on human loss and grief that is, at the same time, a kind of message in a bottle that will console Tsvetaeva after he is gone. An essential aspect of Rilke's poetics, especially in later years, was his belief in the integrity of different aspects of being, the interconnection of worlds and souls, and the remediability — particularly through the poetic medium — of all the sorrows and pains of existence.[72] The first line of his "Elegie" summarizes this whole philosophy as Tsvetaeva absorbed it: "Oh the losses into the All, Marina, the stars that are falling!" [O die Verluste ins All, Marina, die stürzenden Sterne!].[73] Stars only seem, from our limited earthly vantage, to be falling, as souls only seem to be dying. There is a totality of the cosmos and of being that is inaccessible to us in life, Rilke suggests, but that we can intuit through poetry if we have the genius and the fortitude. Thus, he tells Tsvetaeva in his elegy, do not grieve when you seem to lose me... I will be there still, a part of the All.[74]

The elegy goes on to speak of the cyclicity of being by means of various different, loosely related metaphors: "Waves, Marina, we are sea! Depths, Marina, we are heaven. Earth, Marina, we are earth, we are a thousand springtimes, we are larks flung into invisible heights by a song bursting out" [Wellen, Marina, wir Meer! Tiefen, Marina, wir Himmel. / Erde, Marina, wir Erde, wir tausendmal Frühling, wir Lerchen / die ein ausbrechendes Lied in die Unsichtbarkeit wirft]. Rilke's welling waves are quite similar to the undulating curve of Tsvetaeva's poetic inspiration that links life and afterlife in "New Year's Letter." Poetry reverses agency; poets, like larks, fling their song into the heights, even as their *song* propels *them* bodily upward. The depths and the heavens, life and death are joined in an unbreakable circle. It is fascinating to note that Rilke here employs Russian syntax, omitting the present-tense linking verbs that are obligatory in German (in place of "wir *sind* Meer," he writes "wir Meer," and so on). In this way, he transcends the limitations of German even when ostensibly writing *in* German to achieve a kind of Russo-German metalanguage where he and Tsvetaeva can meet.

Later in his "Elegy," Rilke meditates on reincarnation, calling life the "prelife" that precedes rebirth into a higher essence, and claiming that lovers are immune to death. Therefore, he implores Tsvetaeva to praise even the gods of the depths, the gods of death and darkness, with joy and gladness; for even death is part of the whole of existence and hence a reason for celebration. The source of Tsvetaeva's painful depth of feeling, he senses, is her proximity to eternity: "Oh how I understand you, female flower on an eternal stalk" [O wie begreif ich dich, weibliche Blüte am gleichen / unvergänglichen Strauch]. This play on Tsvetaeva's surname (the Russian word *tsvet* means "flower") complements the aquatic play on her first name at the beginning of the poem (*Marina/Meer*). Rilke's understanding of this "flower" that is Tsvetaeva is penetrating: ephemeral and eternal beauty, the feminine and the divine, the fragility of life and the attractiveness of death are all painfully united in a single being.[75]

Rilke's elegy to Tsvetaeva ends with a trenchant meditation on the nature of poets' sexual and romantic desire:

> . . . Frühe erlernten die Götter
> Hälften zu heucheln. Wir in das Kreisen bezogen
> füllten zum Ganzen uns an wie die Scheibe des Monds.
> Auch in abnehmender Frist, auch in den Wochen der Wendung
> niemand verhülfe uns je wieder zum Vollsein, als der
> einsame eigene Gang über der schlaflosen Landschaft.
>
> [The gods long ago learned to counterfeit halves. We, drawn into the cycle, filled ourselves out to the whole, like the disk of the moon. Even in the time of waning, in the weeks of our gradual change, no one could ever again help us to fulfillment, but our own solitary course over the sleepless landscape.]

The "counterfeit halves" of which Rilke speaks are evidently the two genders, which falsely divide the human spirit, leading each half to yearn for the physical union with its opposite that seems to promise wholeness—the wholeness of the full moon. Yet the moon's waxing and waning is, after all, but an optical illusion caused by humanity's limited earthly vantage point; similarly, Rilke suggests, the desire for sexual union with another is but a distraction from the deeper quest for true wholeness in which the poet is engaged. Like the moon, each human is whole within him- or herself; the poet's quest consists in attainment of the psychological, philosophical, and linguistic capacity to experience and express this wholeness. The key to realizing these goals lies not in sexual union with another, but, on the contrary, in traveling a solitary path above the earth's encumbering surface—that is, in traveling the moon's solitary orbit. Thus, Rilke contrasts the false cycles of the moon's phases to the true cycles of the moon's orbit; the former are a product of earthly subjectivity, the latter an objective reality. The true roundness of spiritual wholeness must be achieved not through companionship with another human, but through isolated communion with the empty, echoing spaces of the universe.

This passage is remarkable for its consonance with Tsvetaeva's own beliefs about the role that sexuality plays in the poet's metaphysical striving for unity of being. I cannot understand how it is possible to read Rilke's tone as didactic or condescending here; on the contrary, he is expressing his own painful inner struggle that has arisen in response to Tsvetaeva's intimate presence in his thoughts, belying the geographical distance between them: "How wildly I scatter myself into the night air that in a moment will touch you" [Wie streu ich mich stark in die Nachtluft, / die dich nächstens bestreift]. Rilke senses that Tsvetaeva shares and sympathizes with his emotions. Tsvetaeva, in turn, could not have taken Rilke's lines as a remonstration; on the contrary, she must have gasped in wonderment and recognition. Just recently she had been charting out her own independent path with respect to Pasternak, and, for all her ambivalent feelings about Rilke's need for solitude, she had admitted to Pasternak during the short interlude in her correspondence with the German poet: "In my own best, highest, strongest, most disinterested moments, I myself am the same way" (6:250). For Rilke as for Tsvetaeva, then, the attraction to the opposite sex is merely the deceptive, earthly form of the poet's gravitation toward fundamental metaphysical unity that he or she must, ultimately, attain through the isolated pursuit of a unique poetic path.[76]

For the still earthbound Tsvetaeva, Rilke's image of the moon's cycles, waxing and waning in accordance with the tides of poetic inspiration, is a perfect illustration of the temporal, psychological, and existential roundness that she, moved and guided by his example in poetry as in death, attains in the composition of "New Year's Letter." [77] Tsvetaeva's *poema,* in fact, begins loosely where Rilke's elegy ends—with her calm resignation to the necessary cycles of human intimacy: "The law of departure and abandonment, by which a beloved becomes just anyone, and an incomparable woman is rendered nonexistent" [Zakon otkhoda i otboia, / Po kotoromu liubimaia liuboiu / I nebyvsheiu iz nebyvaloi]. Rilke's death, Tsvetaeva recognizes, is part of the natural order of things, a kind of optical illusion like the moon's phases that nevertheless promises an eventual cyclical return (at the time of her own death, perhaps). In this sense, Rilke's death serves as the ultimate distancing technique through which he—and, in turn, she too—achieves a new, broader poetic perspective. Perversely, then, Tsvetaeva's loss of Rilke becomes a reason for faith and hope.

"New Year's Letter" illustrates the unifying action of Tsvetaeva's new poetic myth in every facet of its structure—like the baobab, it can be contemplated at any distance, minutely or broadly, and the same patterns will nevertheless emerge. Grammar is a key vehicle in the *poema* for conveyance of these patterns. Tsvetaeva's manipulation of expected grammatical logic deautomatizes both language and the thought processes it encodes, in order to express the paradoxical totality that is the legacy of Rilke's death. This procedure recalls similar techniques we have already seen at work in "Attempt at a Room." Here, though, the abstractions of poetic technique that replace real objects and events are not a diminution of possibility as in the earlier *poema,* but encompass instead the infinity of posthumous existence—unutterable in normal human language, and expressible only through the action of paradox.

One example of such grammatical paradox is the mixing of tenses in the oxymoronic "birthday" greeting "he was born tomorrow" [rozhdalsia zavtra]. This formula captures succinctly the idea that Rilke's death is a new beginning (as the end of the old year is the beginning of the next); such temporal recycling is already familiar to us from Tsvetaeva's letters to Rilke ("The past is still ahead"), and the technique is evident throughout "New Year's Letter." Thus, for instance, now that Rilke's death has closed linear time into a circle, the verbs *to begin* and *to end* become synonymous, enabling Tsvetaeva to write of her joy at his passing: "What happiness to end with you, to begin with you!" [Kakoe schast'e / Toboi konchit'sia, toboi nachat'sia!].[78] The miraculous, continued existence of Rilke's soul, now completely liberated from all physical constraints, is likewise conveyed by a play of grammatical paradox: "There is no place where you are not—no, there is: the grave" [mesta / Nest', gde net tebia, net est': mogila]. Here the archaic Russian word *nest'* [there is not] is "unpacked" to reveal that it contains its own refutation: *net, est'* [no, there is]. Rilke's soul is no longer a prisoner in his body; therefore, its absence is transformed into omnipresence. There is yet another level of linguistic play in this assertion, because the archaic Russian *nest'* sounds remarkably like the German *Nest*—a word which was key in Rilke's last letter to Tsvetaeva and which has just appeared in "New Year's Letter" as well: "You don't ask anymore what is *Nest* in Russian?" [Uzh ne sprashivaesh', kak po-russki / *Nest?*].[79] But whereas Tsvetaeva still remains in the earthly realm "of nests and branches" [iz gnezd i vetok], nests, homes, finite and tiny domestic spaces are precisely those places where Rilke is not. As her brilliant rhyming demonstrates, Rilke has given up earthly nests and graves alike, along with the limitations of earthly tongues, to take on the universal proportions and incorporeality of the stars: "The only rhyme, and one that covers all nests: stars" [Edinstvennaia, i vse gnezda / Pokryvaiushchaia rifma: zvezdy].

The undulating wholeness of vision given to Tsvetaeva by Rilke's death is conveyed in "New Year's Letter" not only via grammatical paradoxes, but also through the poem's complex rhetorical structure, which circles repeatedly through successive digressions, always, however, returning to the poem's central concerns. In this way, numerous themes, images, extended metaphors, and grammatical motifs—many of which originate in Tsvetaeva's real correspondence with Rilke—are interwoven in "New Year's Letter" into a complex, infinitely rich web of shimmering meanings that from a certain mental distance might seem inscrutable. Thus, although Hasty convincingly discerns a version of logical, linear development in the *poema*,[80] at the same time the work itself resists such a reading, constantly circling back upon itself in ever more intricate patterns.

Indeed, the *poema* as a whole is, essentially, one gigantic digression away from its core idea, *death* — a word that Tsvetaeva at first refuses to utter at all ("Should I tell, how I learned of yours?" [Rasskazat', kak pro tvoiu uznala?]) and later pronounces only in the distancing context of quotation marks, an asterisk, and a smirk. Yet this typographical *asterisk* [zvezdochka] is, magically, the stellar sign of Rilke's new home, "one of the stars" [odna iz zvezd].[81] Hence, Rilke mirrors Tsvetaeva's skepticism with an intimate, answering sign, as she explains: "Life and death I pronounce with a hidden smirk — you'll touch it with your own!" [Zhizn' i smert' proiznoshu s usmeshkoi / Skrytoiu — svoei ee kosnesh'sia!]. Oddly, the more she estranges herself from death, the closer she comes to it. For, what replaces death in the course of the *poema* is the dead Rilke himself — the source and goal of all Tsvetaeva's digressive ruminations: "Am I digressing? But there is no such thing as digressing — from you. Every thought, any, *Du Lieber* [my beloved], syllable leads into you — whatever the gist might be" [Otvlekaius'? No takoi i veshchi / Ne naidetsia — ot tebia otvlech'sia. / Kazhdyi pomysel, liuboi, *Du Lieber,* / Slog v tebia vedet — o chem by ni byl / Tolk]. What seems to be a circling around and away from is actually a circling toward, into, and within. The negative of Rilke's death negates itself, for he now exists always and everywhere.[82]

The acoustical genius of the rhyme *Du Lieber/by ni byl* is only a fraction of its brilliance; semantically, this rhyme encapsulates the message of the *poema* as a whole. In rhyming the German endearment *Du Lieber* with the untranslatable Russian idiom *whatever might be* [o chem by ni byl], Tsvetaeva — recalling Rilke's use of Russian syntax in his German "Elegy" — creates an extralinguistic bridge that is neither one language nor the other anymore, but a kind of metalanguage of the human soul. Rilke's death obliterates the linguistic differences that divided the two poets during his lifetime. Having mastered all earthly languages, he now proceeds to sing in "Angelic," which Tsvetaeva asserts is her own "most native" language too: "Even if German is more native than Russian, for me Angelic is the most native of all!" [Pust' russkogo rodnei nemetskii / Mne vsekh angel'skii rodnei!].[83] Tsvetaeva's cross-linguistic rhyming mimics Angelic — since the next world is "not a- but omni-lingual" [ne bez- a vse-iazychen] — and anticipates her own attainment of an angelic state of being. At the same time, the Russian idiom *o chem by ni byl* aptly conveys the complex metaphysical condition of the dead beloved [Du Lieber] with which it rhymes, since this idiom's all-inclusive, future-oriented meaning emerges from the unlikely union of a conditional particle [by], a negative particle [ni], and a past-tense verb [byl]. Tsvetaeva thus, through the evidence of rhyme, proves that a similar union of negation (Rilke's death), conditionality (her own hope and belief), and past tense (Rilke's life and poetry) ensures not only the illogical continuity of Rilke's existence, but his omnipresence and continued belovedness on her own spiritual horizon. Like the dangling enjambement that replaces the imaginary room of "Attempt at a Room," the connective cable of rhyme-writ-large here erases the distance between the living poet and the dead one, between the possible and the impossible.

The affinity Tsvetaeva senses between her and Rilke's respective homelands —her own fantastical Russia and Rilke's afterworld—is also a kind of rhyme: "We have a blood tie with the next world: whoever has been in Russia—has seen the next world in this one" [Sviaz′ krovnaia u nas s tem svetom: / Na Rusi byval—tot svet na etom / Zrel]. In fact, the blood tie that binds Tsvetaeva to Rilke can be seen as an image of rhyme itself, all the more so since blood is a metaphor for poetry in her work generally.[84] Besides these figurative and symbolic meanings of the word *blood* in this passage, there is also a purely physical meaning that links Tsvetaeva's experience of the violence of Revolution with Rilke's suffering prior to his death.[85] Rilke died of leukemia; in Tsvetaeva's interpretation in her essay "Your Death" ["Tvoia smert′"] (5:186–205), this disease is the image of his self-sacrificing poetic enterprise: "I know that the illness that killed you is treated by blood transfusions [perelivaniem krovi], i.e. someone close to you, wanting to save you, gives up his own blood. Your illness—began with the transfusion of blood—yours—into all of us. It was the world that was ill, the someone close to it—was you. What can ever save the one who gives away/lets overflow his own blood [Chto kogda spaset perelivshego]!" (5:204).

The idea that each person has a death as unique and as meaningful as his life is one of Rilke's own most cherished beliefs; furthermore, Rilke often expresses this belief through the metaphor of a ripening seed.[86] It is therefore fitting that, in Tsvetaeva's lines about Russia's otherworldliness just cited, the verb *zrel* is ambiguous, for the infinitive *zret′* means both *to ripen* and *to behold;* the verb's subject is *svet* [the world] in the first case and the implicit *kto* [whoever] in the second. Thus, the sentence *Tot svet na etom / Zrel* refers both to a prophetic vision of the next world in this one, and to the ripening of the next world in this one. This may well be a masked reference to Rilke's belief that these two meanings are, in fact, inseparable—a belief that Tsvetaeva apparently shares.

An entire analysis of "New Year's Letter" could be written simply on the basis of its rhymes. Capturing as it does the essence of Tsvetaeva's metaphysical task of reunification in this *poema*, rhyme is not only a metaphor for her relationship to the dead Rilke, but also a code for the identity that she has discovered between the poetic enterprise and a poet's death. As she writes near the *poema*'s conclusion: "Rainer, do you rejoice in the new rhymes? Since understanding the word *rhyme* correctly, what else is death—except—a whole sequence of new rhymes?" [Rainer, raduesh′sia novym rifmam? / Ibo pravil′no tolkuia slovo / *Rifma*—chto—kak ne—tselyi riad novykh / Rifm—Smert′?]. As Tsvetaeva reinterprets Rilke's death in "New Year's Letter," she simultaneously reassesses the efficacy of the instruments of poetry, foremost among which is rhyme. Death comes, in this new understanding, when all the possibilities of earthly poetic

The Dark Lure of Mra

language are exhausted: "Nowhere left to go: language is mastered" [Nekuda: iazyk izuchen]. The answer death makes to life's "masteredness" [izuchennost'] is a new permeating, multiplicitous "resonance" or "echo" [zvuchnost'/sozvuchie] that replaces conventional, binary rhyme; it is this metaphysically liberating resonance that Tsvetaeva emulates in the sonorous sound patterns of "New Year's Letter."

By 1926, Tsvetaeva had begun to feel that she had reached the edge of lyric possibility in her own poetry too. The flow of her short lyrics dramatically slowed after her completion of *After Russia* in early 1925 and would never again resume with the same intensity. Indeed, she portrays her turn toward the genre of the *poema* as resulting from a longing for linguistic challenge similar to that which she ascribes to the dying Rilke: "I offer [my book *After Russia*] as my last lyrical collection; I know that it will be the last. Without sadness. That which one *can* do—should not be done. And that's all there is to it. In that venue I can do anything. Lyricism . . . has served as my faith and my truth, saving me, taking me away—and winding me up each time in its own way, in my own way" (6:272–73). Rilke's attainment, through his death, of a place where "nightingales" (i.e., poets) have never sung means for Tsvetaeva, too, a new creative beginning (in "New Year's Letter"), a complete reconceptualization of the poetic act, a virgin landscape of the imagination in which, for the first time in her life, she has discovered true companionship:

> Сколько мест . . . именно наших
> И ничьих других! Весь лист! Вся хвоя!
> . . . что—мест! А месяцов-то!
> А недель! А дождевых предместий
> Без людей! А утр! А всего вместе
> И не начатого соловьями!
>
> [How much space . . . just our own and no one else's! The whole foliage! The whole underbrush! . . . And what is space! And what about the months! And weeks! And rainy suburbs without people! And mornings! And everything together not even begun by nightingales!]

When Tsvetaeva composes "New Year's Letter," she participates vicariously in Rilke's metaphysical transfiguration and so is able, without actually dying herself, to achieve the liberation from the constraints of earthly language that she has begun to crave.

This liberation is achieved in "New Year's Letter" not only by means of grammatical oxymorons, cyclical rhetorical structure, and revelatory, regenerative rhymes but also by bold, trenchant metaphors that effortlessly bridge the abyss that lies between being and nonbeing like spectacular intergalactic lightning. Perhaps the most potent of these extended metaphors is Tsvetaeva's actualization of her long-awaited meeting and merging with her beloved Rilke in the image of two insubstantial glasses clinking together in a metaphysical New Year's toast:

> Через стол, необозримый оком,
> Буду чокаться с тобою тихим чоком
> Сткла о сткло? Нет—не кабацким ихним:
> Я о *ты*, слиясь дающих рифму:
> Третье.
>
> [Across a table, invisible to the eye, will I clink drinks with you with the quiet clink of glass on glass? No—not with their common bar clinking: *I* against *you*, merging to give a rhyme: a third thing.]

Tsvetaeva's imaginary toast with Rilke is realized through the clinking and clanking of her language in this passage, with its predominance of stops and affricates: *chokat'sia, chokom, stkla, stklo, kabatskim*. Her clanking language, in turn, realizes the resonant chiming and blending of the two pronouns *I* and *you*, marking the achievement of her rigorous poetic quest for genderlessness through love.[87] The key to untying the Gordian knot of her fate has turned out to be her realization that love is synonymous with death. Through this realization, all limitations, divisions, and physical parameters are dissolved; the nighttime circle of Tsvetaeva's creating, insomniac brain is at the same time the infinite sphere of Rilke's entire cosmos, for she embraces infinity in her thoughts: "Night, during which I intuit: instead of my brain's hemisphere—the hemisphere of stars!" [Noch', kotoroi chaiu: / Vmesto mozgovogo polushar'ia— / Zvezdnoe!]. This infinity of profoundly, mutually contained and containing curves that link individual consciousnesses is a welcome replacement for the endlessly linear regression of superficial images in the corridor of mirrors of "Attempt at a Room," where the blindly reflecting surfaces of self and other are completely separate. In "New Year's Letter," Tsvetaeva continues miraculously to exist in the expanse of Rilke's cosmos; while Rilke continues miraculously to exist in the expanse of Tsvetaeva's mind. Her ability to abstract herself from herself and catch glimpses of her faraway self from Rilke's perspective illustrates this spiritual merger, as does the casual, intimate, almost catty tone she uses in addressing the dead poet.[88]

The circles Tsvetaeva realizes in "New Year's Letter" allow her to heal the tormenting sense of incompleteness that has always burdened her poetics. Now it becomes clear that she, like all poets, in life is merely a "reflection" [otsvet] of her true self:

> Из всего *того* один лишь *свет* тот
> Наш был, как мы сами только отсвет
> Нас,—взамен всего сего—весь *тот* свет!

[Of all this world only that light was ours, as we ourselves were only the reflection of ourselves—so instead of all of this—(we'll possess) the whole *other* world!]

The incomparable grammatical, syntactic, and semantic difficulty of this passage illustrates its meaning: the essence of poetry cannot be embodied in human language any more than the poet can be embodied in human form. Tsvetaeva writes, as it were, not for a real audience, but for a virtual, hypothetical one: that is, for Rilke alone, and more specifically, for Rilke's omnilingual soul. Her union with the otherworldly Rilke is not, after all, a union with *an* other, but a union with *the* other—otherness: all the unrealized aspirations and possibilities—that lies within her own soul. Rilke is nothing and everything; he is death and the All, Tsvetaeva's true home, site of her totality, where her poetic intuition ("that light" [*svet* tot]) of the beyond ("the other world" [*tot* svet]) is at last vindicated.

Just as Tsvetaeva in life is just the "reflection" [otsvet] of the integral "light" [svet] that is the "other world" [tot svet],[89] so too, in the acoustical sphere, she is merely the echo to the fullness of original sound that is her otherworldly essence. Rilke himself has already attained this state of original sound, and she congratulates him on his achievement: "Happy new sound, Echo! Happy new Echo, sound!" [S novym zvukom, Ekho! / S novym Ekhom, zvuk!]. Two possible subtexts for these lines illuminate their significance. In Pushkin's poem "Echo" ["Ekho"], the state of isolation that necessarily results from the poet's gift is figured in the metaphor of poet as echo, capable of reproducing any beautiful sound in the world, but incapable of eliciting an answer: "To every sound you beget your answer immediately in the empty air . . . But nothing echoes you... Such are you, poet" [Na vsiakii zvuk / Svoi otklik v vozdukhe pustom / Rodish' ty vdrug . . . / Tebe zh net otzyva... Takov / I ty, poet!].[90] In the second subtext for Tsvetaeva's lines, the Greek myth of Echo and Narcissus, the self-absorbed Narcissus ignores the lovelorn nymph Echo, who pines away in a cave until there is nothing left of her but her voice. Only through Rilke's death are "Echo" and "sound"—lover and beloved, poet and self, self and other—reunited. Tsvetaeva's circular congratulations to Rilke on this occasion are evidence both of newly unhalved wholeness, and of utter self-referentiality. The two half-circles of the doubled preposition *with* [*s;* Cyrillic letter *c*] are closed into a totality. The source of inspiration, located inside the other, is at the same time seated deeply in the self; the circles not only intersect—they are concentric and overlapping.

The curve of the Cyrillic letter *c*—which could, in its own right, be taken both graphically and semantically (in its meaning of "with") as the illustration of Tsvetaeva's new incorporative and incorporeal poetic myth—is rampant in "New Year's Letter" and also participates in a significant way in the orchestration of the *poema*'s merger of selves and essences. For, the Russian preposition *c* embraces a whole concatenation of different meanings: *congratulations* (as in "Happy New Year!" [**S** Novym godom!]), *intrinsic unity* ("you with yourself, you with your own self" [tebia **s** toboi, tebia **s** toboiu zh]), *distance from* ("The first letter to you from yesterday's . . . homeland, which now for you means from one of the stars..." [Pervoe pis'mo tebe **s** vcherashnei . . . / Rodiny, teper' uzhe **s** odnoi iz / Zvezd...]), and *meeting* ("I will clink drinks with you" [Budu chokat'sia **s** toboiu]). The first three meanings of the preposition predominate in the first half of "New Year's Letter"; moreover, the first two (*congratulations; internal unity*), signifying wholeness, are used in reference only to Rilke, thus emphasizing his apparent distance from Tsvetaeva, a distance which the preposition's third meaning (*distance from*), used in reference to each of the poets in turn (and so establishing some degree of reciprocity), attempts to bridge and thus to shorten.

The turning point in the *poema* comes with its central, governing rhyme, located in its very heart and center, when Tsvetaeva cries in distress and exultation: "What should I do in the New Year's hum with this internal rhyme: Rainer—died" [Chto mne delat' v novogodnem shume / **S** etoi vnutrenneiu rifmoi: Rainer—umer]. This passage marks one of Tsvetaeva's first uses in the *poema* of the preposition *c* in its fourth meaning (*meeting*). When the passage occurs, Tsvetaeva has just admitted her utter loneliness in the face of Rilke's death, and as a result she has begun doubting the worth of her entire existence: "For what, with whom will I clink drinks across the table? With what? ... Why? Well, the clock strikes—but what's the point of my being here?" [Za chto, s kem choknus' / Cherez stol? Chem? . . . Zachem? Nu, b'et—a pri chem ia tut?]. Now, Tsvetaeva suddenly recognizes that she has a companion after all: not Rilke himself, but the brilliant slant-rhyme of his name and his death: "Rainer—umer." The "internality" [vnutrennost'] of this rhyme refers both to Rilke's own acoustic affiliation with death (*Rainer* seems to contain the shorter *umer;* moreover, the rhyme occurs internally to the poetic line) and to Tsvetaeva's own deep recognition of that affiliation—her internalization of the rhyme, as it were. This "internality" is, at the same time, an expression of the "third-thingness" or dichotomy-mending wholeness that rhyme generally makes possible in "New Year's Letter." Tsvetaeva enters into the inner truth of Rilke's name, even as she holds the name sacred inside herself; this interpenetration of essences erases any remnants of desire for delimiting, unidirectional sexual penetration and thus erases gender differences, and even the boundaries of the insular self, altogether. Only after Tsvetaeva's reinterpretation of the *Rainer/umer* rhyme as a liberating triumph is she able truly to meet and clink glasses with Rilke at last. The imagined chime of their shared toast across the abyss is, via the circular logic that drives the *poema,* also a metaphor for the transrational resonance of rhyme in this work as a whole.

The Dark Lure of Mra

The four different meanings of the preposition *c* are finally reconciled in the verbal pyrotechnics of the *poema*'s stunning climax. Here, *c* meaning *distance from*—a usage that predominates in the work's opening sections, thereby establishing a connection between Tsvetaeva and her departed addressee—is no longer necessary, whereas the other three meanings of the preposition (*congratulations, internal unity,* and *meeting*) now refer to Tsvetaeva as well as to Rilke, intimating the two poets' indissoluble togetherness and wholeness.[91] This triumph is prepared by the unexpected deautomatization of the expression "do svidan′ia" [goodbye/until we see each other], a shift that acts as a kind of fanfare to the finale still to come:

> —До свиданья! До знакомства!
> Свидимся—не знаю, но—споемся.
> С мне-самой неведомой землею—
> С целым морем, Райнер, с целой мною!
>
> [—Goodbye! Until we see each other! Until our meeting! We'll see each other?—don't know, but—we'll join in song. Happy land unknown to me-myself—happy whole sea, Rainer, happy whole me!]

"Do svidan′ia" is, indeed, not a final farewell, but a salutation redolent with unfaltering hope and belief, as the addition of "Until our meeting!" [Do znakomstva!] reveals. Tsvetaeva never does violence to language, nor does she willfully deform the existential categories and truths that the world has to offer. The action of her genius amounts instead to a poetic harnessing or derivation of essential truths that are already present outside, beyond, in spite of, without reference to herself. Thus, Tsvetaeva's certainty in the meeting that she and Rilke have dreamed about for so long derives from the very etymology of "good-bye." Her meeting with Rilke is fated through language, since, in Russian, there is no such thing as good-bye; there is only "until we meet."

No sooner has Tsvetaeva reiterated her skill at such metaphysical derivations than she carries the implications of Rilke's death to their ultimate extreme, riding high upon the vehicle of the curvaceous *c*. She begins tentatively: "We'll see each other?—don't know" [**S**vidimsia—ne znaiu]. Questions about when and how her meeting with Rilke will take place—questions that were the central, ongoing leitmotif of the two poets' earthly correspondence—are after all simply not a matter of concern. The one thing that matters is the two poets' inspirational union, of which Tsvetaeva is certain: "But—we'll join in song" [No—**s**poemsia]. Unlike her vague promise in a poem to Pasternak (from the cycle "Scythians" ["Skifskie"] [2:164–67]) "sometime, there—we'll meet/sing together!" [kogda-nibud′ tam—spishemsia!], this "we'll join in song" [spoemsia] exudes firm conviction, for the other world that loomed in the far distance as a mysterious unknown in Tsvetaeva's poems to Pasternak is transformed, through Rilke's death, into a familiar landscape.[92]

In the two stunning lines that follow, the meanings of the preposition *c* can no longer be separately parsed:

> С мне-самой неведомой землею —
> С целым морем, Райнер, с целой мною!
>
> [Happy land-unknown-to-me-myself — Happy whole sea, Rainer, happy whole me!]

The unknown afterworld that is Rilke's new home is now figured in the infinite roundness of the marine landscape, which, in turn, Tsvetaeva now accepts as the image of her new self: that "new Marina who can emerge only with you, in you," as she had once written to Rilke. In this metamorphosis, she overcomes her habitual dislike of the aquatic element — which previously has seemed to her tyrannical and threatening and which, in fact, she has associated with Rilke's illness and death — even as she overcomes her fear of death itself.[93] When she becomes like the sea [*more*], grammatically neutral in Russian, she completes her transcendence of human gender. In her joyful exclamation of wholeness, the three remaining meanings of the preposition *c* are inextricably melded: Tsvetaeva congratulates both Rilke and herself on their union with one another, which is at once cause and effect of the newly infinite internal unity and self-sufficiency both have attained through his death.

Just as Tsvetaeva's capacity to embrace the inhuman potentiality of the cosmos lies dormant within her soul until an intimacy with Death reveals her metaphysical strength, so too the genderless, ferocious sea [*more*] is inherent in the tame femininity of her earthly name [Marina]. Likewise, Rilke's genderless fullness after death is foreordained in his name, whose incorporation of all three Russian grammatical genders (Rainer — male; Maria — female; Rilke — neuter) Brodsky has already pointed out.[94] Rilke's full name, in fact, ends "New Year's Letter"; the *poema* thus completes not only Rilke's own destiny, but the circle of Tsvetaeva's love for him as well, for in her very first letter to him she had written a meditation on his name: "Your name willed it, and so you chose that name."[95] Rilke's name, like Tsvetaeva's, aspires toward genderless wholeness; moreover, the two poets' names are acoustically affiliated, as she had previously noted in her dedication to Rilke of her small collection *Poems to Blok* [*Stikhi k Bloku*, 1922]: "My name is an abbreviation of yours — haven't you noticed?"[96] Furthermore, Tsvetaeva and Rilke are linked, through the intertwined coincidence of metaphysical reality and her poetic fantasy in "New Year's Letter," with the sound and essence of Death. For, the primary consonants of the Russian word for "death," *smert'*, are, in fact, the three most important phonemes of the *poema:* the preposition *s* [with/from] (represented in this discussion by

The Dark Lure of Mra

Cyrillic *c*) and the consonants shared between Rilke's initials and Tsvetaeva's first name, *m* and *r*.

This phonetic derivation of the poet's ultimate homeland in death would become even more elaborate several years later in Tsvetaeva's 1932 essay "Art in the Light of Conscience" ["Iskusstvo pri svete sovesti"] (5:346–74):

> Темная сила!
> *Мра*-ремесло!
> Скольких сгубило,
> Как малых — спасло.
>
> [Dark force! *Mra*-craft! How many it has killed, how few it has saved.]

Here, the neologism *Mra-remeslo* (roughly, "death-craft") refers to Tsvetaeva's craft of poetry. Like R.M.R., Marina, *more* [sea] and *smert'* [death], both *Mra* [death] and *remeslo* [craft] share the deathly consonants *m* and *r*.[97] This passage thus corroborates her discovery in "New Year's Letter" that writing poems is akin to dying — a proclivity for which is encoded in the phonemes of the poet's own name from birth and before. She explains that the neologistic *Mra* is the female name of death: "*Mra*, by the way, I use as a female name, a feminine ending, the sound — of death. Mor. Mra. Death [*smert'*] could have been called, and maybe somewhere, sometime indeed was called — Mra" (5:363). This proffered explanation is puzzling, insofar as the Russian word *smert'* is, in fact, already of feminine gender. Evidently, Tsvetaeva feels the need to make certain that death — usually a phenomenon we think of as universal, superhuman, and thus genderless — becomes marked for gender: there is female death, Mra, and there is male death, Mor (this form suggests both *morit'* [to exterminate] and *Morpheus*, ancient Greek god of dreams and sleep).

It is peculiar that Tsvetaeva, whose entire poetic career has been motivated by a desire to escape the limitations of gender and who, in "New Year's Letter," has equated the attainment of death with such an escape, should later engage in this pointed regendering of death itself. Perhaps the solution to this mystery can be located in Tsvetaeva's recognition, once she has emerged from the emotional shock and creative exhilaration of Rilke's death, that there is, after all, a crucial distinction that must be made between the dead Rilke and herself: for she has voluntarily elected, in life, a figurative death to console herself for Rilke's excruciating physical death that he himself wanted to escape.

Indeed, even in her earliest poems (the lyric "A Prayer," for example), death is a figurative mode of being that Tsvetaeva consciously elects, in order to escape from the tangles of her predicament as a female poet. It is this kind of death, rather than the actual, physical phenomenon, which she names "Mracraft." Mra, then, is the disturbingly vicarious, theatrical death necessitated by the woman poet's quest for subjective voice—the attainment of which constitutes her genius.[98] Thus, for the woman poet of genius there are two different kinds of death to contend with: the death-muse that gives her voice, and the death-wish that both induces and arises from creative drought. Out of this deathly duality springs the ambiguity of her fate ("How many it has killed, how few it has saved") and of her unstated fears. That Tsvetaeva is afraid, for all her bravado, is undeniable (though understated), for she begins her explanation of *Mra* with a sentence fragment that she never goes back to complete: "I fear that even when I'm dying..." (5:363). Perhaps she hints here that she is afraid she has become all too adept at manipulating the poetic possibilities of the technique of Mra. Perhaps she, like an opera diva who has died on stage so many times that the exercise has come to seem a game, will be unable to believe in the harsh, physical reality of the other kind of death even on her deathbed. From the beginning, Tsvetaeva has sensed the danger of this metaphysical acrobatics in which she engages, without at first fully believing that the poetic cable she strings between two abysses will someday cease to hold her weight.

At the ecstatic conclusion of "New Year's Letter," however, such sober reevaluations of the implications of her precarious metaphysical stance are still far in the future. Executing her difficult balancing act with dancerly finesse, Tsvetaeva picks her tenuous phonetic path between the Rhone (where Rilke lived) and the Rarogne cliff (where he is buried), between Bellevue (where she lives) and Bellvedere (where Rilke died).[99] The gift she bears for her dead beloved, holding it up high so that her tears do not drench it,[100] is the *poema* itself and, most of all, the rejoined circle of its final rhyme:

> Поверх явной и сплошной разлуки
> Райнеру—Мария—Рильке—в руки.
>
> [Above the obvious and utter separation to Rainer—Maria—Rilke—into his hands.]

Unusually for Tsvetaeva's poetics, the agency of the poetic line here consists in mending a rift, rather than in rending a union. Moreover, the poem's culminating rhyme (*razluki/ruki* [separation/hands]) not only vanquishes the spiritual distance between Tsvetaeva and Rilke but also reunifies the very concepts of *abstraction* and *division* [razluka] with the apparently antithetical concepts of *physicality* and *conjoinment* [ruki].[101] It is a remarkable statement of Tsvetaeva's faith that this poem about death and the dissolution of body ends, miraculously, with its own metaphorical conveyance into Rilke's outstretched hands.

Celebrating Eternity: "Poem of the Air"

If Tsvetaeva derives her crowning poetic myth in the course of "New Year's Letter," then she celebrates it in the exhilarating flight of "Poem of the Air," her purest meditation on the theme of death as liberation. Released from her female predicament, wholly secure in her genius, at the height of her verbal powers, happy and fulfilled in her transcendent love for Rilke and her faith in his inspirational responsiveness,[102] alone yet beloved, apart yet together—this *poema* records a triumph of spiritual and poetic freedom that meets all of Tsvetaeva's most stringent criteria. Indeed, "Poem of the Air," as its title suggests, marks the acme of her poetic achievement and the emotional high point of her life.

This boisterous and difficult work chronicles Tsvetaeva's journey, in step with the ghostly Rilke, into the empyrean heights where he now makes his home. Her escort is in fact never named in the poem, but Rilke's shadowy presence is everywhere palpable, from the work's opening lines, when he stands silently, invitingly, behind her shut door.[103] "Poem of the Air" was composed in May 1927 and is Tsvetaeva's timeless poetic answer to the particular historical event of Charles Lindberg's flight across the Atlantic Ocean to Paris that spring. Humanity's mechanical achievement of flight remains on the distant periphery of the *poema*, however; instead, Tsvetaeva chronicles how, propelled by sound and rhythm, she soars up through seven atmospheric strata—or seven heavens—to the metaphysical height that corresponds to an afterlife.[104]

The shape of "Poem of the Air," like the shape of "New Year's Letter," is a traveling circle; Tsvetaeva's soul retains its essential identity as she ascends—as indicated by the poem's shifting rhythmic patterns and numerous interwoven refrains that repeat anew at each stage of her journey, combining in ever widening, yet ever returning circles of meaning.[105] The *poema*'s circularity is also indicated through the role that lyricism as such plays in Tsvetaeva's cosmogony. For, as she points out in an exuberant flood of specious syllogism, lyricism is not only the province of the seventh heaven (Rilke's new, and true, homeland), but the foundation of the earth as well: "Seven—layers and waves! Seven—*heilige Sieben! Seven* is the basis of the lyre, *seven* is the basis of the world. And since the basis of the lyre—is seven, the basis of the world—is lyricism" [Sem'—plasty i zybi! / Sem'—*heilige Sieben!* / *Sem'* v osnove liry, / *Sem'* v osnove mira. / Raz osnova liry—/ Sem', osnova mira—/ Lirika]. The conflusion in this passage of "layers" and "waves" [plasty i zybi], both of which Tsvetaeva associates with the talismanic number seven, illustrates lyricism's capacity to resolve the apparent structural contradiction in this *poema* between the circle (metaphysical totality) and the vector (flight into the beyond). For, the increasing elevation of each atmospheric layer is, at the same time, just the round crest of one more groundswell. The heights are connected to the depths, and the medium of the commonality of these extremes is, precisely, lyricism.[106]

In this poetic triumph, Tsvetaeva reflects back upon and, in a sense, "completes" a number of her earlier poetic works. Specifically, in "Poem of the Air," she finishes what she has already begun in "Attempt at a Room" and "New Year's Letter"—namely, a poetic solution to the jumbled violence of agency that beset her in "On a Red Steed." Like this earliest *poema,* "Poem of the Air" has a tripartite structure: an introduction, three main movements (each comprising two stages of the poet's flight into the beyond), and a conclusion (comprising the seventh and final stage). This similarity of structure points to the two poems' underlying conceptual similarity: both "On a Red Steed" and "Poem of the Air" are inspirational allegories, almost fablelike in their lucidity of vision and in their clean divorce from the muddled "nitty-gritty" of quotidian reality. Furthermore, in both works, the poet defies the laws (moral laws in the former *poema,* gravitational ones in the latter) that normally govern human existence. Tsvetaeva's perfect union with Rilke in "Poem of the Air" cures the wounds of the painful passion she once dreamed of in "On a Red Steed": not only are the boundaries of life and death, femininity and masculinity overcome, but both participants of the totality she envisions are equally poet and muse, creators and listeners — and both need each other equally. In "Poem of the Air," the horseman's piercing ray of light is curved into a healing circle.

At the same time, "Poem of the Air" may be read as a kind of jubilant coda to Tsvetaeva's more recent *poemy,* both addressed to Rilke, "Attempt at a Room" and "New Year's Letter"; these three works taken together are like a musical composition in three movements, of which the last continually recapitulates and varies the motifs of the former two. In "Attempt at a Room," composed while Rilke was still alive, his illness and impending death were a wedge between him and Tsvetaeva that kept the two of them from meeting in life. Now, after his death, all obstacles to a meeting are removed. The two poets need no longer construct a physical room that will cohere to accommodate their explosive meeting; instead, they can realize their cherished dream through a communion of spirits. Thus, when Tsvetaeva senses Rilke's ghost beckoning at her back, the walls, ceilings, and floors of her room begin to waver: "The door . . . would simply fall off its hinges from the force of his presence behind my back . . . The floor — swam. The door threw itself toward my hand. The darkness — lifted a bit" [Dver′ . . . prosto soshla b s petli / Ot sily prisutstv′ia / Zaspinnogo . . . Pol—plyl. / Dver′ kinulas′ v ruku. / Mrak—chutochku otstupil]. In "Poem of the Air," the dissolution of physical structures is no longer a sign of Rilke's absence, but of his motive presence.

Just as the abstract forms of poetic notation replace physical objects in "Attempt at a Room" and then obliterate death itself in "New Year's Letter," so, too, "Poem of the Air" is characterized by an almost total lack of referentiality to any familiar aspects of concrete being. Instead, it is self-referential and metapoetic in the highest degree, as its opening couplet demonstrates: "Well, there's the first couplet. The first nail" [Nu, vot i dvustish′e / Nachal′noe. Pervyi gvozd′]. This metaphoric "nail" immediately communicates that the poetic edifice Tsvetaeva has set out to construct is, ironically, a coffin for herself — a joyous, buoyant coffin wrought of air and voice that will prove once and for all that death is, as she now knows, not a sorrow, but a celebration to rival all others. Truly, death is the projected destination of this daring flight of fancy; for "Poem of the Air" is fueled not by external reality but by the poet's own breath, sound, language, which consume themselves in the process of her poetic levitation so that, once she is up, there is no longer any way back. The metaphors she uses to explain this process of metaphysical self-consumption are those of a punctured lung breathing out its last air and of a hot-air balloon burning up its last gas: "The suffering is finished in the stony sac of the lung! . . . Bottomless hole of a lung, struck by eternity . . . The suffering is finished in the gas bag of the air. Without a compass—upward!" [Otstradano / V kamennom meshke / Legkogo! . . . Dyra bezdonnaia / Legkogo, porazhennogo / Vechnost'iu . . . Otstradano / V gazovom meshke / Vozdukha. Bez kompasa / Vvys'!]. At one point in the *poema*, Tsvetaeva even makes explicit the suicidal implications of this new conception of the creative act, though her mood is one of great levity only slightly tinged by irony: "But if you yourself are an aeroplane through and through, then what need for a machine? . . . But if you yourself are a lung through and through, then what need for a deadly noose?" [No sploshnoe aero—/ Sam—zachem pribor? / . . . No—sploshnoe legkoe—/ Sam—zachem petlia / Mertvaia?]. Just as the poet, unlike other humans, is able to fly without the aid of a flying machine, so too, Tsvetaeva implies, is the poet able to die without the usual accoutrements of suicide, since poetry itself is a kind of triumphant, progressive, self-inflicted death.

This process of poetic self-relinquishment is initially set into motion in "Poem of the Air" by Tsvetaeva's certainty—recently corroborated in "New Year's Letter"—in the complete reciprocity that exists between her expectation and Rilke's approach. In the *poema*'s opening section, the awaited (though unrealized) knocking of Rilke as otherworldly "guest" [gost'] is both the realized rhythm of her verse and the beating of her heart: "Alive or a ghost—like a guest, in whose wake comes the constant knocking, beyond anyone's endurance—that's what we'll die of—knocking of the hostess's heart: like that of a birch beneath the axe . . . A knock did *not* ensue" [Zhivoi ili prizrak—/ Kak gost', za kotorym stuk / Sploshnoi, ne po sredstvam / Nich'im—ottogo i mrem—/ Khoziaikina serdtsa: / Berezy pod toporom . . . Stuka / *Ne* sledovalo].[107] The Russian *gost'* [guest] and German *Geist* [ghost/spirit]—whose Russian translation, *prizrak* [ghost/spirit] appears in this passage—are often synonymous for Tsvetaeva. Rilke was always pure spirit, she intimates, and thus a guest on this earth; now, as a ghostly presence in her life, he has at last attained his true form.

It does not matter that there is no audible knock on the door; Rilke knocks in Tsvetaeva's heart, as the syncopated rhythms of her *poema* (in this segment, a fast-paced, almost frantic alternation of two-foot and three-foot logaoedic lines of mixed binary and ternary meters) attest without a doubt. What does matter is that her feverish imagination of Rilke's silent knocking is transformed, astonishingly, into his own intent listening and waiting for her on the other side of the metaphysical wall that divides them, in a perfect replication of her own poetic act of faith: "But who on earth waits—without a knock? Certainty in the ear and in fate. Pressing against the wall, certainty in an answering ear. (Yours—in me)" [No kto zhe bez stuka—zhdet? / Uverennost' v slukhe / I v roke. Pripav k stene, / Uverennost' v ukhe / Otvetnom. (Tvoia—vo mne)].

With this achievement of reciprocity, the separate pronouns *I* [ia] and *you* [ty] that clinked against each other in the magical toast of "New Year's Letter" are unified into a single triumphant syllable—*we* [my]—which is now revealed to be the crux of Tsvetaeva's entire inspirational dream: "A dream? But, in the best case—a syllable. And in it? beneath it? Am I imagining? Let me listen carefully: *We,* but a single stride!" [Son? No, v luchshem sluchae—/ Slog. A v nem? pod nim? / Chuditsia? Dai vslushaius': / *My,* a shag odin!]. In "New Year's Letter," Tsvetaeva's "I" and Rilke's "you," self and other, met across the abyss of nonbeing; now self and other merge. The dream in which this miracle occurs is mutual and interpenetrating: "Whether I am dreaming you or you are dreaming me—is a dry question for gray-haired lecturers. Let me feel into it carefully: *We,* but a single sigh!" [Sniu tebia il' snius' tebe,—/ Sush', vopros sedin / Lektorskikh. Dai, vchuvstvuius': / *My,* a vzdokh odin!]. It is appropriate that Tsvetaeva chooses to represent her merger with Rilke through their sharing of a single stride and a single sigh; for these attributes are clearly metaphors for rhythm and voice—the essential ingredients of poetry. Moreover, here as in "New Year's Letter," rhyme is the key to the miraculous simultaneity of Tsvetaeva's and Rilke's consciousnesses: "Complete rhymedness. A rhythm that is mine for the first time!" [Polnaia srifmovannost'. / Ritm, vpervye moi!].

Equals in soul from the start of "Poem of the Air," Tsvetaeva and Rilke are not yet, however, equals in condition—and this is the disparity which her flight in the *poema,* and indeed the *poema* itself, sets out to remedy. Tsvetaeva's suspicion of her own metaphysical inferiority to Rilke had disturbed her even during his lifetime:

I live through him and with him. In all seriousness I am preoccupied with the difference between heavens—his and mine. Mine is not higher than the third, while his, I fear, is the last, meaning—I still have many-many times to live, he has no more than one. My whole intention and task from now on is not to miss the next time (his last). (6:271)

The terraced heavens and hierarchy of gods that make up the afterlife in "New Year's Letter," too, allude implicitly to Rilke's metaphysical seniority over Tsvetaeva. Although she does not dwell on her fears in that work, she does reveal them in passing when she admonishes Rilke in a colloquial idiom intended to lower her addressee to her own metaphysical level: "So as not to miss each other—drop a line ahead of time" [Ne raz"ekhat'sia—cherkni zarane]. However, the real promise of a solution to her worries about inequality in "New

The Dark Lure of Mra

Year's Letter" is the theatrical grand staircase formed by the terraces of paradise: "In the sky is a staircase, one goes up it with Gifts..." [V nebe lestnitsa, po nei s Darami...]. Tsvetaeva can ascend this staircase, if only she can maintain the stamina to continue creating worthy poetic gifts, which will serve as her token or right of passage into the highest heaven—Rilke's abode. Similarly, in "Poem of the Air," although Tsvetaeva at first erroneously attempts to erase the inequality between herself and Rilke by lowering his stature, she ultimately realizes that the only possible solution is her own poetic ascent into his metaphysical league: "It is necessary to even something out: either you lower yourself by an inch . . . Or—and I'm heard: I make no more sound . . . It is necessary to correct something: either you give in by a sigh . . . Or—and I'm released: I breathe no longer" [Chto-to nuzhno vyravniat': / Libo ty na piad' / Sniz'sia . . . Libo—i uslyshana: / Bol'she ne zvuchu . . . Chto-to nuzhno vypravit': / Libo ty na vzdokh / Sdaisia . . . Libo—i otpushchena: / Bol'she ne dyshu].

In this way, gradually, Tsvetaeva passes upward through each successive atmospheric stratum; her poetics propel her into the inhuman beyond with a mechanical inexorability. As she makes the transition from each phase of her journey to the next, she is liberated from all limitations of the previous one. The gaseous attributes of each celestial layer create one of many interwoven refrains in the *poema;* this refrain takes the form of parallel couplets rhymed with one another in a tripartite web of sound that spans the entire *poema* and thereby rounds it into a single unified whole: "Earth illumines. The first sky—is thick. . . Earth absolves. The third sky—is empty. . . Earth excommunicates: the fifth sky—is sound" [Zemleizluchenie. / Pervyi vozdukh—gust. . . Zemleotpushchenie. / Tretii vozdukh—pust. . . Zemleotluchenie: / Piatyi vozdukh—zvuk].[108] At each new sky, first Tsvetaeva's voice, then her breath, then her body is incinerated in the atmosphere.

This last forfeiture is accomplished by a stunning neologism: "A hard body is a dead body: I exgravitated" [Tverdoe telo est' mertvoe telo: / Ottiagotela]. Tsvetaeva combines the common verbs *otiagotet'* [to burden] and *ottiagivat'* [to repulse] to achieve a feat of brilliant poetic unburdening [ottiagotenie]. Because the past-tense verb *ottiagotela* [I exgravitated], referring to Tsvetaeva, is marked for gender, and moreover because she rhymes this verb with *telo* [body], her neologism seems to undo not only the action of gravity and all physical laws upon her body, but her femininity too. Elsewhere in "Poem of the Air," the earth itself is identified with the burden of femininity: "Recoiling powerfully, the ground is like the breast of a woman beneath the stomping of a soldier's boots. (Breast of a mother beneath a child's tiny feet...)" [S sil'noiu otdacheiu / Grunt, kak budto grud' / Zhenshchiny pod stoptannym / Voe-sapogom. / (Materi pod stopkami / Detskimi...)]. These reminiscences of military themes, sexual violence, and the "servitude" of motherhood (motherhood here is implicitly equated with rape!), once again, are strongly reminiscent of "On a Red Steed" as well as of a number of Tsvetaeva's early lyrics. Moreover, here as throughout her oeuvre, the primary goal of poetry is the undoing of physical attraction—elsewhere, figuratively, sexual attraction; here, in the most literal sense, the attraction of physical masses governed by Newtonian gravitational laws—through a miracle of spiritual levitation.

Although Tsvetaeva's quest to escape from body and femininity is a familiar one, her newfound freedom from breath and voice in "Poem of the Air" may at first seem a dubious achievement for a poet. However, in the context of Tsvetaeva's own metaphysics, this freedom is an achievement indeed, because poetry, for her, is the faint echo of some faraway resonance, transcending all the sorrows of temporality, that only the poet's hearing is refined enough to discern. At the height of her journey, she finally enters the realm from which such sweet sounds emerge: "Oh, how resonant the air is, resonant, more resonant than the new year! . . . Oh, how resonant the air is, resonant, more resonant than new grief . . ." [O, kak vozdukh gudok, / Gudok, gudche goda / Novogo! . . . O, kak vozdukh gudok, / Gudok, gudche goria / Novogo . . .].[109] The writing of poetry in ink on paper, in words and sounds, in specific human languages, is only a translation—and, simultaneously, a diminution—of this greater, enveloping poetic essence.[110] Therefore, in "Poem of the Air" as in "New Year's Letter," the loss of a physical means of poetic composition is not at all equivalent to the relinquishment of poetry, but quite the opposite. In the afterlife of "New Year's Letter," miraculously, Rilke continues to be a poet, though he writes not in human languages but in Angelic, not in words but in truths, not physically but abstractly; hence Tsvetaeva's inquiry: "How is it writing . . . without a desk for your elbow, a forehead for your hand (fist)" [Kak pishetsia . . . bez stola dlia loktia, lba dlia kisti / (Gorsti)]. Similarly, in "Poem of the Air," Tsvetaeva envisions a kind of writing from beyond the grave. Death opens up the possibility of poetic creativity that no longer has recourse to the physical instruments of the craft—a writing with spirit instead of with ink.

Thus, in "Poem of the Air," she defines *death* as "a course in aeronautics where everything begins again from scratch, anew" [Kurs vozdukhoplavan'ia / Smert', gde vse s azov, / Zanovo]. The word *az* that appears in the idiom *vse s azov* has a double etymology. On the one hand, it is the old Slavonic word for "I" [ia]; Rilke's death, even as it initiates Tsvetaeva prematurely into the next world, at the same time helps her redefine the core of her poetic selfhood. On the other hand, *az* is the old Slavonic name for the first letter of the Cyrillic alphabet, *A*. Tsvetaeva paradoxically reconceptualizes the regenerative quality of death as a graduation from the poetic word as we know it here on earth to an entirely new kind of alphabet that, at one and the same time, ambiguously looks forward to a spiritual afterlife and backward to the ancient roots of contemporary human speech (we recall her association of Rilke simultaneously with the future and the past tense, though never with the present: "something to look forward to [look backward upon?] . . . The past is still ahead"). Tsvetaeva's new understanding of posthumous poetic activity in "Poem of the Air" assumes the poet's mastery of a language of the soul that exists outside of all time and physicality: "Ancient loss of the body through the ear. To be an ear [i.e., a poet—A. D.] is to be a pure spirit. Leave the alphabet to history" [Staraia poteria / Tela cherez ukho. / Ukhom—chistym dukhom / Byt'. Ostav'te bukvy—/ Veku].[111] These ideas are related to her claims in her 1932 essay "The Poet and Time" ["Poet i vremia"] (5:329-45) that a poet's poems are "older than [he is], because they have longer, farther to live. Older . . . from the future" (5:338) and that, for the poet, "contemporaneity [equals] omnitemporaneity" (5:341).

Tsvetaeva in "Poem of the Air" does, literally, lose herself through her ear when the powerful rhythms of the *poema* propel her into the beyond. This oxymoronically positive "loss" serves as a kind of echoing poetic antidote to the physical tragedy of death by drowning—reminiscent of the Chinese water torture in "Attempt at a Room"—earlier in the poem: "Ancient loss of the body through water (splash of the water closing overhead. A sandy bank...)" [Staraia poteria / Tela cherez vodu / (Vodo-somushcheniia / Plesk. Peschanyi spusk...)]. *Mra* undoes *smert'* in "Poem of the Air"; this is the import of an exultant passage that is set off by its regular dactylic meter from the more heterogeneous logaoedic patterns in the remainder of the work: "Glory to you, who allowed a breach: I weigh no longer. Glory to you, who wrecked the roof: I hear no longer. Part of the sun now, I squint no longer. A spirit: I no longer breathe!" [Slava tebe, dopustivshemu breshi: / Bol'she ne veshu. / Slava tebe, obvalivshemu kryshu: / Bol'she ne slyshu. / Solntseprichastnaia, bol'she ne shchurius'. / Dukh: ne dyshu uzh!]. Having died through her poetry, Tsvetaeva is now impervious to death. One with Rilke, she is no longer blinded by God's aspect; for she is part of it. This is a remarkable escalation of her blasphemous preference for the poet over God in her earlier poems; now she, a poet of genius united with a poet of genius, *is* God.

There is no way back to earth from this infinity. Poetic destiny in "Poem of the Air" consists in an inverse gravitational force that subverts the natural laws of physics, metaphysics, theology—buoying the poet up irrevocably, so that she can never return to earth: "The law of all absences: first the firmament does not hold you, later it will not release you back into weight" [Zakon otsutstvii / Vsekh: sperva ne derzhit / Tverd', potom ne pustit / V ves]. The enjambement of these lines illustrates and enacts the reverse gravity of which they speak. At the same time, Tsvetaeva's poem triumphantly reverses death's conquest of Rilke, which he expresses in his final letter to her in the following terms: "My life is so curiously heavy inside me, often I cannot budge it; the force of gravity, it seems, is forming a new relation to my life—since childhood I have never known such an inertness of spirit."[112] It is likely that the reverse poetic gravity that figures so prominently in "Poem of the Air" is inspired by these lines of Rilke's, as well as by the puzzling image in his "Elegy" of the "larks flung into invisible heights by a song bursting out." [113]

Tsvetaeva's choice of the word *tverd'* [firmament] in the passage just cited aptly conveys the heavens' antigravitational stubbornness. When this word is repeated at the *poema*'s climax, an ingenious play of meanings results. Soaring triumphantly into the seventh heaven, the poet beholds the sky's outer limit and exclaims: "Not everyone—calls [eternity] this. Others say—death.—Earth severs. The sky has ended. Firmament" [Ne vse (vechnost')—/ Tak. Inye—smert'. /—Zemleotsechenie. / Konchen vozdukh. Tverd']. The word *tverd'* [firmament], like the word *svet* [light/world] in "New Year's Letter," has a double meaning; it connotes both *tverd' zemnaia* and *tverd' nebesnaia,* both earth and sky. This "ground of those ungrounded" [Bespochvennykh—/ Grunt] corresponds—without being equivalent—to the earthly "ground, like the breast of a woman" [Grunt, kak budto grud' / Zhenshchiny] from which Tsvetaeva launched her flight in the beginning of the *poema.* Thus, she experiences her arrival in outermost space, where the atmosphere finally thins to nothing and oblivion sets in, as an ironic return to newly firm ground. Death is a mirror image of life—the beginning of another cycle of existence and, thus, a kind of poetic rebirth.

For the poet Osip Mandel'shtam in his 1913 essay "The Morning of Acmeism" ["Utro akmeizma"], the creation of poetry is metaphorically aligned with the construction of a Gothic cathedral: "Building [i.e., writing poetry—A. D.] means doing battle with emptiness, hypnotizing space. The good arrow of a Gothic bell-tower is angry because its entire purpose is to prick the sky, to reproach it for being empty." [114] Moreover, the poet/architect must honor gravity and have "a sincere piety before the three dimensions of space." For Mandel'shtam, then, the Gothic cathedral—and, by extension, poetry—exists in a heavily vectored force field; its bulk is anchored by the weight of tradition even as its spire points unbendingly upward. Tsvetaeva borrows Mandel'shtam's image of the Gothic cathedral for the mystifying conclusion of "Poem of the Air"—but, in so doing, she transforms its meaning entirely:

> Так, пространством всосанный,
> Шпиль роняет храм—
> Дням . . .
>   . . . .
> . . . Не в царство душ—
> В полное владычество
> Лба. Предел?—Осиль:
> В час, когда готический
> Храм нагонит шпиль
> Собственный—и вычислив
> Всё,—когорты числ!

The Dark Lure of Mra 175

> В час, когда готический
> Шпиль нагонит смысл
> Собственный...
>
> [Thus, sucked in by space, the spire drops its cathedral—into time... Not into the kingdom of souls—into the complete dominion of the forehead. What's the limit?—manage this: the hour when the Gothic cathedral will overtake its own spire—having subtracted everything out (cohorts of numbers!)—the hour when the Gothic spire will overtake its own meaning...]

Tsvetaeva's poet removes herself from the sphere of gravity. In the compass of death, the forward arrow of time is curved into an unbroken circle. For Tsvetaeva, then, the enduring Gothic cathedral—resistant to the ravages of history and symbolic of humanity's age-old striving toward beauty and transcendence—is the perfect image of the extratemporal circle sketched by a lyric poem.

At the same time, the Gothic cathedral serves as a kind of diagram that recapitulates the entire metaphysical transformation that Tsvetaeva has just undergone in "Poem of the Air." For, if the spire is symbolically aligned with "soul" and the main church with "body," then the spire's "dropping" its church down into time is an allegory of a painful birth—alleviated only much later when, after a fierce and exhausting race to the finish, the body of the church overtakes its spire (a death allegory), even as the spire overtakes its own essential meaning (poetic rebirth).

The cathedral that completes the circle of "Poem of the Air" is both the constructed coffin that is the *poema* itself—now pounded full of the "nails" of numerous couplets, rhymes, rhythms, echoes—and Tsvetaeva's own self-portrait. The cathedral's spire is her own unremitting thirst for transcendence, whereas the building's hefty main corpus is a simultaneous metaphor for the burden that is her body and for the massive power of her poetic intellect—metonymically indicated, as is typical for her, by the forehead [lob]. Ultimately, "Poem of the Air" is, like most of Tsvetaeva's works, a degendering, reengendering, redefinition of self. In the years that follow her composition of this euphoric poetic masterpiece, she, like the cathedral's symbolic spire, will engage in a race to "overtake her own meaning," primarily through the retrospective and introspective literary genres of essay and memoir. She will continue producing brilliant poetry, too, though not with the frequency of her younger years.

All her life Tsvetaeva has felt an antipathy toward the earth and its conditions. She is therefore surprised, in the early stages of her flight into the beyond, to discover the viscosity of outer space: "Against my expectation: this path is not easy going. Due to resistance of the sphere" [Protivu—mneniia: / *Ne* udobokhozh / Put'. Soprotivleniem / Sfery]. Indeed, she struggles for levity against the force of her own human weight, ties, desires. At last, though, during the latter stages of her upward journey in "Poem of the Air," she is freed of all vestiges of human encumbrance: her "temples are completely torn off from [her] discarded shoulders" and her head sprouts wings [Polnaia otorvannost′ / Temeni ot plech—/ Sbroshennykh . . . Polnoe i tochnoe / Chuvstvo golovy / S kryl′iami].[115] This is the end of her journey; as she herself exclaims frankly and with metapoetic perspicacity, "It's finished!" [Koncheno!]. The nails are all hammered into her coffin; the air is spent in the gas bag of her lungs; death has its due. There is a subtle tinge of nostalgia in the *poema*'s exultant, haunting final lines and images, as Tsvetaeva begins to comprehend deeply that there is truly no way back to earth, breath, life. Nor can she continue to climb any higher; the sky is the limit, and once she has reached the seventh heaven, all limits are exceeded.

4

Ruing Young Orphans
The End of the Line

> It is possible to plan a thing [zadumat' veshch'] only in reverse, from the last step backward to the first—to traverse with seeing eyes the same path one first trod blindly. Reason through the thing [produmat' veshch']. (5:350)
> — "Iskusstvo pri svete sovesti" (1932)

> Стакан твой каждый—будет пуст.
> Сама ты—океан для уст.
>
> [Your every glass—will be empty. You yourself—are an ocean for the lips.]
> — "I esli ruku ia daiu . . ." (1920)

> Я воспевала—серебро,
> Оно меня—посеребрило.
>
> [I sang the praises of silver, and it—silvered me.]
> — "Kogda-to sverstniku . . ." (1940)

Tsvetaeva always felt a creative affinity for the poet Vladimir Maiakovskii, despite their diametrically opposite relationships to the Soviet regime—an affinity that was founded upon the two poets' similarly passionate, reckless way with both words and life.[1] The majority of the Russian émigré community did not share Tsvetaeva's sentiment, however, and she was unpleasantly criticized for some comments she made in praise of Maiakovskii that found their way into print in her husband's pro-Soviet paper *Eurasia*.[2] In April 1930, unexpectedly for some, Maiakovskii put a bullet through his heart. In the conclusion to her 1932 essay "Art in the Light of Conscience" ["Iskusstvo pri svete sovesti"] (5:346–74), Tsvetaeva wrote a moving tribute to his death:

Vladimir Maiakovskii, having served for twelve years in a row [i.e., since the Bolshevik Revolution—A. D.] faithfully and truly, having served with his soul and his body . . .

ended more strongly than with a lyric poem—with a lyric pistol shot. For twelve years in a row the man Maiakovskii was murdering in himself Maiakovskii-the-poet, and in the thirteenth year the poet rose up and murdered the man. If there is such a thing as suicide in this life, then it is not where people think they see it, and its duration was not just the instant when he pulled the trigger, but twelve years of his life. No government censor dealt with Pushkin as efficiently as Maiakovskii with himself. If there is such a thing as suicide in this life, then it is not singular, there are two, and neither is a suicide, for the first—is a feat [podvig], the second—a holiday [prazdnik]. The overcoming of nature and the glorification of nature. He lived like a man and died like a poet. (5:374)

Tsvetaeva, partly in response to a verse fragment contained in Maiakovskii's suicide note that evoked a "love boat smashed on the rocks,"[3] conceives of his death as the climax of a lifelong struggle between the man and the poet within himself. In her eulogistic cycle "To Maiakovskii" ["Maiakovskomu"] (2:273–80), she uses a gruff, humorously colloquial idiom to memorialize Maiakovskii-the-man and prays to God sacrilegiously at the end to "give solace to the soul of Thy departed enemy" [Uspokoi . . . dushu usopshego vraga tvoego].[4]

The questions of death, of suicide, of the poet's fatal struggle between body and soul that Tsvetaeva addresses in her meditation on Maiakovskii's suicide are clearly ones that preoccupied her during the 1930s; indeed, Maiakovskii's smashed "love boat" must have seemed to her an apt metaphor for her own unhappy romantic history. At the same time, the contrast she makes in the conclusion to "Art in the Light of Conscience" between Maiakovskii's crushing self-censorship and Aleksandr Pushkin's persecution by external authority points to her affiliation during this period with yet another dead poetic genius, as evinced in her 1931–33 cycle "Poems to Pushkin" ["Stikhi k Pushkinu"] (2:281–90) and her 1937 autobiographical essay "My Pushkin" ["Moi Pushkin"] (5:57–91).[5] Tsvetaeva shares with "her" Pushkin a vibrant physical energy that expresses itself equally in a love of hiking and a vigorous poetic work ethic; Pushkin, like Tsvetaeva, challenges authority and "rhyme[s] the tsar's censorship . . . with *fool*" [tsarskuiu tsenzuru / . . . s duroi rifmoval] (2:281). Yet Tsvetaeva's Pushkin unites the oppositions that plague both Maiakovskii and herself. In contrast with her own habitual separation of Eros and Logos, Pushkin's physical passion and poetic inspiration are one. Indeed, he is a protean genius, able to be all things to all people simultaneously: "A thorn in the side of the gendarmes, a god to students, gall to husbands, bliss to their wives" [Bich zhandarmov, bog studentov, / Zhelch' muzhei, uslada zhen].

This same metaphysical wholeness that governs Pushkin's life and creativity is manifest in Tsvetaeva's description of his tragic death in a duel:

Кто-то, на фуру
Несший: «Атлета

Мускулатура,
А не поэта!»

То — серафима
Сила — была:
Несокрушимый
Мускул — крыла.

[Someone who carried you to the hearse said: "An athlete's musculature, and not a poet's!" That — was the strength — of a seraph: the indestructible muscle — of a wing.]

True, Pushkin is an athlete of the soul; yet his power is viscerally, palpably physical. When he is shot down by the French assassin Baron Georges-Charles D'Anthès — who stands, in Tsvetaeva's interpretation, for the uncomprehending mob, to whom the language of poetry is incurably alien — his demise equates the raw meat of the stomach with the glory of poetic martyrdom. Thus, Tsvetaeva reminisces: "At three years old I learned definitively that a poet has a stomach . . . In the word *stomach* there is something sacred for me . . . With that shot, they wounded all of us in the stomach" (5:57). Tsvetaeva identifies with the pangs of this human stomach, as she does likewise with Pushkin's persecution by the "mob." (During the last years of her emigration, she felt more and more estranged from the Parisian émigré community; her publications and public readings occurred with rapidly diminishing frequency, while the vociferousness of her resentment increased.[6]) Yet, these affinities aside, the primary question for Tsvetaeva remains whether her own death will emulate Pushkin's and mend the divisions within herself, or whether she walks instead the same tortured path to irrelevant self-destruction that Maiakovskii so recently trod.[7]

Photographs of Tsvetaeva taken during the decade 1930–40 narrate a harrowing progress of aging, worry, and exhaustion. In the late 1920s, Tsvetaeva is still a young and attractive woman with smooth skin, shining green eyes, and silky chestnut hair, who gazes at the camera with a shy, alluring calm. By the end of the following decade, not yet fifty years of age, she has gone prematurely gray, her hair is coarse, her skin lined, her eyes kind but somehow dimmer, her expression one of wisdom and endurance. For a woman like Tsvetaeva with Eros and self-image so much on her mind, this dramatic physical change was surely devastating. According to social convention, old men look stately and distinguished; old women look ridiculous or pathetic. Unlike Akhmatova in her later years, Tsvetaeva proved unable to find an alternative poetic self-image that permitted power to continue to flow into old age; the most she could do was to inscribe her losses in her poetry.[8]

Tsvetaeva's physical erosion, brought on at first by her exhaustion, must also have exacerbated her spiritual condition, so that the aging process only continued to accelerate further. In this way, Tsvetaeva's life comes full circle. Whereas earlier, she renounced bodily desires in favor of poetic transcendence and passion at a distance, now her former "wildness" with words comes home in the body, and she is forced, for the first time, to reinvest genuine value in what is trapped in the flesh. Erotic metaphors of sexual penetration, pregnancy, uterine rebellion—even in the service of pure spirituality—are grounded, after all, in a reminiscence (or at least an imagination) of actual, physical, sensual, sexual, brute biological experience. Gender is inescapable, as are the human consequences of her attempts to escape from gender.

Thus, Tsvetaeva's many hymns to poetic isolation notwithstanding, she recognizes in her later years that such isolation must be an *answer* to a question, proposition, or refusal, stated or unstated. Dreams, visions, and faith in the unseen are ultimately insufficient; as both a woman and a poet, she is still in need of real emotional and inspirational events. She requires dialogue for her life and her art. Without the challenge of a subjectivity—and a body—external to her own, there can be for her neither life nor art; the dearth of a beloved now becomes tantamount to real death (not the fecund metaphoricity of creative Mra, but the barrenness of complete spiritual annihilation). Without a push, there is no shove; Tsvetaeva ultimately finds the dead to be too compliant. She needs a vector; the spiral is not, after all, consistent with her inspirational requirements. She thirsts for a renewal of the exaltation she experienced through her love for Rilke, but the renewal does not come, and the liberating curve of mutuality that she sketched together with him is now transformed through memory's agency into the entrapping circle of endless repetition.

The poems of Tsvetaeva's last decade or so, no less than her prose, constitute a retrospective stock-taking, a leave-taking; even her long works in these years are historical reminiscences connected not only with past events, but with her lost homeland and a lost era (pre-Revolutionary Russia).[9] Her lyric poems are few and far between; she no longer writes as a habit of being, but only as a conscious effort that emanates from urgency or extremity. Her poetic "play" has even ceased to be exhilarating, for she has begun to realize in deadly earnest the toll it has taken on herself and on those dear to her. The leitmotifs of Tsvetaeva's late poetry, therefore, are isolation, loneliness, exhaustion, and the desire for death; her tone is almost always dark, whether searingly ferocious or quietly desperate; and her style, which has always been so flamboyant, now tends toward sparsity, to the point of being telegraphic. More and more, her imagery is heavily gendered and emphasizes motherhood to the exclusion of sexuality—and frustrated motherhood, at that. More and more, she gazes inward; she no longer searches for a muse or a mentor, but turns instead toward the younger generation, in an avowedly futile search for poetic heirs.

Tsvetaeva's Poetic Orphans: Nikolai Gronskii and Anatolii Shteiger

For Tsvetaeva, the admission of body into poetry is the admission of pain, need, illness, vulnerability, and the corpse. Her project in much of her late poetry is to prove the frailty of body under the debilitating burden of poetic drive. Fate cooperated with this aim when it sent her way two young poets whose lives would become, in different ways, exemplary casualties of the human body's transience.

Nikolai Gronskii, for whom Tsvetaeva had served as a poetic mentor and self-designated substitute mother beginning in the spring of 1928,[10] was tragically killed when he fell into the Paris metro at the end of 1934—prompting her poetic cycle "Epitaph" ["Nadgrobie"] (2:324–28), a philosophical and emotional counterweight to "New Year's Letter." Anatolii Shteiger, a homosexual, a friend of Tsvetaeva's poetic arch rival Georgii Adamovich, and a member of the Fascist/neo-Bolshevik organization "Young Russia"[11]—and, for all these reasons, the unlikeliest recipient of her affections—was undergoing a cure for tuberculosis in a Swiss sanatorium when he sent her an admiring letter in the autumn of 1936. The disease was sufficient to activate all of her most robust maternal instincts; so much so that she forgave Shteiger his numerous "sins" and made room for him in her heart: "And if I said *mother*—then it was because that word is the *most* spacious and all-embracing, the vastest and most exact, and—it demands *nothing*. A word before which *all,* all other words are limitations" (7:566). A copious correspondence and the cycle "Poems to an Orphan" ["Stikhi sirote"] (2:337–41) were the result of Tsvetaeva's mostly one-sided long-distance affair with Shteiger.[12]

The relationships that give rise to the cycles "Epitaph" and "Poems to an Orphan" are far more incidental and have far less formative significance for Tsvetaeva's poetic self-definition than did her earlier inspirational infatuations with Blok, Pasternak, and Rilke.[13] Her later relationships no longer hold out to her any promise of a true exit into the alterity of either myth or love; her ambivalent emotional dalliances with Gronskii and then with Shteiger serve, instead, as the occasion for her insular poetic retrospection on the full extent of her subjective isolation. Whereas in the case of Blok, Pasternak, and Rilke, Tsvetaeva strained to rise to their level, levitating upwards and outwards, in the case of Gronskii and Shteiger, by contrast, she must stoop down in order to have anyone at all to talk to.

Indeed, Tsvetaeva's desire to view Gronskii and Shteiger as her potential poetic disciples prompts her to adopt a generous perspective on the less-than-brilliant work of both younger poets. Thus, she rationalizes the weakness she perceives in their writing by her belief that their talent simply has not yet been fully realized. To Gronskii she writes in 1928:

Your poems are younger than you are. To grow up to one's own level and beyond—this is the poet's path. For now you lag behind (you know much that you are not yet able to articulate—because you don't know *enough*)—you'll be your own equal in seven years or so, and after that will come the outgrowing [pererastanie], in all its inevitability, for— the more a poet grows, the greater the human being in him, and the more the human being grows... (7:204–5)

Tsvetaeva almost echoes this passage directly when she tells Shteiger: "You still have to grow up in your poems to the level of yourself in life—that man who is older and deeper and more charismatic [iarche] and more passionate [zharche] than the other" (7:573). After Gronskii's death, when she discovers his unpublished poetry, written during the years since the period of their closest friendship, she apparently feels that he, unbeknownst to her, has fulfilled the poetic promise she sensed in him several years before.[14]

Tsvetaeva's embrace of the idea of motherhood as another name for her intense, antisexual (verbally sublimated) passion is not new; we recall the stepmother in her 1920 *poema* "The Tsar-Maiden" ["Tsar'-devitsa"] (3:190–269), as well as her fascination with the figure of Phaedra. Indeed, Tsvetaeva has often preferred men who betray a hint of androgyny—or "mamas' boys," as she calls them elsewhere.[15] Shteiger's homosexuality apparently aligns him in Tsvetaeva's mind with this male type, to which Rilke also belonged: "There is an unconcealable *feminine* stamp on you: the mark of female hands in your infancy, the same mark that Rilke bore—he *never* became a *man,* although he died at the age of fifty" (7:568). This passage illustrates that Tsvetaeva in the mid-1930s is even beginning to remythologize her relationship with Rilke in terms of the issues that now claim her attention, imagining herself in a mothering relationship to the same sensitive, vulnerable, ailing soul that ten years earlier represented to her the height of poetic invincibility.

In May 1928, during the peak of her friendship with Gronskii, Tsvetaeva addressed to him her lyric poem "Into the Lips of a Youth" ["Iunoshe v usta"] (2:266–67). In this poem, the imagery of physical motherhood is everywhere insistently present. This imagery, in turn, is intimately linked with her own essential identity when she refigures the "foam" [pena] of her marine name as the oozing liquid of female breasts, making the sea of her passion into a giant milk machine that verges on obscenity: "The cream jug of the seas boiled over" [perekipel / Slivochnik morei]. At the same time, there is a telling reversal of desire in which the mother's hunger to *give* is projected as the child's hunger to *take,* as she frantically feeds her own poetry into the mouth of her poetic addressee: "I'm a mother, since I sing, you're a son, since you suck—so suck!" [Mat', koli poiu, / Syn, koli sosesh'—// Sosi zhe!]. The milk of Tsvetaeva's poetry is associated with the unconscious Russian heritage of her young disciple, which he, a mere child at the time he emigrated, hardly remembers: "Suck

The End of the Line

in once again an ancient love: ancestral love! Nomadic love, all of it—from *before* Kii—until Peter" [Staruiu liubov' / Zanovo vsosi: // Tu ee—davno! / Tu ee—shatra, / Vsiu ee—ot *do* / Kiia—do Petra].¹⁶ Just as Phaedra's identity in Tsvetaeva's eponymous cycle was conditioned on the sexual female breast, so too, now that Tsvetaeva has left her Psychean aspirations behind, her own essence emerges from the breast in its maternal hypostasis: "More than just the breast—you suck my essence" [Bol'she nezhel' grud'—/ Sut' moiu sosesh']. Rilke's internal rhyme was with death and the otherworldly ("Rainer—umer"); the internal rhyme here between *grud'* [breast] and *sut'* [essence] equates Tsvetaeva's poetic selfhood with lactation.

A passage that Tsvetaeva excluded from the final version of this poem emphasizes the cyclicity of her predicament:

> Прапамять:
> Всех нянек
> Сердечный щем:
> Что тянешь—
> Тем станешь—
> И канешь—тем!
>
> [Prememory: heartache of all nannies: what you suck—that's what you'll become—and that's how you'll end!]

The threefold verbal rhyme (*tianesh'/stanesh'/kanesh'* [suck/become/end]) that closes this segment has several possible interpretations. It is at one and the same time a merciless summary of Tsvetaeva's recognition of the inescapability of her gender; of the deadly poisonousness of the poetic sustenance she feeds her young pupil; and of the inescapable circle of age and youth. At the same time, her association of her poetry with the "prememory" of all nannies (i.e., wet nurses) indicates the antiquity of her bitter female predicament. Similarly, her allusion to Russia's ancient history ("from *before* Kii—until Peter")—excludes the linearly conceived modern period and so also smacks of prehistorical, mythical cyclicity. Like the wet nurse (who, traditionally, was employed to suckle a stranger's child after the death of her own infant), Tsvetaeva has lost (never found) her true poetic offspring, and she must be satisfied with a mere approximation of her ideal. In this sense, Gronskii here inhabits the same category of poetic orphanhood that Shteiger will later occupy in Tsvetaeva's poetic mythology.

An important subtext in "Into the Lips" is Pushkin's love for his nanny, Arina Rodionovna, whom he immortalized in a number of poems and whose storytelling inspired him to poetic creation even in adulthood, particularly during the period of his 1824–26 Mikhailovskoe exile.¹⁷ In her essay "My Pushkin,"

Tsvetaeva characterizes the importance of Pushkin's nanny thus: "Of all women in the world, Pushkin loved most of all his nanny, who was *not* a woman . . . One can love an old woman—because she is like family—more than a young one—because the young woman is young and even because she is beloved" (5:81).[18] Tsvetaeva, who has always been used to playing the role of the "unbeloved" in every romantic encounter, now glimpses in the fact of her own aging the possibility that she will, after all, find love and fulfillment of a kind. Old age, in a sense, accomplishes the goal that she has been trying to achieve all her life through poetry: it annihilates the dangerous femininity inherent in the female. The question remains, though, whether poetic voice is simultaneously annihilated (Tsvetaeva's desperation in this poem intimates that it is)—and, if so, whether she can survive this loss.

Tsvetaeva, as we have seen repeatedly, has previously found it impossible to participate in the traditional, erotically charged relationship between loving poet and beloved muse. Now, forced back into a reacknowledgment of her bodily origins, she consents to play muse to Gronskii's poet in the immensely powerful sense in which she reinterprets the role of Pushkin's nanny in his poetry: the words and the power are her own, and Gronskii is merely the mouthpiece. Gronskii is, in fact, *all* mouth in this poem—in its title ("Into the Lips of a Youth") as in his incessant sucking. He sucks first on an empty pipe—a "meerschaum mouthpiece"—whose name in Russian [penkovyi mundshtuk] phonetically approximates the milky foam [pena] of Tsvetaeva's waiting teat. He is the embodiment of oral fixation; she is the source of the words that issue forth. When he exchanges his pipe for her teat, a number of ingenious reversals and substitutions occur.

In real life Tsvetaeva, not Gronskii, is the addicted smoker; she confesses her oral fixation in a letter to Shteiger: "I'm exhausted—and the cigarettes got used up ages ago—I suck the empty nipple of a mouthpiece [sosu pustuiu sosku mundshtuka], surprised that nothing—at—all comes out" (7:613). Her imagined exchange of the "masculine" habit of smoking for the feminine nurturance of breast-feeding mimics the switch that Gronskii makes in her poem. Furthermore, it is interesting to note that in her 1920 poem about Pushkin's wife, Natal'ia Goncharova (the poem is tellingly titled "Psyche" ["Psikheia"] [1: 508–9]; this was Goncharova's society nickname), Pushkin himself smokes a meerschaum pipe [penkovaia trubka pyshushchaia], whereas Natal'ia's flouncy ballgown, discarded on the floor, is described as "empty foam" [pustaia pena].[19] When Tsvetaeva associates herself with the nanny rather than the female beloved in "Into the Lips," she reincarnates this ethereal foam as maternal milk and, in so doing, distances herself from her youthful identification with the incorporeal Psyche, while at the same time urging her own hypothetical usurpation of Goncharova's place in Pushkin's mature affections.

As this last point demonstrates, the exchanges that shape "Into the Lips" are by no means capitulations on Tsvetaeva's part. Her new self-image is something bizarrely intermediate between a wet nurse and a muse, and she hopes that in her embrace of this identity will come renewed poetic power: "She is a mother—who gives drink and song" [Mat'—kto poit / I poet]. Indeed, even in her revised female incarnation, Tsvetaeva surreptitiously exchanges the expected lullaby [baiu] of maternal nurturing and nourishment for the military metaphor of her continuing poetic campaign [boi] against—for—within impossibility: "A *battle* or 'lullaby,' a dream or... but all the same" [*Boi* ili 'baiu,' / Son ili... a vse zh]. Tsvetaeva's agenda is never simple—or transparent. In aligning herself with a nanny in this poem with a Pushkinian subtext, she carries out an implicit subversion of the myth of Pushkin's genius. In Tsvetaeva's treatment, Pushkin's nanny—his nonlover and nonmuse—becomes more than his muse: she is the true, native poet who uses Pushkin to speak for her. She is the cause and he the effect; she is the actor and he the acted upon; she is the self and he the object. In a sense, this is not a reversal so much as an extrapolation to infinity of the contours of the traditional inspirational myth. Tsvetaeva takes the myth to its logical conclusion and shows that, at the extreme, it mutates into its opposite.[20]

By the time that Tsvetaeva's cycles to Gronskii and Shteiger were written in 1935–36, she was no longer so certain of either her maternal or her poetic powers. Psychological projection of her emotions onto an unwilling or inanimate recipient is a common technique in her late poetry. In "Epitaph" and "Poems to an Orphan," too, her perception of Gronskii's and Shteiger's childish "orphanhood" is actually a projection of her own extreme isolation onto the male other; the poems and letters she supposedly writes as an antidote to her young lovers' loneliness are really a painful admission of her own. The epigraph to "Poems to an Orphan," with its pathetic "little old lady," indicates her unsparingly accurate awareness of the self-deception in which she engages:

> Шел по улице малютка,
> Посинел и весь дрожал.
> Шла дорогой той старушка,
> Пожалела сироту...
>
> [A little boy went along the street, blue in the face and all shivery. A little old lady went along that road and pitied the orphan...]

These sentimental lines from a popular song of the time ironically return Tsvetaeva in her old age to the schmaltzy "feminine" poetic sensibilities that she has long eschewed. The implication is that, for all her striving for spiritual growth and self-realization over the years, nothing has really changed, and—despite her stunning poetic achievements—no real metaphysical progress has been made.

In a sense, then, she is back again where she started; the difference now is that she is old and weary—and that each repetition of old patterns, by the very fact of its repetitiveness, urges a greater sense of hopelessness, pointlessness, dulling cyclicity (corresponding to the Russian concept of a "bad eternity" [*durnaia beskonechnost'*]). She expresses her feeling of entrapment succinctly in a letter to Shteiger: "Continually repeating chance is *fate*" [Postoianno-povtoriaiu-shchaiasia sluchainost' est' *sud'ba*] (7:617). This kind of impossibility—this existential dead end—is very different from the Romantic poetics of impossibility with which Tsvetaeva began her poetic career. She recognizes now that there is and will be no way for her ever to forge a true relationship between self and other; the outcome of her continued attempts to do so is the breakdown of grammar, meaning, and psychology, as a passage in one of her letters to Shteiger illustrates:

Let me introduce you: *Sie—Ihrer mit Sie—meinem, Sie—Sie mit Sie—ich* [you—yours with *you*—mine, you—you with you—I]. And maybe they—you—will coincide—as criminals' faces and poets' biographies coincide when laid on top of one another. (This is the explanation for the *formulaic* quality that may have troubled you in the last letter. I sometimes think that you—are I, and I don't explain. Whenever you are *not I*—please ask.) But you, at certain moments, are *I*—to the point of strangeness. (7:569)

As if the near nonsensicality of Tsvetaeva's statement is not yet sufficient to convey the acuteness of her psychological disorientation, the German pronouns imbedded in the Russian text further emphasize her state of mental crisis.

The fact that "Epitaph" and "Poems to an Orphan" belong to the genre of the poetic cycle is in itself an important aspect of their meaning. Whereas previously Tsvetaeva was able to transform her isolation into at least a curve of distant mutuality in the genre of the *poema,* here the very cyclicity of form makes any such exit impossible, returning her inexorably to the circle of her lonely fate. In the case of "Epitaph," structural cyclicity is most apparent in the temporal organization of the cycle. The work begins with Tsvetaeva's imagination of Gronskii's last, tragically nonchalant and nonclairvoyant words of parting to his family as he goes out the door to his death: "I'm going out for a few minutes..." [Idu na neskol'ko minut...]. This 1935 cycle ends with a short poem that Tsvetaeva dedicated to Gronskii back in the summer of 1928, whose final words ("God—save!" [Spasi—Bog!]), which originally referred to herself, are ironically transformed in the context of Gronskii's death into a prophetic prayer for him instead.

This reverse chronological strategy in the composition of a poetic cycle (i.e., the completion of the cycle by the inclusion of a poem from the past) is unique in Tsvetaeva's opus; she generally writes all the constituent poems of a cycle within the span of several days at most, and her greatest deviation from strict chronology in any of her other cycles is the appendage of poems "from the future" in final position.[21] In "Epitaph," Gronskii's last words to the living are complemented by Tsvetaeva's last poetic words to him during his life. She is as unable to believe in the reality of his death in retrospect as he was himself in the moments preceding the event, and time turns back upon itself. Moreover, the January of the cycle's composition echoes the new year of "New Year's Letter" and ultimately, perhaps, the January of Pushkin's death as well, since for Tsvetaeva the death of any poet is always an archetype.[22]

Whereas in "New Year's Letter," death is a new beginning, a liberation from the constraints of physical being into new spiritual meanings, Tsvetaeva's view of death is very different in "Epitaph." The cycle's title indicates this change. In contrast to the New Year's greeting she prepares for Rilke, all she is able to muster for Gronskii is an epitaph, a gravestone inscription [nadgrobie] that locates him in his coffin [grob] and so relentlessly stresses his physical decomposition, to the exclusion of any spiritual remnant. She will attempt to recompose him before it is entirely too late; but the poems of "Epitaph" are written *after* the fortieth day after Gronskii's death—thus, after the cessation of his presence on earth and, perhaps, anywhere at all.[23] This contrast between "Epitaph" and "New Year's Letter" is highlighted by the acoustic and morphological near match of their titles: both "Nadgrobie" and "Novogodnee" are compounds, grammatically neutral, and the numerous sounds they share (*n, g, o;* even the stops *b* and *d* and the vowel combinations *ie* and *ee* are similar) result in a kind of slant rhyme between the two. In "Epitaph," the new year's burgeoning spiritual possibility is amended by the ponderous physical finality of a gravestone slab. The open circle of Rilke's death in "New Year's Letter" is closed with Tsvetaeva's return to the death of a poetic beloved in "Epitaph," never to be opened again. The spirit comes home, after all, to the decaying flesh—and afterwards there is nothing left.[24]

The opening poem of "Epitaph" sets the tone for the entire cycle, with its answerless, persistent, despairing questions: "Where did you go? . . . Your soul— where did it go? . . . Your face—where did it go? Your face, your warmth, your shoulder—where did it go?" [Kuda ushel? . . . Tvoia dusha—kuda ushla? . . . Tvoe litso—kuda ushlo? / Tvoe litso, / Tvoe teplo, / Tvoe plecho—/ Kuda ushlo?]. The question is a rhetorical device that Tsvetaeva employs extremely sparingly, because it points to an "external goal, which poems should not have" (5:77). Indeed, this is the case in "Epitaph," in which she utilizes Gronskii's passing to try to come to terms with the finality of real, physical death—the opposite of Mra and of Rilke's transcendence, just as the biological reality of her own aging, yearning body is the opposite of her earlier fantasy of some extrabiological, spiritually feminine yet nonsexual essence.

It is fitting, then, that almost all her questions in this poem mourn the inexorable loss of Gronskii's body: his face, shoulder, corporeal warmth, and indeed the totality of his bodily presence. When she recapitulates, briefly, her earlier focus on spiritual rebirth, she does so almost scornfully: "Since only in fairytales and only in pictures do they rise up to heaven!" [Ved′ v skazkakh lish′ da v kraskakh lish′ / Voznosiatsia na nebesa!]. The contrast between this attitude and Tsvetaeva's ecstatic response to Rilke's death is striking and reflects, at least in part, the different identities of the two men and the different circumstances of their deaths. Rilke's is the greater poetic tragedy and receives a poetic answer; Gronskii's is the greater human tragedy and receives a human answer — an answer that is a nonanswer, just a set of unanswerable questions, since knowledge is given only to the poet. And the poet in Tsvetaeva, in a metaphysical sense, is now absent or inaccessible. She no longer *knows*.

The second poem of "Epitaph," "In vain with my eye" ["Naprasno glazom — kak gvozdem . . ."], reverses one of the refrains of "New Year's Letter" and, simultaneously, of the Romantic, quasi-Symbolist poetics of Tsvetaeva's youth: the ironic poetic identification of life with death and death with life. In "New Year's Letter," we recall, this world and the next, the now and the hereafter are put into communication with one another through the poetic medium, and the result is a new, "third" existential state that is neither life nor death but a philosophical synthesis of the two — a state achieved precisely through Rilke's death: "If you, such an eye, have darkened, it means that life is not life, death is not death" [Esli ty, takoe oko smerklos′, / Znachit zhizn′ ne zhizn′ est′, smert′ ne smert′ est′]. In "In vain with my eye," the separation between life and death is neither transcended nor transgressed but is, on the contrary, reinforced. The circle of Tsvetaeva's limited human vision — her "eye's compass" [oka oborot] — tells her that her lover, far from being made omnipresent by death, has actually been erased from any form of existence: "Here you are not — and are not . . . There you are not — and are not . . . There — is too much there, here — is too much here" [Zdes′ net tebia — i net tebia / . . . Tam net tebia — i net tebia . . . Tam — slishkom tam, zdes′ — slishkom zdes′]. "There" for Tsvetaeva is no longer a place of escape. Moreover, the "nails" of her poetry, which once held fast the liberating coffin of "Poem of the Air," are no longer capable of fastening together a lasting monument to the dead: "In vain with my eye — like a nail — do I pierce the black earth: my consciousness pierces more truly than any nail: here you are not — and you are not" [Naprasno glazom — kak gvozdem, / Pronizyvaiu chernozem: / V soznanii — vernei gvozdia: / Zdes′ net tebia — i net tebia].

Not only does Tsvetaeva no longer believe in a possible meeting of the world of the spirit and the world of the flesh, but she has lost her faith in the inherent meaningfulness of death — and hence, of life — altogether: "However much the priests might sing to us that death is life and life is death, God — is too much God, the worm — is too much a worm" [Chto by ni peli nam popy, / Chto smert′ est′ zhizn′ i zhizn′ est′ smert′, — / Bog — slishkom Bog, cherv′ — slishkom cherv′].[25] Gronskii's death brings home to Tsvetaeva the illegitimacy of her earlier efforts

The End of the Line

to make a clear separation between body and soul: "Inseparable—into corpse and ghost!" [Na trup i prizrak—nedelim!]. Gronskii was not a distant phantom, but a friend whom she knew in the flesh as well as in the spirit; both aspects of his being were dear to her, and thus both are irrecoverable. The result is her recognition of a deep chasm [raskol] left empty in herself by the totality of his passing: "Utterly gone. Gone—with everything" [Sovsem ushel. So vsem—ushel]. In refusing now to give Gronskii up entirely to the "graveyard blooms" [tsvety mogil] that are onomastically linked to her own person, Tsvetaeva renounces her earlier spiritual fictions. Rilke is everywhere; Gronskii is nowhere, except in living memory: "And if somewhere you *are*—then it's just—in us" [I esli gde-nibud′ ty *est′*—/ Tak—v nas]. At last, she has come to value life and body intrinsically—but only when it is already too late.

Once upon a time, Gronskii's friendship and youthful enthusiasm provided Tsvetaeva with a reprieve from her despair; now, in the third poem of "Epitaph," she tries to repay her debt to him by establishing a memorial reciprocity: "Because once, young and brave, you didn't allow me to rot alive among soulless bodies, to fall in a dead faint between walls—I will not allow you—to die completely!" [Za to, chto nekogda, iun i smel, / Ne dal mne zazhivo sgnit′ mezh tel / Bezdushnykh, zamertvo past′ mezh sten—/ Ne dam tebe—umeret′ sovsem!]. Yet this effort to keep Gronskii in memory through the creation of a poetic epitaph is admittedly futile, as the cycle's following poem, "A blow muffled" ["Udar, zaglushennyi godami zabven′ia . . ."], makes clear; for Tsvetaeva has already forgotten him. The effort to remember (the governing impulse behind "Epitaph" as a whole) is, in fact, something of an empty gesture—regretfully empty, but empty all the same:

> Грех памяти нашей—безгласой, безгубой,
> Безмясой, безносой!
> Всех дней друг без друга, ночей друг без друга
> Землею наносной
>
> Удар—заглушенный, замшенный—как тиной.
>
> [The sin of our memory—voiceless, lipless, meatless, noseless! Of all our days without one another, nights without one another—a blow—muffled by riverborne soil as by mire, overgrown with moss.]

The blow of Gronskii's death is muted in Tsvetaeva's emotions by the temporal distance between them (it has been nearly seven years since the summer of their friendship), as well as by his physical absence now: the lack of his voice (not the poetic voice, which does live on, but Gronskii's actual vocal timbre), lips, flesh, nose. These are aspects of the human that Tsvetaeva hardly valued before and certainly would not have identified with the totality of a person's being. Their absence now is tantamount to Gronskii's nonexistence—a sign of her own essential nonexistence, too, because she has never been at home in her body.

This is already a painful state of affairs; but the hesitant final stanza of "A blow muffled," which departs metrically from the rest of the poem, hints cryptically at an even more grisly prospect:

> А что если вдруг
> . . . .
> А что если вдруг
> А что если — вспомню?
>
> [And what if suddenly... And what if suddenly, and what if — I remember?]

Tsvetaeva's palpable horror here makes clear that her fear of remembering (what? — she does not exactly specify) no longer relates directly to Gronskii, so much as to her own deep philosophical and psychological crisis. If she remembers the body, all that she has lost, not just in Gronskii but throughout her life (her nonlife), all that she has renounced for the sake of her poetry — then... what? There is no then and no what, but the poet's stammering, elliptical terror in these final lines, as well as the extreme spareness of her style, akin to muteness, suggests that in "Epitaph" she narrates not just Gronskii's disappearance, but also her own.

Tsvetaeva's emerging sense of an exitless circle enclosing her biography and her resultant feelings of irredeemable loss shape both her correspondence with Shteiger and the poetic cycle that she dedicates to him. In her letters and poems to Shteiger, his tuberculosis, like Gronskii's death in "Epitaph," serves ultimately as a template for her consideration of her own metaphysical dilemmas. She implicitly admits as much when she compares Shteiger's physical illness to her own spiritual one:

Let's *suppose* that your illness is essentially incurable, that you will never again be a healthy person. Let's take this — and try to find a cure to incurability, an exit from an evident dead-end. I *always* think according to examples and outside of such examples I can understand nothing. (7:609)

Shteiger's predicament, then, is an "example" [primer] or foil for Tsvetaeva's own. Another passage points to the fact that Shteiger is really just a third-person stand-in for Tsvetaeva's own "I":

Go on living as you do *auf der Höhe* [in the heights] (like myself: *in der Höhle* [in a cave]) — break through occasionally in episodes of "happiness," "life" — even if these are just furloughs, *plongeons* [plunges] — gulp and grab as much as you possibly can — and return — into yourself. (7:611–12)

The parallelism here between Shteiger's *Höhe* (the Swiss Alps) and Tsvetaeva's self-deprecating *Höhle* emphasizes his function as her male alter ego. Likewise, her advice to her interlocutor to plunge periodically from his elevated state of isolation into the incomprehensible, foreign realm of "life" and "happiness" has little to do with Shteiger himself, but in fact evokes her own reckless psychological patterns. Shteiger is, in this sense, a tool for Tsvetaeva's self-inflicted psychoanalysis.

Her awareness of Shteiger's unsuitability for her as either a lover or a disciple —even, perhaps, as a friend—necessitates her realization that she is "using" him in order to perform an emotional and poetic experiment on herself. This last epistolary romance is a futile reprise of earlier inspired turning points in Tsvetaeva's creative life. Accordingly, in her letters to Shteiger, she executes a studious recapitulation of many of the themes and refrains from her letters to Pasternak and Rilke—sometimes almost to the exact turn of phrase—with sham innocence and wheedling, desperate passion. For instance, there is her familiar proclamation of the superiority of love in absentia [zaochnaia liubov'] over meeting in person:

And here you and I—through sight and *hearing* [voochiiu i *voushiiu*]—have become friends, having, if you like, *skipped over* the necessity of becoming acquainted. (7:579)

There is her renunciation of her own love and her conjuring of her lover's desired advances:

Do *not* expect *my* request for your visit. (*I want*—is not a reason, and maybe even— is a reason against.) I am a backwards activist: for refusal. "*Entbehren sollst du, selbst entbehren* [You should be the one to want, you yourself]." (7:583)

There are her dreams of an imaginary room, a Psychean palace, where the two lovers could meet:

But I would like to be with you *absolutely* without other people, absolutely alone in a huge womb—a castle—and we would be waited upon by *hands,* as in the fairytale "The Little Scarlet Flower" . . . [And] in the end we would—imperceptibly—fade into the *walls* and when *others* came—they would find no one. (7:575)[26]

Finally, for all her professions of self-denial, there is her constant planning and replanning, in letter after letter, of the logistics of her desired meeting with Shteiger.[27]

In Tsvetaeva's epistolary romances with Pasternak and Rilke these themes were occasional, interwoven into a larger and more complex mythopoetic fabric (Psyche's renunciation of Eros; Rilke's reunification of the cosmos) that imbued the leitmotif of thwarted desire with poignancy and power. In her letters to Shteiger, on the contrary, the only context for her laments is her own wry awareness of their fictiveness and of the ephemerality of her emotion—her protests of eternal love, past and future, notwithstanding: "I have the feeling that you and I have to live through our whole life together—backwards and forwards" (7:570). Such maudlin confessions sound less than ingenuous in light of Tsvetaeva's open admission to herself and even to Shteiger of her mendaciousness and his mere incidentalness in her life. Indeed, her "love" for him is just a temporary delusion that serves the selfish interests of her poetic path:

How many times has this happened already? And do I really not know that everything ends, and do I really believe that (this feeling in me for you) will end sometime, will at some point set me free, that I will empty of you: become again an empty—and cold—and vacant house: *domaine?*[28] (7:574)

Neither her cloyingly sentimental overtures to Shteiger nor her galling confessions, of course, can be hoped to endear her much to the younger poet. Tsvetaeva knows this well herself, and her bitterness shows through her ostensibly tender passion both in her letters to Shteiger and, even more so, in her poems.

Indeed, whereas in her correspondence with Shteiger she usually feigns innocence, assuring him repeatedly of her complete belief in their spiritual kinship, her cycle "Poems to an Orphan," on the contrary, exudes a biting self-awareness.[29] This is a reversal of the situation that obtained in Tsvetaeva's relationship with Pasternak, where she often kept at arm's length in the correspondence, only to write numerous passionate poems about their indestructible spiritual bond. Her letters to Shteiger are a kind of charade, enabling her to summon the creative will to eke out just a few more poems. Yet she knows from the beginning that nothing will come of her mistaken love for Shteiger, if not poetry. Like a girl who has cried wolf too many times, she has come to doubt her own veracity and to doubt, in fact, any direct connection of her endless words, words, words with reality. From now on, she fears, every wolf is really a sheep in a wolf's hide.[30]

In fact, although it is true that Tsvetaeva is often undeservedly harsh in her critiques of others, she is harshest and most relentlessly analytical when it comes to herself.[31] In "Poems to an Orphan," she extends the groundwork of self-criticism that she has laid down previously in such works as the scathing 1922 "Hands—and into the circle" ["Ruki—i v krug . . ."] (2:121). In this lyric as in "Poems to an Orphan," she uses cyclical patterns to voice her tormented memory of the nameless multitudes who have fallen victim to her romantic "conquests": "Hands—and into the circle of overselling and overcompromising! If only I can avoid mixing up lips, mixing up hands!" [Ruki—i v krug / Pereprodazh i pereustupok! / Tol'ko by gub, / Tol'ko by ruk mne ne pereputat'!]. Moreover, Tsvetaeva associates her passion with her beloved's (her victim's) death, and so sardonically pictures her poetry—inspired as it is by these murderous loves—as a garbage pit or a mass graveyard: "So that in verse (the garbage dump of my Majesties!) you won't wither, you won't dry up as all the others did" [Chtoby v stikhakh / (Svalochnoi iame moikh Vysochestv!) / Ty ne zachakh, / Ty ne usokh napodob'e prochikh].

Like "Hands—and into the circle," "Poems to an Orphan" is a self-damning exercise, from beginning to end, in impossibility and irrevocability. In other words, the cycle as a whole and each of its constituent poems make it clear (as Tsvetaeva's letters to Shteiger do not) that she is absolutely aware that her infatuation with Anatolii Shteiger is nothing more than an opportunistic poetic experiment to prove not his, but her own orphanhood. This is not, however, to deny the sincerity of her emotions. Her conscious poetic utilization of Shteiger and her intense feeling for him are by no means mutually exclusive; in fact, this paradox deepens Tsvetaeva's tragedy. She already knows well enough that Shteiger will not be able to provide her with an exit into true love and true alterity, and, indeed, she no longer strives for such an exit. Her only poetic ambition now is to provide the fullest possible statement of her inevitable metaphysical isolation.

"Poems to an Orphan," like "Epitaph," is once again governed by cyclical patterns, most often on the level of imagery. The cycle's brief first poem, "An icy tiara" ["Ledianaia tiara gor . . ."], which, suspiciously, does not invoke Shteiger's presence at all, unites images of circular containment—a tiara, a frame, a castle—with descriptions of nature to evoke the poet's exaggerated devolution from the spiritual to the vegetable plane of existence.[32] Instead of any human lover in this poem, there is the tiara of mountains which crown her; the ivy on her castle that she parts like human hair; the pine tree's slim figure that she embraces, and the tulip that she caresses. Yes, this is a return to physical love, but a strange return indeed: only plants and inanimate objects, which cannot protest against Tsvetaeva's self-projections onto them, are suitable lovers. The scale of her desire is extravagantly enormous—she loves as a mountain loves, as a castle loves, as a tree loves. Her foray into the aconscious, elemental world of nature brings her relief both from the exertion of communication with humans, and from her own unrelenting pursuit of consciousness that has sapped her poetic resources.[33] Yet there is also an ethical aspect to Tsvetaeva's retreat from humanity in "An icy tiara"—as there is, too, in her discussion of nature in her essay "Art in the Light of Conscience":

Is nature holy? No. Sinful? No. But if a work of art is also a work of nature, then why do we ask a poem to be accountable, but not a tree (in the best case we regret that it grows crooked)?

Because the earth, when it gives birth, is not responsible, but a person, when he creates, is responsible. Because the sprouting earth has one will: to sprout, but a person should will the sprouting of the *good* that he is capable of knowing. (5:347)

When Tsvetaeva turns toward nature in "Poems to an Orphan," she exhibits her jealousy of the moral irresponsibility—the freedom from soul—that is the law of nature's creativity, even as her own creative drive is founded upon the necessary transgression of morals.

The second poem of the cycle, "I embrace you with my horizon" ["Obnimaiu tebia krugozorom . . ."], builds upon the implicit self-portrait Tsvetaeva has painted of herself in "An icy tiara" as an irrepressible, irresponsible phenomenon of nature. Her notes in her workbook testify to this poem's almost geometrical origin in the very idea of circularity: "Unambiguously *round* things are needed: flowerbed, tower, horizon, valley."[34] Here again, she figures her love in the metaphorical "caresses" of natural elements for one another: a mountain range encloses a valley; a well encompasses its own depths; ivy curls around a stone. These caresses are unintentional; they are simply accidents of proximity, just as her long-distance, poetic "caress" of Shteiger is an "accident" of fate. Such imagery conveys not only the immensity of Tsvetaeva's passion but, at the same time, its reticence, its independence from both herself and her object (Shteiger), its complete self-sufficiency. She expects nothing at all of her beloved and professes to make no demands:

> Но не жимолость я—и не плющ я!
> Даже ты, что руки мне родней,
> Не расплющен—а вольноотпущен
> На все стороны мысли моей!
>
> [But I am not honeysuckle—and I am not ivy! Even you, who are more dear to me than my own hand, are not crushed, but set free in all the directions of my mind!]

In the early poems of *After Russia*, honeysuckle is Tsvetaeva's recurrent metaphor for the secret, forbidden sweetness of human flesh, while ivy stands for her determination to hold onto even an unwilling lover at all costs.[35] The ingenious sound play in this stanza (*pliushch/raspliushchen/volnootpushchen* [ivy/crushed/set free]) captures the paradox inherent in her passion for Shteiger: he is free, and she demands nothing of him, nor does she cling—because he exists for her only, really, as a manifestation of her own poetic thought process [mysli moei].

Thus, Shteiger's "orphanhood" is the objective correlative for Tsvetaeva's inability to go beyond the parameters of her own insular selfhood. She expresses this idea by a play on the polysemous adjective *kruglyi,* which can mean either "round," "mutual," or "complete":

> Обнимаю тебя . . .
> . . . .
> . . . Кругом клумбы и кругом колодца,

> Куда камень придет — седым!
> Круговою порукой сиротства, —
> Одиночеством — круглым моим!
>
> [I embrace you . . . with the roundness of a flowerbed and the roundness of a well so deep that even a stone reaches bottom gray-haired! With the round/mutual bond of orphanhood — with my round/complete loneliness!]

Tsvetaeva's attitude toward Shteiger in "I embrace you" is characterized by an unsettling mixture of passion and indifference, possessiveness and distance. She projects her own needs onto her beloved and so internalizes his anticipated response to her emotion: incomprehension and disdain. She has come a long way since her unbridled fervor for Blok in "Poems to Blok," which made her position so vulnerable; now she incorporates in her own being both the poet's desire and the muse's insouciance. The beautifully lyrical lines "Do you know — this ivy, which embraces a stone — with one hundred four hands and streams?" [Znaesh' — pliushch, obnimaiushchii kamen' — / V sto chetyre ruki i ruch'ia?] are a testament to the inhumanity or superhumanity of her need for her beloved (104 hands and streams!). He is merely an anchoring place for her multifarious loneliness — a bit of fertile ground where a poem can take root.

Yet, even as Tsvetaeva entangles him, so too is she entangled in the remnants of her own desire. Indeed, the gray strands interspersed in her hair echo the tangles of ivy earlier in the poem: "That's how more than one silvery tress became entangled with my reddish curls!" [Ták vplelas' v moi rusye priadi — / Ne odna serebristaia priad'!]. Fittingly, this is an image of self-entanglement, of the complex interaction of Tsvetaeva's past (young, passionate, golden-haired) self with her present one (aging, despairing, gray) — rather than of any relationship with her lover. At the same time, these lines echo a poem from Akhmatova's 1914 collection *Rosary* [*Chetki*], which begins: "How a silvery-white tress became entangled with my dark hair — only you, voiceless nightingale, will be able to understand this torment" [Kak vplelas' v moi temnye kosy / Serebristaia belaia priad' — / Tol'ko ty, solovei bezgolosyi, / Etu muku sumeesh' poniat'].[36] Akhmatova's poem, like Tsvetaeva's, is an enigmatic love lyric that uses nature imagery and the theme of aging to allude to her creative solitude (Akhmatova's nightingale waits tensely for "another's song" [pesnia chuzhaia]). Yet Tsvetaeva writes a corrective to Akhmatova's merely superficial, symbolic utilization of the imagery of female aging (when Akhmatova's poem was written, she was all of twenty-three years old) with her own trenchant portrayal of the wrenching psychic changes that the real aging process entails.

Until now, love has, for Tsvetaeva, been associated with a split in subjectivity necessitated by her attempt to interact with a human other, as was the case most vividly in her relationship with Pasternak. Now, however, absorbed in her own body and her own private hopes and sorrows, she takes her position to the other extreme. She cannot establish any true relationship to Shteiger—not even one based on mutual aloneness (this ideal is conveyed by her phrase "the round bond of orphanhood" [krugovaia poruka sirotstva]). For, having discovered the insularity of her loneliness, she is no longer willing to be divided even insomuch as to acknowledge Shteiger's alterity. He is, for her, simply an island in the unified stream of her consciousness; she creates this island during a momentary dalliance, only to drown it once again in her depths: "And [I embrace you] with a river, split into two—so as to create, and embrace, an island" [I rekoi, razoshedsheisia ná dve—/ Chtoby ostrov sozdat'—i obniat']. In one of her final, bitterly disappointed letters to Shteiger, Tsvetaeva quotes this passage from "I embrace you" by way of enunciating her resistance to the truth of his otherness—since recognizing this truth would require her unwilling renewal of her earlier psychic split:

I am a person of such deep [serdtsevinnoi], inborn adherence to principles, of such *unity,* that I am not at all sure that anyone else needs this or is at least glad of it—alone, for myself, because of myself, alone with myself, alone before myself, on the strength of my nature I *cannot* divide my being otherwise than that river in my poems: so as to create, and embrace, an island. (7:622)

For all the distance that she still admits into her passion, the older Tsvetaeva is no longer willing to love blindly, in fantasy alone. By the end of her correspondence with Shteiger, she will come to feel that he, friend of Adamovich and those she terms the other Parisian "Bohemians," is eminently unworthy even of her respect, let alone her tenderness. Tsvetaeva, in loving him, would not be herself: her love is for the sake of poetry, and his "sin" is an aesthetic one, a poetic one. A human sin she could forgive, a poetic one—no. She will insist on the roundness, the wholeness of her being, which comes at such a cost. She will no longer be divided; if reality does not correspond to fantasy, then she will relinquish both.

In "I embrace you," however, Tsvetaeva is still willing to try the fantasy out for a little longer. The poem's final stanza is a fitting reprise of its opening stanza, as she returns to the images of the encircling mountain range and the horizon—acoustically transposed now from *krugozor* into its synonym *gorizont,* which is linked paronomastically with *gory* [mountains]—to figure her own long-distance poetic embrace of her beloved. She makes use, as she does so, of the double meaning of *khrebet* [spine/ridge] in order to realign her bodily self with this powerful natural imagery: "And—breaking my spine/the mountain ridge part way—I embrace you with my blue horizon—and my two hands!" [I—nemnozhko khrebet nadlomia—/ Obnimaiu tebia gorizontom / Golubym—i rukami dvumia!]. Tsvetaeva's ambivalence toward her addressee and her distrust of her emotion for him culminate in a subtle yet ironic last insult: in order to embrace the younger, inferior, and—what is perhaps most important—spiritually alien Shteiger, she must bend down double so that her back almost breaks.

A straight spine and erect posture have consistently been for Tsvetaeva a metaphor for a fierce work ethic, as well as for poetic integrity—a principle that takes the place of moral integrity, since her feminine inspirational impasse inevitably requires moral transgression for the achievement of poetic flight. A self-portrait in verse from 1920 provides the best example of such symbolism: "There is in my figure—an officer's erectness, there is in my ribs—an officer's honor. I take on every torture without balking: I have a soldier's endurance!" [Est' v stane moem—ofitserskaia priamost', / Est' v rebrakh moikh—ofitserskaia chest'. / Na vsiakuiu muku idu ne upriamias': / Terpen'e soldatskoe est'!] (1:565).[37] Tsvetaeva dislikes being on either end of a spiritually unequal relationship and often uses the symbolism of the bending or breaking spine to illustrate her unease; she feels, for instance, that Rilke's superiority is such that he is forced to bend down to her too deeply, too graciously:

The depth of a bow [glubina naklona]—is a measure of height. He bowed deeply to me ... what did I feel? HIS STATURE. I knew him even before, now I know him *on me*. I wrote to him: I will not demean myself, that will not make you higher (nor will it make me lower!), it will only make you *even more lonely,* because on the island *where we were born*—*everyone is like us*. (6:253; emphasis in the original)

Similarly, Tsvetaeva represents the unequal footing of her short-lived, though intense passion for the nonpoet Aleksandr Bakhrakh (a literary critic) in 1923 by a deep bend—on her part this time—in the poem "A Bow" ["Naklon"] (2:213–14): "I have for you an inclination of the forehead, which patrols the upper reaches" [U menia k tebe naklon lba, // Doziraiushchego ver—khov'ia]. Throughout this poem, she plays ingeniously on the double meaning of the Russian word *naklon,* meaning both "bow" and "inclination."

Clearly, Tsvetaeva's breaking spine at the end of "I embrace you" indicates that she is fully conscious of Shteiger's complete unsuitability for the role into which she has placed him. In the last throes of their embittered correspondence, her stubbornly straight spine will be the metaphor she uses to describe the spiritual equanimity she maintains at the cost of her human sorrow: "That was a blow to my chest (in which you resided) and, if I did *not* fall down—then only because no *human* force can knock me flat any more, because I no longer permit *this* to humans, because I will die—standing up" (7:620). From the beginning, Tsvetaeva's position with respect to Shteiger is false, and—as these recurrent images attest—she knows it. Her bitterness is mostly against herself, after all: an indication of her own culpability in the fiasco of this romance.

"The Cave" ["Peshchera"], the next lyric of "Poems to an Orphan," has an intricately cyclical form that reiterates the predetermined impossibility of Tsvetaeva's and Shteiger's ever meeting on equal, or indeed any, terms. The poem begins with the wish "If I could—I would take you . . ." [Mogla by—vziala by . . .] and ends with a repetition of these very same words. The fantasy that Tsvetaeva "would if she could" unravels in sounds and images in the interval between these two wistful avowals, in a kind of laconic reprise of "Attempt at a Room." This poem is acoustically, rhythmically, rhetorically, and imagistically complex; its ideas modulate gradually from one sound pattern to the next in a kind of mantra or prayer, though a prayer devoid of any hope. Tsvetaeva's portrait in images of her own metaphysical dead end is haunting:

> Могла бы—взяла бы
> В утробу пещеры:
> В пещеру дракона,
> В трущобу пантеры.
>
> [If I could—I would take you into the womb of the cave: into the cave of the dragon, into the panther's thicket.]

Not the wise and disembodied Sibyl Tsvetaeva imagined in her youth, she is not the cave's voice but its monstrous womb, all need. In this chaotic lair dwells a beast (her soul) that lies in wait like a dragon or panther to devour its victims.

This is a horrifying realization of the womb/tomb dialectic of birth and death, which the Russian play *lono/lozhe* [bosom/bed] in this poem also captures: "Into the bosom of nature, onto nature's nuptial bed" [Prirody—na lono, prirody—na lozhe]. Similarly, the granite of gravestones is juxtaposed with mother's milk, whereas the bond of kinship (two lovers' clasped hands) is equated with the interlaced fingers of a corpse: "[I would take you] there, where in granite, and in bast, and in milk, hands are clasped for all the ages . . ." [Tuda, gde v granite, i v lyke, i v mleke, / Spletaiutsia ruki na vechnye veki . . .]. The hands here, as in the concluding line of "I embrace you," stand for physical passion; this is in contrast to the eloquent gesture of Rilke's disembodied hands at the end of "New Year's Letter."

Tsvetaeva has always preferred the dynamism of painful longing to the stasis of sexual gratification. When in "The Cave" she collapses the handclasp of two lovers—self and other—into the image of a single, obsessively self-contained corpse, she signals her replacement of the hypothetical amorous paradise for which she once purportedly yearned with the atemporal circle of hell that she now openly prefers: "So that there would be no knock on my door, no yell into my window, so that in future—nothing *happened,* so that—there would never be any end!" [Chtob v dver'—ne stuchalos', / V okno—ne krichalos', / Chtob vpred'—ne *sluchalos',* / Chtob—vvek ne konchalos'!]. The realization of passion would be tantamount for Tsvetaeva to spiritual death; in order to avert this catastrophe, which would destroy her poetry, she does not grant to her beloved the possibility of becoming real. Like the black widow spider who kills her mate to feed her newly hatched offspring, Tsvetaeva needs the demise of her potential lover to nourish her poems. This has been the pattern until now; but now that she sees the full horror of her position, even this triumph is insufficient: "But the cave—is not enough, and the thicket—is not enough!" [No malo—peshchery, / I malo—trushchoby!].

The following two lyrics of "Poems to an Orphan" are a pair; both end with the same tongue-twisting, hypnotizing line ("My beloved, desired, pitied, painful one!" [Liubimyi! zhelannyi! zhalennyi! boleznyi!]), and both make use of the imagery of extremity to express the intensity of Tsvetaeva's despair. She loves Shteiger, she confesses, on an iceberg, standing on a mine, in Guiana (the French punishment colony, equivalent to Russia's Siberia), in the like-sounding Gehenna (hell). She desires him in a wound, from the grave, with the last contraction of her uterus. Her desire is the desire of a skeleton; only teeth and bones are left. In other words, she loves Shteiger *in extremity only;* this is an opportunistic lovemaking, a temporary insanity, spurred on by the prospect of encroaching, certain death. Had she any choice—she would have chosen another. But these are her last moments, and he is the last unworthy human whom fate has thrown in her path. He is hardly real at all, just a whiff of air or a paper cut-out: "My fragile one! hardly alive! transparent! paper-thin!" [Khílyi! chut'-zhívyi! skvoznoi! bumazhnyi!].

Tsvetaeva loves him and desires him as a way of coming to terms with the cessation of her need to love, the cessation of her desire. No real hell on earth is equivalent to the abyss of Marina Tsvetaeva's self-loathing love for Anatolii Shteiger:

> Последнею схваткою чрева—жаленный.
> И нет такой ямы, и нет такой бездны—
> Любимый! желанный! жаленный! болезный!

[I desire him with the final contraction of my uterus. And there is no such pit, and there is no such abyss (that could encompass her passion—A. D.)—my beloved, desired, pitied, painful one!]

Tsvetaeva's love is really profound pity—for herself even more than for Shteiger. Her love for him is a reflection of the extent to which her soul is incapable of recolonizing her decrepit body, hardly female anymore. The consequence of her feeling of bodily alienation is her extreme alienation from poetry, too—a state of mind that would have been unthinkable for her earlier. This dire logic is captured by means of a brilliant shorthand in the poem: "From pharynx to womb—a vertical slash" [Ot zeva do chreva—prodol'nym razrezom]. She is split vertically down the center (down her spine), from her mouth to her womb. The orifice of female poetic creativity is linked with the orifice of female biological procreativity by rhyme (*zeva*/*chreva* [pharynx/womb]) and by a linking, vertical wound. In contrast to the waist-high, horizontal split between Tsvetaeva's supposedly ungendered soul and gendered body that tormented her in earlier years, now body and soul together form the relentlessly erect axis upon which she spins. In order to escape this condition—she must escape from both.

In the context of the self-deprecating irony, bitterness, and sarcasm that give shape to "Poems to an Orphan" as a whole, the cycle's sixth poem is an anomaly. In it, Tsvetaeva movingly asserts the sincerity and tenderness of her feelings for Shteiger and imagines his reciprocation of her own intense need for affection, which, even in this poem, admittedly verges on the pathological (the need is "mortal"):

> Наконец-то встретила
> Надобного—мне:
> У кого-то смертная
> Надоба—во мне.
>
> Что для ока—радуга,
> Злаку—чернозем—
> Человеку—надоба
> Человека—в нем.
>
> [At last I met the one I need: someone who has a mortal need—of me. What a rainbow is for the eye, what black earth is for grain—is for a person a person's need of him.]

The metrical and rhetorical structure of this poem are far simpler than in the cycle's other lyrics, creating the impression of a rare, quiet interlude amid the overpowering *Sturm und Drang* of Tsvetaeva's exitless passion.[38] Even the poem's finale, with its suggestion that Tsvetaeva's bond with Shteiger is based on a shared experience of agony, does not go so far as to question the mutuality of this experience: "And for the fact that you brought me the palm of your hand with an *ulcer*—I would plunge my own hand into the fire for you in a moment!" [I za to, chto s *iazvoiu* / Mne prines ladon'—/ Etu ruku—srazu by / Za tebia v ogon'!]. Tsvetaeva here shows herself to be a masterful orchestrator, a far more versatile practitioner of the nuances of silence and sudden decrescendo than she is often given credit for. The effect of this simple, tender, underspoken lyric in the ferocious context of those which surround it is deeply, almost unbearably tragic. Tsvetaeva's voice here is her human one, sad, lonely, hopeful, hopeless, without the armor of bristling pride—a voice she rarely allows us to hear. She has, indeed, begun to break.

After such an intermezzo, the cruelty of the cycle's final poem, "Lost in thought" ["V mysliakh ob inom, inakom . . ."], comes as a great shock. This shock is further deepened by this poem's reminiscence of the opening lyric of "Poems to an Orphan," in which Tsvetaeva plucks a tulip—an act both tender and cruelly self-indulgent—in reference to the risk she takes in courting Shteiger's love: "Today I took a tulip—like a child by the chin" [Ia segodnia vziala tiul'pan—/ Kak rebenka za podborodok]. The verb *took* [vziala] is ambiguous in these lines; it is not clear whether she is actually taking (picking) the tulip or, as the following simile suggests, simply caressing it as one "takes" a child by the chin. This ambiguity between literal and figurative meanings is finally resolved in "Lost in thought," when Tsvetaeva's amoral plucking is chillingly revisited upon her: "Step by step, poppy by poppy—I beheaded the entire garden . . . Just so, someday, in a dry summer, on the edge of a field, death with a careless hand will pluck off my own head" [Shag za shagom, mak za makom—/ Obezglavila ves' sad . . . / Tak, kogda-nibud', v sukhoe / Leto, polia na kraiu, / Smert' rasseiannoi rukoiu / Snimet golovu—moiu].[39]

In my view, critical attempts to psychoanalyze Tsvetaeva are redundant at best, offensive at worst—because, as is the case in "Lost in thought," she psychoanalyzes herself more trenchantly and with more brutal honesty than any outsider can ever hope to do. In this poem, she conceives of her failures at love as the purposeful, systematic "beheading" of her lovers/victims like flowers, one by one, in selfish pursuit of the rarified beauty of her own poetic genius. The price she will pay for her inhuman experiments in love and loneliness will be her own, equally senseless, nonpoetic and nonheroic death. Like the graveyard blooms [tsvety mogil] that she derives from her own name in "Epitaph," her destiny is the tomb. All of her poetic metaphors are brought back to their physical origins at the conclusion of "Poems to an Orphan," even as her powerfully evocative language is brought back to its source: her amoral utilization of others to her own poetic ends. The circle is already closed, Tsvetaeva seems to be saying, and there is no escape. In retrospect, she now feels that it was closed from the very beginning—by her gender, by her feminine inability to establish legitimate poetic voice. She has written herself out of existence, just as she has always written out all her potential lovers; now, there is no one left but herself, and she is the one who will answer.

Coming Full Circle: The Last Judgment

Fifteen years earlier, in "On a Red Steed," Tsvetaeva had created a myth that gave her an outlet into the infinity of inspiration—making possible her precarious acrobatic equilibrium, which once seemed capable of endlessly summoning the abyss of sublimity out of the refuse of body, real life, and interpersonal relationships. In her fantasy, she conceived of poetic language as an inviolable absolute, unbeholden to the relationships that govern reality. Between her willful creation of new etymologies through the paronomastic rearrangement of syllables, morphemes, and phonemes on the one hand, and her hypothesized creation of an alternate realm of spiritual existence on the other hand, she placed hardly so much as a long dash. Usurping God's creative powers, she imagined that her poetic Logos possessed an independent reality that allowed her to conjure up whole new worlds at will. She deliberately ignored the fact that language is a composite emanation of human traditions and desires, and that her own word weavings were therefore susceptible to the destructive fire of her poetic passion. Language was the unflagging tightrope that divided the two existential abysses between which she carried out her poetic negotiations; she knew that it was possible to fall, but she never considered that the cable itself might fray or even break.

In "Poems to Blok" and "Poems to Akhmatova" we have seen the blasphemous implications of Tsvetaeva's transgressive poetic inspiration; in "On a Red Steed" the rider's red horse smacks of hellfire as it plunges to destroy Christ's altar in the cathedral. Yet in all these works, the demonic nature of Tsvetaeva's muse is never openly stated; it is as if she herself is attempting not to see. This may not be a simple case of moral evasion, but a result of the considered complexity of Tsvetaeva's poetic project. Northrop Frye writes of the usual alignment of the desirable and the moral in literature:

The relation of innocence and experience to apocalyptic and demonic imagery illustrates ... displacement ... in the direction of the moral. The two dialectical structures are, radically, the desirable and the undesirable. Racks and dungeons belong in the sinister vision not because they are morally forbidden but because it is impossible to make them objects of desire. Sexual fulfillment, on the other hand, may be desired even if it is morally condemned. Civilization tends to try to make the desirable and the moral coincide.[40]

In "On a Red Steed," Tsvetaeva, faced with the need to transcend the limitations of her gender, transgresses civilization's habitual proscriptions insofar as she pursues her desire not only outside the sanctioned limits of human morality, but even outside the bounds of the desirable itself. In other words, she makes Frye's figurative "racks and dungeons"—that is, the psychological torture of guilt, and the erotic torture of her bondage to the absent horseman—the impossible objects of her desire.[41] In the process, Frye's antithetical categories of the apocalyptic and the demonic merge; Tsvetaeva's holy quest for spiritual apotheosis is at the same time a headlong rush toward damnation. This identity is not a moral choice as such; rather, it is conditioned by the parameters of her metaphysical plight. As she writes to Pasternak: "Boris, *it's all the same to me, where I'm flying to.* And maybe my deep amorality (ungodliness) consists precisely in this" (6:249; emphasis in the original). Tsvetaeva's only choice is a primal one: to be, or not to be, a poet. Once she has decided in the affirmative, there is a haunting inevitability to the path she follows. In this austere dialectic between freedom and fate is contained the kernel of her poetic greatness and the key to her personal tragedy.

By the end of her relationship with Shteiger, Tsvetaeva has obviously begun to think through these issues, to take stock of her poetic achievements and the sacrifices and compromises they have demanded throughout her life. In the process, she begins to reconceptualize her lifelong battle *for* poetry as necessarily a bid *against:* not merely against her old enemies—flesh, sexuality, drudgery, creative barrenness—but also against humanity, morality, goodness. In her attempts to separate body from soul, necessitated by the paradox of her female gender, she has reviled the sanctity of human life in all its complex duality of essence. This certainly was not her intent; but nor has she done anything to prevent this outcome. She has served poetry exclusively, never admitting the possibility of split loyalties. Her 1932 essay "Art in the Light of Conscience"—written almost a full decade before her suicide—grows out of the despairing ethical inquiry that haunted her in her final years. The ideas that shape this important philosophical work, however, are not recent ones but have been developing gradually in her poetry over time.

As early as 1925, even before Tsvetaeva's encounter with Rilke, we find among the last poems of *After Russia* a number of lyrics that express her growing poetic weariness, as she begins to shift her attentions away from the spiritual travails of her impossible romance with Pasternak and back to her practical obligations in daily, familial life. One such lyric is "Alive and not dead" ["Zhiv, a ne umer . . ."] (2:254), in which she returns to the allegory of the muse to describe her inspirational impasse—only to discover that her muse has metamorphosed from the stern, salvational angel of "On a Red Steed" into a torturing demon:[42]

> Жив, а не умер
> Демон во мне!
> В теле как в трюме,
> В себе как в тюрьме.

> [Alive and not dead is the demon in me! Being in my body is like being locked inside a ship's hold, being in myself is like being in prison.]

In the remainder of this poem, Tsvetaeva imagines that all poets are allied in a (necessarily self-defeating) campaign against their own physical being—a rebellion that she, pursuing a dangerous train of logic, couches as a battle against a supposedly paternalistic tradition of embodiment:

> (Только поэты
> В кости как во лжи!)

> Нет, не гулять нам,
> Певчая братья,
> В теле как в ватном
> Отчем халате.

> [(Only for poets is being incarnate in the skeleton a lie!)
> No, it's not for us to amble, lyrical brotherhood, in the body as in a paternal quilted dressing gown.]

The playfulness of Tsvetaeva's poetics, which results from her penetrating sense of the irreality and conditionality of the world around her, is now brought home to its very real, tragic consequences:

> Мир—это стены.
> Выход—топор.
> («Мир—это сцена»,
> Лепечет актер).
>
> [The world—is walls. The exit—an axe. ("The world—is a stage," the actor babbles).]

Earlier Tsvetaeva was able to treat the world as a puppet stage, playing in it when she was so inclined: treating the people around her as marionettes that could be set in motion by her poetic will—and ruining the thing when she grew weary, stepping easily over an imaginary, safe threshold into the bliss of non-being. Now, however, she intuits that such irresponsible play is not innocuous, and that the escape from her imaginary world into reality will entail violence of one kind or another: "The exit—an axe."

In "Alive and not dead," Tsvetaeva's alliance with the spiritual at first seems complete and vigorous to the extreme, sustained as it is by a numbing litany of insults against body as captivity: "ship's hold" [trium], "prison" [tiur′ma], "walls" [steny], "stage" [stsena], "glory" [slava],[43] "toga" [toga], "lie" [lozh′], "dressing gown" [khalat], "stall" [stoilo], "cauldron" [kotel], "swamp" [top′], "crypt" [sklep], and finally "utmost exile" [krainiaia ssylka]. However, from the poem's beginning we also sense the troubling hint of a fissure in her bond with her demonic muse. This fissure expands into a definite rift with lightning speed in the poem's final three lines (the last of them extra-stanzaic):

> В теле—как в тайне,
> В висках—как в тисках
>
> Маски железной.
>
> [In my body—as in a secret; in my temples—as in the vice grip of an iron mask.]

Suddenly, shockingly, Tsvetaeva's poetic identity—metonymized by her "temples" [viski]—has become a stifling vice grip [tiski] that threatens to crush her entirely.[44] That a poet haunted by a demonic muse is subject to such suffering suggests that Tsvetaeva's poetic efforts are not merely superhuman, but super-demonic. Even as she suffocates in her muse's harsh embrace, though, she gaspingly reverses her previous pronouncements on the body. The body is a secret, she confesses. True, a painful one—yet a desired one. Suddenly, all that she has reviled in her poetry is imbued with real value, although her losses can no longer be salvaged. Despite all her raging against the confines of physicality, she now admits that the body is a mystery she cannot penetrate, cannot possess, any more than she can possess the reality of any of her poetic beloveds. Her rage is, in this sense, a bluff for her desire, just as her pride is often a bluff for deep hurt.

Several scholars have speculated that, for all Tsvetaeva's apparent sexual bravado in poetry as in life, sexual fulfillment for its own sake eluded her, with the possible exceptions of her lesbian relationship with Sofiia Parnok and her later brief but passionate liaison with Konstantin Rodzevich.[45] Of course, there is no way for us to judge the reliability of these conjectures, but Tsvetaeva's own repeated statements (in her letters to Voloshin, Pasternak, and Rilke, as well as elsewhere) that sex for her is a means to penetrate the shell of the body and bare her lover's soul—a necessary trial in pursuit of spiritual wholeness, akin to walking through a wall of fire—bolsters the probability that this hypothesis is not, after all, too far from the truth.[46] Aside from subtle hints, though, Tsvetaeva never condescends to "give the body its due" so much as to delve openly into these issues in a poetic forum; instead, she retreats defensively into her poetic pride, as in another brief lyric of 1925: "Arrogance—is my caste. Rather than [admit] lack—renunciation . . . And the rest—is a secret: they'll cut it out with my tongue" [Vysokomer'e—kasta. / Chem nedokhvat—otkaz . . . / A ostal'noe—taina: / Vyrezhut s iazykom] (2:260).

The final lines of "Alive and not dead" echo undeniably in "Art in the Light of Conscience," where Tsvetaeva's muse again is explicitly identified as a demon:

The demon (the elemental) pays his victim. You give me—your blood, life, conscience; I'll give you—such a feeling of power (for the power is mine!), such mastery over everyone (except yourself, for you are mine!), such freedom in my vice grip [v moikh tiskakh], that every other power will be laughable to you, every other kind of mastery will be too little, every other brand of freedom will be too narrow

—and every other prison [tiur'ma] will be too wide.

Art does not pay its victims. It does not even know them. The master, not the lathe, pays the servant. The lathe can only leave him without an arm. (5:369)

Here again is the paradoxically liberating "vice grip" [tiski] of poetic servitude; here again, too, is the prison [tiur'ma] which, in "Alive and not dead," was ostensibly a metaphor for the body. In the context of this essay, however, it becomes clear that the alternate "self" that Tsvetaeva constructs in her poetry is, ironically, as much of a prison—a mode of enslavement—as the body which that new self rejects. Not only is life a theater, a fiction, but poetry is, too; words alone cannot propel the poet into the absolute. "Art in the Light of Conscience" thus deepens the ambiguities of "Alive and not dead" and makes manifest the poem's subtle suggestion that Tsvetaeva is beginning to acknowledge both the real, human price she has paid (and will continue to pay) for her poetic license, and the ultimate insufficiency of the poetics to which she has sacrificed so dearly.

Poetry's vice grip on Tsvetaeva may be associated both with the unflinching, unflagging effort of will and self-discipline required to tame the poetic impulse into a finished work of art (her poetic work ethic[47]), and with the sheer pressure of her unrelenting creative drive—which she describes elsewhere in "Art in the Light of Conscience," using the French words, as a maddeningly ceaseless alternation between the states of *obsession* and *possession* (5:366). This paradoxical state is not so very different, after all, from the frenzy of sexual desire and dependence that Tsvetaeva so fears and shuns. Even poetic language emanates originally from human and bodily experience; the temples that symbolize poetic freedom also codify bodily incarceration, so that poetry is just one more version of nonfreedom. Poetic language is ultimately just as confining as the body from which it emerges.

Therefore, the "iron mask" that ends "Alive and not dead" suggests yet another, more sinister meaning: poetry itself—that is, the shell of words with which Tsvetaeva surrounds herself; the imagined identity that she fantasizes on the page as a replacement for her own humble, human, female form—is a colossal game of incognito, in which she has lost herself even to herself. The mask will not come off. Indeed, the fact that the iron mask occurs extra-stanzaically suggests that it contains even the poem itself. This outcome is not unreasonable, given Tsvetaeva's numerous poetic "manifestoes" devoted to the idea that poetry is a beautiful lie; an example is the 1914 poem "Insanity—and wisdom" ["Bezum'e—i blagorazum'e . . ."] (1:233–34), in which she declares: "I am a virtuoso of virtuosos in the art of the lie" [Ia virtuoz iz virtuozov / V iskusstve lzhi]. This lie, this mask, is required by Tsvetaeva's female gender and her resulting problematic subjectivity; indeed, if she is to be a poet at all, she is required to forge an alternate identity for herself in order to achieve access to the alterity of poetic inspiration. There is thus a pernicious element of self-deceit inherent in her poetic stance. She knows that the alternate reality she imagines is not and can never be made real. The pitilessly crushing iron mask is, truly, a condition of her identity as poet.

Like the iron mask, the cruel lathe [stanok] in the passage cited from "Art in the Light of Conscience" is an image for the inescapability of the vicious inspirational circle in which the female poet finds herself. Just as words are conditional upon body, so too body is affected by words; the endlessly rotating disk of the poetic machine can obliviously lop off an arm—or lop away a loved one. Body invades poetry; words are merely a force field within which the poet seeks to manipulate and transform real desires, real emotions. Tsvetaeva's ventures into the poetic realm have not brought her access to the ideal otherness that she desired. Rather, she has entered into a cycle of perpetual yearning and frustration in which the sexual and the poetic are, for all her rebelliousness, ultimately inseparable.

In the early part of "Art in the Light of Conscience" Tsvetaeva seems to picture this entrapping cycle in a positive light reminiscent of the salvational circles of "New Year's Letter," when she invokes the inviolable wholeness of being to which poetry gives access:

> As long as you are a poet, you cannot perish in the elements, for everything returns you to the element of all elements: the word.
>
> As long as you are a poet, you cannot perish in the elements, for it would not be death, but a return to the bosom.
>
> A poet's destruction is in his renunciation of the elemental. It's simpler just to slit one's veins with no further ado. (5:351)

This passage reads like a mantra or a prayer, due to an underlying melody of archaic and biblical diction (*gibel'* [death], *ibo* [for], *slovo* [word], *lono* [bosom]). Yet the magical circle of words within which the poet finds direct entry into the elements is like a charm: it operates through belief and can collapse in a moment of hesitation. Tsvetaeva's salvation in "Art in the Light of Conscience" is by no means assured. By renaming "death" a "return to the bosom," she reiterates the conditions of creative Mra which also give shape to "New Year's Letter" — but, at the same time, she casts doubt upon the efficacy of this myth when she claims, contrary to usual categories of human cognition, that a poet's only real death lurks is in her renunciation of poetry — an act equivalent to suicide.

In other words, Tsvetaeva willfully shifts the definitions of metaphysical realities as if they are free-floating algebraic variables: creative barrenness is renamed death, and real suicide becomes a return to the elemental Logos. Furthermore, the particular suicidal method she selects is uncomfortably close to her metaphors elsewhere of poetry as bloodletting, as in her well-known poem "I opened my veins" ["Vskryla zhily . . ."] (2:315). The female poet is in a double bind. If she writes poetry — she kills herself; if she does not write poetry — she kills herself. The only difference is in what the two kinds of death are called; *Mra* is a kind of paradoxical spiritual salvation, whereas *smert'* is the worm and the tomb. The poet is poised precariously between the abyss of life (body) and the abyss of death (spirit), which circle around her and become indistinguishable from one another. In the absence of a true muse in Tsvetaeva's inspirational mythology, traditional hierarchies are overturned; inspiration is not bestowed but is stolen, self-induced.

The more hopeless her entrapment, the more intensely Tsvetaeva's poet thirsts for inspiration. It is no accident that Goethe's *Faust* is a recurrent motif in "Art in the Light of Conscience." Excluded from the salvational channels that Rilke follows into angelhood, Tsvetaeva makes a subversive pact with the devil. Her object is not the glorification of God, but the intoxicating power of contact with the elemental: "I don't know for whose glory, and I think that here the question is one not of glory, but of power" (5:346). Indeed, the words *sila* [strength] and *vlast'* [power, mastery] are recurrent motifs in "Art in the Light of Conscience" as well. The origin of poetic power is explicitly located "beyond good and evil," in the service of spiritual suffering: "This is the poet's innermost kernel [zerno zerna]—*obligatory* artistry on behalf of—*the power of anguish*" (5:364). Poetry is no longer an end in itself, but merely a means to experiencing the thrill of demonic power.

Tsvetaeva is trapped forever in the endless cycle of striving and failing, of metaphysical intermediacy—and the salvational circle she once envisioned for herself through Rilke's death quickly closes into a Dantesque circle of damnation. Moreover, this metaphysical trap is enacted in the obsessive, convoluted circularity of the language that describes it:

In relation to the spiritual world—art is a kind of physical world of the spiritual.

In relation to the physical world—art is a kind of spiritual world of the physical.

Leading away from the earth—the first millimeter of air above its surface is already sky (for either the sky begins immediately above the earth, or it does not exist at all. This can be tested by extrapolating to a great distance, which will clarify the phenomenon).

Leading down from the sky—that same first millimeter over the earth becomes the last from above, which means that it is almost the earth, and from the greatest height of heaven—it *is* the earth. (5:361)

This is a corruption of the infinitely terraced structure of being that Tsvetaeva imagines in "New Year's Letter" and "Poem of the Air." In those earlier works, the widening circles of meaning lead progressively outward and upward, so that she is successful in climbing far beyond the lowest, almost palpable spiritual sky that is earthly poetry, beyond words and sounds altogether, into new realms of continual growth and striving. By the end of "Art in the Light of Conscience," on the contrary, the circles have all collapsed into one. The poet is inside, trapped between her physical and spiritual aspects. She can no longer climb beyond the lowest strip of poetic "sky" that is all that is available to her in life; she has no exit into an outside perspective, and the result is that, whereas earlier she was alienated only from body, now she is alienated from poetry as well in her strivings toward higher spiritual realms.

Eventually, then, Tsvetaeva comes to see her poems themselves as physical objects that, like her skin and bones, she yearns to shed and leave behind entirely. Even the soul that she had once so glorified seems to be now just a tiny

The End of the Line

step above body in the context of the spiritual infinity that Rilke's death first revealed to her:

> In the same way the soul, which the common person considers to be the height of spirituality, is, for a spiritual person, almost flesh . . . The entire event of poetry—from the poet's inspiration to the reader's reception—transpires entirely in the soul—in that first, lowest sky of the spirit. . .
>
> O poet, poet! The most animated/inspired [samyi odushevlennyi], yet how often—maybe even precisely by virtue of this animation—the most inanimate/uninspirited object/being [samyi neodukhotvorennyi predmet]! (5:361)

This last outcry captures perfectly Tsvetaeva's artistic predicament throughout her life: her feeling of overwhelming inspiration ("samyi odushevlennyi"), her inability to locate that feeling in any valid higher spiritual reality ("samyi neodukhotvorennyi"), and her resultant inability to be transformed from a mere female "object" [predmet] into a true self.[48]

Despite—or perhaps because of—the incalculable losses Tsvetaeva narrates in "Art in the Light of Conscience," the essay as a whole is vociferous, argumentative, and by and large assertive of her rightness—poetic, though not moral rightness—in the way she has lived her life, in the works she has written and the way she has written them, and in her convictions and beliefs. Throughout the essay, she repeatedly alternates between ruminations on her uniquely female poetic predicament and efforts to find poetic examples outside herself that can justify her own comportment—instances in which male poets, too, dabble dangerously with death, spurred by artistic necessity, with sometimes damaging results. As is the case in her statement comparing the deaths of Pushkin and Maiakovskii that ends "Art in the Light of Conscience," so, too, throughout the entire essay, she seems to be searching for poetic archetypes that may reassure her of the fatedness of her life's achievements (in both a positive and a negative sense) and give her some insight into her own eventual end.

The archetypes Tsvetaeva discovers in her essay are numerous and varied. Pushkin taking refuge from cholera and the spiritual plagues of his own time in his reimagination of history in *Feast during a Plague* [*Pir vo vremia chumy*], then killing off his hero Walsingham in order to save himself. The suicide of Goethe's Werther—a fictional "event" that awakened a dangerous suicidal wave among contemporary youth. Maiakovskii's political gamble to silence his own lyrical instinct by "stepping on the throat of his own song"—a tactic that could not end otherwise than in the extrapolation of this figurative self-destruction to its literal end.[49] In each case, Tsvetaeva asks, implicitly or explicitly: "Are they guilty?" And the resounding, repeated judgment that comes down is the following: "As a person—yes, as an artist—no" (5:353).[50] With this answer, too, she provocatively ends her essay, implicitly daring the reader (whom she thought of at this time in her life—and probably rightly so—as sharply critical: a petty, nitpicking human parody of the inflexible Old Testament God) to apply the same standard of judgment and forgiveness to her as he applies to Pushkin, Goethe, and Maiakovskii. She outlines the standard thus:

It is more important to be a person, because it is more useful . . . With the exception of parasites in all their various forms—everyone is more useful than we [poets] are.

And knowing this, having signed my name to it in full possession of my faculties of reason and being of firm memory, I attest that I would not exchange my own occupation for any other. Knowing the greater, I do the lesser. Therefore there can be no forgiveness for me. At the Last Judgment of conscience, only those such as I will be called to accounting. But if there is a Last Judgment of the word—there I am innocent. (5:374)

Both the subject matter and the stylized phraseology here ("having signed my name . . . in full possession of my faculties and being of firm memory . . .") indicate that this passage, albeit ironic to a degree, is intended as Tsvetaeva's last will and testament—her last defiant answer to her merciless critics and, most of all, to the merciless critic seated within her self. It is a function of her extra-temporal poetic stance that she pens these resonant "final words" a full decade before her death.

Yet, although this may indeed be Tsvetaeva's last answer in "Art in the Light of Conscience," it is not the only answer she offers within the space of the essay to the hypothetical charge that her poetics are immoral (in trumping up this accusation against herself, incidentally, she also puts a smoking gun into the hands of future literary critics). Instead, there is another tentative, frightened answer muffled in the essay's center. Rather, this is not even an answer, but an alternative life course, a brief glimpse of the path not taken. I refer to the section of the essay entitled "Art without Artifice" ["Iskusstvo bez iskusa"] (*iskus* may also mean "bite" or "seductiveness"), in which Tsvetaeva meditates on the artless but moral, poetically bad but ethically good "poems" of several poetic ingénues:

The mark of such works is their effectiveness combined with the insufficiency of their means, an insufficiency which we would not for anything in the world exchange for any kind of sufficiency and superfluity and which we notice only when we attempt to figure out how the thing is made . . .

Not quite art, yet more than art.

Such works often belong to the pen of women, children, the self-taught—the humble creatures of this world. (5:356)

Tsvetaeva includes in this category of "artless art" verses composed by a four-year-old boy, a seven-year-old lame girl, and a nun of the Novodevichii Monastery, as well as the poems of her precocious daughter Alia, written at the age of six. All these works are characterized by an unevenness of composi-

The End of the Line 211

tion; linguistic awkwardness inadvertently resulting, on occasion, in linguistic originality; emotional poignancy; a charming yet pitiful naïveté of themes and means; and—most important—absolute sincerity and human goodness. As Tsvetaeva explains, such poems are quite impossible to cope with by usual critical means:

To call these lines "brilliant" would be heresy, and to judge them as a literary production would be simply petty—for this is all so far beyond the threshold of *art's great smallness* (like that of earthly love) . . .

But maybe only such poems are true poems after all? (5:357)

This question, of course, is ironic coming from the pen of Tsvetaeva, whose definition of poetry is as far as can be from such artless ingenuousness, and whose whole creative life has been dedicated to severing herself completely from this stereotypical brand of women's writing.

At the same time, though, the question clearly haunts her. Such "artless" souls present her with a dramatic foil to the governing principles of her own life. Moral goodness, she intimates, is necessarily linked with unconscious innocence. Good deeds produce weak words; bad deeds—and the doer's painful awareness of his guilt—produce strong words. Tsvetaeva has opted for the path of consciousness and strength that goes contrary to her feminine destiny, and she has had to abandon morality in the process. She has traded in the "circular bond of kindness" [krugovaia poruka dobra] that she finds so moving in the nun's poem for the "circular bond of orphanhood" [krugovaia poruka sirotstva] that torments and isolates her. She has traded in innocence for the creative pangs of conscience. In so doing, she reverses Pushkin's message in his play *Mozart and Salieri* (to which she alludes elsewhere in "Art in the Light of Conscience" [5:368]) to argue that not only is it untrue that "genius and evil are incompatible" [genii i zlodeistvo / Dve veshchi nesovmestnye],[51] but that genius necessitates evil.

Ultimately, then, try as she might to emulate male poets like Pushkin and Maiakovskii, the implication is that Tsvetaeva believes that for her, as a female, the standards do and must differ. This is why, when she contemplates her own poetry in the soft moral light shed by the artless works of the women she "should" resemble, she feels a strange admixture of tenderness and remorse:

These poems are my favorites of all poems that I have ever read or written, my favorites of all poems in the world. When after reading them I read (or write) my own, I feel nothing but shame. (5:358)

By absenting herself from the endless circle of human goodness, Tsvetaeva hints, she has damned herself to the exitless circle of the metaphysical void. This passage is at one and the same time a playful simulation of the traditional female sentimentality and female lack of aesthetic taste that she has long since left behind, and a serious statement of her overwhelming feeling of shame and moral responsibility for the transgressions required by her poetic destiny.[52]

In fact, such ambivalent admissions of moral responsibility are characteristic of Tsvetaeva's poetic stance from the earliest stage; her existential guilt is an inherent part of her poetic mythos, as demonstrated by the recurrent motif of the Last Judgment in her writing. Her guilt seems to emerge not as a result of any of her specific actions or even specific poems, but from the very fact of her aspiration to be a poet that is, in and of itself, a transgression of human (i.e., feminine) norms. Nevertheless, despite the different origins of her guilt, the judgment upon her is consistent with that meted out to Pushkin, Goethe, and Maiakovskii in "Art in the Light of Conscience": she is guilty as a human being, innocent as a poet. Many examples of the doomsday motif in Tsvetaeva's writing can be cited, spanning all the years of her creative life. For example, from 1913:

> Идите же! Мой голос нем
> И тщетны все слова.
> Я знаю, что ни перед кем
> Не буду я права.
> . . . .
> Но помните, что будет суд,
> Разящий, как стрела,
> Когда над головой блеснут
> Два пламенных крыла.
>
> [Go on then! My voice is dumb and all my words are in vain. I know that I will never be in the right before anyone . . . But remember that there will be a judgment, penetrating as an arrow, when above our heads will flash two flaming wings.]

From 1915:

> Заповедей не блюла, не ходила к причастью . . .
> Богу на Страшном суде вместе ответим, Земля!
>
> [I did not keep the commandments, I did not take communion . . . Earth, we will answer God together at the Final Judgment!]

From 1918:

> Закинув голову и опустив глаза,
> Пред ликом Господа и всех святых—стою.
> Сегодня праздник мой, сегодня—Суд.
> . . . .

Так, смертной женщиной, — опущен взор,
Так, гневным ангелом — закинут лоб,
В день Благовещенья, у Царских врат,
Перед лицом твоим — гляди! — стою.

[With my head thrown back and eyes cast downward, before the image of the Lord and all the saints—I stand. Today is my holiday, today is—the Judgment... Just so, like a mortal woman—my gaze is averted; just so, like a wrathful angel—my forehead is thrown back. On the day of the Annunciation, at the Tsar's gates, before your face—behold!—I stand.]

From 1920:

И будем мы судимы — знай —
Одною мерою.
И будет нам обоим — Рай,
В который — верую.

[And know that we will be judged by a single measure. And we will both reach Paradise, in which I believe.]

From 1935:

О, с чем на Страшный суд
Предстанете: на свет!
Хвататели минут,
Читатели газет!

[Oh, what will you present at the Final Judgment: to the world! Grabbers of minutes, readers of newspapers!]

It is impossible for Tsvetaeva to make her Faustian bargain for poetic power only in words and not in life. Her tactic of utilizing metaphors of willful neglect, violence, and even murder wholly outside of their moral context—for purely symbolic, metaphysical ends—must ultimately fail because, if she is a true poet (which she is), then she necessarily believes in poetry's transformative, physical reality.

By the very execution of her experiment, therefore, Tsvetaeva forces the fair-minded critic to participate in her own dangerously dissociative state of consciousness and, in so doing, to echo her own self-judgment: guilty as a human, as a poet—no. The co-creative critic, in other words, finds herself manipulated into echoing willy-nilly Tsvetaeva's own perilous intellectual dichotomies. The vicious circle in which Tsvetaeva spins sucks her ideal reader in as well; perhaps resistance to this threat is the secret to the condescension and censure that have often sounded in critical responses to this poet's life and works, in her time as in ours.

Very occasionally, as we have observed, Tsvetaeva writes from the "human" stance rather than the "poetic" one, painfully avowing her feeling of indelible guilt before those she loves and wounds by her irrepressible quest for the maximal experience of passion (read: transgression) that fires her poetry. Such instances in her oeuvre are few, muted, and often heavily encoded, but they do, nevertheless, exist. Often, in such cases, Tsvetaeva's guilt is articulated yet rationalized, at the same time, by some version of a motif of stark reciprocity that justifies her actions by presenting them as ultimately fated. The poet's free choice accomplishes her destiny; this complex dialectic is characteristic, we recall, of "On a Red Steed" and, in fact, of Tsvetaeva's ontology as a whole. A cryptic example of such rationalized self-condemnation is found in a brief poem from as far back as 1918:

> Кто дома не строил—
> Земли недостоин.
>
> Кто дома не строил—
> Не будет землею:
> Соломой—золою...
>
> —Не строила дома.
>
> [Whoever has built no home—is not worthy of the earth. Whoever has built no home—will not become earth: but straw—ash...—I built no home.]

Here, what at first seems to be Tsvetaeva's acknowledgment of moral culpability for her undomestic ways is then twisted implicitly into a proof of her poetic greatness, because the earth of which she is "unworthy" in the first stanza becomes, in the second, unworthy of her—whom immortality awaits. It is interesting that her transgression against home and family is presented here in a transgendered, purely human context: she evokes the domesticity usually associated with women via the metaphor of building, a stereotypically male sphere of activity. This strategy is similar to her attempts to align her own guilt with that of other, male poets in "Art in the Light of Conscience."

But Tsvetaeva, woman that she is, feels compelled to scrutinize her personal mistakes and weaknesses—particularly as they affect her spouse and her children—in a way that male poets, it seems, rarely do. Just as in "Poems to an Orphan" she castigates herself for her ill-treatment of her adoptive poetic "lovers" and "children," so too in other poems does she confront the damage done to her real family by her inveterate poetic need to love in extremis only. For example, in poems written to her husband Sergei Efron in anticipation of their reunion in 1922,[53] Tsvetaeva envisions a stark economy of payment for sins (i.e., her adulterous strayings, most of them probably accomplished in thought only, during their years apart) that is often colored by an ascetic Christian ideology. In "I sit without light, and without bread" ["Sizhu bez sveta, i bez khleba..."] (1:537), the poet imagines that by undergoing extreme hardships, she can demonstrate her full repentance and, by this means, "buy back" her endangered mate from the clutches of fate: "I sit—since morning, not a stale crust—nurturing such a dream that maybe, with all my obedience—my Warrior!—I will earn you back" [Sizhu,—s utra ni korki cherstvoi—/ Mechtu takuiu poliubia / Chto—mozhet—vsem svoim pokorstvom /—Moi Voin!—vykupliu tebia]. In the somewhat later cycle "Good News" ["Blagaia vest'"], written immediately after Tsvetaeva learned that Sergei Efron was, in fact, alive and well and living in Prague, this theme modulates into another vein. Now she must pay, not for sins committed, but for undeserved happiness: "I am defeated, struck with terror. Now what will be extracted—in exchange?" [Oglushena, / Ustrashena. / Chto zhe vzamen—/ Vyrvut?].

Tsvetaeva's desperate poetic "mothering" of Gronskii and Shteiger later in life may have been, in part at least, a reaction to her deepening feeling of responsibility for the real-life tragedies—each unique—of her three real children of the flesh, Ariadna (Alia), Irina, and Georgii (Mur). Most dramatic and troubling of these tragedies, of course, is little Irina's death of starvation in an orphanage in 1920—an event to which Tsvetaeva devoted a single poem, "Two hands resting lightly" ["Dve ruki, legko opushchennye..."] (1:518), in which, as David Bethea claims, she "presents the loss of one daughter and the preservation of the other as a kind of romanticized and unavoidable 'Sophie's Choice.'"[54] However, this horrifying analysis implies a kind of agency that Tsvetaeva, in fact, does not exercise in the poem. Instead, she is guilty of the maternal ineptitude that emerges from her poetic strength—or, as she puts it elsewhere: "my adventurism, my careless attitude toward difficulties, and finally—my health, my monstrous endurance" (6:153). Irina's death is a result of her mother's inattention, for Tsvetaeva is occupied with her "poetic" offspring—that is, her older daughter Alia, who was recovering from malaria during this time. Tsvetaeva was very close to Alia, with her sharp wit and precociously creative bent, whereas she seems to have felt alienated from the listless, needy, sweet, and pitiful Irina.[55]

Tormented in retrospect by the memory of this split allegiance and relying upon her sense of the grim reciprocity that governs the relationships between sin and responsibility, free will and fate, Tsvetaeva attempts in "Two hands resting lightly" to mythologize Irina's death by reconceiving the tragedy as the unwitting result of her own choice of poetry over life, thereby reiterating her own poetic destiny. She communicates this meaning by the symbolic divorce of her own two hands in the poem: "Two hands—and suddenly one of them in the course of a single night turned out to be extra" [Dve ruki—i vot odna iz nikh / Zá noch' okazalas' lishniaia]. The symbolic motif of a conflict between the poet's right and left hands often expresses the profound psychological split in Tsvetaeva's own concept of self.[56] Hence, in "Two hands resting lightly," she tacitly presents her guilt as that of an immortal being before the suffering and demise of a mere human—not a causal guilt, but an existential one. Tsvetaeva is guilty, in her poetic reimaginings, less by virtue of what she did or did not do to help her daughter than by what she *is*. In this way, she achieves a philosophical expansion of the very concept of moral responsibility—an expansion that is tantamount to her crossing the line into the realm of the divine or the inhuman.

Evidently, it is easier for Tsvetaeva to take responsibility on herself than to admit the randomness of Irina's tragedy. Fate, for Tsvetaeva, must always have a shape and a meaning; fate must always be poetic. In truth of fact, Tsvetaeva's predicament at this time was dire, and Irina's death, although perhaps avoidable, was certainly unforeseeable—nor was it unique: indeed, such deaths of children placed in orphanages by their desperate parents during these hungry years were something of an epidemic. Yet, in the throes of despair, Tsvetaeva—ever the poet—attempts to imagine an aesthetically satisfying (though morally abhorrent) rationale for her child's calamitous, wrenching death, a tragedy that is otherwise unbearable. Poetry is Tsvetaeva's only means of coping with life and her only means of communicating; this inadequacy is the true location of her guilt, if such there be.

The moral responsibility that Tsvetaeva feels before her older daughter Alia is of a very different kind. She recognizes that, just as her own mother bled into the young Marina enough artistic and romantic frustration to suffice for a lifetime of pain, so too the grown Tsvetaeva unintentionally tortures her elder daughter by the very intensity of her love.[57] The torment of poetry is to Alia what the burden of music was to Tsvetaeva as a girl. When Alia spends some time with friends in the country in the summer of 1921, Tsvetaeva reflects with merciless self-awareness on the relief her daughter must feel in exiting her mother's sphere of influence:

I don't miss Alia—I know that she's having fun, my heart is reasonable and fair—the way other people's is *when they do not love*. She writes to me infrequently: left to herself, she's becoming a child, i.e. a forgetful creature who avoids anything painful (and it is true that I bring pain to her life, I am *the pain of her life*). I write rarely: I don't want to dampen her spirits, every letter of mine will cost her several pounds of lost weight, therefore in nearly a month—only two letters . . . I am beginning to think—in all seriousness—that I am harmful to Alia . . . Alia laughs when she is with others, but with me she cries, with others she grows fat but with me she grows thin . . . Without me, of course, she will not write any poems, she won't even look at her notebook, because poems are—me, the notebook is—pain. (6:181–82)

A powerful two-poem cycle that Tsvetaeva addressed to Alia in October 1919 ("To Alia" ["Ale"] [1:485–86]) expresses her chagrin at the creatively domineering, almost sadistic role she has come to play in her daughter's fragile psyche. The metaphor she uses in the cycle's first poem is a forced walk across a tightrope:

> Ни кровинки в тебе здоровой.—
> Ты похожа на циркового.
>
> Вон над бездной встает, ликуя,
> Рассылающий поцелуи.
> . . . .
> Что, голубчик, дрожат поджилки?
> Все как надо: канат—носилки.
>
> Разлетается в ладан сизый
> Материнская антреприза.
>
> [Not a healthy droplet in you. You look like a circus acrobat. There above the abyss he stands up, rejoicing, sending around kisses . . . What, my little dove, do your knees tremble? Everything is as it should be: the tightrope—the stretcher. The maternal enterprise scatters into the gray mist of incense.]

This tightrope [kanat] is the very cable above the abyss that Tsvetaeva herself treads in her poetry. The poetic gamble she makes in so doing, she recognizes here, risks not only her own life and well-being, but also those of the vulnerable creature closest to her.

Indeed, whereas Tsvetaeva is a robust poetic acrobat, her portrait of Alia recalls Picasso's haunting images of emaciated saltimboques.[58] The untranslatable "materinskaia antrepriza" [maternal enterprise/undertaking/theatrical business] that goes flying into the hazy netherworld is at once both Tsvetaeva's life-and-death poetic "play" for which her own existence is the stage, and her nonpoetic, human offspring Ariadna, drawn into the spectacle perforce. The two meanings are inseparable; Tsvetaeva's exhilarating metaphysical plunge is her daughter's bone-smashing, winding, terrifying crash into an all-too-real abyss. Moreover, Tsvetaeva's austere tutelage, intended to dissolve for her daughter the limitations of female gender against which she herself has always rebelled, goes terribly wrong in the second poem of "To Alia":

> Упадешь—перстом не двину.
> Я люблю тебя как сына.
>
> Всей мечтой своей довлея,
> Не щадя и не жалея.

> Я учу: губам полезно
> Раскаленное железо
>
> Бархатных ковров полезней —
> Гвозди — молодым ступням.
>
> А еще в ночи беззвездной
> Под ногой — полезны — бездны!
>
> Первенец мой крутолобый!
> Вместо всей моей учебы —
> Материнская утроба
> Лучше — для тебя была б.

[If you fall — I won't move a finger. I love you like a son. All my dreams suffice; I am unsparing and unpitying. I teach: hot iron is good for the lips, and nails are better for young soles than velvet carpets. And also on starless nights, abysses beneath the feet are useful! My firstborn with your steep forehead! Instead of all my teachings — a mother's womb would have been better for you.]

This poem, cited here in its entirety, is remarkable for its brutal honesty; Tsvetaeva spares and pities herself no more than she does her daughter. Her teachings are fit for a saint or a martyr, but not for a sensitive little girl, intelligent though she might be. One of Alia's own childhood poems that Tsvetaeva published in her collection *Psyche* speaks eloquently of the strain that the girl experienced in growing up with such a mother: "You stand like an ancient statue leaning on a saber, and I, a leaf from the maple tree, drifted down to your stern feet" [Vy stoite kak statuia staraia / Operevshis′ na sabliu, / I ia, listik s klenovogo dereva, / Obletel k surovym nogam].[59]

When her long-desired son was born, Tsvetaeva may have thought that he was the miraculous, saintly offspring she had always dreamed of. These hopes were dramatically misguided; however, the extent to which Tsvetaeva was aware of Mur's shortcomings and of the failures of her own parenting in his regard remains a mystery that is intimately bound up with the reasons for her suicide. In any case it is clear that, by the end of her life, she had come to feel that she was more a burden and a hindrance to her son alive than she would be dead.[60] Mariia Belkina demonstrates how Tsvetaeva's earlier formula "as long as I am *alive* — Mur should be *well*" transmutes into its opposite: "I must depart, so as not to get in Mur's way." [61] Tsvetaeva's longing for a son was an obsession long before his actual birth and was surely bound up in her mythopoetic attempts to enter the line of male literary descent. In fact, chillingly, the very first poem she wrote after "Two hands resting lightly" — entitled "Son" ["Syn"] (2:519) — is a fantasy about the son who will, implicitly, someday replace the daughter she has just lost so tragically. She metaphorizes him as her crowning poetic masterpiece:

> И как не умереть поэту,
> Когда поэма удалась!
>
> Так, выступив из черноты бессонной
> Кремлевских башенных вершин,
> Предстал мне в предрассветном сонме
> Тот, кто еще придет—*мой сын*.
>
> [And how can the poet keep from dying, when he has achieved his masterpiece! Thus, stepping out from the insomniac blackness of the Kremlin towers' heights, in the predawn crowding, he who is yet to come appeared to me—*my son*.]

During Tsvetaeva's pregnancy with Mur and after his birth, her letters are full of him. She imagines him as a male hypostasis of her own self and dotes on him with an intensity that goes beyond motherly love to attain the frantic pitch of near-religious fervor. In the poem "Beneath My Shawl" ["Pod shal'iu"] (2:240), written during her pregnancy, there is even the overt suggestion that Mur is, indeed, a modern-day saint. Tsvetaeva's bizarre discussions in her correspondence of her son's behavior in utero conforms to the conventions of Byzantine saints' lives.[62] Her decision to name the boy Georgii—always her favorite saint and the patron saint of Moscow—likewise speaks of her fantastically inflated hopes for her child.

After Mur's birth, from the time of his infancy, Tsvetaeva's passionate love for him is all-consuming; she pours her whole self into him. At the same time, she force-feeds him the Russia he has never seen, as in "Poems to My Son" ["Stikhi k synu"]: "I, who pounded all of Russia into you, as with a pump!" [Ia, chto v tebia—vsiu Rus' / Vkachala—kak nasosom!] (2:301). She dreams of living alone with him on an island—the island she has previously associated with poetic exile and the homeland of her lonely soul—where they will be united in the perfect circle of mutual love, without the threat of outside intruders.[63] Tsvetaeva's love for her son is thus, in a sense, her consummate attempt at the merger with her own "male essence" or alter ego toward which she has been striving throughout her creative life. Sadly, she seems to have been largely unwilling to face (or at least to admit) the fact that Mur, for all his intelligence and precocity, was a sullen and unpleasant child, by many accounts selfish, inconsiderate, rude, and emotionally somehow stunted (his laconic diary jottings after his mother's death are revealing in this respect).

Still, it is probable that Tsvetaeva is, after all, deeply cognizant of her failure in Mur's upbringing, although she can never bear to voice fully this most painful secret. As early as 1935, she hints obtusely in a brief, desolate poem at Mur's unhappiness and its tragic resemblance to her own inhuman anguish:

> И если в сердечной пустыне,
> Пустынной до краю очей,
> Чего-нибудь жалко — так сына, —
> Волчонка — еще поволчей!
>
> [And if in my heart's wilderness, wild to the edge of vision, I'm sorry for anything — then it's my son, a wolf cub — even more wolfish!]

The lonely, disturbed ten-year-old boy of this poem is even more of an outcast from humanity than is his dangerous, perpetually ravenous wolflike mother. Whereas she retains at least the vestiges of memories that once bound her to life, he — thanks to the isolation in which she has selfishly kept him — has never known anything but wilderness and is incapable of being tamed.

During her last years, Tsvetaeva evidently comes to feel that she has driven everyone potentially close to her far away — not only her imaginary poetic lovers, but the children and husband with whom she shares her daily life and with whom, as the years pass, she has less and less true rapport. Body and soul are linked after all, and the rift between the two that is necessitated by the coincidence of Tsvetaeva's female gender and poetic bent is, at the same time, a very real and powerfully dangerous rift in the fabric of life itself. Tsvetaeva, true to herself to the last, follows this logic through to its inevitable destination. Indeed, in the few lyric poems that she writes during the final years of her life, her poetic myth consists in her shutting herself irrevocably into the abyss of her own loneliness — the exitless purgatory of her impossible fate. There is no company in this metaphysical wasteland of any kind; even the muse does not venture into its entrapping circles. The result is no longer a poetics of frustratingly gendered passion, but of inanimate objects eerily animated.[64]

Such are the cycles "A Bush" ["Kust"] (2:317–18) and "Desk" ["Stol"] (2:309–14), both written during the period 1933–35. In the former work, a flowering bush, reminiscent perhaps of the biblical burning bush out of which God speaks to Moses, becomes the enigmatic incarnation of Tsvetaeva's inspiration, challenging her new sense of spiritual emptiness with its own lush fullness: "What does the bush need — from me? The possessor — from the possessionless? . . . What, full cup of the bush, do you find in this — empty place?" [Chto nuzhno kustu — ot menia? / I mushchemu — ot neimushchei! // . . . Chto, polnaia chasha kusta, / Nakhodish' na sem — meste puste?].[65] By the end of this cycle, Tsvetaeva completely relocates her poetic impulse from passion to despair.

In "Desk," similarly, she finds poetic inspiration not in any human form, but in the disciplining companionship of her writing desk, which at the same time subordinates itself to her creative will in a way no human beloved ever could or would:

The End of the Line 221

> Мой письменный вьючный мул!
> Спасибо, что ног не гнул
> Под ношей, поклажу грез —
> Спасибо — что нес и нес.
>
> Строжайшее из зерцал!
> Спасибо за то, что стал
> — Соблазнам мирским порог —
> Всем радостям поперек.
>
> [My writing mule, beast of burden! Thank you for not bending your legs beneath the weight, — thank you for hauling and hauling the load of daydreams. Strictest of mirrors! Thank you for standing — a barrier to worldly temptations — across the path to all joys.]

The desk is the ideal, genderless lover Tsvetaeva has been seeking all her life; she has simply failed to recognize until now what has been literally right in front of her nose. Her inhuman "marriage" with the desk, whose thirtieth anniversary (the impetus for this cycle) she now celebrates, has been a physical and sensual one — as the following tender reminiscence makes clear:

> Я знаю твои морщины,
> Изъяны, рубцы, зубцы —
>
> Малейшую из зазубрин!
> (*Зубами* — коль стих не шел!)
> Да, был человек возлюблен!
> И сей человек был — стол
>
> Сосновый.
>
> [I know your wrinkles, flaws, scars, jags — your tiniest notches! (I *gnawed* you — when the verses didn't come!) Yes, a person was beloved! And this person was — a pinewood desk.]

Tsvetaeva's union with her writing table transcends sexual as well as all other boundaries that normally limit human potential. Theirs is a perfect reciprocity, without the moral guilt that attaches to her attempts to pound the seemingly wooden exteriors of real human beings into the image of her own soul; rather, the table bequeaths its death (its deadwood — its surface) to her so that she can bring it back to life: "Thank you for the fact that, having given up your trunk to me so that it could become a desk — you remained — a live trunk!" [Spasibo za to, chto stvol / Otdav mne, chtob stat′ — stolom, / Ostalsia — zhivym stvolom!].

This is precisely the relationship of mutual, almost symbiotic (one might say parasitic) exchange of physical and spiritual essences — the very merging of alterity and autonomy—that Tsvetaeva has always sought with her human lovers:

> . . . Скорей—скалу
> Своротишь! И лоб—к столу
> Подстатный, и локоть *под*—
> Чтоб лоб свой держать, как свод.
> . . . .
> Спасибо тебе, Столяр,
> За доску—во весь мой дар,
> За ножки—прочней химер
> Парижских, за вещь—в размер.

[One could sooner move a cliff! And my forehead—well-matched with the desk, and my elbow *under*—so as to hold my forehead, like the arch of heaven . . . Thank you, Carpenter, for a board—the size of my gift, for legs—stronger than Parisian gargoyles, for a thing—the right size.]

Now, at last, she recognizes in her desk her true, and only possible poetic equal—the perfect mate who has, unbidden, faithful to the last, returned her every poetic pressure with an equal and opposite impulse.

With these poems, Tsvetaeva has truly reached the outermost edge of human possibility. Her isolation now is not simply a state of mind, but an inexorable metaphysical condition of absolute proportions, as is evident in poems such as "That was my life singing—howling" ["Eto zhizn′ moia propela—provyla . . ."] (2:317), "The age thought not about the poet" ["O poete ne podumal . . ."] (2:319), "The Garden" ["Sad"] (2:320), and the wrenching "When I gaze at the drifting leaves" ["Kogda ia gliazhu na letiashchie list′ia . . ."] (2:344).[66] Her only escape from the cage of herself is further and further inward: "Isolation: exit into yourself, like the forefathers into their fiefdoms. Isolation: seek in your breast and find freedom" [Uedinenie: uidi / V sebia, kak pradedy v feody. / Uedinenie: v grudi / Ishchi i nakhodi svobodu] (2:319). The ultimate result of this existential collapse will and must be that, like a black hole whose forces all suck only inward, Tsvetaeva will reduce all the matter of her being to a single point that is, at last, independent of her eternal enemies space, body, gender, desire, and time (i.e., those very attributes that attach other humans to "life"): "Celebrate and bury the victory of isolation in my breast. Isolation: exit, life!" [Spravliai i pogrebai pobedu // Uedineniia v grudi. / Uedinenie: uidi, // Zhizn′!]

Chilling words, these—as are the words of many of Tsvetaeva's last poems, which are made even more poignant by the fact that they tend to be far quieter and gentler in tone than her feisty earlier works. Over and over again, she prepares herself for death, accustoms herself to the idea in various symbolic, metaphoric, and mythical contexts. In what is perhaps her most despairing poem of

The End of the Line

all, an incantatory fragment of just four lines written in February 1941, half a year before her death, she seems to prepare her own corpse for burial:

> Пора снимать янтарь,
> Пора менять словарь,
> Пора гасить фонарь
> Наддверный...
>
> [It's time to take off the amber necklace, time to change to a new lexicon, time to put out the lamp above the door...]

Yet there is no regret here; Tsvetaeva's tone is maximally restrained, and her statements are purely factual. There is no question in her mind that it is time; as she has already written in the privacy of her diary the previous year:

No one sees—or knows—that for a year (approximately) already I have been searching with my eyes for a hook, but there is none, because electricity is everywhere. No more chandeliers... For a *year* I have been trying on—death. Everything is ugly and—terrifying. Swallowing pills—loathsome, jumping—repugnant: the *primordial* repulsiveness of *water*. I don't want to frighten (posthumously), it seems to me that I already—posthumously—fear myself. I don't want to *die,* I want *not to be.* Nonsense. As long as I am needed... But, Lord, how small I am, how incapable of *anything!*

> Доживать—дожевывать
> Горькую полынь—
>
> [To finish living out life—is to finish chewing the bitter wormwood—]

How many verses are lost! I write nothing down. With that—I am finished. (4:610)

Tsvetaeva's life has closed full circle; yet there is, remarkably, hope implied even in the midst of her deepest despair: "It's time to change to a new lexicon" [Pora meniat' slovar']. In "New Year's Letter" and "Poem of the Air," she has dreamed of new realms where she can escape the limitations that torment her and those she loves; in "Art in the Light of Conscience," she has imagined poetry as only the lowest of innumerable levels of spiritual transcendence. Now, she is about to undertake the final and most immutable test of her poetic faith: death. Even her last surviving poem (addressed to the young poet Arsenii Tarkovskii) is a love poem—but the love poem of a ghost: "You set the table for six, but six do not exhaust the world's possibilities. Rather than be a scarecrow among the living—I want to be a ghost—with your people (my own)" [Ty stol nakryl na shesterykh, / No shesterymi mir ne vymer. / Chem pugalom sredi zhivykh—/ Byt' prizrakom khochu—s tvoimi, // (Svoimi)] (2:369). The sixth sense, fourth dimension, and fifth season of the year in which Tsvetaeva once imagined herself dwelling with Pasternak are soon to be her own as she becomes a magical, otherworldly "seventh"; she anticipates this change of scenery with compelling courage and even wit.

In her lucid moments, Tsvetaeva realizes that this apparent exit is not an exit at all, just as her "escape" from the Hades of emigration into Stalin's Soviet Union is anything but salvation. Even on the point of death, she remains implicated in the same emotional and poetic tangles that have always held her. Her January 1940 letter to the critic Evgenii Tager presents a mythopoetic summation of her unseverable double bonds to both earth and heaven, and of the gruesome spiritual nourishment she has cultivated throughout her life upon the "sacrificial blood" of her various beloveds:

> Remember Antaeus, who gathered strength from (the lightest!) brushing against the earth, who was held aloft in the air—by the earth. And the souls of Hades who only spoke when they had sipped of sacrificial blood. All of this—both Antaeus's earth and Hades' blood—is the same thing, that without which *I* am not alive, *not I*—am alive! This is the only thing that is *outside* myself, that I am unable to create and without which I *do not exist...*
>
> And one thing more: when it is absent, I forget it, live without it, forget as if it never existed (everywhere that I write "it" put in "real love"), I even deny that it exists at all and try to prove to everyone like two times two that it's all nonsense; but when it does exist, meaning when I again chance to fall into its live stream—then I *know* that it is the only true thing and that I myself exist only at those times when *it* exists, that my whole other life is imaginary, the life of a Hadean shade who has not drunk his blood: *non*-life. (7:678)[67]

It is impossible to say, in the final analysis, whether Tsvetaeva's death should be read as the capitulation of poetic inspiration to the dark tyranny of nothingness, or, on the contrary, as the triumph of the poet's creative will over the limitations of earthly being. In other words, it is impossible to say whether Tsvetaeva's death kills her muse, or the other way around. The only possible answer to this question is that it has no answer; Tsvetaeva's suicide is, in any case, immensely overdetermined.[68] There is no way out; as she writes in her suicide note to her son, she has reached a dead end: "Let Papa and Alia know—if you see them—that I loved them until the last moment, and explain that I *got stuck in an impasse* [popala v tupik]" (7:709; emphasis in the original).

Tsvetaeva's greatest tragedy is not, after all, her suicide per se, but the fact that even that heroic final act (heroic—because necessitated by the whole shape and development of her poetics and her life) fails, ultimately, to resolve the insuperable divide that she intends it to mend: the rift in her between the lonely, needy, shy, remorseful woman and the raging poet beset by a demonic muse. Death cannot mend this divide, any more than life can; it can simply cancel out the offending terms, erase the parameters. There is no exit for Tsvetaeva, even

The End of the Line

in death; the perpetual machine of impossibility goes on grinding around in circles into eternity. Her last bid for entry into a higher heaven, her last attempt to escape the vicious cycle of desire and loneliness, is, at the same time, her last betrayal of those she loves and who need her most: her husband, daughter, and sister, all in prison and awaiting her food packages—and, most of all, her unruly and unhappy teenage son.

Unlike Pushkin, Tsvetaeva is not fated to die a poetic martyr. Even at the end of her life, there is to be no contact with otherness; she must perish by her own hand, for death has grown in her organically for nearly half a century. When she is ready at last, she has only to loop the rope of her poetry—which once she trod, balancing precariously, high above the abyss—into one final, entrapping circle.

Postscript

> Я найду в своих стихах
> Всё, чево не будет в жизни!
>
> [I will find in my verses everything that I will not have in life!]
>
> — "Serdtse, plameni kapriznei . . ." (1913)

> Ибо раз голос тебе, поэт,
> Дан, остальное — взято.
>
> [For if voice is given to you, poet, all the rest — is taken away.]
>
> — "Est' schastlivtsy i schastlivitsy . . ." (1934)

The two epigraphs above, taken from poems written two decades apart, demonstrate just how consistent, despite the brilliant variety of her poetic creation, was Marina Tsvetaeva's conviction in the essential incompatibility of life and poetry throughout the whole course of her creative lifetime. As a result, poetic narratives replace life as such, canceling out in the process any communion or companionship with a real, human other. Tsvetaeva's terse summation of her credo in a letter of 1916 — "My whole life is a romance with my own soul" [Vsia moia zhizn'—roman s sobstvennoi dushoiu] (6:25) — turns out to be self-fulfilling. This reflexive romance, this poetic game, substitutes for true intimacy, so that she herself becomes like the two-headed beings on her childhood playing cards about which she reminisces in her 1935 essay "The Devil" ["Chert"]:

What was the point of playing with them . . . when they themselves played, they themselves were — the game: played with themselves and inside themselves. It was a whole, live, inhuman, dwarfish tribe, frighteningly powerful and not quite beneficent, childless and grandfatherless, living nowhere . . . but for that reason — how strong! (5:39)

Tsvetaeva, together with her mythic double Psyche, achieves complete autonomy in the course of her romantic and poetic fantasies to reign supreme over all the earthly limitations of gender, sex, age, geography, death, and indifference. This triumph, however, is highly ambivalent. Although in early years her metamorphosis into pure spirit promises a release into genius and alternate realms of being, in the last years of her life this mythic transformation becomes a formula for inescapable doom.

In the foregoing chapters, I have traced the development of Tsvetaeva's Psyche myth in her poetry and thought through a close analysis of her most important poetic encounters and the works inspired by those passionate "non-meetings." We have seen that she uses the simultaneous archaism and flexibility of mythological thought patterns—the simultaneous power of myth both to validate and to liberate—in her quest to revise, rather than overcome, the poetic tradition, in order to forge her own place in the poetic "brotherhood" as a woman poet of genius. In fact, all of Tsvetaeva's writing (not just the autobiographical prose of the 1930s) can be said, on one level, to be about her poetic genesis. She is compelled, over and over again, to "make use" of her encounters with other beloved poets in order to rework and relive her own metamorphosis from woman into poet: a transformation that she experiences in a rawly visceral, pagan, truly mythological vein—a metamorphosis from flesh into fire. Tsvetaeva's muse, who provides the impetus for this miracle, is far more than a simple metaphor for inspiration. It (he) is also the quintessential masculine spirit whose guardianship is key to her own poetic legitimacy.

Tsvetaeva, in her encounters with other poets, does not merely engage in dialogue with them (in fact, even in poems addressed to them, she rarely quotes them directly). Rather, she enters the alien poet at a deeper level—she enters into his poetics, his personality, his worldview, his mythology—and then she manipulates his system to include herself, trying to adapt it to her own emotional and poetic needs. Birdlike in her love of exhilarating, metaphysical flight and perpetually homeless, she occasionally comes to roost in the other, improvising a nest for herself out of the poetic materials he or she provides. Therefore, when she writes poems to Blok, Akhmatova, Pasternak, or Rilke, she is not just in search of a muse, but in search of a workable poetic myth—in search of a new self and a complete way of seeing, hearing, and being. Ultimately, she finds fulfillment only when she crosses the line between fact and fantasy so that it is no longer she rewriting the myth, but the myth rewriting her. She conveys over and over again in her writing the danger and exhilaration of this imaginative eternal loop: the tightrope-walking Eurydice of "Wires" and "There are lucky men and women" ["Est' schastlivtsy i schastlivitsy..."] (2:323–24); the room that dissolves even as it begins to take shape in "Attempt at a Room"; the snake climbing out of its own skin in "Seven, seven" ["Semero, semero..."] (2:61); the cyclical chain of being in "New Year's Letter" and "Poem of the Air"; and the metaphysical cycles and circles of "Epitaph" and "Poems to an Orphan" are just a few examples.

In considering the development of Tsvetaeva's poetics and the course of her human fate, we observe a continuing tension between change and constancy that is one reason why it is so hard, if not impossible, ever to organize a final, definitive interpretation of her poetic path. On the one hand, there is evolution; she does mature, achieve new heights, new depths, new metaphysical landmarks of various kinds. On the other hand, the same fracturing dichotomies that give rise initially to her poetic career relentlessly repeat throughout the duration—there truly is no exit. As a result, the dialectic between cause and effect breaks down; the two poles merge and become indistinguishable. But is this merging evidence, ultimately, of Tsvetaeva's poetic failure, or of success?

It is difficult to answer unequivocally, especially given the facts of her life and death. Her suicide, for the same reasons, is impossible to read unambiguously. Does it represent her ultimate poetic triumph—her last inspired move from a poetry of words into a poetry of acts—poetry of the next, superhuman existential level that Rilke already posthumously inhabits? Or is it, on the contrary, an acknowledgment of her utter defeat ("there's nowhere left to go" [dal'she nekuda], as she says in "Poem of the End" [3:47]) on all fronts, human and poetic? The very unanswerability of these questions—their forever shimmering, haunting ambiguity—is evidence that Tsvetaeva remains a poet of genius to the very end. Her suicide is richly nuanced; it is a brilliant rebinding of soul to body even in the moment of forceful unbinding (death thus bestows a simultaneity that she was constitutionally incapable of achieving during her life). Indeed, Tsvetaeva's suicide supplies the story of existential impossibility that unfolds in her poetry with a suitable and symbolic conclusion. It is her final poetic act: an act of greatness and courage, as well as of tragedy.

The wholeness and melding of gendered opposites within one selfhood that is possible for male poets of Tsvetaeva's acquaintance as diverse as Rilke, Mandel'shtam, and Maksimilian Voloshin was simply not an option for her. Her response to this impossibility was to seek wholeness through active, cocreative poetic dialogue with various other poets. Yet it is curious that Sergei Efron, her chosen husband, was specifically *not* a poet by inclination or trade—and was, moreover, a far weaker person and personality than she was herself, as she knew well from the beginning. Perhaps Tsvetaeva's choice of Efron as a mate was yet another facet of her project to segregate her daily life from her passions, to attempt "ordinary female happiness" with a typical man in one compartment of her life, while leaving herself "free" elsewhere to figure out the poetry of it all. Or perhaps the marriage was the result of her own reckless self-damning, knowing ahead of time what unhappiness it was destined to lead to—she knew, after all, where her real allegiance lay from a very young age. Of course, the most likely explanation is that the match was an honest mistake, born of youthful enthusiasm and the sacrificial naïveté of first love.

In any case, Tsvetaeva's lifelong passion for the underdog and her need to take care of the more vulnerable Efron prevented her from ever "abandoning" her husband, for all the aplomb with which she proclaims in her poetry the benefits of love at a distance. She knew the responsibility for their shared tragedy was, ultimately, hers; they were not equals and thus not free to part ways. It is tempting to imagine how Tsvetaeva's life and poetics might have turned out differently had she left her husband early on—grown into her own strength independently, without any automatic casualties ensuing from the flexing of her poetic muscles; or, alternatively, had she broken out of the controlling narrative of the Psyche myth and gone to Pasternak, attempting the union of poetic and sexual passion that always seemed to her so impossible and that so terrified her throughout her life.

Now, however, these can be no more than idle musings. Repeatedly buffeted by the winds of her ceaseless desire against the rocks of her desperate need for creative solitude, Tsvetaeva was never able to accomplish a true meeting with any human beloved. Unique yet incongruous, gifted but awkward, she remained for the duration an otherworldly "guest" who could not settle fully into the humble pleasures of family or the mutuality of genuine intimacy. Her necessities were other people's luxuries, and vice versa; hence her incommensurability with mortal life. The meaning of love in Tsvetaeva's metaphysical vocabulary was forever inseparable from the anguish of parting and the pangs of intense loneliness. In this respect she was not so different, for all the ferocity of her nature, from her other poetic sisters of genius in other times and places, few and far between though they be. Among these, Emily Dickinson has left behind a stern, sad poem that is a moving tribute to the emotional price the woman poet pays for the privilege of pursuing her destiny. Tsvetaeva surely would have sympathized with this hymn to feminine renunciation.

> I cannot live with You—
> It would be Life—
> And Life is over there—
> Behind the Shelf . . .
>
> . . . .
> So We must meet apart—
> You there—I—here—
> With just the Door ajar
> That Oceans are—and Prayer—
> And that White Sustenance—
> Despair—

Notes
Index

Notes

Preface

1. Throughout this book, unless otherwise attributed, all volume and page references to Tsvetaeva's works refer to the following edition: *Sobranie sochinenii v semi tomakh,* (Moscow: Ellis Lak, 1994–95). All translations from the original Russian and German are mine unless otherwise noted.

Introduction

1. See Catriona Kelly's discussion of this problem in the specific context of Russian Romanticism, *A History of Russian Women's Writing 1820–1992* (Oxford, England: Clarendon Press, 1994), 13.

2. I refer here to Robert Graves's classic and eccentric study *The White Goddess: A Historical Grammar of Poetic Myth,* rev. ed. (New York: Farrar, Straus & Giroux, 1966), which traces in detail the historical development of the myth of the poetic muse in the Western European context. The first chapter of Catherine Ciepiela's monograph ("Falling for the Poet," in *The Same Solitude: Boris Pasternak and Marina Tsvetaeva,* in press) provides an overview of the development of this same myth in the specific context of Russian Symbolism.

3. See Svetlana Boym's discussion of the poetess's attributes (*Death in Quotation Marks: Cultural Myths of the Modern Poet* [Cambridge, Mass.: Harvard University Press, 1991], 192–93); Boym convincingly argues that Tsvetaeva simultaneously uses and satirizes the feminine poetic mask (i.e., she uses it in order to transgress it).

4. See Svetlana El'nitskaia's study "Poeticheskii mir Tsvetaevoi: Konflikt liricheskogo geroia i deistvitel'nosti," *Wiener Slawistischer Almanach* 30 (1990): 1–396.

5. In this respect Tsvetaeva goes beyond the "usual" transgressions of the female writer into the male symbolic domain (cf. the following discussions of the vilification of writing women: Toril Moi, *Textual/Sexual Politics: Feminist Literary Theory* [London: Methuen 1985], 167; and Elizabeth Grosz, *Sexual Subversions: Three French Feminists* [Sydney, Australia: Allen & Unwin, 1989], 68) into a nebulous no-man's-territory outside the scope even of the "masculine" creative consciousness.

6. Grosz, "Bodies and Knowledges: Feminism and the Crisis of Reason," in *Feminist Epistemologies,* ed. Linda Alcoff and Elizabeth Potter (New York: Routledge, 1993),

210. Grosz's formulation applies to the work of French feminist theorist Luce Irigaray but is equally applicable to Tsvetaeva's poetry.

7. I refer here to essays by poststructuralist feminist theorists Julia Kristeva ("About Chinese Women," in *The Kristeva Reader,* ed. Toril Moi [New York: Columbia University Press, 1986], 138–59) and Hélène Cixous (*Readings: The Poetics of Blanchot, Joyce, Kafka, Kleist, Lispector, and Tsvetayeva,* ed. and trans. Verena Andermatt Conley [Minneapolis: University of Minnesota Press, 1991], 110–51).

8. Simon Karlinsky's pioneering studies *Marina Cvetaeva: Her Life and Art* (Berkeley: University of California Press, 1966) and *Marina Tsvetaeva: The Woman, Her World, and Her Poetry* (Cambridge, England: Cambridge University Press, 1985) laid the groundwork for Western scholarship on Tsvetaeva and arguably still serve as the best introduction to this complex poet.

9. An emphasis on bodily imagery is central to Barbara Heldt's *Terrible Perfection: Women and Russian Literature* (Bloomington: Indiana University Press, 1987), 135–37; Sibelan Forrester's "Bells and Cupolas: The Formative Role of the Female Body in Marina Tsvetaeva's Poetry," *Slavic Review* 51, no. 2 (1992): 232–46; and Pamela Chester's "Engaging Sexual Demons in Marina Tsvetaeva's 'Devil': The Body and the Genesis of the Woman Poet," *Slavic Review* 53, no. 4 (winter 1994): 1025–45. The "poetic journal" approach to Tsvetaeva is most explicitly formulated in Jane Taubman's *A Life through Poetry: Marina Tsvetaeva's Lyric Diary* (Columbus, Ohio: Slavica, 1988) but also informs Viktoria Schweitzer's *Tsvetaeva,* trans. Robert Chandler and H. T. Willetts; poetry trans. Peter Norman; ed. Angela Livingstone (New York: Farrar, Straus & Giroux, 1992) and Lily Feiler's *Marina Tsvetaeva: The Double Beat of Heaven and Hell* (Durham, N.C.: Duke University Press, 1994). The fascination with Tsvetaeva's suicide and its psychoanalytic and psycholinguistic implications is characteristic of the work of poststructuralist critics Kristeva and Cixous, cited earlier; Svetlana Boym draws on their theories in her own analysis as well.

10. A number of short studies that put Tsvetaeva's writing first although not neglecting consideration of gender issues have influenced my thinking a great deal: see especially Antonina Filonov Gove's "The Feminine Stereotype and Beyond: Role Conflict and Resolution in the Poetics of Marina Tsvetaeva," *Slavic Review* 36, no. 2 (June 1977): 231–55; Anya M. Kroth's "Androgyny as an Exemplary Feature of Marina Tsvetaeva's Dichotomous Poetic Vision," *Slavic Review* 38, no. 4 (December 1979): 563–82; and, more recently, Stephanie Sandler's "Embodied Words: Gender in Cvetaeva's Reading of Puškin," *Slavic and East European Journal* 34, no. 2 (1990): 139–57; Catriona Kelly's chapter on Tsvetaeva in *A History of Russian Women's Writing: 1820–1992,* 301–17; Catherine Ciepiela's "The Demanding Woman Poet: On Resisting Marina Tsvetaeva," *PMLA* 111, no. 3 (May 1996): 421–34; Sibelan Forrester's "Not Quite in the Name of the Lord: A Biblical Subtext in Marina Cvetaeva's Opus" *Slavic and East European Journal* 40, no. 2 (summer 1996): 278–96; and Liza Knapp's "Marina Tsvetaeva's Poetics of Ironic Delight: The 'Podruga' Cycle as Evist Manifesto," *Slavic and East European Journal* 41, no. 1 (1997): 94–113.

11. Robyn R. Warhol and Diane Price Herndl, "About Feminisms," in *Feminisms: An Anthology of Literary Theory and Criticism,* ed. Robyn R. Warhol and Diane Price Herndl (New Brunswick, N.J.: Rutgers University Press, 1997), x.

12. Tsvetaeva makes a similar point in her 1934 essay "Mother and Music" ["Mat' i

muzyka"], where she defines the chromatic scale thus: "The Chromatic is a whole spiritual structure, and that structure is mine. Because the Chromatic is the very opposite of the grammatical—the Romantic. And the Dramatic... The chromatic scale is my spinal column, a live staircase, along which those who know how to frolic in me—do. And when they play—they play along my vertebrae" (5:16). Tsvetaeva's emphasis in such passages on incorporeal music over physical body resonates with Judith Butler's investigations into the ways in which not only gender, but sex and body too are constructed (Judith Butler, *Bodies That Matter* [New York: Routledge, 1993]).

13. Margaret Homans, *Women Writers and Poetic Identity: Dorothy Wordsworth, Emily Brontë, and Emily Dickinson* (Princeton, N.J.: Princeton University Press, 1980), 216.

14. For Kristeva, significantly, only a male writer can renovate the symbolic order; a female writer, positioned as she is at its limit, can do nothing but transgress (cf. Nancy Fraser, "The Uses and Abuses of French Discourse Theories for Feminist Politics," in *Revaluing French Feminism: Critical Essays on Difference, Agency, and Culture,* ed. Nancy Fraser and Sandra Lee Bartky [Bloomington: Indiana University Press, 1992], 189). Tsvetaeva, on the contrary, believes that it is possible to enter into the symbolic order—in this case, poetic tradition—and to renovate it precisely through her transgression of its sacred space.

15. Indeed, a state of productive tension between antithetical desires and essences is vitally important to Tsvetaeva's poetics. See the discussion in Olga Peters Hasty's *Tsvetaeva's Orphic Journeys in the Worlds of the Word* (Evanston, Ill.: Northwestern University Press, 1996), 158-59.

16. Cf. Catherine Ciepiela's "Inclined toward the Other: On Cvetaeva's Lyric Address," in *Critical Essays on the Prose and Poetry of Modern Slavic Women,* ed. Nina Efimov, Christine D. Tomei, and Richard L. Chapple (Lewiston, N.Y.: Edwin Mellen Press, 1998), 117-34.

17. Tsvetaeva's repetition of the word *there* subtly transforms the Symbolist dichotomy between "here" (the mundane world) and "there" (the spiritual beyond) into this evocation of the mothers' earthbound perspective on space: "here, and there, and there again..." In 1909 when "In the Luxembourg Garden" was written, the Symbolist literary movement in Russia was showing signs of going defunct.

18. This rebellion, of course, will eventually declare itself overtly, as in one famous line from Tsvetaeva's defiant 1920 poem "Placing my hand on my heart" ["Ruku na serdtse polozha..."] (1:539): "I am a rebel in mind and womb" [Ia—miatezhnitsa lbom i chrevom].

19. Compare the opening lines from a poem of 1919: "But in my mind—know that stars are burning!" [A vo lbu moem—znai!—/ Zvezdy goriat] (1:480). In Greek mythology, the gods often grant humans immortality by transforming them into stars or constellations. The star as symbol and locus of poetic immortality takes on primary importance in Tsvetaeva's *poema* "New Year's Letter."

20. For examples of this symbolism in Tsvetaeva's later works, see the following: "Dumali—chelovek!..." (1:291-92), "Kak sonnyi, kak p′ianyi..." (1:298-99), "Vekami, vekami..." (2:53), "Gordost′ I robost′—rodnye sestry..." (2:55), "Sivilla vyzhzhena, sivilla: stvol..." (2:136), "Sakhara" (2:207-8), "Zapechatlennyi, kak rot orakula..." (2:240), "Dom" (2:295-96). As Olga Peters Hasty notes in the context of

her discussion of Tsvetaeva's Sibylline lyrics: "The closed eyes are emblematic in this cycle and elsewhere in Tsvetaeva's writings of a perceptual transvaluation. The tyranny of phenomenal vision is replaced by transcendent imaginative perception" (*Tsvetaeva's Orphic Journeys,* 92).

21. Elisabeth Bronfen in *Over Her Dead Body: Death, Femininity, and the Aesthetic* (New York: Routledge, 1992) provides a wide-ranging survey of various artistic media and cultural traditions to argue that the ideal of feminine beauty is closely affiliated with the mask of death.

22. Of course, this kind of subjectivity could no longer be known in the world of humans; this limitation is not really a problem for Tsvetaeva, for whom the world of spirits is as real as, or even perhaps more real than, the world of live people. For a feminist critical consideration of these matters, see Margaret Higonnet, "Speaking Silences: Women's Suicide," in *The Female Body in Western Culture: Contemporary Perspectives,* ed. Susan Rubin Suleiman (Cambridge, Mass.: Harvard University Press, 1986), 68–83.

23. Cf. Iurii Freidin's "Tema smerti v poeticheskom tvorchestve Mariny Tsvetaevoi," in *Marina Tsvetaeva: One Hundred Years,* ed. Viktoria Schweitzer et al. (Berkeley, Calif.: Berkeley Slavic Specialties, 1994), 249–61.

24. The theme of "myself against the world" occurs countless times in Tsvetaeva's poetry and prose and is an essential element of her poetic self-definition. Perhaps her most eloquent statement of this defiantly lonely stance—once again in the metaphorical context of a military battle—occurs in the 1921 poem "Roland's Horn" ["Rolandov rog"] (2:10): "Beneath the fool's whistle and the bourgeois's laughter—I am alone of everyone—for everyone—against everyone!" [Pod svist gluptsa i meshchanina smekh—/ Odna iz vsekh—za vsekh—protivu vsekh!].

25. Sandra M. Gilbert and Susan Gubar have discussed this problem in several articles: "'Forward into the Past': The Complex Female Affiliation Complex," in *Historical Studies and Literary Criticism,* ed. Jerome McGann (Madison: University of Wisconsin Press, 1985), 240–65; "Infection in the Sentence: The Woman Writer and the Anxiety of Authorship," in *Feminisms: An Anthology of Literary Theory and Criticism,* eds. Robyn R. Warhol and Diane Price Herndl (New Brunswick, N.J.: Rutgers University Press, 1997), 21–32; and "Tradition and the Female Talent," in *The Poetics of Gender,* ed. Nancy K. Miller (New York: Columbia University Press, 1986), 183–207. Gilbert and Gubar theorize that Harold Bloom's "anxiety of influence" (in his *The Anxiety of Influence: A Theory of Poetry* [New York: Oxford University Press, 1973])—which assumes that typically "male," competitive instincts dominate in the creative arena as in the military one—is replaced for the female writer or poet by an "anxiety of authorship" when she attempts to break into the forbidden realm of literary speech. Hence, her primary concern is not to distance herself from her (female) predecessors and contemporaries, who are few and far between, but, rather, to establish her right to an affiliation with them. Tsvetaeva does, indeed, value such affiliations with a broad range of female literary figures (Sappho, Karolina Pavlova, Bettina von Arnim, Mariia Bashkirtseva, Adelaida Gertsyk, Cherubina de Gabriak, Anna Akhmatova, and others) and makes a point of emphasizing these in her writing; cf. Sibelan Forrester's "Reading for a Self: Self Definition and Female Ancestry in Three Russian Poems," *The Russian Review* 55, no. 1 (Jan. 1996): 21–36. Nevertheless, Tsvetaeva is much more concerned with her links to her poetic brothers, fathers, and grandfathers. She engages directly with her

imposing male poetic forebears and peers on their own terms in her attempts to define her particular poetic voice; moreover, for all her sympathy with other women writers, she often portrays herself as a rank above their ilk. An examination of how Tsvetaeva negotiates the space between the "two" poetic traditions (male and female) that she inherits, although outside the scope of this inquiry, might yield fascinating insights into the workings of her poetic method.

26. Svetlana Boym writes that the poetess is "an exalted literary weaver, who by mistake picked up the wrong textures/textiles for domestic knitting—words instead of threads" (*Death in Quotation Marks,* 193); according to this logic, Tsvetaeva's spinning female captive and tooting shepherdess are one and the same.

27. Tsvetaeva would drum her fingers rhythmically on her desk when a new poem began to take shape; only after she had entered fully into its rhythmic contour would she begin filling in the words: "The indicator is an aural path to the poetic line: I hear the melody, but I don't hear the words. I seek the words" (5:285). Her early training in music had much to do with this method; cf. her essay "Mother and Music."

28. Tsvetaeva's predilection for long walks is often the basis for her affinity with others who share this fondness, including Maksimilian Voloshin, Aleksandr Pushkin, Nikolai Gronskii, and Konstantin Rodzevich (cf. "Zhivoe o zhivom" [4:160–61], "Preodolen'e . . ." [2:287–88], "Poet-al'pinist" [5:435–59], "Poema gory" [3:24–30], "Poema kontsa" [3:31–50], "Oda peshemu khodu" [2:291–94]).

29. The figure of the drummer boy was inherently tragic for Tsvetaeva since early childhood, as she indicates in her essay "My Pushkin" ["Moi Pushkin"]: "When the drummer boy left for the war and then never returned—that was love" (5:68).

30. On the importance of chronology to Tsvetaeva's poetics, see Olga Peters Hasty's article "*Poema* vs. Cycle in Cvetaeva's Definition of Lyric Verse": "Lest this insistence on chronology appear surprising, if not altogether contradictory, on the part of a poet who in so much of her work proclaimed war on the measurement of time and on the restrictions of temporality, it is necessary to understand that its source lies in an attempt to transpose the dialectical relation of whole and part [in lyric poetry] into the realm of temporal phenomena" (*Slavic and East European Journal* 32, no. 3 [1988]: 392).

31. In a questionnaire sent to her by Pasternak in 1926, Tsvetaeva listed Derzhavin, along with Nekrasov, as her favorite Russian poet of the past. In her 1934 essay "Poet-Mountaineer" ["Poet-al'pinist"], she claims a family relationship to Derzhavin: "Between me and Derzhavin—there is a family resemblance. I cannot recognize myself, let's say, in a single line by Baratynskii, but I see myself fully in Derzhavin's 'The Waterfall' ['Vodopad']—in everything, even to the wisdom of his remarks about the insanity of such visions" (5:458). Critics have detected Derzhavin's influence in a number of Tsvetaeva's works, while Gleb Struve has connected Tsvetaeva's exploitation of contrasts between high and low style in her mature work with Derzhavin's poetics. For more on Tsvetaeva's affinity with Derzhavin, see Michael Makin, *Marina Tsvetaeva: Poetics of Appropriation* (Oxford, England: Clarendon Press, 1993), 43, 108–9, 228, 299; Karlinsky, *Marina Cvetaeva: Her Life and Art,* 131, 223; E. Kononko, "G. R. Derzhavin v tvorchestve M. Tsvetaevoi," *Voprosy russkoi literatury,* vyp. 2 (L'vov, Ukraine: Izdatel'stvo L'vovskogo universiteta, 1985): 44–49; Anna Lisa Crone and Alexandra Smith's two co-authored essays, "Cheating Death: Derzhavin and Tsvetaeva on the Immortality of the Poet" (*Slavic Almanach: The South African Year Book for Slavic, Central and East Euro-*

pean Studies 3, nos. 3–4 [1995]: 1–30) and "Death Shall Have No Dominion" (*Russian Literature,* in press); and Tamara Fokht, "Derzhavinskaia perifraza v poezii M. Tsvetaevoi," *Studia Russica Budapestinensia* 2–3 (1995): 231–36.

32. The full text of "The Bullfinch" can be found in Gavriil Derzhavin, *Stikhotvoreniia* (Leningrad: Sovetskii pisatel', 1957), 283.

33. In her essay "My Pushkin," Tsvetaeva makes explicit her dislike for the question: "The question in poetry is an irritating device, if only because every *why* demands and promises a *because* and in this way weakens the self-contained value of the process, turns the whole poem into an interval, fettering our attention to the final external goal, which poems should not have. Persistent questions turn poems into riddles and puzzles, and if every poem is itself a riddle and a puzzle, then not that riddle for which there is a ready explanation, and not that puzzle whose solution can be found in an answer key" (5:76–77).

34. Ariadna Efron gives a penetrating description of the working of Tsvetaeva's poetics in this respect: "Her acquaintances in the artistic world sometimes were irritated or scared off by the persistence with which Marina, inculcating herself into their personal melodies, reshaped and reorganized them in her own peculiar, strong, alien key, with the help of her peculiar, strong, alien language, character, her very essence" (*O Marine Tsvetaevoi* [Moscow: Sovetskii pisatel', 1989], 140).

35. On Tsvetaeva's mythopoetics, see Svetlana El'nitskaia's two works *Poeticheskii mir Tsvetaevoi: Konflikt liricheskogo geroia i deistvitel'nosti* and "'Vozvyshaiushchii obman': Mirotvorchestvo i mifotvorchestvo Tsvetaevoi" (in *Marina Tsvetaeva: 1892–1992,* ed. Svetlana El'nitskaia and Efim Etkind [Northfield, Vermont: The Russian School of Norwich University, 1992], 45–62) and Zbigniew Maciejewski's "Priem mifizatsii personazhei i ego funktsiia v avtobiograficheskoi proze M. Tsvetaevoi" (in *Marina Tsvetaeva: Trudy 1-go mezhdunarodnogo simpoziuma,* ed. Robin Kemball [Bern, Switzerland: Peter Lang, 1991], 131–41). Goul's comment is cited in Karlinsky's *Marina Tsvetaeva: The Woman,* 176. The idea of poetic appropriation is at the basis of Makin's study of Tsvetaeva; he claims that Tsvetaeva never develops her own myths but only borrows them ("It may well be that she could not 'invent' a plot" [*Poetics of Appropriation,* 10]). In my view, this tendency of Tsvetaeva's is not absolute, and even when her texts are borrowed, as I have just argued, they are live entities that simultaneously "borrow" her (cf. her letter to Pasternak upon her completion of "The Swain" ["Molodets"], a reworking of an Afanas'ev folktale: "I just finished a big *poema* [it's necessary to call it something!], not a *poema,* but an obsession [navazhdenie], and it wasn't I who finished it, but it me—we parted as if tearing ourselves asunder [rasstalis', kak razorvalis']!" [6:236]).

36. Olga Peters Hasty, *Tsvetaeva's Orphic Journeys,* 6.

37. Thus, for instance, Olga Peters Hasty notes that Tsvetaeva's dichotomous interpretation of female sexuality finds expression simultaneously in "Ophelia's insistence on sexuality and Eurydice's assertion of the asexual fraternity of poets" and goes on to add that "once again it is language that successfully unites these antithetical demands" (*Tsvetaeva's Orphic Journeys,* 160).

38. Northrop Frye notes that this "playfulness" can be seen as the very feature that marks the dividing line between reality and art: "In poetry the physical or actual is opposed, not to the spiritually existential, but to the hypothetical ... The transmutation of

act into mime, the advance from acting out a rite to playing at the rite, is one of the central features of the development from savagery into culture . . . the release of fact into imagination" (*Anatomy of Criticism* [New York: Atheneum, 1969], 148).

39. Even when Tsvetaeva's lyrical protagonists are ostensibly fictional, she often claims (extratextually) a personal affiliation with them. For example, she writes to Pasternak that she is Marusia, heroine of her *poema* "The Swain" ("For I myself—am Marusia" [6:249]); she likewise identifies herself with the heroine of her Romantic play *The Blizzard* [*Metel'*] ("I, silently: 'The lady in the cloak—is my soul, no one can play her' " [4:298]).

40. Genrikh Gorchakov, "Marina Tsvetaeva: Korrespondent—Adresat," *Novyi zhurnal* 167 (1987): 158–59.

41. I do not mean to suggest that, in reality, Tsvetaeva was utterly alone, nor that she had no audience for her writing. Indeed, despite her protestations to the contrary, her letters give copious evidence that, even at times when she was publishing little, she always had friends and admirers who took her seriously as a poet and recognized her genius. Nevertheless, her poetic investigations into the scope and limitations of her own subjectivity were consistently manifested in the grandiloquent self-absorption that marks her lyrical performances, conveying the illusion of her complete isolation—an illusion that she herself cultivated, especially during her years in emigration (cf. Karlinsky, *Marina Tsvetaeva: The Woman*, 176–78).

Chapter 1. Battling Blok and Akhmatova

1. Ariadna Efron, *O Marine Tsvetaevoi* (Moscow: Sovetskii pisatel', 1989), 89.

2. Cited by Anna Saakiants in the commentary to M. Tsvetaeva, *Sochineniia v dvukh tomakh*, ed. Anna Saakiants (Moscow: Khudozhestvennaia literatura, 1980), 1:494.

3. The line in quotes is from Tsvetaeva's poem "You pass by," discussed later in this chapter. This passage comes from a letter to Pasternak in which she is mustering the evidence of her past nonmeeting with Blok against a present meeting with Pasternak; I address this topic at length in the next chapter. Pasternak becomes the (deferred) audience for Tsvetaeva's solitary poetic experiment.

4. For a full explication of Tsvetaeva's equation of Blok with Orpheus, see Hasty, *Tsvetaeva's Orphic Journeys in the Worlds of the Word* (Evanston, Ill.: Northwestern University Press, 1996), 14–25. See also Ariadna Efron's letter to E. O. Voloshina of 1921: "Marina and I are reading mythology . . . And Orpheus reminds us of Blok: pitiful, able to touch stones" (Ariadna Efron, *O Marine Tsvetaevoi*, 245).

5. See Tsvetaeva's letters to Akhmatova (6:200–203) and accompanying commentary (6:204–7).

6. Viktoria Schweitzer, for instance, characterizes the lyrics of "Poems to Akhmatova" as "poems of rapturous, adoring eulogy" and adds that the "selfless generosity of Tsvetaeva's raptures is as startling as their extravagance" (*Tsvetaeva*, trans. Robert Chandler and H. T. Willetts; poetry trans. Peter Norman; ed. Angela Livingstone [New York: Farrar, Straus & Giroux, 1992], 116); Schweitzer's comments that Tsvetaeva "ranked [Blok] with the immortals" (174) and regarded him with "worshipful awe" (180) are common critical parlance. Jane Taubman, on the contrary, recognizes that for Tsvetaeva "Akhmatova was an elder sister, the object of both affection and rivalry" (*A Life*

through Poetry: Marina Tsvetaeva's Lyric Diary [Columbus, Ohio: Slavica, 1988], 94) and asks tantalizingly whether the "lost" manuscript of Tsvetaeva's prose work in memory of Blok might not actually have been destroyed by its author—evidence that she had "finally 'overcome' Blok as, much earlier, she 'overcame' Akhmatova" (93). Olga Peters Hasty likewise recognizes the challenge that Blok represents to Tsvetaeva: "Tsvetaeva continued to avoid all those moments of joy, power, and glory which the myth affords Orpheus to focus instead on his apparent failures. It is possible to construe this representation as an attempt on her part to disenfranchise Orpheus and thus also those male poets she designates as his embodiments in order that they be more readily overcome" (*Tsvetaeva's Orphic Journeys in the Worlds of the Word*, 25).

7. Ariadna Efron, *O Marine Tsvetaevoi*, 89.

8. The 1916 cycle "Poems to Blok" consists of eight poems, first published in Tsvetaeva's collection *Milestones I* (1922). I deal exclusively with these eight lyrics, rather than with poems written in 1920–21 under the same dedicatory heading. Critical discussions of the first Blok cycle can be found in the following sources: David A. Sloane, "'Stixi k Bloku': Cvetaeva's Poetic Dialogue with Blok," in *New Studies in Russian Language and Literature* (Columbus, Ohio: Slavica, 1986), 258–70; N. V. Ozernova, "'Stikhi k Bloku' Mariny Tsvetaevoi," *Russkaia rech': Nauchno-populiarnyi zhurnal* 5 (Sept.–Oct. 1992): 20–24; Andrew Field, "A Poetic Epitaph: Marina Tsvetaeva's Poems to Blok," *Triquarterly* (spring 1965): 57–61; Seweryn Pollak, "Slavosloviia Mariny Tsvetaevoi (Stikhi k Bloku i Akhmatovoi)," in *Marina Tsvetaeva: Trudy 1-go mezhdunarodnogo simpoziuma,* ed. Robin Kemball (Bern, Switzerland: Peter Lang, 1991), 179–91; two articles by L. V. Zubova ("Semantika khudozhestvennogo obraza i zvuka v stikhotvorenii M. Tsvetaevoi iz tsikla 'Stikhi k Bloku,'" *Vestnik Leningradskogo universiteta,* seriia istorii, iazyka i literatury 2 [1980]: 55–61; and "Traditsiia stilia 'pletenie sloves' u Mariny Tsvetaevoi Stikhi k Bloku 1916–21 gg., Akhmatovoi 1916 g.," *Vestnik Leningradskogo universiteta,* seriia 2, istoriia, iazykoznanie, literaturovedenie 9, no. 2 [Apr. 1985]: 47–52); V. N. Golitsyna, "M. Tsvetaeva ob Al. Bloke (tsikl 'Stikhi k Bloku')," in *Biografiia i tvorchestvo v russkoi kul'ture nachala XX veka,* Blokovskii sbornik IX, Uch. zap., vypusk 857 (Tartu, Estonia: Tartuskii gosudarstvennyi universitet, 1989), 100–102; Jane Taubman, *A Life through Poetry,* 88–93; Catherine V. Chvany, "Translating One Poem from a Cycle: Cvetaeva's 'Your Name is a Bird in my Hand' from 'Poems to Blok,'" in *New Studies in Russian Language and Literature* (Columbus, Ohio: Slavica, 1986), 49–58; and Olga Peters Hasty, "Tsvetaeva's Onomastic Verse," *Slavic Review* 45, no. 2 (1986): 245–56. The last two studies deal primarily with the first poem of the cycle.

9. Tsvetaeva believed in complete seriousness that a poet's destiny can be derived from his or her name; in numerous works she meditates on the meanings inherent in other poets' names and her own ("Marina" she associates variously with the Russian word *more* [sea], with the Latin expression *memento mori,* with Marina Mniszek, and with Pushkin's Mariula). On the fascinating and rich subject of Tsvetaeva's onomastic poetics, see Olga Peters Hasty, "Tsvetaeva's Onomastic Verse"; M. V. Gorbanevskii, "'Mne imia—Marina . . .': Zametki ob imenakh sobstvenykh v poezii M. Tsvetaevoi," *Russkaia rech': Nauchno-populiarnyi zhurnal* 4 (July–Aug. 1985): 56–64; K. G. Petrosov, "'Kak ia liubliu imena i znamena . . .': Imena poetov v khudozhestvennom mire Mariny Tsvetaevoi," *Russkaia rech': Nauchno-populiarnyi zhurnal* 5 (Sept.–Oct. 1992): 14–19;

Sibelan Forrester, "Not Quite in the Name of the Lord"; and Liza Knapp, "Tsvetaeva's Marine Mary Magdalene," *Slavic and East European Journal* 43, no. 4 (winter 1999): 597-620.

10. Tsvetaeva's 1920 poem "An Earthly Name" ["Zemnoe imia"] (1:548) is an extended meditation on the unquenchable spiritual longing that both prompts and results from this replacement of earthly desire with an "earthly name."

11. David A. Sloane, "'Stixi k Bloku,'" 261.

12. Along similar lines, Catherine Ciepiela convincingly argues that in "Poems to Blok," Tsvetaeva's "half-worshipful, half-erotic address mimics Blok's own relation to the Beautiful Lady. In this cycle, Tsvetaeva remakes Blok in the image of the symbolist muse" (*The Same Solitude: Boris Pasternak and Marina Tsvetaeva*, in press).

13. For the text of Pushkin's "What is in my name for you?" cf. A. S. Pushkin, *Sochineniia v trekh tomakh* (Moscow: Khudozhestvennaia literatura, 1985), 1:468. Roman Jakobson analyzes the pronominal patterns in this poem in his "Poeziia grammatiki i grammatika poezii," in *Roman Jakobson: Selected Writings,* ed. Stephen Rudy (The Hague, Netherlands: Mouton Press, 1981), 3:78-86. Monika Greenleaf's penetrating comment that this poem amounts to Pushkin's "virtual synopsis of . . . epitaphic, fragmentary, and intersubjective theories of language . . . [instructions] for his past lover and future reader" is apropos here (*Pushkin and Romantic Fashion: Fragment, Elegy, Orient, Irony* [Stanford, Calif.: Stanford University Press, 1994], 54).

14. The diagnosis of wounded narcissism is a key concept in Lily Feiler's psychoanalytical study of Tsvetaeva; without actually using the term *megalomania*, she also claims that for Tsvetaeva depression "is temporarily overcome by feelings of 'grandiosity' —superiority and contempt" (*Marina Tsvetaeva: The Double Beat of Heaven and Hell* [Durham, N.C.: Duke University Press, 1994], 4).

15. Olga Peters Hasty notes that both transcendence and transgression are valid interpretations of the Orphic myth: "This ambivalence was not lost on Tsvetaeva, who juxtaposes Orpheus alternately with Christ—an emblem of grace—and with the vampire swain—an emblem of damnation. Both are true guises of the prototypal poet" (*Tsvetaeva's Orphic Journeys,* 82).

16. Ariadna Efron, *O Marine Tsvetaevoi,* 90.

17. See the tragic opening sentence of "Mother and Music" ["Mat' i muzyka"] (5:10).

18. For Tsvetaeva, every being who has an impact on her creative existence attains mythical status, whereas all the rest are simply nonexistent, the "refuse" of real life: "Everything is myth, since there is no non-myth, no meta-myth, no extra-myth—since myth has anticipated and cast the form of everything once and for all" (5:111).

19. Tsvetaeva here refers to characters and events from Pushkin's Byronic *poema* "The Gypsies" ["Tsygany"].

20. Olga Peters Hasty, *Pushkin's Tatiana* (Madison: University of Wisconsin Press, 1999), 233.

21. Ibid. I do not completely agree with Hasty's claim that Tsvetaeva's notions depart from those of the Romantics and post-Symbolists "in that she assigns women an active, responsible role within the literary tradition. In her account, they are neither the embodiment nor the essence of poetry; nor are they muses exciting creativity in others." Although this is true at those times when Tsvetaeva aligns herself with the women she

describes, at other times, when her intention is to align herself with the male poet, she takes a very different stance (see, for instance, her extremely ungenerous treatment of Pushkin's wife in her essay "Natal'ia Goncharova" [4:80-90]).

22. There may be several associations at work simultaneously in this swan's call. It is fabled that a swan sings just before its death; Tsvetaeva thus hints that Blok's poetry is a "swan song" in the sense of the English expression—the hauntingly beautiful and seductive call of death itself. Yet the swan's call is at the same time a motif in Blok's own poetry—as, for example, in his cycle "On Kulikovo Field" ["Na pole Kulikovom"], where it is an omen of doom. There may be a more general Blokian equation of birds (wings) with poetry present here too. The association of the dead and dying Blok with a swan recurs in several poems of Tsvetaeva's 1920-21 cycle "Poems to Blok." A similar association of swan with poet shapes Derzhavin's poem "Swan" ["Lebed'"], which Tsvetaeva may also have in mind.

23. For an analysis of the significance of this type of stanzaic aberration in Tsvetaeva's poetics generally, cf. R. D. B. Thomson, "Extra-Stanzaic Elements in the Lyric Poetry of Marina Cvetaeva," *Russian Literature* 45 (1999): 223-43.

24. Olga Peters Hasty writes: "Tsvetaeva suggests an equivalence between Blok and Bog [God] but stops ambiguously just short of sacrilege and leaves to the reader the realization of the line" ("Tsvetaeva's Onomastic Verse," 250). Catherine Chvany denies that there is even an implication of blasphemy present ("Translating One Poem," 53).

25. "Vecherniaia pesn' Synu Bozhiiu sviashchennomuchenika Afinogena" (cited in Catherine Chvany, "Translating One Poem," 58 n. 8).

26. David A. Sloane, "'Stixi k Bloku,'" 269. It is important to note that Sloane does not distinguish between the two separate Blok cycles, considering them rather as a whole.

27. I am disagreeing here with Catherine Chvany's contention that Tsvetaeva throughout "Poems to Blok" merely follows an innocuous tradition of comparing the Poet's sacrifice to that of Christ ("Translating One Poem," 53). Although she does not say so explicitly, Chvany may be trying to write a corrective to Ariadna Efron's interpretation, which overstates the case for Tsvetaeva's worship of Blok.

28. This is the choice that underlies Tsvetaeva's admission in a lyric of August 1916: "This is why I cry a lot, because—I fell in love with God's dear angels more than God himself" [Ottogo i plachu mnogo, / Ottogo—/ Chto vzliubila bol'she Boga / Milykh angelov ego] (1:316).

29. Here there is both a biblical subtext, and a reminiscence from Blok's own poetry ("When in foliage" ["Kogda v listve syroi i rzhavoi . . ."] from the cycle "Faina"). See David A. Sloane, "'Stixi k Bloku,'" 263.

30. Tsvetaeva often associates renunciation of her beloved with a state of physical and emotional paralysis or "polnyi fizicheskii stolbniak" (5:85).

31. Fire is a symbol of Tsvetaeva's poetic essence that encodes for her the irreconcilability of poetry and reality, as for example in this manifesto-like poem of 1918: "Whatever others don't need—bring to me: everything must burn up in my fire! I summon both life and death into the light gift of my fire. A flame loves light substances: last year's brushwood—wreaths—words... A flame blazes up with this kind of fodder! And you yourselves will arise—purer than ash!" [Chto drugim ne nuzhno—nesite mne: / Vse dolzhno sgoret' na moem ogne! / Ia i zhizn' maniu, ia i smert' maniu / V legkii dar moemu ogniu. // Plamen' liubit legkie veshchestva: / Proshlogodnii khvorost—venki—slova... /

Plamen' pyshet s podobnoi pishchi! / Vy zh vosstanete—pepla chishche!] (1:424). The introduction to Tsvetaeva's essay "A History of One Dedication" ["Istoriia odnogo posviashcheniia"] contains a potent description of her inspired pyromania; fire also plays a central role in several of her longer poetic works, notably "On a Red Steed" and "Poem of a Staircase" ["Poema lestnitsy"].

32. In the Russian Bible, *stezia* is the word often used to describe the path of Christ; see for example Matthew 3:3, Mark 1:3, and Luke 3:4.

33. See Catherine Ciepiela's discussion of Tsvetaeva's apostrophic poetics in the context of this poem in her article "The Demanding Woman Poet: On Resisting Marina Tsvetaeva," *PMLA* 11 (May 1996): 421–34.

34. It is interesting to note that, in retrospect, Tsvetaeva's understanding of Blok's poetic path darkens significantly. Years after his death, she writes in her essay "Poets with a History and Poets without a History" ["Poety s istoriei i poety bez istorii"] (1933) that the whole course of Blok's life consisted of his ripping himself apart: "Blok in the course of his whole poetic path did not so much grow, as tear himself to pieces [ne razvivalsia, a razryvalsia]" (5:409). This is quite different from the inexpressible ideal of angelic wholeness Blok presents in Tsvetaeva's 1916 "Poems to Blok."

35. For a discussion of this meeting and of Akhmatova's condescending attitude toward Tsvetaeva and her poetry, see Viktoria Schweitzer, *Tsvetaeva*, 356–58.

36. Tsvetaeva records Mandel'shtam's tale in "An Otherworldly Evening" (4:287); apparently Akhmatova denied its having any veracity after reading Tsvetaeva's memoir in later years (cf. Roberta Reeder, *Anna Akhmatova: Poet and Prophet* [New York: St. Martin's Press, 1994], 94).

37. The only poem Akhmatova ever addressed directly to Tsvetaeva ("A Belated Answer" ["Pozdnii otvet"]) was written several months before their 1941 meeting, but even this she decided to keep to herself, and Tsvetaeva never knew of the poem's existence. In contrast to Tsvetaeva's poems to Akhmatova with their passionate inquiries into poetic essentials, Akhmatova's poem to Tsvetaeva portrays her addressee first and foremost not as a poet, but as a sister sufferer at the cruel hands of the Soviet regime. Some scholars believe there was little room in Akhmatova's heart and sensibilities for Tsvetaeva as a poet; she was moved, rather, by Tsvetaeva's human tragedy (see the discussion in Viktoria Schweitzer, *Tsvetaeva*, 119; see also Simon Karlinsky, *Marina Tsvetaeva: The Woman, Her World, and Her Poetry* [Cambridge, England: Cambridge University Press, 1985], 237). On the other hand, Anatolii Naiman (in his article "O sviazi mezhdu 'Poema bez geroia' Akhmatovoi i 'Poemoi vozdukha' Tsvetaevoi," in *Marina Tsvetaeva: 1892–1992*, ed. Svetlana El'nitskaia and Efim Etkind [Northfield, Vermont: The Russian School of Norwich University, 1992], 196–205) has suggested that Akhmatova's "Poem without a Hero" ["Poema bez geroia"] has affinities with Tsvetaeva's "Poem of the Air" ["Poema vozdukha"], while Natalia Roskina writes in her memoir ("Good-bye Again," in *Anna Akhmatova and Her Circle*, ed. Konstantin Polivanov, trans. Patricia Beriozkina [Fayetteville, Ark.: The University of Arkansas Press, 1994], 190) that Akhmatova described Tsvetaeva as a "powerful poet." For further discussions of the poetic and personal relationship between Akhmatova and Tsvetaeva, cf. Vladimir Kornilov, "Antipody: Tsvetaeva and Akhmatova," in *Marina Tsvetaeva: 1892–1992*, 186–95; Veronika Losskaia, *Pesni zhenshchin: Anna Akhmatova i Marina Tsvetaeva v zerkale russkoi poezii XX veka* (Paris, France: Moskovskii zhurnal, 1999); and Irma Kudrova, "Sopernitsy (Tsve-

taeva i Akhmatova)," in Kudrova's *Posle Rossii. O poezii i proze Mariny Tsvetaevoi: Stat'i raznykh let* (Moscow: Rost, 1997), 201–17.

38. This cycle was first published in *Milestones I* (1922); it consisted of eleven poems. In addition to the cycle of poems to Akhmatova, Tsvetaeva also wrote several separate lyrics addressed to her sister-poet between 1915 and 1921 ("Uzkii, nerusskii stan . . ." [1:234–35], "A chto esli kudri v plat . . ." [1:310], "Sorevnovaniia korosta . . ." [2:53–54], "Kem polosyn′ka tvoia . . ." [2:79–80]; cf. also the notes in Marina Tsvetaeva, *Stikhotvoreniia i poemy v piati tomakh* [New York: Russica, 1980–90], 2:383). Other critical discussions of "Poems to Akhmatova" can be found in the articles by Pollak and Zubova already cited, as well as in Jane Taubman's *A Life through Poetry,* 97–100; Viktoria Schweitzer's *Tsvetaeva,* 116–18; and Simon Karlinsky's *Marina Cvetaeva: Her Life and Art* (Berkeley: University of California Press, 1966), 182–83.

39. Joseph Brodsky, "The Keening Muse," in *Less Than One: Selected Essays* (New York: Farrar Straus & Giroux, 1986), 35. Akhmatova chose her pseudonym, the surname of her Tartar grandmother, when her father protested that a woman poet would bring shame on his family name.

40. Viktoria Schweitzer, *Tsvetaeva,* 116, 119.

41. Alexander Zholkovsky, "Anna Akhmatova: Scripts, Not Scriptures," *Slavic and East European Journal* 40, no. 1 (spring 1996): 138. See also Zholkovsky's extended treatment of this subject in his "Strakh, tiazhest′, mramor (Iz materialov k zhiznetvorcheskoi biografii Akhmatovoi)," *Wiener Slawistischer Almanach* 36 (1995): 119–54.

42. The tradition of Petersburg in Russian literature—beginning with Pushkin's *poema* "The Bronze Horseman" ["Mednyi vsadnik"], continuing throughout the works of Gogol′ and Dostoevskii, and revived again in the poetry of the Symbolists—as a dangerous, phantasmagorical place where demons roam in the mists is so pervasive that no more than this nuance is required for the specter of the whole Petersburg hell to arise in Akhmatova's person here.

43. Zholkovsky, "Anna Akhmatova: Scripts, not Scriptures," 138–39.

44. Drawing, as she is prone to do, on gypsy thematics, Tsvetaeva terms the entire race of poets a "roaming brotherhood" [bratstvo brodiachee] in "Poem of the End" ["Poema kontsa"] (3:37). This idea is also conveyed in a number of other lyrics where Tsvetaeva equates the urge toward parting and wanderlust with her commitment to poetry's mandate (cf. "Tsyganskaia strast′ razluki! . . ." [1:247], "Kakoi-nibud′ predok moi byl—skripach . . ." [1:238], "Ditia razgula i razluki . . ." [1:506]).

45. Many social anthropologists have interpreted the phenomenon of gift giving as a power ploy (cf. Peter B. Hammond, *An Introduction to Cultural and Social Anthropology* [New York: Macmillan, 1971], 136).

46. This metaphorical ardor is reminiscent of the *zaria/zarit′sia* play in "Poems to Blok." It is possible that the burning cupolas of "O, Muse of lament" are not only a metonymic attribute of Tsvetaeva's creative space, but a metaphor for Tsvetaeva's own body and self, as Sibelan Forrester argues in her article "Bells and Cupolas: The Formative Role of the Female Body in Marina Tsvetaeva's Poetry," *Slavic Review* 51, no. 2 (1992): 232–46.

47. Simon Karlinsky notes that the Russian themes of the cycles to Blok and Akhmatova (both Petersburg poets) define not only Tsvetaeva's poetic identity, but also her national identity, which has hitherto been somewhat confused: "In her poems of

early 1916 . . . she assumed the identity of a Pole and of a noblewoman of ancient lineage (*boliarynia*), to neither of which she really had any right" (*Marina Tsvetaeva: The Woman,* 61).

48. See V. Vinogradov's discussion of mirroring in Akhmatova's poetics in his *O poezii Anny Akhmatovoi* (Leningrad: Tipografiia khimtekhizdata, 1925), 56. Akhmatova's inspirational tactics can be seen at work most explicitly in her 1911 poem "To the Muse" ["Muze"].

49. For brief discussions of the technical and thematic aspects of Tsvetaeva's Akhmatovan stylizations in this cycle, see Simon Karlinsky, *Marina Cvetaeva: Her Life,* 182–83, and Jane Taubman, *A Life through Poetry,* 102–3.

50. In essence, Tsvetaeva here restores Akhmatova to her patrilineal descent (and to the harsh semantics and rough, nonexotic, nonaristocratic, Ukrainian nuances of her birth name) and removes her pretension to matrilineality (Akhmatova's pseudonym references an exotic Tartar great grandmother). Elsewhere, Tsvetaeva elaborates: "Every literary pseudonym is first of all a rejection of paternity, since it does not include the father, excludes him. Maksim Gor'kii, Andrei Belyi—who are their fathers? Every pseudonym is a subconscious refusal of continuity, heredity" (4:264). Such a rejection of male poetic heritage is unthinkable to Tsvetaeva herself, however ambivalent her attitude to it may be.

51. Tsvetaeva is, however, selective in her paronomastic play. It is significant that she never uses the word *gore* [grief] in this poem, although it could easily arise as yet another echo of *Gorenko.* She selects the unsympathetic emotion of "bitterness" rather than the purer and less self-interested one of "grief." Nor does she use the word *goret'* [to burn] in connection with Akhmatova, who is portrayed on the contrary as a chill force of conservatism; the passionate, destructive heat of fire Tsvetaeva associates instead with her own poetics.

52. For "I erected a monument," cf. A. S. Pushkin, *Sochineniia,* 1:586; for "In Tsarskoe Selo," cf. Anna Akhmatova, *Sochineniia v dvukh tomakh* (Moscow: Khudozhestvennaia literatura, 1986), 1:23–4. The theme of the monument, in the context of Tsvetaeva's oeuvre, evokes not just Pushkin's poem but the figure of Pushkin in general (in the guise of the Moscow Pushkin Monument, her childhood impressions of which she describes at length in "My Pushkin").

53. This opposition between her own dynamic fluidity and the perceived stony stasis of a beloved is one that Tsvetaeva often uses to illustrate her chosen other's lack of comprehension of her complicated selfhood and, simultaneously, to assert her artistic superiority; cf. "You—are stone, but I sing" ["Ty—kamennyi, a ia poiu . . ."] (1:527). Tsvetaeva is a kind of reverse Pygmalion, whose art renders flesh-and-blood beings back into cold, poetic stone.

54. For a brief discussion of the function and theology of icons in the Orthodox church, see Ernst Benz, *The Eastern Orthodox Church: Its Thought and Life,* trans. Richard and Clara Winston (Garden City, N.Y.: Anchor Books, 1963). As Benz explains: "The two-dimensionality of the icon . . . and its golden nimbus are intimately bound up with its sacred character" (6).

55. In a 1921 poem addressed to Akhmatova ("Kem polosyn'ka tvoia . . ." [2:79–80]), this imputation of blame is made more explicit; Akhmatova is pictured as an indifferent wizardess who manipulates lives, unintentionally but irresponsibly sending her loved ones up for sacrifice without a twinge (the poem was written shortly after the tragic

deaths of Blok and Gumilev). In my understanding, this poem is a continuation of Tsvetaeva's examination of the consequences of Akhmatova's poetics, rather than a literal condemnation of Akhmatova as a human being.

56. One might surmise that this difference in approach indicates a kind of sexism on Tsvetaeva's part: Blok is judged to be the personification of Poetry itself, whereas Akhmatova is stripped of her magic and reduced to just another sullen female.

57. It is significant that Tsvetaeva chooses the genre of the *poema;* "On a Red Steed" is her first mature work in this genre. As she explains: "Lyric poetry is a dotted line that seems whole and dark from afar, but look closely: it's full of omissions between the dots—an airless space—death . . . In a book (a novel or *poema, even* an article!) this is not the case, it has its own rules. A book does not abandon its writer, the people—fates—souls about whom one writes want to live, want to live on, every day more so, don't want to end! (Parting [rasstavanie] with a hero is always a rupture [razryv]!)" (6:234). In "On a Red Steed," Tsvetaeva selects the embracing wholeness of the *poema* over the dotted line of the lyrical cycle, indicating her hope that the myth she is creating will continue to have meaning outside its own bounds and her fantasy achieve a superreality more compelling than reality itself.

58. Because Lann is a far weaker poet than Akhmatova and Blok, Tsvetaeva is superior and thus can "use" him for her own poetic purposes in a way she has discovered she cannot use Akhmatova and Blok. At the same time, Lann's emotional distance guarantees against any risk of a creatively deadening consummation of the relationship, as Tsvetaeva frankly explains to him in a letter: "Please recognize the alienness to me of your talent and take from this the most flattering conclusion for yourself . . . Since—it's too easy—for me—to love Blok and Akhmatova!" [6:174].)

59. Ariadna Efron, *O Marine Tsvetaevoi,* 92.

60. Simon Karlinsky, *Marina Tsvetaeva: The Woman,* 103-4.

61. David M. Bethea, " 'This Sex Which Is Not One' versus This Poet Which Is 'Less Than One': Tsvetaeva, Brodsky, and Exilic Desire," in *Joseph Brodsky and the Creation of Exile* (Princeton, N.J.: Princeton University Press, 1994), 185.

62. Catherine Ciepiela, *The Same Solitude.*

63. Both Bethea (in " 'This Sex Which Is Not One,' " 184-85) and Ciepiela (in *The Same Solitude*) read the snowstorm as the key to an intertextual connection between "On a Red Steed" and Blok's *poema* "The Twelve."

64. It is interesting that, in the same letter to Akhmatova cited earlier, Tsvetaeva claims to be planning to convey the manuscript of "On a Red Steed" via Blok to Akhmatova; apparently she feels that this scheme, by transposing her poetic experiment back onto the space of real life, would somehow magically reinforce her poetic coup. Yet clearly she made no effort at all to carry out the plan; this example emphasizes once again how difficult it is to separate the real and the fantastic, cause and effect in Tsvetaeva's life and writing.

65. In the former example, a Maiakovskian subtext (his 1915 *poema* "A Cloud in Trousers" ["Oblako v shtanakh"], in which the hero's heart catches on fire) makes the internal origin of Tsvetaeva's fire clear. The latter example once again recalls the *zaria/zarit'sia* play from "Poems to Blok"; "On a Red Steed," incidentally, ends at dawn rather than dusk—this is a tale of beginnings.

66. Timothy Clark, *The Theory of Inspiration: Composition as a Crisis of Subjectivity*

in Romantic and Post-Romantic Writing (Manchester, England: Manchester University Press, 1997), 27.

67. Elsewhere (in her 1926 essay "The Poet about the Critic" ["Poet o kritike"]) Tsvetaeva elaborates on her belief that the act of reading is necessarily co-creative: "The reader's weariness is not a draining [opustoshitel'naia] weariness, but a creative one. Co-creative [sotvorcheskaia]. It brings honor both to the reader and to me" (5:293).

68. David Bethea, "'This Sex Which Is Not One,'" 184.

69. The negative semantic resonance of dolls in literature of the grotesque—suggesting automatism, superficiality, and demonic manipulation—may also be an influence here.

70. Tsvetaeva succinctly expresses this idea in one poem: "I—am a rebel in brow and womb" ["Ia—miatezhnitsa lbom i chrevom..."] (1:539). In later works such as the cycles addressed to Nikolai Gronskii and Anatolii Shteiger that I address in chapter 4, imagery of motherhood and female reproductive organs comes ironically to symbolize the inhuman depths of Tsvetaeva's loneliness and the destructive voraciousness of her poetic appetite.

71. Catherine Ciepiela, *The Same Solitude.*

72. Ibid.

73. David M. Bethea, "'This Sex Which Is Not One,'" 186.

74. Similarly, see Tsvetaeva's poem "Dagger" ["Klinok"] (2:219), where a usually phallic sword, agent of the poet's imagined suicide pact with her muse and lover, enacts her poetic transcendence (through death) of both sex and gender.

75. A similar use of prolepsis to indicate the complex interaction of poetic inspiration with reality can be found in Pushkin's well-known poem "I remember a miraculous moment" ["Ia pomniu chudnoe mgnoven'e..."]. Here the absent muse's reappearance in the fifth stanza is strangely preceded by the poet's inspirational passion: "My soul experienced an awakening: and then again you appeared..." [Dushe nastalo probuzhden'e: / I vot opiat' iavilas' ty...] (Pushkin, *Sochineniia,* 1:352).

76. This vow of celibacy can be read both as an allegory of Tsvetaeva's poetic work ethic and as a literal challenge to her roaming heart. At the same time, by swearing eternal faithfulness to her muse, she damns herself to a life of intense loneliness; as she writes in another poem: "My path does not lead past your house. My path does not lead past anyone's house... Wives are not jealous of me: I—am voice and vision" [Moi put' ne lezhit mimo domu—tvoego. / Moi put' ne lezhit mimo domu—nich'ego. / ... Ko mne ne revnuiut zheny: / Ia—golos i vzgliad] (1:524–5). Although this state of affairs is not necessarily a result of Tsvetaeva's female gender, still the absoluteness of the choice she makes diverges significantly from the male poet's ability to love real women even while he is in service to his muse. The male poet can remain a man; but Tsvetaeva, in choosing poetry, feels obligated to renounce her womanhood.

77. These Russian phrases are excerpted from the definition of *genii* provided by Vladimir Dal' in his *Tolkovyi slovar' zhivogo velikorusskogo iazyka* (Moscow: Gosudarstvennoe izdatel' stvo inostrannykh i natsional'nykh slovarei, 1955), 1:348.

78. The figure of the horseman/muse does not disappear from Tsvetaeva's oeuvre after "On a Red Steed"; instead, this image appears periodically in her writing, each time showing evidence of growth and change. In one poem ("Da, drug nevidannyi, neslykhannyi..." [1:524]), for instance, Tsvetaeva herself ironically becomes the ghostly

male rider of the fiery horse. It is interesting to note that, whereas originally both horse (fiery Pegasus) and horseman (inspiring muse) are emblems of Poetry, in later versions, horse and rider fuse; the result is an image of the archetypal poet in his mutually antagonistic, yet ultimately inseparable, bodily and spiritual aspects (cf. Tsvetaeva's letters to Rilke of 12 May and 13 May, 1926).

Chapter 2. Conjuring Pasternak

1. Besides the Psyche motif in Tsvetaeva's eponymous collection, there are numerous other references to the myth scattered throughout her poetry, correspondence, and other writings (cf. "Punsh i polnoch' . . ." [1:508–9], "Ne samozvanka—ia prishla domoi . . ." [1:394], "Golubinaia kupel' . . ." [2:182], "Popytka komnaty" [3:117], and "Prikliuchenie" [3:459–64]; cf. also Michael Makin, *Marina Tsvetaeva: Poetics of Appropriation* [Oxford, England: Clarendon Press, 1993], 38–39, 68, 269). In *Psyche,* Tsvetaeva also incorporates twenty brief poems composed by her young daughter Alia (Ariadna Efron) and titles this segment "Psyche"; Tsvetaeva's association of Alia with Psyche apparently springs from her daughter's girlish innocence: she is a prenubile, pure spirit that has not yet become a truly gendered, sexual body. Tsvetaeva may have read Apuleius's tale of Psyche in S. T. Aksakov's well-known Russian translation, and/or she may have known the myth from La Fontaine's expanded, semihumorous version in his *Les Amours de Psyche et de Cupidon.* In 1924, Tsvetaeva read Erwin Rohde's study of the ancient Greeks' belief in the soul's immortality (*Psyche: Seelencult und Unsterblichkeitsglaube der Griechen,* 2 vols. [Tübingen: J. C. B. Mohr, 1903]), which made an enormous impression on her. Ieva Vitins, in her excellent article "The Structure of Marina Cvetaeva's 'Provoda': From Eros to Psyche" (*Russian Language Journal* 41, no. 140 [1987]: 143–56), makes use of the Psyche myth in reading one particular poetic cycle and also suggests in passing the myth's relevance to several other poems. Konstantin Azadovskii notes the importance of Psyche to Tsvetaeva's poetic identity in his introduction (titled "Orfei i Psikheia" [10–47]) to *Nebesnaia arka: Marina Tsvetaeva i Rainer Mariia Ril'ke,* ed. Azadovskii (St. Petersburg: Akropol', 1992).

2. It is possible to read Tsvetaeva's 1922 folktale "The Swain," which she dedicated to Pasternak, as a variation on the Psyche myth, where the vampire with his demonic lure stands in for the more positively valenced Olympian deities. Tsvetaeva even overtly identifies herself with Marusia, the heroine of "The Swain": "For I myself am Marusia: keeping my word as honestly as I should (impossibly firmly), defending myself, shielding myself from happiness, half-alive . . . obedient to my own constraints upon myself without truly knowing why, and even when I move toward that cherubic realm, I follow—voices, someone else's will, not my own" (6:249).

3. The majority of Tsvetaeva's short lyric poems addressed to Pasternak are included in *After Russia*. In fact, even love poems addressed to other lovers (notably, Vishniak and Bakhrakh) in *After Russia* echo surreptitiously with hints and references to Pasternak. Longer works of poetry addressed to Pasternak include the *poemy* "From the Sea" ["S moria"] and "Attempt at a Room" ["Popytka komnaty"]. Prose works focused, at least in part, on Pasternak's poetry are the essays "A Downpour of Light" ["Svetovoi liven'"], "Epic and Lyric of Modern Russia" ["Epos i lirika sovremennoi Rossii"], and "Poets with a History and Poets without a History." The correspondence between Tsve-

taeva and Pasternak consists of over one hundred letters in total, but many of these have not survived; the originals of her letters to Pasternak were lost and the content of those we have today has been reconstructed from the drafts in her notebooks. The edition of Tsvetaeva's works I use here, *Sobranie sochinenii v semi tomakh* (Moscow: Ellis Lak, 1994–95), includes twenty-three of Tsvetaeva's letters to Pasternak; excerpts from several others can be found in the memoirs of Ariadna Efron. A number of Pasternak's letters to Tsvetaeva are published in *Perepiska Borisa Pasternaka,* ed. E. V. and E. B. Pasternak (Moscow: Khudozhestvennaia literatura, 1990).

4. Although many of the poetic works to emerge from Tsvetaeva's relationship with Pasternak have yet to be examined in detail, the relationship itself has been treated at some length in the following sources, among others: Ariadna Efron, *O Marine Tsvetaevoi* (Moscow: Sovetskii pisatel', 1989), 140–65; Jane Taubman, "Marina Tsvetaeva and Boris Pasternak: Toward the History of a Friendship," *Russian Literature Triquarterly* 2 (1972): 304–21; Jane Taubman, *A Life through Poetry: Marina Tsvetaeva's Lyric Diary* (Columbus, Ohio: Slavica, 1988), 160–219; and Viktoria Schweitzer, *Tsvetaeva,* trans. Robert Chandler and H. T. Willetts; poetry trans. Peter Norman; ed. Angela Livingstone (New York: Farrar, Straus & Giroux, 1992), 273–99. Catherine Ciepiela's forthcoming monograph (*The Same Solitude: Boris Pasternak and Marina Tsvetaeva,* in press) promises to be a wonderful contribution to the critical literature on this rich subject.

5. Erich Neumann, *Amor and Psyche: The Psychic Development of the Feminine,* trans. Ralph Manheim (New York: Pantheon Books, 1956). This volume includes both Apuleius's original tale (in English translation) and Neumann's commentary, which is extremely helpful to a symbolic interpretation of the Psyche myth, although Neumann's primarily psychoanalytic agenda at times leads to questionable overinterpretations.

6. Neumann, *Amor and Psyche,* 61.

7. Ibid., 90.

8. Ibid., 89.

9. As Tsvetaeva writes to Pasternak in a letter of July 10, 1926: "Please understand: this is the insatiable, primordial hatred of Psyche for Eve, in whom I share no part. Everything in me is from Psyche. Psyche—abandoned for Eve! Understand the cascading heights of my abhorrence (men never abandon a Psyche for another Psyche). [They abandon] a soul for a body . . . I never look at [men], I simply do not see them. They don't like me; they have a sense of smell. *Sex* doesn't like me [ia ne nravlius' *polu*] . . . You don't understand Adam, who loved only Eve. I don't understand Eve, whom everyone loves. I don't understand the flesh as such, don't recognize that it has any rights—especially the right to a voice" (6:263–64). Pamela Chester has developed the notion of an "anti-Edenic" theme that shapes Tsvetaeva's biographical prose in her article "Engaging Sexual Demons in Marina Tsvetaeva's 'Devil': The Body and the Genesis of the Woman Poet" (*Slavic Review* 53, no. 4 [winter 1994]: 1025–45). Cf. also Liza Knapp's "Marina Tsvetaeva's Poetics of Ironic Delight: The 'Podruga' Cycle as Evist Manifesto," *Slavic and East European Journal* 41, no. 1 (1997): 94–113.

10. It is interesting to note that the structure of "On a Red Steed" in its original version is similar to that of the Psyche myth: there are three trials, followed by a fourth, spiritual encounter (in the cathedral) and the final sacrifice/meeting of the lovers/apotheosis.

11. Erich Neumann, *Amor and Psyche,* 105. For Neumann, the ancient symbol of the uroboros represents the primordial union of the sexes.

12. Ibid., 108.

13. Elisabeth Bronfen in *Over Her Dead Body: Death, Femininity, and the Aesthetic* (New York: Routledge, 1992) argues that the female artist's suicide must be understood as the logical result of her pursuit of the aesthetic, because the "male" tradition has always objectified feminine beauty, implicitly equating it with the mask of death. Tsvetaeva's lyric "The sunset flamed" ["Zaria pylala, dogoraia . . ."] (1:549) develops a similarly fateful logic: there is a direct connection between the female poet's/soldier's artistic "cross-dressing" and her eventual suicide.

14. Catherine Ciepiela, *The Same Solitude*.

15. The ability to cause pain is an essential feature of Tsvetaeva's muse, and all candidates for the position (whether real ones like Blok, Akhmatova, and Pasternak, or imaginary ones like the horseman of "On a Red Steed" or the vampire of "The Swain") are identified by this characteristic. Pain for Tsvetaeva is synonymous with unrealized desire, which in turn is the upward vector that inspires and guarantees poetic production. This dynamic can be seen as a paradoxically outward-striving masochism. She seeks others to do the damage she plots against herself.

16. In the privacy of her notebook, a sisterly minded Tsvetaeva appended the following dedication to her cycle "The Two" ["Dvoe"] (2:235–38): "To my brother in the fifth season, the sixth sense, and the fourth dimension—Boris Pasternak" (Marina Tsvetaeva, *Stikhotvoreniia i poemy v piati tomakh* [New York: Russica, 1980–90], 3:463). This cycle is Tsvetaeva's most wrenching statement of the impossibility of a union between equals on this earth—an idea that also underlies the cycle "Wires," discussed at length later in this chapter: "In a world where everything—is mold and ivy, I know: you alone—are equal to me" [V mire, gde vse—/ Plesen' i pliushch, / Znaiu: odin / Ty—ravnosushch // Mne]. She expresses a similar thought in one of her first letters to Pasternak: "I would give up my whole life for you. (Yours is worth mine. For the first time)" (6:246).

17. Ariadna Efron, *O Marine Tsvetaevoi*, 155.

18. This is a very Pushkinian notion of freedom; and indeed, Tsvetaeva's sensibility of her real-life responsibilities to husband and children is superimposed upon her absolute faith in her fantasy of Pasternak as her "true" mate in a way that once again echoes Pushkin's *dolia/volia* dichotomy. Tsvetaeva herself acknowledges this link in a letter to Pasternak: "Our lives are alike, I also love those with whom I live, but that is—*fate* [dolia]. Whereas you are my own free choice, in a Pushkinian sense [volia moia, pushkinskaia], in place of happiness" (6:244).

19. Tsvetaeva's unique forehead symbolism calls to mind Minerva's birth from Zeus's splitting headache—in contrast to Aphrodite's sensual and soft genesis from sea foam. Through such imagery, Tsvetaeva here implicitly rejects her own marine onomastic origins (proclaimed, for example, in a poem of 1920 ["Kto sozdan iz kamnia . . ."] [1:534]), in favor of militant poeticism.

20. Later Tsvetaeva would succinctly express this opposition between the two poets' respective conceptions of life in a letter to Pasternak of 1927: "You turn the visible into the invisible (you make the manifest mysterious [iavnoe delaesh' tainym]), whereas I turn the invisible into the visible (I make the mysterious manifest)" (cited in Ariadna Efron, *O Marine Tsvetaevoi*, 159).

21. Ibid., 144.

22. A concise statement of the relationship of the arrow of love to the fated trajec-

tory of parting can be found in the brilliant paronomastic play of "Poem of the End": "Love—means an archer's bow tautened: a bow: parting" [Liubov′—eto znachit luk / Natianutyi: luk: razluka] (3:35).

23. These remarks are far from purely theoretical; many of Tsvetaeva's later letters to Pasternak recount her recent dreams in great detail. In her light-hearted 1926 *poema* "From the Sea," addressed to Pasternak, she writes of a miraculous experience of mutual dream. In her wistful and visionary "Attempt at a Room," written immediately after "From the Sea," the poet ends up alone in the vacuum of impossibility, surrounded by the shreds of her imagined meeting with her lover; this work was originally titled "Instead of a Letter" ["Vmesto pis′ma"].

24. See H. A. Guerber, *The Myths of Greece and Rome: Their Stories, Signification, and Origin* (London: G. G. Harrap & Co., 1907), 344: "[The mythologists'] school interprets the [myth of Cupid and Psyche] as a beautiful allegory of the soul and the union of faith and love." The connection of Psyche with the idea of faith is also an outstanding feature of Tsvetaeva's interpretation of the myth.

25. Pasternak, apparently, had somewhat different intentions toward Tsvetaeva. He is typically restrained in his letters of this period and does not make his thoughts and intentions clear; however, by 1926 as his marriage is disintegrating, he declares himself ready to leave his family and come to Tsvetaeva, if she will only say the word.

26. The relevant passage from Tsvetaeva's letter to Pasternak on the subject of her missed meeting with Blok was quoted in chapter 1, p. 36.

27. Tsvetaeva realizes the complexity of the secret language in which she and Pasternak communicate. Their relationship is supported entirely by this ornate, at once rugged and fragile poetic fabric (in which even silence and reticence play a meaningful part), and their connection weakens precisely at those times when their messages are not transmitted as intended. Examples of such "communication gaps" are Pasternak's failure to understand her loving intentions (reticence as a mythical act of self-abnegation) when she sends on Rilke's letter to him unaccompanied by a letter of her own (6:254); her own difficulty in understanding Pasternak's reactions to her *poema* "The Ratcatcher" ["Krysolov"] (6:261); and, more seriously, her utter incapability of empathizing with his depression in later years (6:277). For Tsvetaeva, the meaning of words is heavily colored by their impersonal, mythological associations; whereas for Pasternak, language means primarily in a rawly personal way.

28. Lawrence Lipking, *Abandoned Women and Poetic Tradition* (Chicago: University of Chicago Press, 1988), xvii. See also Joan DeJean's corrective to Lipking's ideas in her article "Fictions of Sappho" (*Critical Inquiry* 13 [summer 1987]: 787–805).

29. There may be an oblique reminiscence here of Valerii Briusov's 1902 poem "In Answer" ["V otvet"] in which he compares his muse to an ox that he lashes with a whip: "Gallop on, dream, my faithful ox! By force, if not willingly! I'm close to you, my whip is harsh, I'm laboring myself, so you work too! We should not rest a single moment" [Vpered mechta, moi vernyi vol! / Nevolei, esli ne okhotoi! / Ia bliz tebia, moi knut tiazhel, / Ia sam truzhus′, i ty rabotai! / Nel′zia nam miga otdokhnut′] (*Izbrannoe* [Moscow: Prosveshchenie, 1991], 81–2).

30. See a similar word play in Tsvetaeva's poem "The Lute" ["Liutnia"] (2:167), addressed to Pasternak and composed the same day as this letter.

31. Elsewhere, as already noted, Tsvetaeva makes a similar pun: "The heart: more

a musical organ than an anatomical one" [Serdtse: skoree orgán, chem órgan] (4:476). The heart is for her an instrument for the torment of poetry, rather than the muscle of happy love.

32. Ariadna Efron, *O Marine Tsvetaevoi,* 146. Cf. Joseph Brodsky's powerful discussion of Tsvetaeva's influence on Pasternak in his article "Primechaniia k kommentariiu," in *Marina Tsvetaeva: One Hundred Years,* ed. Viktoria Schweitzer et al. (Berkeley, Calif.: Berkeley Slavic Specialties, 1994), 262-84.

33. Tsvetaeva reiterates this point succinctly in a later letter to Pasternak: "I cannot tolerate presence, nor can you. Our songs would merge [my by spelis']" (6:265).

34. A wrenching passage from "Poem of the End" reveals the identity of Tsvetaeva's self-protective and self-destructive impulses when she drives away her potential lover: "One way or another, friend—rip the seams! Slivers and fragments! The only merit is that you burst yourself: burst, rather than unraveling slowly! And, that beneath the basting is live, red flesh, not rot! Oh, whoever rips cannot lose!" [Tak ili ínache, drug,—po shvam! / Drebezgi i oskolki! / Tol'ko i slavy, chto tresnul sam: / Tresnul, a ne raspolzsia! // Chto pod nametkoi—zhivaia zhil' / Krasnaia, a ne gnil'! // O, ne proigryvaet—/ Kto rvet!] (3:46).

35. The imagery of this poem suggests a subtextual link to Pushkin's "The Prophet" ["Prorok"], in which the poet's visitation by a six-winged seraph is instrumental in his poetic genesis; in both poems, lavish wing motifs symbolize the transcendence of poetic inspiration (A. S. Pushkin, *Sochineniia,* 1:385).

36. Elsewhere in a letter to Pasternak, Tsvetaeva writes: "The sea is a dictatorship, Boris. A mountain—is divinity" (6:252). The Nereid's flight thus represents Tsvetaeva's liberation from the body's dictates into the genderless freedom of the poetic soul.

37. Further evidence that Pasternak is latently present in "Phaedra" is contained in frequent references to secrets and concealment in both poems of the cycle: "hidden" [skryt], "hide" [spriach'], "as in a crypt" [kak v sklepe], "great secret" [velikaia taina], "silence" [molchanie], "Hippolytus's secret" [Ippolitova taina]. Mystery [taina] is a motif in Pasternak's own poetry, and—perhaps as a direct result—Tsvetaeva also experiences Pasternak's communications with her as somehow secretive and mysterious. Cf. her letter to Pasternak of 11 November 1923: "I am beginning to guess at some secret of yours. Secrets . . ." (6:233).

38. See too another poem ("Tsvetok k grudi prikolot . . ." [2:246]), where Tsvetaeva proclaims her insatiable craving for a love so intense that it confuses life with death: "Unquenched is my hunger for grief, for passion, for death" [Nenasytim moi golod / Na grust', na strast', na smert']. This stance is reminiscent of the suicidal poetic passion in her early poem "A Prayer."

39. The former stance is exemplified in a 1911 letter from Tsvetaeva to the poet Maksimilian Voloshin (6:47); the latter stance shapes an episode recalled by Tsvetaeva's acquaintance Vera Zviagintseva, who once accidentally intruded upon Tsvetaeva's tryst with a man Zviagintseva herself was interested in: "She lay on top of him and was casting her spell with words. She often said that her main passion was to communicate with people; that sexual relationships were necessary because that was the only way to penetrate a person's soul" (cited in Lily Feiler, *Marina Tsvetaeva: The Double Beat of Heaven and Hell* [Durham, N.C.: Duke University Press, 1994], 105).

40. In her essay "The Poet and Time" ["Poet i vremia"], Tsvetaeva writes: "Every

poet is in essence an emigrant, even in Russia. An emigrant from the Heavenly Kingdom and the earthly paradise of nature" (5:335).

41. See Tsvetaeva's poem "Nights without my beloved—and nights with my unbeloved" ["Nochi bez liubimogo—i nochi s neliubimym . . ."] (1:408).

42. This strategy is in contrast to the Symbolist choice (Blok's, for example) of living with one's muse physically but as if she is pure spirit.

43. Tsvetaeva's imagery resonates with both the Old Testament, in which the Hebrew God marks His covenant with a rainbow arched across the heavens, and the ancient Sumerian epic *Gilgamesh,* in which the goddess Ishtar vows her remembrance of human suffering by raising her necklace of "azure blue" jewels in a celestial half-circle. Cf. Alexander Heidel, *The Gilgamesh Epic and Old Testament Parallels,* 2d ed. (Chicago: University of Chicago Press, 1949), 259. Ishtar, the Babylonian goddess of sexuality and fertility, is but another manifestation of Psyche's nemesis Aphrodite; Ishtar plays a central role in Tsvetaeva's cycle "Scythians" ["Skifskie"], which is also addressed to Pasternak.

44. A book and three articles to date have been devoted to readings of "Wires": Anna Majmieskulow's *Provoda pod liricheskim tokom (Tsikl Mariny Tsvetaevoi "Provoda")* (Bydgoszcz, Poland: Wyższa Szkoła Pedagogiczna w Bydgoszczy, 1992); Ieva Vitins's "The Structure of Marina Cvetaeva's 'Provoda' "; Bruce Holl's " 'The Wildest of Disharmonies': A Lacanian Reading of Marina Tsvetaeva's 'Provoda' Cycle in the Context of Its Other Meanings" (*Slavic and East European Journal* 40, no. 1 [spring 1996]: 27–44); and Olga Zaslavsky's "In Defense of Poetry: Cvetaeva's Poetic Wires to Pasternak" (in *Critical Essays on the Prose and Poetry of Modern Slavic Women,* eds. Nina Efimov, Christine Tomei, Richard Chapple [Lewiston, N.Y.: Edwin Mellen Press, 1998], 161–83). Majmieskulow's book is a painstaking analysis of the linguistic and cultural significance of the complex imagery in "Wires." Holl's analysis is interesting in that his Lacanian approach allows him to focus on Tsvetaeva's problematic relationship to alterity which is also at the center of the present study; nevertheless, he overlooks the alternative exit from self afforded to Tsvetaeva by myth. Similarly, Olga Zaslavsky asserts that "Wires" is a prime example of Tsvetaeva's belief in the "tragic antinomy in the poetic existence," but she does not link this belief to the Psychean subtext in the cycle.

45. Tsvetaeva calls attention to this effect when she writes to Pasternak: "Do you notice that I give myself away to you *in fragments* [vrazdrob']?" (6:258). Another letter to Pasternak contains a similar allusion to her self-fragmentation: "I am tired of tearing myself, breaking myself into the shards of Osiris. Each book of verse is a book of partings and severings, with Doubting Thomas's finger probing the wound between one poem and the next" (6:273).

46. Compare the poem "More capacious than an organ" ["Emche organa i zvonche bubna . . ."] (2:250), which reduces (thus focuses, intensifies) all poetic speech to an acoustically and semantically evocative series of three prelinguistic cries: "And growing red-hot in flight—in the preheroic darknesses—the irresistible exclamations of the flesh: oh!—eh—ah!" [I—raskalias' v polete—/ V prabogatyrskikh t'makh—/ Neodolimye vozglasy ploti: / Okh!—ekh!—akh!].

47. See, for instance, the discussion of "big," "great," and "high" poets in Tsvetaeva's essay "Art in the Light of Conscience" ["Iskusstvo pri svete sovesti"] (5:358–60). She

also believes in a tiered afterlife and an almost Buddhist ranking of human souls; see her comments about Rilke's metaphysical advancement ("In all seriousness I'm troubled by the difference in the heavens—his and mine. Mine are no higher than the third, his, I'm afraid, are the highest" [6:271]) and her *poema* "New Year's Letter."

48. Incidentally, this is the critical point upon which my reading differs from Holl's; in my opinion, he reads the quintessentially Romantic, Tiutchevan paradox of "silentium" that underlies Tsvetaeva's poem too reductively. Tsvetaeva's poetics of the inexpressible is a more vectored idea than the deconstructionist tangle by means of which poetry expresses nothing so much as its own inexpressibility. For Tsvetaeva, it is not that the ineffable cannot be uttered, but that it can be uttered only in agonizing stages or fragments. Poetry for her always points outside itself; it is the instrument of a higher truth than the human.

49. Of course, in these lines Tsvetaeva is also engaged in staking out her own poetic territory: great as are Shakespeare and Racine, they do not really know the woman's unique sorrow—but Tsvetaeva does know.

50. Ariadna Efron, *O Marine Tsvetaevoi,* 144–45.

51. See the poignant poem "Omens" ["Primety"] (2:245), in which the poet observes the torments of her desirous body, whose claims she has renounced, as if from a great distance with a scientific, wry curiosity. Here, too, her physical pain translates ultimately into lyricism, as her broken throat metamorphoses into a Pasternakian broken voice, and the rift [shchel'] between body and soul is sublimated in a poetic trill. The motif of mutual cremation as a seal on Tsvetaeva's incestuous sibling bond with Pasternak can be found in a letter to him ("Pasternak, I want you not to be buried, but cremated" [6:230]), as well as in two poems of *After Russia,* titled, appropriately, "Sister" ["Sestra"] (2:198) and "Brother" ["Brat"] (2:209–10).

52. We recall that the motif of fire represents Tsvetaeva's poetic appropriation of life's raw materials. The miracle of the burning bush, which burns but is not consumed, could well be taken as a symbol of her impossible poetics (cf. her cycle "A Bush" ["Kust"] [2:317–18]). In a brief comment to Pasternak, she defines the logic of her poetic pyromania: "That which burns up without leaving behind any ashes is—God" (6:249); Tsvetaeva's fiery imagery thus encodes her own striving away from the physical and toward the divine realm of pure spirit. Sergei Efron's damning 1924 letter to Voloshin co-opts Tsvetaeva's own metaphor: "Marina is a gigantic stove, which in order to be heated requires wood, wood, and more wood. The useless ash is thrown away, and the quality of the wood is not so important. As long as the chimney draws well—everything turns to flame. Wood of poorer quality burns up faster, better wood takes longer. I don't even have to tell you that I haven't been able to feed the fire for a long time already" (cited in the original Russian version of Viktoria Schweitzer's *Tsvetaeva,* titled *Byt' i bytie Mariny Tsvetaevoi* [Moscow: SP Interprint, 1992], 316).

53. Tsvetaeva may also be recollecting Derzhavin's ode "God" ["Bog"], in which he derives God's existence from his own through a sequence of verbal permutations: "You were, you are, you will always be! . . . I am—of course, you are also!" [Ty byl, Ty est', Ty budesh' vvek! . . . Ia esm'—konechno, est' i Ty!]. For the full text of this poem, cf. Gavriil Derzhavin, *Stikhotvoreniia* (Leningrad: Sovetskii pisatel', 1957), 114–16.

54. In Tsvetaeva's 1933 essay "Poets with a History and Poets without a History," she distinguishes the trajectory of "pure geniuses" like Pushkin from that of "lyrical

geniuses" like Pasternak: "Thought—is an arrow. Feeling—is a circle" (5:403). Tsvetaeva, predictably, fits exclusively into neither of her two categories.

55. The contrast between Tsvetaeva's insular poetics at this time and Pasternak's expansive concept of poetic inspiration is well illustrated in her poem "Thus they listen" ["Tak vslushivaiutsia . . ."] (2:193-94), her poetic response to Pasternak's 1921 poem "Thus they begin" ["Tak nachinaiut. Goda v dva . . ."] from his collection *Themes and Variations* [*Temy i variatsii*]. These two works narrate the beginnings of each poet's extraordinary linguistic sensibilities in distant childhood. Words for Pasternak emerge as a result of the poet's confrontation with the objective reality of nature; whereas in Tsvetaeva's corrective, poetic language is innate and self-perpetuating and contradicts the very existence of any objective, natural world. For Tsvetaeva, then, poetic genius consists in the poet's hyperawareness of her own most intense desires and sensations.

56. The fact of Pasternak's Jewishness accords well with Tsvetaeva's concept of the poet as a cosmic outsider. Thus, in "The Emigrant," Pasternak is a "native of Vega" [Vegi—vykhodets] (2:163); just as Blok was affiliated with a comet, so too Pasternak is an emigrant from the star Vega of the constellation Lyra, often associated with Orpheus and Apollo. Similarly, in the first poem of "Scythians," Tsvetaeva refers to Pasternak as "my young, dark-skinned Syrian" [molodoi, smutnyi moi / Siriets]—"Syrian" here is both a reference to Pasternak's Semitic origins, and to the star Sirius, the brightest in the sky. It is also possible that Tsvetaeva intends an echo of the Russian *sirota* [orphan]—a concept that often characterizes for her the lot of the poet.

57. Atlas himself has already appeared in "Wires" in the cycle's first poem, as the embodiment of the telegraph poles: "These are piles, onto them Atlas lowered the racecourse of the gods" [Eto—svai, na nikh Atlant / Opustil skakovuiu ploshchad' / Nebozhitelei]. Incidentally, in 1926 after a break with Pasternak, Tsvetaeva would describe him as a "liberated Atlas" (*Rainer Maria Rilke, Marina Zwetajewa, Boris Pasternak: Briefwechsel,* eds. E. B. Pasternak, E. V. Pasternak, Konstantin Asadowskij [Frankfurt am Main, Germany: Insel Verlag, 1983], 239). The echo of Atlantis, too, intensifies the suggestion that the world of bodies and companionship is a lost continent in the sea of Tsvetaeva's new spiritual isolation. Cf. her poem "The Pedal" ["Pedal'"] (2:190-91), where she speaks of the Russian Atlantis, Kitezh, as the humming [gudiashchii] kingdom of memory—her soul's reminiscence of its ancient, drowned human past.

58. Incidentally, the word *vel'mozha* is prominent in the titles of well-known poems by both Derzhavin ("Vel'mozha," 1774-94) and Pushkin ("K vel'mozhe," 1830); the word is thus associated with the masculine poetic legacy with which Tsvetaeva affiliates herself.

59. In a letter to Pasternak written much later (on the eve of the new year 1930), Tsvetaeva meditates on the reasons for the long periods of silence in their correspondence: "We have nothing but words, we are doomed to them. And everything that for other people is communicated without words, through the air, that warm cloud *from—to*—for us is stated in words, voiceless ones, without the corrective of the human voice . . . The soul must be sustained by life, but here one soul consumes another soul: self-cannibalism, entrapment" (6:275).

60. The poet, in contrast, finds spiritual sustenance in the company of living forests in Tsvetaeva's cycle "Trees" ["Derev'ia"]: "Trees! I come to you! To be saved / From the roar of the marketplace! / In your upward wavings / How the heart is breathed clean!"

[Derev'ia! K vam idu! Spastis'/ Ot reva rynochnogo! / Vashimi vymakhami vvys'/ Kak serdtse vydyshano!] (2:143).

61. Yet the poetry is so forceful that it has undoubtedly colored interpretations of Tsvetaeva's personality and biography even, paradoxically, by people who knew her (including her own daughter, who describes aspects of Tsvetaeva's character and physical appearance using imagery and vocabulary obviously taken directly from her poems). This is, of course, something of a "chicken-and-egg" question, especially posthumously, and it cannot be argued with complete conviction either way. Still, I believe that it is important (and fair) to recognize, as most of Tsvetaeva's critics have failed to do, that she was essentially an extremely private, shy, and reticent person (she herself mentions this repeatedly in her writing and especially in her correspondence). Her poetry is her mask rather than the only truth of who she is—in real life, quite possibly, she may have been the opposite of the persona whom she inhabited in her poetry.

62. Nevertheless, this fantasy continues to shape the remaining poems of *After Russia*, many of which repeat the ideas and sometimes even the words of "Wires" almost verbatim (cf. especially "Poets" ["Poety"] [2:184–86], "The Crevasse" ["Rasshchelina"] [2:201], "Sahara" ["Sakhara"] [2:207–8], "I wander" ["Brozhu—ne dom zhe plotnichat'..."] [2:233–34], "Graying temples" ["V sedinu—visok..."] [2:257], and "Distance—versts, miles" ["Ras—stoianie: versty, mili..."] [2:258–59]).

63. The "beloved" in this poem is simultaneously Pasternak and Rainer Maria Rilke. It is interesting to note that Tsvetaeva, despite the crowded circumstances in which she often lived during her emigration, does not dream primarily of a Woolfian "room of one's own"; her greatest need is not solitude, but love.

64. Other examples of this symbolic function of the dash in Tsvetaeva's poems to Pasternak can be cited. In "Graying temples," the long dash is the sign of the two poets' private poetic conspiracy: "There are distant marriages, different marriages! As at the sign of a dash—like a secret sign—our eyebrows tremble—do you suspect?" [Braki roznye est', raznye est'! / Kak na znak tire—/ Chto na tainyi znak / Brovi vzdragivaiut— / Zapodazrivaesh'?]. Moreover, the dash's simultaneous linking and rending action is illustrated both graphically and morphologically in the very first word of *After Russia*'s penultimate poem, "Dis—tance: versts, miles." Pasternak remarks on the symbolic function of stylistic elements in cementing the two poets' peculiar bond in his letter to Tsvetaeva of 14 June 1924: "A shock passes through the stuff of habit as if through water... And when the heart contracts, Marina!... And how much *ours* that contraction/density [szhatost'] is—because it is thoroughly stylistic!" (*Perepiska Borisa Pasternaka*, 309).

Chapter 3. Losing Rilke

1. Rilke was born in 1875 into the German minority community of Prague, which at the time was part of the Austro-Hungarian Empire. His lifelong interest in Slavic cultures was first piqued during his formative years in Prague. For a concise biography of Rilke and introduction to his works, see Patricia Pollock Brodsky, *Rainer Maria Rilke* (Boston: Twayne Publishers, 1988). For a discussion of the importance of Russia to Rilke, see Anna Tavis, *Rilke's Russia: A Cultural Encounter* (Evanston: Ill.: Northwestern University Press, 1994).

2. See Olga Peters Hasty, *Tsvetaeva's Orphic Journeys in the Worlds of the Word*

(Evanston, Ill.: Northwestern University Press, 1996), 138–41. The correspondence between Tsvetaeva and Rilke, all of which was conducted in German, is published in *Rainer Maria Rilke, Marina Zwetajewa, Boris Pasternak: Briefwechsel,* eds. E. B. Pasternak, E. V. Pasternak, Konstantin Asadowskij [Azadovskii] (Frankfurt am Main, Germany: Insel Verlag, 1983). Tsvetaeva had been trilingual in Russian, German, and French since early childhood, a fact that allowed her to read in a deeply meaningful way not only Rilke's German poetry, but also his French collection *Vergers,* which he sent to her shortly after its publication. For a perceptive discussion of how Tsvetaeva's trilingualism shapes her poetry, see Elizabeth Klosty Beaujour, *Alien Tongues: Bilingual Russian Writers of the "First" Emigration* (Ithaca, N.Y.: Cornell University Press, 1989). All in all, the known Tsvetaeva–Rilke correspondence includes nine letters and a postcard that Tsvetaeva wrote to Rilke during his life; he sent her six letters and his "Elegie an Marina Zwetajewa-Efron." However, Tsvetaeva claimed that Rilke had written her seven letters, and in fact, in writing to Pasternak immediately following Rilke's death, she makes mention of a final letter from Rilke dated 6 September (6:266); Rilke's last known letter to Tsvetaeva is dated 19 August. Although scholars may, of course, be correct in assuming that Tsvetaeva counted Rilke's "Elegie" as a separate letter in order to arrive at the number seven—her and Rilke's lucky favorite (*Briefwechsel,* 112)—and that Tsvetaeva's memory in her letter to Pasternak and in another to Nanny Wunderly-Volkart (7:355), moreover, is simply distorted, there is nevertheless a possibility that there was, indeed, a seventh letter from Rilke that has been lost. This possibility is important not only for textological reasons, but also because many critics have assumed that Rilke ended the correspondence as a result of his supposed negative reaction to Tsvetaeva's letter of 22 August. If there was a 6 September letter from Rilke, then such interpretations are clearly invalid.

3. This kinship is evinced in striking similarities in poetic themes, concerns, symbols, and myths. Rilke's artistic preoccupation with the theme of death (see Patricia Pollock Brodsky, *Rainer Maria Rilke,* 29–30), especially, is important in the context of his relationship with Tsvetaeva, in which his own death was to play such a central role. Brodsky also mentions "the cluster of images of falling, ascending and descending" ("On Daring to Be a Poet: Rilke and Marina Cvetaeva," *Germano-Slavica* 3, no. 4 [fall 1980]: 265) that both poets share. However, Hasty points out that despite their many similarities, Tsvetaeva and Rilke operate in almost opposite ways: "What Tsvetaeva's poet achieves in the privileged space of language Rilke's poet attains within himself, arriving at a harmony, equilibrium, and self-sufficiency alien to Tsvetaeva. Thus too Rilke seeks peace and solitude whereas Tsvetaeva seeks wrenchingly impossible encounters—meetings to be realized only in poetry" (*Tsvetaeva's Orphic Journeys,* 162).

4. *Briefwechsel,* 104.

5. Ibid., 105. Rilke also sent Tsvetaeva his *Sonnets to Orpheus;* see the whole of Hasty's *Tsvetaeva's Orphic Journeys* for an immensely satisfying discussion of the importance of the Orpheus myth to Tsvetaeva's poetics.

6. *Briefwechsel,* 118.

7. As Tsvetaeva writes later to Pasternak, "I have loved no one for years—years—years. The last time—in real life—was what 'Poem of the End' came out of" (6:275). Tsvetaeva felt that Rodzevich, the stimulus for "Poem of the End," was the only man who had ever loved her as a woman rather than a poet (see Lily Feiler, *Marina Tsvetaeva: The*

Double Beat of Heaven and Hell [Durham, N.C.: Duke University Press, 1994], 145–47). If the less than laudatory reminiscences of contemporaries are to be trusted, then perhaps this because he simply was incapable of appreciating her as a poet, and uninclined to do so.

8. Tsvetaeva kept Rilke's "Marina Elegie" a secret from everyone except Pasternak until 1936, when she sent it to Anna Tesková, her Czech friend and correspondent (see the accompanying letter to Tesková [6:443–44]); the poem had already become known, however, on the basis of Rilke's drafts. Rilke had, in fact, written several other short works besides the "Elegie" before his death. Interestingly, Anna Tavis reads the poetic epitaph that he composed for himself shortly before his death ("Rose, oh pure contradiction, delight / At being no one's sleep under so many / Lids" [Rose, oh reiner Widerspruch, Lust / Niemandes Schlaf zu sein unter soviel / Lidern] [trans. Patricia Pollock Brodsky, *Rainer Maria Rilke,* 27]) as a final response to Tsvetaeva (Anna Tavis, "Russia in Rilke: Rainer Maria Rilke's Correspondence with Marina Tsvetaeva," *Slavic Review* 52, no. 3 [fall 1993]: 508–9).

9. James Beasley Simpson, comp., *Simpson's Contemporary Quotations: The Most Notable Quotes since 1950* (Boston: Houghton Mifflin, 1988), 344.

10. In her dedication to Rilke of a copy of her collection *Psyche,* sent to him shortly after her first letter, Tsvetaeva seems to inhabit the Psyche mask and equate him with Eros when she writes: "For Rainer Maria Rilke, my most beloved on earth and above earth (*over* the earth!)" (*Briefwechsel,* 111).

11. Tsvetaeva's muse Eros thus metamorphoses into Asrael, the Islamic and Hebrew Angel of Death, for whom, as for Eros, the bow and arrow are the tools of his trade (cf. Michael Naydan, commentary to Marina Tsvetaeva, *After Russia,* trans. and ed. Michael Naydan [Ann Arbor, Mich.: Ardis, 1992], 238 n. 57). Tsvetaeva, with her keen ear, could not have failed to note the phonetic similarity of the two mythological names "Eros" and "Asrael." Cf. Tsvetaeva's two poems about Asrael ("Azrail" [2:168], "Opereniem zim . . ." [2:168-69]); in the second of these she terms him her "ultimate lover" [poslednii liubovnik].

12. We recall again Tsvetaeva's association of lyricism with a circle and thought with an arrow in her essay "Poets with a History and Poets without a History" (5:97–428).

13. Konstantin Azadovskii provides a wealth of factual and background information in his notes and commentaries to both the German edition (*Briefwechsel*) and the Russian edition (*Rainer Mariia Ril'ke, Boris Pasternak, Marina Tsvetaeva: Pis'ma 1926 goda,* eds. K. M. Azadovskii, E. B. Pasternak, E. V. Pasternak [Moscow: Kniga, 1990]) of the Tsvetaeva–Rilke correspondence. Rilke scholars have tended to ignore entirely the significance of this correspondence to Rilke; one welcome exception, however, is Walter Arndt's commentary: "The Rainer–Marina relationship was absolutely the only one in his life in which his mind and another of equal rank confronted, recognized, and electrified each other" (*The Best of Rilke,* trans. Walter Arndt [Hanover, N.H.: University Press of New England, 1989], 147). Such omissions perhaps have encouraged the tendency of Tsvetaeva scholars to assume that the passion in this unique epistolary exchange was largely one-sided. Nevertheless, this one side, at least, has been discussed in numerous works. Key among these are Olga Peters Hasty's *Tsvetaeva's Orphic Journeys* (chapters 6 and 7) and the following three works by Anna Tavis: "Russia in Rilke"; *Rilke's Russia* (chapter 9); and "Marina Tsvetaeva through Rainer Maria Rilke's Eyes" (in *Marina Tsve-*

taeva: 1892–1992, ed. Svetlana El'nitskaia and Efim Etkind [Northfield, Vermont: The Russian School of Norwich University, 1992], 219–29). Tavis's reference to Tsvetaeva's "[increasing self-indulgence and] demands for personal intimacy [zhutkaia intimnost']" ("Russia in Rilke," 503) and Hasty's perception that Tsvetaeva is "aggressive" (162) and that her "claims and demands" on Rilke amount to a "siege" (161) are characteristic of the very strong language that, unfortunately, has often been used in relation to the Tsvetaeva–Rilke correspondence. I rather prefer Patricia Pollock Brodsky's assessment, in her article "On Daring to Be a Poet," that Tsvetaeva "treats [Rilke] in her letters with a rather endearing mixture of awe and impudence" (263). Brodsky, who is well-versed in the poetry of both Rilke and Tsvetaeva, succeeds admirably in providing a clear-sighted and balanced view of both correspondents; as she writes: "Rilke found in Tsvetaeva an unexpected and challenging late friendship; she found in him an artistic equal and a friend whose letters helped her survive her degradations" (262).

14. *Briefwechsel,* 124.

15. Cf. for instance the editorial comments in *Boris Pasternak, Marina Tsvetayeva, and Rainer Maria Rilke: Letters Summer 1926,* eds. Yevgeny Pasternak, Yelena Pasternak, and Konstantin M. Azadovsky (New York: Harcourt Brace Jovanovich, 1985), 127.

16. *Briefwechsel,* 108.

17. Ibid., 105.

18. Tsvetaeva writes: "I would not be able to live with you, not because of a lack of mutual understanding, but because of how well we do understand. To suffer from someone else's rightness which is simultaneously my own ... that humiliation I would not be able to bear" (6:262).

19. *Briefwechsel,* 235.

20. Tsvetaeva proposed a joint trip to London; this trip, however, never materialized. Her long-awaited meeting with Pasternak, when it finally came—during his brief visit to an anti-Fascist literary congress in Paris, in June of 1935, in the darkest years of Stalinism—is the mistaken earthly nonmeeting she had feared so many years before. Later, in Moscow, Pasternak was helpful to Tsvetaeva and her family; but the intense intimacy of their early letters was never matched in real life.

21. *Briefwechsel,* 237.

22. We recall that Tsvetaeva writes in a similar vein of her "missed" meeting with Blok: "In life—by the will of poetry—I missed a great meeting with Blok (if we'd met—he wouldn't have died)" (6:36). Although some have read only immense egotism and a severely imbalanced sense of reality into this comment, I believe that it must, like everything Tsvetaeva writes, be apprehended with a poetic imagination. There is a complex philosophical (albeit idiosyncratic) logic imbedded in Tsvetaeva's terse statement: Blok's death and her own nonmeeting with him are linked not causally, but through the equal degree to which both events are fated. Changing any piece of the puzzle of reality would render everything conditional and so, potentially, change the entire picture.

23. Tsvetaeva welcomes Rilke as the incarnation of her equestrian muse, revised and reconstrued, even from the very beginning of their correspondence: "Rainer, I am no collector, and the man-Rilke, who is greater than the poet ... because he carries the poet (knight and steed—Rider!), I love inseparably from the poet" (*Briefwechsel,* 119).

24. *Briefwechsel,* 157.

25. Pushkin explores the inspirational effects of such an awareness of ephemerality in

his poem "Autumn (A Fragment)" ["Osen' (Otryvok)"]; perhaps it is not a coincidence that, in Tsvetaeva's next letter (of 14 June), she apparently paraphrases Rilke's poem by the same title ("Autumn" ["Herbst"]; cf. *Pis'ma 1926 goda,* 246 n. 9).

26. *Briefwechsel,* 175.

27. Ibid. Rilke's generosity reverses belatedly the unpaid debts of Tsvetaeva's long-ago poetic tributes to Blok and Akhmatova. As Tsvetaeva explains: "Rilke, my whole life long I have given myself away in parcels of verse—to everyone. Including poets. But I always gave too much, I always drowned out the possible answer. The answer was scared away. I anticipated the entire echo" (*Briefwechsel,* 175).

28. *Briefwechsel,* 174.

29. Ibid., 208.

30. Ibid., 231-32.

31. Ibid., 114. This passage is consonant with Rilke's own dislike of organized religion and traditional authoritarian figures, and with his association of divinity with creativity (see Patricia Pollock Brodsky, *Rainer Maria Rilke,* 1, 29).

32. *Briefwechsel,* 121.

33. Ibid., 232.

34. It is curious that the Latin word for "world" is *mundus,* which is phonetically close to *Mund,* the German word for "mouth"; one wonders whether Tsvetaeva has in mind this translinguistic play on words.

35. Tsvetaeva here apparently misconstrues the meaning of the word *Untiefe,* which actually means "shallows, shoal" (see the note in *Letters Summer 1926,* 196).

36. *Briefwechsel,* 232.

37. Ibid., 236.

38. Ibid., 237.

39. Ibid., 237-38.

40. Ibid., 239.

41. Ibid., 229.

42. Hasty, *Tsvetaeva's Orphic Journeys,* 161.

43. I am here disagreeing with Hasty, who accuses Tsvetaeva of wounded pride: "Rilke had no intention of injuring Tsvetaeva, but she read [his] remarks as an assertion of his unattainable superiority and as a rejection of her own poetic identity" (*Tsvetaeva's Orphic Journeys,* 156).

44. *Briefwechsel,* 125-26.

45. Ibid., 236.

46. Cf. "Death—means no" ["Smert'—eto net . . ."] (1:555-56), "Life lies inimitably" (2:132-33), and especially the first poem of the cycle "Poets" (2:184), where the poet's role is to "conjure a detour" [kriuk vymorochit'] between Life and Death, Yes and No. It is not that Tsvetaeva does not comprehend Rilke's coming death, but that she refuses to accept it as absolute. The "calendar's lie" [kalendarnaia lozh'] (1:556) is not the whole truth.

47. *Briefwechsel,* 237.

48. Ibid., 236-37.

49. Ibid., 241. This was the lone inscription on a postcard Tsvetaeva sent to Rilke in early November.

50. *Briefwechsel,* 236. The last sentence appears as a footnote in Tsvetaeva's original letter; it is an inexact quotation from one of Rilke's poems (cf. *Briefwechsel,* 301 n. 9; *Pis'ma 1926 goda,* 252–53 n. 13).

51. *Briefwechsel,* 238.

52. Ibid., 239.

53. Ibid., 230.

54. Tsvetaeva suggests as much in her letter to Pasternak immediately following Rilke's death, when she paraphrases her final appeal to Rilke ("Do you still love me?"); now, she intimates, her question has been belatedly answered—by Rilke's explanatory death—in the affirmative. (6:266)

55. Here I use imagery suggested by Tsvetaeva's immensely evocative poem "Seven, seven" ["Semero, semero . . ."] (2:61).

56. See for example the poem "The Lesson of Thomas" ["Nauka Fomy"] (2:219–20).

57. In her cycle "Desk" ["Stol"], Tsvetaeva calls her desk "the sternest of mirrors" [strozhaishee iz zertsal] (2:309); whereas the black surface of a piano is her "first mirror" in her autobiographical essay "Mother and Music" (5:28).

58. We recall how, years before, Tsvetaeva's metaphorical thought process was a barrier to companionship in her poem "In the Luxembourg Garden."

59. Rilke as Tsvetaeva's tour guide into the realm of death is a kind of Dantesque figure—but this Dante leads, rather than being led. Although Dante is not explicitly mentioned in "Attempt at a Room," a phonetically similar name—Danzas—does occur when Tsvetaeva tells Rilke, "You grow up like Danzas—from behind" [Vyrastesh' kak Danzas—/ Szadi]. Konstantin Danzas was Pushkin's friend and the second at Pushkin's fatal duel; like his phonetic twins Dante and D'Anthès (Pushkin's murderer), Danzas is for Tsvetaeva an emissary of death—though a benign one.

60. *Briefwechsel,* 114.

61. Ibid., 239.

62. See Joseph Brodsky's brilliant essay "Footnote to a Poem" (in *Less Than One: Selected Essays* [New York: Farrar, Straus & Giroux, 1986], 195–267) and the final chapter of Olga Peters Hasty's *Tsvetaeva's Orphic Journeys,* 163–222.

63. Hence the immense difference of "New Year's Letter" from previous poems Tsvetaeva has written to dead beloveds, where infinity seems insurmountable (cf. "Osypalis' list'ia nad Vashei mogiloi . . ." [1:212]).

64. Cf. a trio of poems that Tsvetaeva wrote in the spring of 1913: "I dedicate these lines" ["Posviashchaiu eti stroki . . ."] (1:176), "You pass by as I once did" ["Idesh', na menia pokhozhii . . ."] (1:177), and "To my poems, written so early" ["Moim stikham, napisannym tak rano . . ."] (1:178). Numerous other examples could be cited.

65. Joseph Brodsky, "Footnote to a Poem," 231.

66. Ibid., 211–12.

67. This imagery is found in Tsvetaeva's poems "Take, my darling, these rags . . ." ["Na tebe, laskovyi moi, lokhmot'ia . . ."] (1:401), "The Emigrant" (2:163), and "The Soul" (2:163–64).

68. For an immensely evocative reading of this first line of "New Year's Letter," cf. Joseph Brodsky, "Footnote to a Poem," 205–12.

69. The date of Rilke's "new year" (new life)—1927—has a kind of poetic perfec-

tion, since seven is his and Tsvetaeva's favorite number. Furthermore, the composition date of "New Year's Letter" — 7 February, which, in the European style, would be coded 7.2.27 — is in itself a kind of open circle.

70. A fractal is a mathematical figure in which a set pattern of relationships between growth nodes repeats ad infinitum; ideally, all trees are fractals. This image is very different from the vectored tree symbolism of an earlier poem ("V snovidiashchii chas moi..." [2:17–18]). For more on the symbolism of trees in Tsvetaeva's poetry, see O. G. Revzina, "Tema derev'ev v poezii M. Tsvetaevoi," in *Uchenye zapiski Tartuskogo universiteta*, 576, *Tipologiia kul'tury: Vzaimnoe vozdeistvie kul'tur*, ed. Iurii Lotman (Tartu, Estonia: Tartuskii gosudarstvennyi universitet, 1982), 141–48 and Alyssa Dinega, "Ne serdtse, a serdtsevina: The Metaphysics of Trees in Tsvetaeva's Poetry" (work in progress).

71. *Briefwechsel*, 158.

72. These are, in particular, the organizing themes of Rilke's poetic masterpieces, *Duino Elegies* and *Sonnets to Orpheus*, which he had sent to Tsvetaeva together with his first letter. For an overview of these cycles, see Patricia Pollock Brodsky, *Rainer Maria Rilke*, 138–63.

73. The English translations given here of passages from Rilke's "Marina Elegie" are taken from *The Selected Poetry of Rainer Maria Rilke*, ed. and trans. Stephen Mitchell (New York: Random House, 1982). I have modified Mitchell's version in several places for greater accuracy.

74. Both Anna Tavis and Olga Peters Hasty read Rilke's "Elegie" as a "warning" to Tsvetaeva against possessiveness and as a sign that he wishes to discontinue the correspondence, and both scholars contend that Tsvetaeva herself interpreted the "Marina Elegie" as such. I cannot agree with this interpretation. Rather, Rilke offers his own accumulated wisdom and tranquility with all his heart, knowing the cost at which it has come, and desiring—on his deathbed, as it were—to share it with Tsvetaeva, who, he senses from her letters, is in need of consolation and succor. Tsvetaeva, in turn, accepts the gift with all her heart.

75. Incidentally, Tsvetaeva herself occasionally uses the flower in a similarly symbolic way — a fact that has not been remarked in critical articles on her onomastic poetics, which have focused on her play with her first name and patronymic (cf. "Idesh', na menia pokhozhii..." [1:177], "Tsvetok k grudi prikolot..." [1:246], "Poem of the End" [3:35]). In all these poems, the flower, symbolic of poetry, is at the same time associated with the graveyard, blood, and pain.

76. This sublimation of sexual love is a central theme in Rilke's life and work: "Over the years Rilke developed a vision of an ideal love, the *gegenstandslose* or *besitzlose Liebe* (objectless love, or love without possession). This was a state in which the lover is so strong and sure in his, or more often her, love that the object, the specific person, becomes superfluous. The lover loves outward, as it were, in an expenditure of pure energy, of pure, intransitive loving . . . It has been suggested, of course, that in developing his theory . . . [Rilke] was providing a poetic and philosophical defense for his own inability to receive and reciprocate love in an ordinary fashion" (Patricia Pollock Brodsky, *Rainer Maria Rilke*, 33).

77. In Tsvetaeva's lyric poems she several times uses the epithet "round" [kruglyi] to describe paradise; elsewhere in "New Year's Letter" she plays on the similarity of the Russian word for paradise, *rai*, to Rilke's first name.

78. Similarly in her 1927 essay "Your Death" ["Tvoia smert'"] (5:186–205), written shortly after "New Year's Letter," Tsvetaeva claims that Rilke's death links all discrete human deaths into a single whole and bends the linearity of time into an unbroken circle: "Many buried in one [grave] and one buried in many. There, where your first grave and your last merge—on your own headstone—the row closes into a circle. Not only the earth (life), but also death is round" (5:186). For an excellent reading of "Your Death," see Olga Peters Hasty, "'Your Death'—The Living Water of Cvetaeva's Art," *Russian Literature* 13 (1983): 41–64. Hasty shows that the essay is designed around a symmetry of opposites, with Rilke as the supporting fulcrum, and that this structure can be discerned on every level of the work.

79. Rilke in his final letter to Tsvetaeva had somewhat ironically envisioned the two poets as two halves of one nest where lives "a large bird, a predatory bird of the spirit" (*Briefwechsel*, 236).

80. Hasty reads "New Year's Letter" as the trajectory of Tsvetaeva's ultimate Orphic journey, during which the poet's distance from Rilke is gradually obliterated until she finally "arrives" in Rilke's sphere.

81. This star recalls the star symbolic of unattainable poetic destiny in Tsvetaeva's early poem "Only a Girl," as well as the cosmic imagery inspired by Blok's transcendence in "Poems to Blok." Now, at last, Tsvetaeva is affiliated with the star that earlier seemed so inaccessible—that is, through her intimacy with Rilke both before and after his death, she achieves certainty in her own poetic genius.

82. This mutual cancellation of negatives has the very opposite effect of the double negative in Russian which, on the contrary, only intensifies the degree of negativity. Rilke's death thus alludes to a new, liberating grammar of essences that provides an exit from the traps of earthly grammar.

83. See Tsvetaeva's discussion of Rilke's French collection *Vergers* in her 6 July letter to him, where she writes: "Writing poetry is already translating, from the mothertongue—into another, whether French or German doesn't matter. No tongue is the mothertongue" (*Briefwechsel*, 206). See, too, Tsvetaeva's comments about *Vergers* to Pasternak after Rilke's death: "He was tired of the language of his birth . . . He was weary of omnipotence, began longing for apprenticeship, seized the language most inhospitable to poets—French . . . and again he *could*, once more he *could*, and he immediately tired of it. The problem turned out to be not with German, but with Human. His thirst for French turned out to be a thirst for Angelic" (6:267).

84. Cf. the well-known poem "I opened my veins" ["Vskryla zhily: neostanovimo . . ."] (2:315).

85. I draw here on Joseph Brodsky's convincing reading of these lines (cf. "Footnote to a Poem," 227).

86. Cf. the discussion in Patricia Pollock Brodsky, *Rainer Maria Rilke*, 30.

87. That the usage of these pronouns is metalinguistic, so that not only the referents of the pronouns merge, but in fact the pronouns themselves (i.e., the language is altered) is suggested both by the italics and by the fact that "you" [ty] occurs in the nominative, rather than the expected accusative case.

88. See Joseph Brodsky's discussion of these astonishing shifts of perspective ("Footnote to a Poem," 216–19).

89. Hasty provides a rich discussion of the double meanings of the words *svet* [world/

light], *krai* [edge/realm], and *mesto* [place/expanse] in "New Year's Letter": "Tsvetaeva uses the polysemy of key words in the poem to represent the difference between the two distinct worlds of existence but also to highlight their contiguity in language" (*Tsvetaeva's Orphic Journeys,* 181).

90. For the full text of Pushkin's poem, cf. A. S. Pushkin, *Sochineniia v trekh tomakh* (Moscow: Khudozhestvennaia literatura, 1985), 1:503.

91. This wholeness at the same time undoes the divisiveness of Tsvetaeva's *poema* "From the Sea" ["S moria"], a work addressed to Pasternak in the summer of 1926. With Rilke, distance *from* [s + genitive case] becomes union *with* [s + instrumental case].

92. With Pasternak, such a union threatened Tsvetaeva's poetic prowess ("Our songs would merge" [my by spelis'] [6:265]); with Rilke, on the contrary, the earthly meeting that never took place ("Nothing worked out for you and me. To such a degree, so cleanly and simply nothing . . ." [Nichego u nas s toboi ne vyshlo. / Do togo, tak chisto i tak prosto / Nichego . . .]) is replaced by a dynamic, metalinguistic paradise where Tsvetaeva's poetic aspirations are no longer plagued by the ambiguities and divisions of earthly language.

93. During the May–June rift in her correspondence with Rilke, Tsvetaeva writes to Pasternak that Rilke is like a cold sea, in no need of human company (6:252, 258). Cf. Stephanie Sandler's "Embodied Words: Gender in Cvetaeva's Reading of Puškin," (*Slavic and East European Journal* 34, no. 2 [1990]:139–57) for a discussion of Tsvetaeva's childhood memories of Pushkin's poem "To the Sea" ["K moriu"] as she presents them in her 1937 essay "My Pushkin."

94. Joseph Brodsky, "Footnote to a Poem," 245.

95. *Briefwechsel,* 105.

96. This dedication is given incorrectly in *Briefwechsel* (111); Hasty cites the correct text (*Tsvetaeva's Orphic Journeys,* 139).

97. Tsvetaeva borrows the concept of "craft" from the nineteenth-century female poet Karolina Pavlova, whose lines she cites as the epigraph to her own 1923 collection *Craft* [*Remeslo*] (cf. commentary in Marina Tsvetaeva, *Stikhotvoreniia i poemy v piati tomakh* [New York: Russica, 1980–90], 2:363–65).

98. Indeed, there is a theatrical element to "New Year's Letter" as well, as Joseph Brodsky points out ("Footnote to a Poem," 257–58). For Tsvetaeva, "paradise—is an amphitheater" [rai—amfiteatr] where "the curtain is lowered on someone" [zanaves nad kem-to spushchen]; she imagines Rilke's "elbows resting on the rim of the theater box" [prioblokotias' na obod lozhi]. This theatrical motif suggests an irreverent playfulness not in keeping with the usual somberness of death.

99. In Tsvetaeva's essay "Your Death," this symmetry is extended further: Rilke's death is temporally situated between the deaths of Tsvetaeva's two acquaintances, the French Ioanna (Jeanne Robert) and the Russian Ioann (the retarded boy Vania) (5:205).

100. This precautionary act recalls the flood of "Wires" in which an Atlantic Ocean of tears overflows its own shores.

101. Joseph Brodsky explains that the *poema*'s final line can also be read, in a purely prosaic manner, as a postal instruction—signaling the triumph of the genre of the love lyric over the competing genre of the funereal lament ("Footnote to a Poem," 266–67).

102. Tsvetaeva interprets Rilke's posthumous appearance in her dreams as evidence of his continuing involvement with her, as she explains to Pasternak in her letter of 9 Feb-

ruary 1927 (6:269–71); supposedly, Rilke's first visitation took place on 7 February, the day on which "New Year's Letter" was completed.

103. In this passage, the poet mistakes the silent Rilke for a fir tree; in "New Year's Letter," Rilke dies in the presence of firs, and firs are likewise associated with the Savoy where he and Tsvetaeva had planned to meet the following spring.

104. Here as elsewhere, the number seven is a magical sign of Tsvetaeva's bond with Rilke.

105. For a thorough analysis of the poetic patterning of "Poem of the Air," see M. L. Gasparov's article " 'Poema vozdukha' Mariny Tsvetaevoi: Opyt interpretatsii" (*Uchenye zapiski Tartuskogo universiteta,* 576, *Tipologiia kul'tury: Vzaimnoe vozdeistvie kul'tur,* ed. Iurii Lotman [Tartu, Estonia: Tartuskii gosudarstvennyi universitet, 1982], 122–40).

106. At the same time the word *plast* (which is sometimes used to mean "gravestone") is an image of heaviness and stasis—the negative face of death; Tsvetaeva here infuses this image, paradoxically, with the continual dynamism of "waves" [zybi] to express her new understanding of the afterlife.

107. The use of the slang verb *mrem* [we'll die] in this passage recalls Tsvetaeva's concept of Mra, whereas the poet's expectation of a ghostly guest's knock suggests that Pushkin's play *The Stone Guest* [*Kamennyi gost'*] may be a subtext in Tsvetaeva's "Poem of the Air." Pushkin's statue is the spirit of death who comes for Don Guan (a poet, like Tsvetaeva); he stands watch silently outside the door as does Rilke's spirit here. The statue's sudden knock is the sign that Don Guan's time has run out.

108. It is possible that in forging this disseminated rhyme reminiscent of terza rima and in giving the *poema* its tripartite structure, Tsvetaeva is playing with the structure of *The Divine Comedy;* we recall that in "Attempt at a Room" there was an obtuse hint of Tsvetaeva's association of Rilke with Dante; the terraced heavens and staircases of "New Year's Letter" are likewise a reference to Dante's conception of the afterlife (Joseph Brodsky remarks wittily that Tsvetaeva's notion of paradise as amphitheater is a "grandiose statement fusing all of Alighieri's efforts into a single phrase" ["Footnote to a Poem," 257]). In "Poem of the Air," Rilke is Tsvetaeva's guide into the outer circle of heaven, just as Virgil once guided Dante into the inner circle of hell.

109. This passage refers subtly to "New Year's Letter," with its resonant interpretation of the "new year" of Rilke's death. In her essay "The Poet about the Critic," Tsvetaeva describes the poetic process as the honing of her entire being into intense listening: "My directive is the auditory path to a poem: I hear the melody [napev], but I don't hear the words. I seek the words . . . To hear correctly—this is my task. I have no other" (5:285). The poet Osip Mandel'shtam, incidentally, had a similar concept, which Nadezhda Mandel'shtam describes in her memoir of her husband: "The whole process of composition is one of straining to catch and record something compounded of harmony and sense as it is relayed from an unknown source and gradually forms itself into words (*Hope against Hope,* trans. Max Hayward [New York: Atheneum, 1983], 71).

110. Cf. Tsvetaeva's comment about Rilke in a letter to Anna Tesková: "I am still convinced that when I die—he will come for me. He will transport/translate [perevedet] me into the next world as I now translate [perevozhu] him (holding his hand) into the Russian language. This is the only way I understand translation." (6:375)

111. Here as elsewhere, Tsvetaeva may be associating the idea of "purity" with Rilke

himself, given that his first name, Rainer, can be paronomastically linked with the German adjective *rein* [pure]. This motif is reiterated in the poema a few lines later: "Are we propelled by pure hearing or pure sound?" [Chistym slukhom / Ili chistym zvukom / Dvizhemsia?].

112. *Briefwechsel,* 230.

113. Related to the reverse gravity of "Poem of the Air" is Tsvetaeva's portrayal of the heavens as her future burial ground in a number of poems (cf. "Cherdachnyi dvorets moi..." [1:488], "Vysoko moe okontse!..." [1:494], "Priamo v efir..." [2:50], "Bez samovlastiia..." [2:67], "Na naznachennoe svidan'e..." [2:202]). Joseph Brodsky seems to have adopted from Tsvetaeva the idea of this reverse gravitational force—appropriately so, because he, like Tsvetaeva, often uses metaphors of flight (birds, astronauts, etc.) to speak about poetic inspiration. Examples can be found in Brodsky's poems "Great Elegy to John Donne" ["Bol'shaia elegiia Dzhonu Donnu"] and "The Hawk's Cry in Autumn" ["Osennii krik iastreba"]. Cf. also Alyssa Dinega, "Poet as Aeronaut: Brodsky's Dialogue with Tsvetaeva on Aging and the Poetic Death-Wish" (conference paper, AATSEEL National Conference, Chicago, 1999).

114. Osip Mandel'shtam, *Sochineniia v dvukh tomakh* (Moscow: Khudozhestvennaia literatura, 1990), 2:143. Tsvetaeva had an intense friendship with Mandel'shtam during the spring of 1916. More broadly, on the relationship of "Poem of the Air" to Acmeism, see Alexandra Smith, "Surpassing Acmeism?—The Lost Key to Cvetaeva's 'Poem of the Air,'" *Russian Literature* 45, no. 2 (February 1999): 209–22.

115. It is interesting to note that here Tsvetaeva recants the poetic self-image she had sketched in "On a Red Steed," where her wings grew from her shoulders, and it was the horseman/muse, on the contrary, whose temples had sprouted wings.

Chapter 4. Ruing Young Orphans

1. Elsa Triolet's description of Maiakovskii could be applied equally well to Tsvetaeva herself: "[Maiakovskii carried] within himself all of human misery ... [He] demanded of love, happiness, life, the impossible, the immortal, the boundless ... he possessed in the highest degree what the French call *le sens d'absolu,* the need for total, maximal intensity in friendship and love" (cited in Victor Erlich's *Modernism and Revolution: Russian Literature in Transition* [Cambridge, Mass.: Harvard University Press, 1994], 263). A passage from Maiakovskii's "The Backbone-Flute" ["Fleita-pozvonochnik"] could have been written by Tsvetaeva: "I stretched out my soul above the abyss like a tightrope, and, juggling words, I swayed above it" [Ia dushu nad propast'iu natianul kanatom, / zhongliruia slovami, zakachalsia nad nei] (Vladimir Maiakovskii, *Sobranie sochinenii v dvenadtsati tomakh* [Moscow: Pravda, 1978], 1:256). Indeed, Tsvetaeva obviously borrows her hyperbolic fire imagery in the first scene of "On a Red Steed" from Maiakovskii's *poema* "A Cloud in Trousers" ["Oblako v shtanakh"]. Maiakovskii himself was critical of Tsvetaeva (perhaps unbeknownst to her), despite her frank admiration of him. For Tsvetaeva's views on Maiakovskii, see her essay "Epic and Lyric of Modern Russia" (5:375–96); cf. also Anna Saakiants, "Vladimir Mayakovsky and Marina Tsvetaeva," *Soviet Studies in Literature* 19, no. 4 (fall 1983): 3–50.

2. Cf. the discussion of this episode in Lily Feiler's *Marina Tsvetaeva: The Double Beat of Heaven and Hell* (Durham, N.C.: Duke University Press, 1994), 191–92.

3. The line is "Liubovnaia lodka razbilas' o byt"; Tsvetaeva uses it as an epigraph to the fourth poem of her cycle "To Maiakovskii."

4. For a discussion of Tsvetaeva's writings on Maiakovskii's suicide, cf. Svetlana Boym, *Death in Quotation Marks: Cultural Myths of the Modern Poet* (Cambridge, Mass.: Harvard University Press, 1991), 221–25 and Olga Peters Hasty, "Reading Suicide: Tsvetaeva on Esenin and Maiakovskii" (*Slavic Review* 50, no. 4 [winter 1991]: 836–46).

5. On the significance of Pushkin in Tsvetaeva's writings, see Alexandra Smith, *The Song of the Mocking Bird: Pushkin in the Work of Marina Tsvetaeva* (Bern, Switzerland: Peter Lang, 1994); Alexandra Smith, "Rol' pushkinskikh podtekstov v poetike Tsvetaevoi," *Studia Russica Budapestinensia* 2–3 (1995): 237–44; Peter J. Scotto, "The Image of Puškin in the Works of Marina Cvetaeva" (Ph.D. Diss., University of California, Berkeley, 1987); and Stephanie Sandler, "Embodied Words: Gender in Cvetaeva's Reading of Puškin" (*Slavic and East European Journal* 34, no. 2 [1990]: 139–57).

6. Simon Karlinsky gives a penetrating portrait of Tsvetaeva's complex relationship to the Russian émigré culture from which she felt increasingly alienated in the 1930s (*Marina Tsvetaeva: The Woman, Her World, and Her Poetry* [Cambridge, England: Cambridge University Press, 1985], 176–78). Cf. also Viktoria Schweitzer's discussion of this matter in *Tsvetaeva* (trans. Robert Chandler and H. T. Willetts; poetry trans. Peter Norman; ed. Angela Livingstone [New York: Farrar, Straus & Giroux, 1992], 310–15).

7. Interestingly, Maiakovskii and Pushkin are two strong male poets with whom Tsvetaeva does not have the kind of intense half-competitive, half-worshipful relationship that she does with other male poets; presumably this is due to their distance from her—political and ideological distance in the case of Maiakovskii, historical distance in the case of Pushkin.

8. Tsvetaeva's later, grim poems on the aging process are very different from her earlier poems on this theme, which tend to view old age as a trophy, symbolic of wisdom's triumph over body. Examples of such early poems on aging are the lyrics "The gold of my hair" ["Zoloto moikh volos . . ."] (2:149) and "These are the ashes of treasures" ["Eto peply sokrovishch . . ."] (2:153–54), as well as the cycle "The Sibyl" ["Sivilla"] (2:136–38); all these works are included in *After Russia*.

9. Examples of such retrospective *poemy* are "The Little Red Bull" ["Krasnyi bychok"] (1928), "Perekop" (1929) and "Poem about the Tsar's Family" ["Poema o tsarskoi sem'e"] (1929–36). Cf. M. S. Smith, "Marina Tsvetaeva's *Perekop:* Recuperation of the Russian Bardic Tradition," *Oxford Slavonic Papers* 32 (1999): 97–126. Smith argues that in "Perekop" Tsvetaeva delves backward into history far beyond the Russian Revolution which is the ostensible theme of the *poema,* to the ancient Russian poetic tradition of "The Lay of Igor's Campaign" ["Slovo o polku Igoreve"].

10. Tsvetaeva became friends with the eighteen-year-old Gronskii shortly before his mother, a talented sculptor, left the family to be united with her lover in September 1928. Tsvetaeva expresses great sympathy for Gronskii's mother, interpreting her illicit desire as "a thirst for *that other* self—not of the world of ideas, but of the chaos of hands and lips. A thirst for the secret self. The last self. The imaginary self" (7:204). In Tsvetaeva's understanding, Gronskii's mother abandons the ascetic realm of art to realize herself sexually—something Tsvetaeva has never been able to do. Tsvetaeva and Gronskii

gradually grew apart as time passed; his parents may have disapproved of their friendship and so may have been instrumental in this outcome.

11. For background on Shteiger and his correspondence with Tsvetaeva, cf. Lily Feiler, *Marina Tsvetaeva: The Double Beat,* 228; Viktoria Schweitzer, *Tsvetaeva,* 323; and the commentary to the published letters (7:626 n. 9).

12. Tsvetaeva wrote nearly thirty letters to Shteiger in August and September 1936 alone. On the other hand, her friendship with Gronskii was, by and large, carried out in person, and the correspondence that remains consists primarily of short notes passed to him through various acquaintances in order to arrange meetings and outings or ask for practical favors. Aside from brief discussions of Tsvetaeva's relationships with Gronskii and Shteiger in literary biographies, not much has been written on these encounters. The exceptions are two short articles that appear in *Marina Tsvetaeva: Trudy 1-go mezhdunarodnogo simpoziuma,* ed. Robin Kemball (Bern, Switzerland: Peter Lang, 1991): Simon Karlinsky's " 'Puteshestvuia v Zhenevu...': Ob odnoi neudavsheisia poezdke M. I. Tsvetaevoi," 72–80, and V. Morkovin's " 'Krylataia i bezrukaia' — (M. Tsvetaeva i N. P. Gronskii)," 221–26.

13. Moreover, it is important to note that both "Epitaph" and "Poems to an Orphan" were organized as cycles not at the time of composition of their constituent lyrics but in 1940, after Tsvetaeva's return to the Soviet Union, when she was, at the urging of friends, attempting to put together a new collection of poetry—a project that never in fact materialized (cf. Viktoria Schweitzer, *Tsvetaeva,* 364–67).

14. This reevaluation is the subject of Tsvetaeva's essay "Poet-Mountaineer" ["Poetal'pinist"] (5:435–59), as well as of her brief review of Gronskii's posthumous poetry collection (5:460–62). "Poet-Mountaineer" was published only in Serbo-Croatian translation during Tsvetaeva's lifetime; its first Russian publication was under the title "A Posthumous Gift" ["Posmertnyi podarok"]. Anna Lisa Crone and Alexandra Smith discuss "Poet-Mountaineer" in "Cheating Death: Derzhavin and Tsvetaeva on the Immortality of the Poet" (*Slavic Almanach: The South African Year Book for Slavic, Central and East European Studies* 3, nos. 3–4 [1995]: 1–30) and "Death Shall Have No Dominion" (*Russian Literature,* in press), although these two articles mainly focus on the importance of Derzhavin in Tsvetaeva's works. Tsvetaeva's additional discussions of Shteiger's poetry can be found in her letters to him of 1 September, 7 September, and 10 September 1936 (7:592–94, 599–603, 605–7). In general, she is kinder to Gronskii, for he is a poet resembling her in spirit, style, and themes. Shteiger's work is much harder for her to admire; she summarizes his gift thus: "You have an *ascetic* gift. Servile. Reclusive [zatvornicheskii]. God gave you a *gift* and—to go along with it—a *lock* [zatvor]" (7:612).

15. In this category Tsvetaeva has included such varied company as the young Bolshevik Boris Bessarabov, Pasternak, and Rilke, not to mention her own Sergei Efron. As she puts it: "Evidently ... I can be loved only by boys who loved their mothers madly and who are lost in the world—this is my sign [primeta]" (6:180).

16. Kii was the legendary founder of the city of Kiev and thus, by extension, of the ancient kingdom of Kievan Rus'; Tsar Peter the Great built the city of St. Petersburg in the eighteenth century and modernized Russian society.

17. Tsvetaeva possibly associates her own exile in Paris with Pushkin's exile and iso-

lation in Mikhailovskoe, roughly one hundred years earlier. We recall the importance of the hundred-year interval to Tsvetaeva's poetic mythmaking; on Pushkin's significance for Russian Modernism in general, see Irina Paperno, "Pushkin v zhizni cheloveka Serebrianogo veka," in Boris Gasparov et al., *Cultural Mythologies of Russian Modernism: From the Golden Age to the Silver Age* (Berkeley: University of California Press, 1992), 19–51. Cf. also Gasparov's introduction to the same volume, "The 'Golden Age' and Its Role in the Cultural Mythology of Russian Modernism," 1–16.

18. For a discussion of the role that Pushkin's nanny plays in Tsvetaeva's poetics, see Liza Knapp's perceptive recent essay "Marina Tsvetaeva's Poetics of Ironic Delight: The 'Podruga' Cycle as Evist Manifesto" (*Slavic and East European Journal* 41, no. 1 [spring 1997]: 94–113).

19. Cf. Tsvetaeva's 1929 memoir "Natal'ia Goncharova" (4:64–129); this essay is primarily about the contemporary painter who was the namesake of Pushkin's wife, but Tsvetaeva discusses the first Natal'ia Goncharova in it as well. Cf. Liza Knapp's analysis of the essay, "Tsvetaeva and the Two Natal'ia Goncharovas: Dual Life," in the volume *Cultural Mythologies of Russian Modernism*, 88–108. Cf. also Alexandra Smith's chapter on Goncharova and the Cnidus myth in *The Song of the Mocking Bird*, 63–80.

20. At the same time, Tsvetaeva's new interpretation of the role of Pushkin's nanny reverses her earlier feeling of poetic inferiority to her male counterparts, which she had once bemoaned in a letter to Pasternak: "Most of all I loved a poet when he was hungry or when he had a toothache: this made me feel close to him on a human level. I was a *nanny* to poets, the gratifier of their lower needs—not at all a poet! nor a Muse!—but a young (sometimes tragic, but even so)—nanny! With a poet I always would forget that I myself—am a poet" (6:229).

21. This is the case, for instance, in Tsvetaeva's cycle "Trees" ["Derev'ia"] (2:141–49); all of the cycle's poems were composed in September–October 1922, except for the last two, which were written the following May. She self-consciously footnotes this transposition.

22. As Tsvetaeva once wrote to Rilke: "Pushkin, Blok—and in order to name them all at once—ORPHEUS—cannot be dead, for he is dying even now (always!)" (*Rainer Maria Rilke, Marina Zwetajewa, Boris Pasternak: Briefwechsel* [Frankfurt am Main, 1983], 115–16). The January snow figures prominently in her account of Pushkin's fatal duel in the opening of her essay "My Pushkin," which she wrote for the 1937 centennial anniversary of Pushkin's death. When she recopied "Epitaph" in January 1940, she yet again drew attention to the meaningful sequence of Januaries by adding the following inscription after the cycle's concluding poem: "Gironde, Ocean, summer 1928—Golitsyno, Snow, January 1940" (Marina Tsvetaeva, *Stikhotvoreniia i poemy v piati tomakh* [New York: Russica, 1980–90], 3:487).

23. In her notebook, Tsvetaeva noted her thoughts after Gronskii's death as follows: "31 of December 1934—the fortieth day. I stood on his grave and thought: he is not here, and he is not there. Here—is too close (narrow), there—is too spacious; here—is too here, there—is too there. *Where* then?" (Marina Tsvetaeva, *Stikhotvoreniia i poemy v piati tomakh,* 3:487). The concepts of "here" [zdes'] and "there" [tam] that emerge from Symbolism have always been important to Tsvetaeva's poetics (cf. the early poems "In Paradise" ["V raiu"] [1:123] and "Neither Here Nor There" ["Ni zdes', ni tam"]

[1:123–24]); we recall that in "In the Luxembourg Garden," her intuition of an otherworldly "there" separates her from the geographical boundedness of other women. In "Epitaph," she no longer has such an exit into faith.

24. Viktoria Schweitzer offers an important caveat to this discussion of Tsvetaeva's contrasting philosophical views on death in "New Year's Letter" and "Epitaph": "It would be wrong . . . to conclude with any certainty that Tsvetaeva had lost her belief in immortality. It may simply be that Rilke was the only one of these poets whom she saw as an 'immortal' genius" (*Tsvetaeva,* 293). However, when the wider context for these divergences is taken into account, it is clear that in her last years Tsvetaeva does reevaluate real, physical existence; a new appreciation for the absoluteness of death is the logical outcome of this process. Moreover, the growing pessimism and bitterness of her late poetry is unmistakable.

25. Derzhavin's spiritual ode "God" ["Bog"] is an important subtext here (cf. Gavriil Derzhavin, *Stikhotvoreniia* [Leningrad: Sovetskii pisatel', 1957], 114–16). Derzhavin's poet contemplates the majesty of the universe and the miracle of his own existence and arrives thereby at a joyful faith in God and in the interconnectedness of all things: "You exist—and I already am not nothing! . . . I am the connection between worlds existing everywhere, I am the highest level of matter; I am the focus of all life; the starting point of Divinity; I rot like a body in the dust, I command thunder with my mind, I am tsar—I am slave—I am worm—I am God!" [Ty est'—i ia uzh ne nichto! / . . . Ia sviaz' mirov, povsiudu sushchikh, / Ia krainia stepen' veshchestva; / Ia sredotochie zhivushchikh; / Cherta nachal'na Bozhestva; / Ia telom v prakhe istlevaiu, / Umom gromam povelevaiu, / Ia tsar'—ia rab—ia cherv'—ia Bog!]. For Tsvetaeva in "In vain with my eye," on the contrary, faith is lost and the different aspects of being have splintered irreparably.

26. Similarly, in a 1928 letter to Gronskii, Tsvetaeva admits that she associates S. T. Aksakov's tale "The Little Scarlet Flower" ["Alen'kii tsvetochek"] with the Psyche myth (7:203)—indicating, perhaps, that she first read Apuleius's tale of Psyche and Eros in Aksakov's well-known Russian translation.

27. When a brief meeting between Tsvetaeva and Shteiger did, finally, materialize, it was close to disastrous, although Tsvetaeva narrates the event with wry humor in her miniature essay "My Geneva" ["Moia Zheneva"] (7:595–99), which she sends to Shteiger afterwards in the form of a letter. Cf. Simon Karlinsky's discussion of this essay in " 'Puteshestvuia v Zhenevu.' "

28. Cf. Tsvetaeva's 14 February 1925 letter to Pasternak where she writes: "I have made my soul into a home (*maison son lande*), but never my house—into a soul. I am absent from my life, I am *not* at home. A soul in a house, a soul-house, is unthinkable to me, in fact I don't think about it" (6:243). Cf. also Tsvetaeva's 1931 poem "House" ["Dom"] (2:295–96), in which a dilapidated, abandoned house becomes her self-portrait. It is interesting to compare these texts to her discussion of Pushkin's Natal'ia Goncharova. Whereas the male poet Pushkin, in Tsvetaeva's interpretation, requires that his muse be an empty vessel into which he can pour the immensity of his talent and genius, the female Tsvetaeva has herself become an uninhabited vessel, unable to speak poetically unless she is "filled" with the image of her lover.

29. Even in the correspondence, there are occasional candid moments when Tsvetaeva confesses that she does not, after all, delude herself into believing in the reciprocity of Shteiger's emotions or, even, in the genuineness of her own: "*I know everything,* and

if I haven't sold my soul until now in exchange for this live heat, then only because no one has ever needed that sale, that betrayal. God only knows what I've done with my immortal soul and upon what consolations—my own—I've ground my teeth, but—where is up and where down, where is God and where Idol, where I am and where I am not, I have *always* known" (7:611). This passage directly contradicts Tsvetaeva's claim in her earlier letter (already cited) that she has undergone a subjective merger with Shteiger ("But you, at certain moments, are *I*—to the point of strangeness" [7:569]).

30. I make use here of Tsvetaeva's own animal symbolism. In her writing, wolves represent the poet generally or her specifically: lonesome, wild, proud, and free, alien and dangerous to human society. Sheep, in contrast, are highly negative for Tsvetaeva—as is the sheeplike activity of rumination—for they represent the thoughtless masses, hostile to poets and poetry. Cf. Tsvetaeva's overt reversal of the usual fairy-tale symbolism of wolves and sheep in "My Pushkin" (5:68), as well as L. B. Savenkova, "Obraz-simvol volk v lirike M. I. Tsvetaevoi," *Russkii iazyk v shkole* 5 (September–October 1997): 62–66.

31. Even Tsvetaeva's friends were sometimes not immune from such treatment. An example is her essay "My Answer to Osip Mandel'shtam" ["Moi otvet Osipu Mandel'shtamu"] (5:305–15), which ends: "How can a great poet be a small human? . . . My answer to Osip Mandel'shtam—is this question to him." Mandel'shtam had apparently enraged Tsvetaeva by his negative attitude to the White Army in his memoir *The Noise of Time* [*Shum vremeni*].

32. Tsvetaeva was living at this time in a castle (the Château d'Arcine) in the Savoy—where, incidentally, she and Rilke had once planned to meet. Her cycle "To Maiakovskii" had been composed during her previous trip to the Savoy in August 1930; her hyperbolic expressions of love in "An icy tiara" and her recourse to natural imagery on a grand scale are reminiscent of Maiakovskii's style.

33. This was the case long ago, too, in the cycle "Trees," where Tsvetaeva's companionship with trees provides a respite both from daily cares ("Trees! I come to you! To be saved from the marketplace din!" [Derev'ia! K vam idu! Spastis' / Ot reva rynochnogo!]) and from the constant creative pressure she puts on herself ("Cast away my manuscripts!" [Zabrosit' rukopisi!] [2:143]).

34. Cited in Marina Tsvetaeva, *Stikhotvoreniia i poemy v piati tomakh,* 3:491.

35. For examples of Tsvetaeva's symbolic use of honeysuckle, cf. "Liutaia iudol'" (2:118–19), "Daby ty menia ne videl . . ." (2:122), "Kogda zhe, Gospodin . . ." (2:126–28), "Nepodrazhaemo lzhet zhizn' . . ." (2:132–33); for ivy symbolism, cf. part 8 of "Poema kontsa" (3:41).

36. For the full text of Akhmatova's poem "How a silvery-white tress," cf. Anna Akhmatova, *Sochineniia v dvukh tomakh* (Moscow: Khudozhestvennaia literatura, 1986), 1:70–71.

37. Ariadna Efron remarks in her memoirs on her mother's starkly upright posture: "She had a stern, slender carriage: even bending above her desk, she maintained the 'steely angle of her spine'" (*O Marine Tsvetaevoi* [Moscow: Sovetskii pisatel', 1989], 33). This posture is also evident in Efron's drawing of her mother at work at her desk (reproduced in *O Marine Tsvetaevoi,* 32). Tsvetaeva maintained this dignified posture until the very end of her life; Lidiia Chukovskaia reminisces about her meeting with Tsvetaeva in Chistopol' just days before the poet's suicide: "What was new for me in her

story was: the precision [otchetlivost'] of her pronunciation, *corresponding to the precise inflexibility of her upright figure* and the precise sharpness of her abrupt movements, yes and also the precision of her thought" ("Predsmertie," in *Marina Tsvetaeva: Trudy 1-go mezhdunarodnogo simpoziuma,* 123; my emphasis).

38. Tsvetaeva was criticized for her stylistic "loudness" in the émigré press. As Viktoria Schweitzer remarks: "No one appears to have noticed that Tsvetaeva also wrote 'quiet' poems" (*Tsvetaeva,* 272).

39. For a discussion of the classical significance of this symbolism, cf. Aminadav Dykman, "Poetical Poppies: Some Thoughts on Classical Elements in the Poetry of Marina Tsvetaeva," in *Literary Tradition and Practice in Russian Culture: Papers from an International Conference on the Occasion of the Seventieth Birthday of Yury Mikhailovich Lotman,* ed. Valentina Polukhina, Joe Andrew, and Robert Reid (Amsterdam: Rodopi, 1993), 163–76.

40. Northrop Frye, *Anatomy of Criticism* (New York: Atheneum, 1969), 155–56.

41. Or, as Tsvetaeva puts it metaphorically in "Art in the Light of Conscience": "So then the artist is like the earth, giving birth, and giving birth to everything. For the glory of God? And what about spiders? (they are present in works of art too)" (5:46). For Tsvetaeva, art does not exclude the darker aspects of existence but, on the contrary, often emanates from a contemplation of them, if not an outright desire for them.

42. Other poems of this period that sum up Tsvetaeva's darkening poetics in a particularly evocative way are "Conversation with a Genius" ["Razgovor s geniem"] (2:267–68) and "Naiada" ["The Naiad"] (2:270–72). In "Conversation with a Genius," Tsvetaeva's muse forces her to continue singing painfully, even when she has nothing left to say and the only sound she can produce is a dry gullety rasp. In "The Naiad," as a result of her constant poetic striving for the impossible, Tsvetaeva is deeply and irremediably estranged from her life, her muse, and her own self. Cf. Michael Makin's discussion of the literary subtexts in this poem: "Marina Tsvetaeva's 'Nayada,'" in *Essays in Poetics: The Journal of the British Neo-Formalist Circle* 11, no. 2 (September 1986): 1–17. Cf. also the discussion of "Conversation with a Genius" and "The Naiad" in Alyssa Dinega, "Exorcising the Beloved: Problems of Gender and Selfhood in Marina Tsvetaeva's Myths of Poetic Genius" (Ph.D. Diss., University of Wisconsin–Madison, 1998), 315–23. It is interesting to note that "Conversation with a Genius" makes subtextual use of Derzhavin's poem "The Bullfinch," just as did Tsvetaeva's poem-manifesto "The Drum" with which, long ago, she commenced her poetic rebellion.

43. "Glory" is a relentlessly negative category for Tsvetaeva, representing as it does humility before the whip of public opinion that she sees as unbefitting to a poet. Cf. the poems "Quiet, praise!" ["Tishe, khvala! . . ."] (2:262) and "Glory falls like plums" ["Slava padaet tak, kak sliva . . ."] (2:260), as well as the essay "The Poet about the Critic," where Tsvetaeva weighs in on the relative value to a poet of money versus glory in typically iconoclastic fashion: "I admit glory into a poet's life in the capacity of an advertisement—for financial ends" (5:287).

44. Laura Weeks notes that, in poems from the period of *After Russia* onward, the temple [visok] sometimes stands in for the forehead [lob] as the locus of the "mark of the poet" in Tsvetaeva's vocabulary of signs ("The Search for the Self: The Poetic Persona of Marina Cvetaeva" [Ph.D. Diss., Stanford University, 1985], 47). An example can

be found in the poem "Graying temples" ["V sedinu—visok . . ."] (2:257), where the poet's graying temples presage her passage into the beyond.

45. Lily Feiler, for example, speculates that Tsvetaeva's affair with Parnok was "probably the most passionate, and sexually the most gratifying, of Tsvetaeva's life" (*Marina Tsvetaeva: The Double Beat*, 66), whereas Tsvetaeva herself expresses her intuition that her passion for Rodzevich will for the first time make her wholly incarnate: "Yes, there is in me a [woman] too. Scarcely—weakly—in swoops—reflections—inklings . . . Maybe . . . I really will become a human being, become fully embodied [sdelaius' chelovekom, dovoploshchus']" (6:616). Viktoria Schweitzer considers that most, if not all, of Tsvetaeva's love affairs were motivated by something other than sexual desire: "What she was in search of was a kindred soul. She hungered and thirsted, she soared to ecstasy and was plunged into disenchantment, as she went from one infatuation to another. It was not just sex. Perhaps it wasn't sex at all, or was sex of a sort unknown to ordinary mortals . . . Perhaps there is in poets a sort of spiritual vampirism, crudely mistaken for a sexual manifestation?" (*Tsvetaeva*, 198–99).

46. Cf. Tsvetaeva's letters to Voloshin of 18 April 1911 (6:47), to Pasternak of 10 July 1926 (6:264), and to Rilke of 2 August 1916 (*Briefwechsel*, 232).

47. Even under the most adverse circumstances, Tsvetaeva held to a rigorous schedule, spending several hours at her writing desk each morning. Ariadna Efron provides a vivid description of Tsvetaeva's poetic work habits in her memoirs: "Having filled herself a small mug of boiling hot black coffee, she would place it on her desk, to which she went each day of her life like a laborer to his assigned place—with that same *feeling of responsibility,* inevitability, impossibility of doing otherwise. She would move aside everything extra that turned up on the desk at the given moment, freeing up, with an already automatic gesture, a place for her notebook and her elbows. She buried her forehead in her palm, plunged her fingers into her hair, and began concentrating instantaneously" (*O Marine Tsvetaevoi,* 37). In her essay "Mother and Music," Tsvetaeva opposes poetry's liberating, syncopated rhythms to the tyrannical beat of the metronome; yet, in her last years, even poetry itself seems just another version of mechanical compulsion: "And what if someday the spring—never unwinds, and what if I—can never get up from the stool, never get out from under the tick-tock, tick-tock . . . The metronome was a coffin, and death lived inside it" (5:21). One of Tsvetaeva's last, laconic diary entries (from January 1941) reads: "Write every day. Yes. I've been doing that my entire (conscious) life" (4:615).

48. It is instructive to compare this formula with the male inspirational economy explored in Pushkin's lyric "The Poet": "As long as the poet is not called . . . perhaps he is more insignificant than anyone" [Poka ne trebuet poeta . . . / Byt' mozhet, vsekh nichtozhnei on]. Tsvetaeva's problem, in contrast to Pushkin's, is not the attainment of a feeling of inspiration—indeed, she lives in a frustrating state of perpetual inspiration with no valid outlet, akin to a state of perpetual sexual arousal. Rather, her difficulty is with the conceptualization and mythopoetic foundation of her unceasing poetic desire.

49. The quotation comes from Maiakovskii's 1930 poem "At the Top of my Voice" ["Vo ves' golos"] (*Sobranie sochinenii v dvenadtsati tomakh,* 6:175–80).

50. The counterexample to this formula is Nikolai Gogol', who burns the manuscript of the second part of his novel *Dead Souls* and, in so doing, effectively bequeaths him-

self to the fire. Tsvetaeva writes: "Gogol', burning the work of his hands, also burned his own glory . . . Gogol''s half-hour at the hearth did more *for* goodness and *against* art than did all the many years of Tolstoi's sermon" (5:355).

51. The text of Pushkin's play *Mozart and Salieri* can be found in A. S. Pushkin, *Sochineniia v trekh tomakh* (Moscow: Khudozhestvennaia literatura, 1985), 2:442–50.

52. Svetlana Boym argues convincingly that Tsvetaeva often adopts an ambiguous stance with regard to feminine stereotypes, playing at female "lack" while making serious poetic statements: "Tsvetaeva's ambivalent attitude toward the cultural myth of femininity manifests itself in a series of self-defensive performances: on the one hand, the female narrator often attempts to distance herself from the traditional feminine heroine . . . and on the other hand, she becomes infatuated with aesthetically obscene, 'oversweet,' and overly romantic 'feminine' discourse which she tries to reinvent despite all critical taboos" (*Death in Quotation Marks*, 203). See too Antonina Gove's seminal article "The Feminine Stereotype and Beyond: Role Conflict and Resolution in the Poetics of Marina Tsvetaeva," *Slavic Review* 36, no. 2 (June 1977): 231–55.

53. Tsvetaeva and her husband, who fought with the Whites during the Russian Civil War, were separated for approximately four years. During this period they had no contact, and Tsvetaeva did not know whether he was alive or dead until she received news of him through Il'ia Erenburg in July 1921.

54. David M. Bethea, " 'This Sex Which Is Not One' versus This Poet Which Is 'Less Than One': Tsvetaeva, Brodsky, and Exilic Desire," in *Joseph Brodsky and the Creation of Exile* (Princeton, N.J.: Princeton University Press, 1994), 189.

55. I like very much Catherine Ciepiela's forceful observation that "Two hands resting lightly" should be read *not* as a "denial of complicity . . . but . . . as a confession of failure and crisis" ("The Demanding Woman Poet: On Resisting Marina Tsvetaeva," *PMLA* 111, no. 3 [May 1996]: 430)—although ultimately, as I argue, Tsvetaeva reconceptualizes this failure as fault, not because she truly *is* at fault in the tragedy, but because she cannot bear the terribleness of Irina's death as a naked, random, unpoeticized fact.

56. Especially relevant here is a 1918 lyric "I don't embarrass, I don't sing" ["Ne smushchaia, ne poiu . . ."] (1:434), in which an elaborate symbolic logic serves to associate the left hand with falsehood (underhandedness), whereas the right hand, used for writing inspired poetry and for making the sign of the cross, is an emblem of truth and faith.

57. In her 1934 autobiographical essay "Mother and Music," Tsvetaeva locates the source of her own poetry in her mother's unrealized artistic yearnings—a transfer that sets into motion an uncanny mechanism of intergenerational parasitism: "It was as if Mother buried herself alive inside us—for life eternal . . . Mother gave us to drink from the open vein of Lyricism, just as we later, having mercilessly opened our own veins, attempted to succor our children with the blood of our personal anguish. *Their* happiness—that *we* did not succeed, *ours*—that *she* did! After such a mother I had only one option: to become a poet. In order to rid myself of her gift to me, which would otherwise have suffocated me or turned me into a transgressor of all human laws" (5:14).

58. The word *ladan* [incense] is often associated with death, as in the expression *dyshat' na ladan* [to have one foot in the grave].

59. Marina Tsvetaeva, *Stikhotvoreniia i poemy v piati tomakh*, 2:317.

60. This feeling stems not merely from Tsvetaeva's strained relationship with her

troubled teenaged son, but also from her awareness of the political danger that she—a returned émigré writer whose husband, daughter, and sister are already in Stalin's prisons—poses to her young son in the poisonous climate of the Soviet Union of the early 1940s. Both Simon Karlinsky (*Marina Tsvetaeva: The Woman*, 244) and Lily Feiler (*Marina Tsvetaeva: The Double Beat*, 259–60) raise the possibility that Tsvetaeva's political position in her final days was even more precarious than any of her friends realized, if a memoir by Kirill Khenkin is to be believed. Khenkin, an acquaintance of Sergei Efron during his years with the NKVD, claims that Tsvetaeva was called upon to become an informer on other evacuated writers shortly after her arrival in Elabuga (Karlinsky, however, is careful to point out that the veracity of these allegations is doubtful).

61. Mariia Belkina, *Skreshchenie sudeb* (Moscow: Rudomino, 1992), 324–25.

62. See Tsvetaeva's letter to Ol'ga Kolbasina-Chernova of 25 November 1924: "My son always behaves extremely calmly in my womb, from which I conclude that he does not take after me!" (6:693). Tsvetaeva's testaments to her son's remarkably accelerated development after his birth are likewise in keeping with the conventions of saints' lives. Thus, in her 26 May 1925 letter to Pasternak, Mur is beginning to talk: "In a few days he'll be 4 months old, he's very big and solid, he speaks [completely clearly, with a French r: 'Reuret'], he smiles and laughs" (6:246). Not even a month later, in her letter to Pasternak of 21 June, the miraculous five-month-old infant is already walking in circles: "Mur can walk, but oh, get this! only on the beach, in circles, like an orbiting planet. In a room or a garden he doesn't want to move, you stand him up—he doesn't go. At the seaside he tears himself from your arms and indefatigably revolves [and falls]" (6:259). In reading such obviously preposterous tales, it is important to keep in mind that Tsvetaeva, in her correspondence as in her poetry, is an artist of the word. Although it may well be true that her maternal pride does indeed distort her perception of her child, it is also true that she is consummately aware of literary genres and traditions and exploits them for her own expressive ends. Such is the use she makes here of Byzantine hagiographic tropes.

63. Tsvetaeva writes to Ol'ga Kolbasina-Chernova: "In general, I have the feeling with Mur that we are on an island, and today I caught myself thinking that I already dream of an island with him, a real one, so that he would have *no one else* (you must recognize the full extent of my cowardice!) but me to love" (6:742). In later years she would resist sending her son to school so as to avoid exposing him to the corrupting influences of strangers' children and to insulate him as much as possible from French society.

64. There is a striking parallel here to Joseph Brodsky's later verse, with its emphasis on "thingness" and its quiet but wrenching irony; an excellent example of this tendency is "Dedicated to a Chair" ["Posviashchaetsia stulu"] from Brodsky's collection *Urania* [*Uraniia*] (Ann Arbor, Mich.: Ardis, 1987).

65. For a discussion of the "mesto pusto" in this poem and elsewhere in Tsvetaeva's works, cf. L. V. Zubova, *Iazyk poezii Mariny Tsvetaevoi: Fonetika, slovoobrazovanie, frazeologiia* (St. Petersburg: Izdatel'stvo Sankt-Peterburgskogo universiteta, 1999), 108–19.

66. The imagery of this last poem is hauntingly reminiscent of Pushkin's 1821 lyric "I outlived my desires" ["Ia perezhil svoi zhelan'ia . . ."]; Tsvetaeva amends the youthful, romanticized *ennui* of Pushkin's poem to create her own personal cry of anguish free from all cliché.

67. At the time this letter was written, Tsvetaeva was briefly infatuated with Tager; several of her last poems are addressed to him.

68. I echo Lily Feiler's judgment here (*Marina Tsvetaeva: The Double Beat*, 264). Or rather, as Joseph Brodsky puts it, Tsvetaeva's "tragic quality was not exactly a product of her life experience; it existed prior to it. Her experience only coincided with it, responded to it, like an echo" ("A Poet and Prose," in *Less Than One: Selected Essays* [New York: Farrar Straus & Giroux, 1986], 182). Tsvetaeva knew, when she decided to return to the Soviet Union, that she was returning to her death; see, for example, her poignant letter to Anna Tesková of 7 June 1939, written during her preparations for the trip: "Oh God, what anguish! Now, in the heat of the moment, in the utter fever of hands—and head—and weather—I still don't completely feel it, but I know what awaits me: I know—myself! *I'll wring my own neck*—in gazing backwards: at you, at your world, at our world..." (6:479; my emphasis). This is Tsvetaeva's penultimate letter to Tesková, her confidante and correspondent of many long years. Tsvetaeva's final letter to her Czech friend is written on the train en route to Moscow and reads like a farewell to life itself; it is as if she describes her own corpse laid out ceremoniously for burial: "I am departing in *your* necklace and in a coat with *your* buttons, and on my waist is *your* buckle. All these things are modest and madly beloved, I'll take them with me to the grave, or burn together with them. Farewell! Now this is no longer difficult, now this is already—fate" (6:480).

Index

Abraham and Isaac, 79
abstraction, process toward, 7, 132, 138–39, 144–47, 150, 155–56, 160, 168–69, 172, 254*n52*. *See also* figurative language, power and perils of
acrobatic motifs, 5, 8, 32, 82, 128, 136, 144, 166, 201–2, 217–18, 225, 266*n1*
Adamovich, Georgii, 181, 196
Afanas′ev, Aleksandr, 238*n35*
agency, ambiguity of, 14–15, 68, 78, 80, 84–85, 88–89, 152–53, 167–68, 184–85, 215, 221. *See also* freedom and constraint; responsibility, claiming of
aging process, 179–80, 183–87, 195, 198–99, 267*n8*
Akhmatova, Anna, 4, 29, 37–38, 56–77, 87–89, 179, 195, 227, 236*n25*, 239–40*nn5–6*, 243*nn35–37*, 244*n39*, 245–46*nn48–51*, 55–56, 58, 64, 250*n15*, 260*n27*
—works of: "A Belated Answer" ["Pozdnii otvet"], 243*n37*; "In Tsarskoe Selo" ["V Tsarskom Sele"], 67; "Poem without a Hero" ["Poema bez geroia"], 243*n37*; *Rosary* [*Chetki*], 195; "To the Muse" ["Muze"], 245*n48*
Aksakov, Sergei, 248*n1*, 270*n26*
alterity. *See* otherness, problem of
androgyny, 24, 26, 87, 115, 182, 228. *See also* gender difference: erasure of
Antaeus, 224
anxiety of influence, 21, 25, 38, 71, 75–76, 104–6, 236–37*n25*, 267*n7*
Aphrodite, 93–94, 150, 250*n19*, 253*n43*
Apuleius, Lucius, 91, 248*n1*, 249*n5*, 270*n26*
Ariadne, 116, 118, 120
Arndt, Walter, 258*n13*
Arnim, Bettina von, 236*n25*

asexual love. *See* ideal love
Asrael, 258*n11*
Azadovskii, Konstantin, 248*n1*, 258*n13*

Bakhrakh, Aleksandr, 91, 121, 197, 248*n3*
Bal′mont, Konstantin, 33
Baratynskii, Evgenii, 237*n31*
Bashkirtseva, Mariia, 236*n25*
Beaujour, Elizabeth Klosty, 257*n2*
Belkina, Mariia, 218
Belyi, Andrei, 44–45, 53, 54, 245*n50*
Benz, Ernst, 245*n54*
Bethea, David, 75, 79, 83–84, 215, 246*n63*
blasphemy, 49–50, 69, 89, 120, 151, 173, 202, 208, 242*n24*
blind man, figure of, 61, 65, 119, 130
Blok, Aleksandr, 29, 35–56, 57, 58, 65, 66–67, 69–77, 87–89, 98, 101–3, 106, 120, 129, 130, 147, 181, 195, 227, 239–40*nn3–4, 6*, 241*n12*, 242*nn22, 24, 29*, 243*n34*, 246*nn55–56, 58, 64*, 250*n15*, 251*n26*, 253*n42*, 255*n56*, 259*n22*, 260*n27*, 263*n81*, 269*n22*
—works of: "Faina," 242*n29*; "On Kulikovo Field" ["Na pole Kulikovom"], 242*n22*; "The Twelve" ["Dvenadtsat′"], 246*n63*
blood as metaphor for poetry, 158, 205, 207, 216, 224, 262*n75*, 274*n57*
Bloom, Harold, 236*n25*
body: Tsvetaeva's attitude toward, 6, 16, 27, 30, 36, 39, 43–46, 78, 82, 92, 96–97, 107–8, 112, 126, 166, 175, 180, 182–85, 187–90, 196, 199, 201, 203–6, 208, 222–23, 234*n9*, 235*n12*, 247*n70*, 248*n1*, 249*n9*, 251–52*nn31, 39*, 253*n46*, 273*n45*, 276*n68*; vs. soul, 33, 47, 50–51, 76, 94, 97–101, 103, 106–10, 115, 120, 125, 128, 138, 150, 156, 175, 179, 189, 203, 205, 208–9, 219–20, 228, 248*n78*,

277

body (*continued*)
  249*n9*, 251*n24*, 252*nn36, 39*, 254*n51*. See also aging process; disembodiment; gender difference; physical pain; sex and sexuality
Boym, Svetlana, 233*n3*, 234*n9*, 237*n26*, 274*n52*
Briusov, Valerii, 6
— work of: "In Answer" ["V otvet"], 251*n29*
Brodsky, Joseph, 147, 150, 164, 252*n32*, 264*nn98, 101*, 265*n108*, 266*n113*, 275*n64*, 276*n68*
— works of: "Dedicated to a Chair" ["Posviashchaetsia stulu"], 275*n64*; "Great Elegy to John Donne" ["Bol'shaia elegiia Dzhonu Donnu"], 266*n113*; "The Hawk's Cry in Autumn" ["Osennii krik iastreba"], 266*n113*
Brodsky, Patricia Pollock, 256*nn1, 3*, 259*n13*
Bronfen, Elisabeth, 236*n21*, 250*n13*
brotherhood of poets, 22–27, 39, 122, 149, 203, 209–14, 218, 227, 236*n25*, 242*n21*, 244*n44*, 267*n7*. See also poetic tradition; sisterhood
Butler, Judith, 235*n12*

Chester, Pamela, 234*n9*, 249*n9*
Christian themes, 39, 49, 67–69, 70, 74, 80, 89, 121, 151, 202, 214–15, 219, 241*n15*, 242*nn27, 29*, 243*n32*, 245*n54*, 275*n62*. See also Old Testament
chronology, 24, 72–73, 90, 186–87, 237*n30*, 269*n21*
Chukovskaia, Lidiia, 271*n37*
Chvany, Catherine, 242*nn24, 27*
Ciepiela, Catherine, 75, 83–84, 96, 233*n2*, 234*n10*, 240*n12*, 243*n33*, 246*n63*, 274*n55*
circles and vectors, 23, 29, 30, 48, 53–55, 61, 62, 85–87, 99, 119, 120, 132, 146, 149–76, 180, 183, 186–87, 190, 192–94, 197, 198, 201, 206–8, 211, 213, 219–20, 223–25, 250*nn15, 22*, 254*n48*, 255*n54*, 258*n12*, 262*nn69–70*, 263*n78*
Cixous, Hélène, 234*n9*
clairvoyance valued over physical gaze, 11–12, 16, 21, 44, 61, 77, 95, 117, 118–19, 121
cosmic imagery, 16–17, 51–53, 64, 76–77, 113, 150, 153–57, 160, 164, 166–76, 235*n19*, 255*n56*, 263*nn81, 83*
creative paralysis, danger of, 50–51, 62, 63–64, 71, 76, 77, 78, 88, 123, 125, 134, 166, 190, 198–99, 203, 208, 224, 242*n30*
Cumaean Sibyl, 28, 198, 236*n20*

Dante Alighieri, 208, 261*n59*, 265*n108*
D'Anthès, Baron Georges-Charles, 82, 179, 261*n59*
Danzas, Konstantin, 261*n59*
death, poetics of, 17–19, 30, 34, 49, 50, 78, 118, 124–25, 132, 134, 143–76, 183, 224–25, 228, 242*n22*, 247*n74*, 257*n3*, 258*n11*, 262*n75*, 265*n110*. See also transcendence and transgression
demonism. See blasphemy
Derzhavin, Gavriil, xii, 25–27, 237*n31*, 255*n58*, 268*n14*
— works of: "The Bullfinch" ["Snigir'"], 25–27, 272*n42*; "God" ["Bog"], 254*n53*, 270*n25*; "Swan" ["Lebed'"], 242*n22*; "The Waterfall" ["Vodopad"], 237*n31*
Dickinson, Emily, 229
disembodiment, 85, 87, 97, 99, 114–15, 122, 138, 161, 166, 171–72, 203–4. See also gender difference: erasure of
dolia/volia paradox, 56, 81, 250*n18*. See also freedom and constraint
doll imagery, 13–14, 74, 80–82, 107, 247*n69*
domestic drudgery, xii, 8, 23, 124, 126–27, 203, 214. See also mundane reality
Dostoevskii, Fedor, 244*n42*
dreams, importance of, 16–17, 41–42, 45–49, 76, 97–98, 100, 170, 180, 191, 251*n23*, 264*n102*

Echo and Narcissus, 161
Efron, Ariadna (Alia), 35–37, 43, 72, 75, 90, 97, 99, 105, 119, 210, 215–18, 224–25, 238*n34*, 239*n4*, 242*n27*, 248*n1*, 249*n3*, 256*n61*, 271*n37*, 273*n47*, 275*n60*
Efron, Georgii (Mur), 126, 215, 218–20, 224–25, 275*nn60, 62–63*
Efron, Irina, 79, 215–16, 274*n55*
Efron, Sergei, 126, 177, 214–15, 224–25, 228–29, 254*n52*, 268*n15*, 274*n53*, 275*n60*
Esenin, Sergei, 33
ethics vs. aesthetics, 5, 7, 30–31, 71, 80, 168, 193–94, 196–97, 201–25, 274*nn50, 57*. See also transcendence and transgression
Eurydice, 28, 36, 94, 103, 117, 227, 238*n37*
Eve, 93–94, 122

Index

Feiler, Lily, 234*n9*, 241*n14*, 273*n45*, 275*n60*, 276*n68*
female roles, 9, 12–13, 22–23, 38, 54–55, 81, 110, 228, 246*n56*, 274*n52*; rejection of, 26, 28, 42, 73–74, 77, 82, 102, 107, 117, 124–26, 171–72, 210–12, 217–18. *See also* gender difference: erasure of; marriage; motherhood
feminine self-expression: trivialization of, 6, 12, 23, 26, 185, 233*n3*; valorization of, 210–12, 236*n25*, 274*n52*
femininity and poetry, disjunction between, 4–8, 9, 13, 16, 17, 19, 27, 32, 44–46, 91, 92, 95, 117, 124–27, 149, 199–201, 203, 206–7, 209, 212, 220, 224, 226–27
feminist criticisms, 4, 6, 234*nn9–10*, 236*n22*
figurative language, power and perils of, 78–83, 85, 105, 137–39, 165, 201–25. *See also* abstraction, process toward
fire imagery, 60–61, 77, 80–81, 95–96, 200, 227, 242*n31*, 244*n46*, 245*n51*, 246*n65*, 254*n52*, 266*n1*
flight as metaphor for poetry, 29, 30, 40–41, 84–88, 106–7, 147, 149–50, 153, 166–76, 197, 202, 227, 253*n46*, 263*n79*, 266*n113*. *See also* wings, motif of
Forrester, Sibelan, 234*nn9–10*, 244*n46*
freedom and constraint, xii, 8, 28–32, 47–48, 56, 74, 79, 81–84, 103, 114, 120, 151, 159, 165–66, 171, 173–76, 194, 202, 205–12, 214–16, 223–25, 227–29, 273*n47*, 276*n68*. *See also* agency, ambiguity of; *dolia/volia* paradox; responsibility, claiming of
Frye, Northrop, 202, 238–39*n38*

Gabriak, Cherubina de, 236*n25*
Gasparov, Mikhail, 265*n105*
gender difference, 5, 21, 27, 28, 32–33, 41, 43, 46, 49, 50, 96, 106, 123, 138, 154–55, 180, 183, 200, 206, 222, 235*n12*, 247*n76*, 248*n1*; erasure of, 6–7, 21, 23, 39, 41, 46, 50, 55, 77–78, 82, 87, 93, 106, 114, 124, 126, 137, 160, 162, 164–65, 168, 175, 184, 202, 214, 217–18, 247*nn74, 76*, 249*n11*, 252*n36*. *See also* disembodiment; female roles: rejection of
Gertsyk, Adelaida, 236*n25*
gift giving, 61, 78, 131, 143, 166, 171, 244*n45*, 262*n74*, 274*n57*
Gilbert, Sandra M., 236*n25*

Goethe, Johann Wolfgang von, 207–10, 212, 213
Gogol', Nikolai, 69, 244*n42*, 273–74*n50*
Goncharov, Ivan, 140
Goncharova, Natal'ia, 184, 242*n21*, 268*n19*, 270*n28*
Gorchakov, Genrikh, 33
Gor'kii, Maksim, 245*n50*
Goul, Roman, 28
Gove, Antonina Filonov, 234*n10*
Graves, Robert, 4, 233*n2*
gravity, 143, 155, 168, 171–76, 222, 266*n113*
Greenleaf, Monika, 241*n13*
Gronskii, Nikolai, 30, 181–90, 215, 237*n28*, 247*n70*, 267*n10*, 268*nn12, 14*, 269*n23*, 270*n26*
Grosz, Elizabeth, 233–34*nn5–6*
Gubar, Susan, 236*n25*
Gumilev, Nikolai, 65, 246*n55*

Hades, 36, 94, 101, 113, 114, 116, 124, 128, 224
Hasty, Olga Peters, 28, 45, 147, 156, 235*nn15, 20*, 237*n30*, 238*n37*, 239*n4*, 240*n6*, 241*nn15, 21*, 242*n24*, 257*n3, 5*, 258*n13*, 260*n43*, 262*n74*, 263*nn78, 80, 89*
Heldt, Barbara, 234*n9*
Holl, Bruce, 253*n44*, 254*n48*
horseman, figure of, 38, 71–89, 91, 94, 110, 135, 148, 202, 247–48*n78*, 250*n15*, 259*n23*, 266*n115*
human and poet, rift between, 25, 78–79, 82–83, 91, 92, 112–13, 117, 125–27, 161, 171, 175–76, 178–79, 196, 197, 200–225, 229, 247*n70*, 254*n48*, 255*n57*, 259*n23*

ideal love, 24, 76, 77, 87, 100, 104, 112, 116, 135, 136, 148, 159–76, 183, 193, 219, 221–22, 224. *See also* reciprocity in love
ideal reader. *See* ideal love
Ilovaiskaia, Nadia, 44–46
immortality, attainment of. *See* poetic destiny
inspirational allegories, 4, 28–31, 37–38, 51, 55–56, 61–62, 76, 83, 91, 92, 98, 118, 121, 137, 152, 161, 163–64, 168, 170, 185, 201–3, 206–8, 209, 220, 224, 227, 245*n48*, 247–48*n78*, 266*n113*, 273*n48*. *See also* muse, the; myths and mythopoetics
Irigaray, Luce, 234*n6*
Ishtar, 253*n43*

isolation, will toward, 12, 21, 22, 24, 27, 31, 45, 72, 74, 87, 91, 93, 103, 106, 108, 109, 113, 115, 117–18, 127, 130, 135, 152, 154–55, 167, 180–81, 185, 191, 193–201, 211, 219–25, 226, 229, 239*n41*, 244*n44*, 247*nn70, 76,* 255*n59,* 256*n63,* 257*n3,* 261*n58,* 268*n17,* 269–70*n23,* 271*n30*

Jakobson, Roman, 241*n13*
Job, 79

Karlinsky, Simon, 75, 234*n8,* 244*n47,* 245*n49,* 267*n6,* 275*n60*
Kelly, Catriona, 233*n1,* 234*n10*
Khenkin, Kirill, 275*n60*
Knapp, Liza, 234*n10*
Kolbasina-Chernova, Ol'ga, 275*nn62–63*
Kristeva, Julia, 234*n9,* 235*n14*
Kroth, Anya M., 234*n10*
Kuzmin, Mikhail, 56

La Fontaine, Jean de, 248*n1*
Lann, Evgenii, 73, 246*n58*
Larina, Tat'iana, 44–45, 55–56
Last Judgment, 30–31, 209–10, 212–20
laughter. *See* theatrical play
Lipking, Lawrence, 102
loneliness. *See* isolation, will toward

Maiakovskii, Vladimir, 177–79, 209–12, 246*n65,* 266*n1,* 267*nn4, 7*
—works of: "The Backbone Flute" ["Fleita-pozvonochnik"], 266*n1;* "A Cloud in Trousers" ["Oblako v shtanakh"], 246*n65,* 266*n1*
Majmieskulow, Anna, 253*n44*
Makin, Michael, 238*n35*
Mandel'shtam, Osip, 56, 57, 174, 228, 243*n36,* 265*n109,* 266*n114,* 271*n31*
—works of: "The Morning of Acmeism" ["Utro akmeizma"], 174; *The Noise of Time* [*Shum vremeni*], 271*n31*
marriage, 13–14, 44, 78, 93, 94, 107, 124, 126, 221, 228
masculine ideal, 25, 61, 75, 94, 96, 99, 191, 218–19, 227
military ethos, 14–15, 20–21, 22–27, 38, 74, 84, 171, 185, 203, 236*n25,* 250*nn13, 19*
Moi, Toril, 83, 233*n5*
motherhood, 8, 10–13, 14, 23, 74, 82, 107, 123–24, 126–27, 171, 180–85, 214–20, 247*n70,* 274*n57,* 275*n62. See also* female roles
Mra, 165–66, 173, 180, 187, 207, 265*n107*
mundane reality: conflict between art and, 19–20, 22, 30, 32, 48, 50, 81, 87–88, 95, 97, 99–101, 108, 117, 123–26, 148, 150–51, 168–69, 175, 215, 226, 228–29, 242*n31,* 246*n57,* 255*n55,* 263*n82,* 264*n92,* 270*n28;* as source of poetry, 4, 41, 95, 97, 137, 145–46, 149, 201, 224, 247*n75,* 255*n55. See also* domestic drudgery; transcendence and transgression
muse, the, 4, 28–31, 35–89, 102, 112, 113, 119–20, 130, 143, 166, 168, 180, 184–85, 195, 202–5, 207, 224, 227, 241*nn12, 21,* 247*nn75–76,* 250*n15,* 251*n29,* 259*n23,* 266*n115,* 269*n20;* as poetic lover, 38, 41, 71–89, 100, 106, 120, 127, 135, 148, 184, 199, 220, 247*n74,* 253*n42,* 258*n11,* 270*n28. See also* inspirational allegories
myths and mythopoetics, 7, 22, 27, 28–33, 36–38, 44, 71, 82, 91, 95, 98–99, 101–3, 117, 131–32, 134, 137, 148, 161, 166, 181, 182, 183, 201–2, 207, 215–16, 218, 220, 224, 227, 238*n35,* 241*n18,* 246*n57,* 251*n27,* 268*n17,* 273*n48. See also* inspirational allegories

Naiman, Anatolii, 243*n37*
names, poetics of, 39–43, 49, 52, 53, 54–59, 62–64, 66, 71, 73, 86–87, 89, 154, 164–66, 182, 189, 201, 240*n9,* 250*n19,* 262*nn75, 77,* 266*n111*
Nekrasov, Nikolai, 237*n31*
Neumann, Erich, 93–94, 103, 249*nn5, 11*
nonmeetings, Tsvetaeva's preference for, 36, 38, 53, 55–56, 72, 84, 92, 100, 112–13, 120, 130, 132, 143–47, 191, 197, 227, 229, 239*n3,* 251*n23,* 257*n3,* 259*nn20, 22,* 264*n92,* 270*n27*

Old Testament, 70, 79, 93, 120, 210, 220, 253*n43,* 254*n52. See also* Christian themes
onomastic poetics. *See* names, poetics of
Ophelia, 28, 238*n37*
Orpheus, 28, 36, 94, 117, 120, 129, 239*n4,* 240*n6,* 241*n15,* 255*n56,* 257*n5,* 263*n80,* 269*n22*
otherness, problem of, 9, 21, 28, 30–32, 61–62, 71, 76, 77, 87, 93, 160–62, 170, 180–81, 185–86, 191, 193, 195–96, 198, 206–7,

221–22, 225, 226–27, 245*n53*. *See also* problematic subjectivity

Parnok, Sofiia, 205, 273*n45*
paronomasia. *See* sound play
Pasternak, Boris, 29–30, 91–127, 129, 130, 133–35, 137, 139, 140, 143–44, 148, 155, 163, 181, 191–92, 195, 202, 203, 205, 224, 227, 229, 237*n31*, 238*n35*, 239*nn39, 3*, 248–49*nn2–4, 9*, 250*nn15–16, 18, 20*, 251*nn23, 25–27, 30*, 252*nn32–33, 36–37*, 253*nn43, 45*, 254*nn51–52*, 255*nn54–57, 59*, 256*nn63–64*, 257*nn2, 7*, 258*n8*, 259*n20*, 261*n54*, 263*n83*, 264*nn91–93, 102*, 268*n15*, 270*n28*, 275*n62*
—works of: *My Sister—Life* [*Sestra moia—zhizn'*], 92, 95–99; *Themes and Variations* [*Temy i variatsii*], 96, 255*n55*; "Thus they begin" ["Tak nachinaiut. Goda v dva . . ."], 255*n55*
Pasternak, Leonid, 129
Pavlova, Karolina, 236*n25*, 264*n97*
Persephone, 94, 127
physical pain, 40, 42, 44–45, 50, 59–60, 65–67, 84–85, 95, 96, 97, 105, 107, 119–20, 124–25, 165, 169, 179, 181, 198, 200, 202–7, 216–18, 250*n15*, 254*n51*, 262*n75*, 269*n20*. *See also* body: Tsvetaeva's attitude toward
poetic destiny, 9–10, 21, 22, 29, 38–56, 71–89, 91, 94, 114, 118, 130, 164, 173, 211–12, 214, 215–16, 220, 229, 240*n9*, 263*n81*, 272*n44*
poetic dialogue, 9, 25–27, 29, 42, 71, 75–76, 130, 140, 180, 227, 228
poetic genius, 4, 21, 27, 32, 39, 43, 57, 78, 87–89, 95, 102, 113, 117, 118, 127, 130, 148–49, 153, 163, 166, 167, 173, 178, 185, 201–2, 227–28, 239*n41*, 254–55*nn54–55*, 263*n81*, 270*nn24, 28*
poetic tradition, 5, 7, 27, 30, 33, 38, 42–43, 80, 84, 124, 185, 202, 207, 209, 227, 235*n14*, 237*n25*, 245*n50*, 250*n13*, 255*n58*. *See also* brotherhood of poets
posthumous existence, 95, 148–76, 223–24, 228, 264*n102*
problematic subjectivity, 9, 14–15, 18–19, 21, 23, 28–30, 32–33, 71, 76, 81, 82, 84–85, 88–89, 92–93, 107, 124, 145, 150–51, 154, 162, 166, 172, 175, 185, 194–95, 205–6, 209, 216, 218, 236*n22*, 239*n41*, 271*n29*. *See also* otherness, problem of

Psyche and Eros: myth of, 29, 91–128, 135, 149, 150, 183, 184, 191, 226–27, 229, 248*nn1–2*, 249*nn5, 9–10*, 251*n24*, 253*nn43–44*, 258*nn10–11*, 270*n26*; central teachings of, 95; retelling of, 93–94
Pushkin, Aleksandr, 42–43, 45, 53, 55, 67–68, 101, 161, 178–79, 183–85, 209–12, 225, 237*n28*, 240*n9*, 241*nn13, 19*, 245*n52*, 254*n54*, 255*n58*, 261*n59*, 267*nn5, 7*, 268–69*n17*, 269*nn18–20, 22*, 270*n28*, 273*n48*
—works of: "Autumn (A Fragment)" ["Osen' (Otryvok)"], 260*n25*; "The Bronze Horseman" ["Mednyi vsadnik"], 244*n42*; "Echo" ["Ekho"], 161; *Feast during a Plague* [*Pir vo vremia chumy*], 209; "The Gypsies" ["Tsygany"], 240*n9*, 241*n19*; "I erected a monument" ["Ia pamiatnik sebe vozdvig nerukotvornyi . . ."], 67–68; "I outlived my desires" ["Ia perezhil svoi zhelan'ia . . ."], 275*n66*; "I remember a miraculous moment" ["Ia pomniu chudnoe mgnoven'e . . ."], 247*n75*; *Mozart and Salieri* [*Motsart i Sal'eri*], 211; "The Poet" ["Poet"], 273*n48*; "The Prophet" ["Prorok"], 252*n35*; *The Stone Guest* [*Kamennyi gost'*], 265*n107*; "To the Sea" ["K moriu"], 264*n93*; "What is in my name for you?" ["Chto v imeni tebe moem? . . ."], 42–44, 241*n13*

reciprocity in love, 29, 38, 44–45, 49, 50, 54–56, 76, 81, 84, 87–88, 93–95, 120, 141, 148–49, 167–70, 180, 181, 186, 196–97, 200, 219, 221–22, 229, 251*n23*, 270*n29*. *See also* ideal love
Remizov, Aleksei, 33
renunciation of desire, xii, 29, 43, 45, 51, 71, 74, 91, 92, 98–99, 101–6, 109, 112, 114, 120, 124–27, 130, 132, 135, 136, 147, 148, 154, 175, 180, 190–91, 207, 229, 242*n30*, 250*n15*, 251*n27*. *See also* sublimation of physical urges
responsibility, claiming of, 7, 17, 31, 47–48, 80, 83–84, 89, 209–25, 250*n18*, 273*n47*, 274*n55*. *See also* agency, ambiguity of; freedom and constraint
rhyme, 82, 156–59, 162, 166, 170, 171, 183, 199
Rilke, Rainer Maria, 29–30, 129–76, 180–83, 187–89, 191, 197, 198, 205, 208–9, 227, 228, 251*n27*, 254*n47*, 256*nn63, 1*, 257*nn2–3, 5*,

Rilke, Rainer Maria (*continued*)
258*nn8, 10, 13,* 259*n23,* 260*nn25, 27, 31, 43, 46, 49,* 261*nn50, 54, 59, 69,* 262*nn72–74, 76–77,* 263*nn78–83,* 264*nn91–93, 98–99, 102,* 265*nn103–4, 107–11,* 268*n15,* 269*n22,* 270*n24,* 271*n32*
— works of: "Autumn" ["Herbst"], 260*n25;* *Duino Elegies,* 129, 130, 262*n72;* "Elegie an Marina Zwetajewa-Efron," 131, 136, 153–55, 157, 174, 257*n2,* 258*n8,* 262*nn73–74;* epitaph, 258*n8; Sonnets to Orpheus,* 257*n5,* 262*n72; Vergers,* 263*n83*
risk-taking, 24, 32–34, 36, 42, 47, 49, 71, 79, 81, 101, 104, 137, 204–6, 209, 217
Rodzevich, Konstantin, 31, 130, 205, 237*n28,* 257*n7,* 273*n45*
Rohde, Erwin, 248*n1*
Roskina, Natalia, 243*n37*

Sandler, Stephanie, 234*n10,* 264*n93*
Sappho, 236*n25*
Schnabel, Artur, 131
Schweitzer, Viktoria, 59, 234*n9,* 239*n6,* 243*n35,* 270*n24,* 272*n38,* 273*n45*
selfhood. *See* problematic subjectivity
seven, the number, 36, 167, 174, 176, 182, 223, 257*n2,* 261*n55,* 262*n69,* 265*n104*
sex and sexuality, 5, 27, 29, 32, 41, 43, 55, 65, 71, 78, 92–93, 95, 98, 107–10, 119, 123, 125, 138, 154–55, 162, 171–72, 180, 183, 184, 193, 202, 203, 205–7, 229, 235*n12,* 241*n12,* 249*n9,* 252*n39,* 262*n76,* 267*n10,* 273*nn45, 48;* dissolution of sexuality, 84–87, 97, 113, 115, 124, 137, 152, 162, 172, 182, 187, 221, 247*n74*
Shteiger, Anatolii, 30, 181–86, 190–201, 202, 215, 247*n70,* 268*nn11–12, 14,* 270*nn27, 29*
sisterhood, 96–97, 109, 112, 115, 134, 243*n37,* 250*n16,* 254*n51. See also* brotherhood of poets
Sloane, David, 42, 49, 242*n26*
Smith, Alexandra, 266*n114*
Smith, M. S., 267*n9*
Solov'ev, Vladimir, 33
sound play, 26, 39–40, 58, 62–63, 66, 85–86, 87, 106, 114, 151, 156, 160, 164–65, 194, 196, 201, 245*n51,* 250–51*n22*
Struve, Gleb, 237*n31*
sublimation of physical urges, 23, 27, 39, 41–42, 47, 77, 119, 124, 172, 198, 241*n10,* 262*n76. See also* renunciation of desire
suicide, 7–8, 19, 94, 114, 120, 124, 166, 169, 177–79, 203, 207, 209, 218, 222–25, 228, 234*n9,* 247*n74,* 250*n13,* 252*n38,* 267*n4,* 271*n37. See also* Tsvetaeva, Marina: significance of biography
Suvorov, Aleksandr, 25–26
syncopated rhythms, 23, 26, 167, 169, 173, 237*n27*

Tager, Evgenii, 224, 276*n67*
Tarkovskii, Arsenii, 223
Taubman, Jane, 234*n9,* 239*n6*
Tavis, Anna, 258*nn8, 13,* 262*n74*
Tesková, Anna, 258*n8,* 265*n110,* 276*n68*
theatrical play, 30, 32–34, 36–38, 47–48, 69–70, 165–66, 180, 204–5, 217, 226, 238–39*n38,* 264*n98,* 274*n52*
Thomas (Apostle), 144–45, 253*n45*
Thomson, R. D. B., 242*n23*
transcendence and transgression, 5, 15–18, 22–24, 30, 32–34, 39, 41, 43, 49–51, 61, 74, 76–78, 83–85, 92, 94–96, 113, 121–22, 124, 132, 138, 149, 164, 171–76, 180, 187–88, 194, 197, 202, 212–25, 233*nn3, 5,* 235*n14,* 241*n15,* 247*n74,* 252*n35,* 263*n81,* 274*n57. See also* ethics vs. aesthetics
tree imagery, 53–54, 112–13, 125, 151–52, 155, 255*n60,* 262*n70,* 265*n103,* 271*n33*
Tsvetaeva, Anastasiia, 225, 275*n60*
Tsvetaeva, Marina: and Acmeism, 150, 174, 266*n114;* adolescence, 9, 15, 18–19, 43, 115, 130; and Akhmatova (biographical context), 37–38, 56–58, 72, 243*n35;* and Blok (biographical context), 35–39, 72; and Classicism, xii, 25, 272*n39;* critical responses to, 5–6, 32, 79, 131, 135, 141, 200–201, 210, 213, 234*nn9–10,* 256*n61;* earthly love affairs, 8, 31, 79, 84, 92, 112, 121, 126, 214, 221; and Gronskii (biographical context), 181–82, 267*n10;* and Pasternak (biographical context), 92, 133–35, 259*n20;* and Pasternak (correspondence), 99–102, 104, 111–13, 205, 248–49*n3;* and Rilke (biographical context), 129–32; and Rilke (correspondence), 131, 132–43, 173, 205, 248*n78,* 257*n2,* 258*n13,* 260*n49;* and Romanticism, xii, 4, 18–20, 26, 31, 38,

Index

45, 91, 98, 127, 186, 188, 233*n1*, 235*n12*, 241*n21*, 254*n48;* and Shteiger (biographical context), 181–82; and Shteiger (correspondence), 181, 186, 190–93, 196, 197, 268*nn12, 14;* significance of biography, 6, 8, 79; and Symbolism, 12, 31, 33, 41, 83–84, 188, 233*n2*, 235*n17*, 241*nn12, 21*, 244*n42*, 253*n42*, 269–70*n23;* work ethic, xii, 178, 197, 206, 247*n76*, 271–72*n37*, 273*n47*
—works of: *After Russia* [*Posle Rossii*], 91, 92, 121, 126, 149, 159, 194, 203, 248*n3*, 254*n51*, 256*nn62, 64*, 267*n8*, 272*n44;* "The age thought not about the poet" ["O poete ne podumal..."], 222; "Alive and not dead" ["Zhiv, a ne umer..."], 203–6; "Art in the Light of Conscience" ["Iskusstvo pri svete sovesti"], 101, 165, 177–78, 193, 203, 205–12, 214, 223, 253*n47*, 272*n41;* "Attempt at a Room" ["Popytka komnaty"], 128, 132, 143–47, 150, 155, 158, 160, 167–68, 173, 198, 227, 248*n3*, 251*n23*, 261*n59*, 265*n108;* "Beneath My Shawl" ["Pod shal'iu"], 219; *The Blizzard* [*Metel'*], 239*n39;* "Boring Games" ["Skuchnye igry"], 81; "A Bow" ["Naklon"], 197; "Brother" ["Brat"], 254*n51;* "The Bus" ["Avtobus"], 13; "A Bush" ["Kust"], 220, 254*n52;* "A Captive Spirit" ["Plennyi dukh"], 44–45, 53, 54; "Conversation with a Genius" ["Razgovor s geniem"], 272*n42; Craft* [*Remeslo*], 264*n97;* "Dagger" ["Klinok"], 247*n74;* "Dawn on the Rails" ["Rassvet na rel'sakh"], 100; "Desk" ["Stol"], 220–22, 261*n57;* "The Devil" ["Chert"], 226; "Dis—tance: versts, miles" ["Ras—stoianie: versty, mili..."], 256*n64;* "A Downpour of Light: Poetry of Eternal Masculinity" ["Svetovoi liven': Poeziia vechnoi muzhestvennosti"], 96, 248*n3;* "The Drum" ["Baraban"], 9, 22–27, 28, 38, 55, 272*n42;* "An Earthly Name" ["Zemnoe imia"], 241*n10;* "The Emigrant" ["Emigrant"], 112, 255*n56;* "Epic and Lyric of Modern Russia" ["Epos i lirika sovremennoi Rossii"], 248*n3*, 266*n1;* "Epitaph" ["Nadgrobie"], 181, 185–90, 201, 227, 247*n70*, 268*n13*, 269–70*nn22–23*, 270*nn24–25;* "Eurydice to Orpheus" ["Evridika—Orfeiu"], 117; *Evening Album* [*Vechernii al'bom*], 9; "From the Sea" ["S moria"], 248*n3*, 251*n23*, 264*n91;* "The Garden" ["Sad"], 222; "The gold of my hair" ["Zoloto moikh volos..."], 267*n8;* "Good News" ["Blagaia vest'"], 215; "Graying temples" [V sedinu—visok..."], 256*n64*, 273*n44;* "Gypsy passion for parting" ["Tsyganskaia strast' razluki..."], xi—xii; "Hands—and into the circle" ["Ruki—i v krug..."], 192–93; "A History of One Dedication" ["Istoriia odnogo posviashcheniia"], 88, 243*n31;* "House" ["Dom"], 270*n28;* "The House at Old Pimen" ["Dom u starogo Pimena"], 44–46; "I—am a rebel in brow and womb" ["Ia—miatezhnitsa lbom i chrevom..."], 247*n70;* "I don't embarrass, I don't sing" ["Ne smushchaiu, ne poiu..."], 274*n56;* "Insanity—and wisdom" ["Bezum'e—i blagorazum'e..."], 206; "In the Luxembourg Garden" ["V Liuksemburgskom sadu"], 9, 10–13, 14, 16, 21, 22, 24, 125, 228, 235*n17*, 261*n58*, 269–70*n23;* "Into the Lips of a Youth" ["Iunoshe v usta"], 182–85; "I sit without light, and without bread" ["Sizhu bez sveta, i bez khleba..."], 215; "Isolation: exit" [Uedinenie: uidi..."], 222; "It's time to take off the amber" ["Pora snimat' iantar'..."], 223; "I wander" ["Brozhu—ne dom zhe plotnichat'..."], 128; "Life lies inimitably" ["Nepodrazhaemo lzhet zhizn'..."], 97–99; "The Lute" ["Liutnia"], 251*n30; The Magic Lantern* [*Volshebnyi fonar'*], 9; *Milestones* [*Versty*], 25, 37, 240*n8*, 244*n38;* "More capacious than an organ" ["Emche organa i zvonche bubna..."], 253*n46;* "Mother and Music" ["Mat' i muzyka"], 83, 234–35*n12*, 237*n27*, 241*n17*, 261*n57*, 273*n47*, 274*n57;* "My Answer to Osip Mandel'shtam" ["Moi otvet Osipu Mandel'shtamu"], 271*n31;* "My Pushkin" ["Moi Pushkin"], 44–46, 53, 72–73, 81, 82, 83, 178, 183–84, 237*n29*, 238*n33*, 245*n52*, 264*n93*, 269*n22*, 271*n30;* "The Naiad" ["Naiada"], 272*n42;* "Natal'ia Goncharova", 242*n21*, 269*n19;* "New Year's Letter" ["Novogodnee"], 132, 147–72, 174, 181, 187–88, 198, 207, 208, 223, 227, 235*n19*, 254*n47*, 261*nn63*,

Tsvetaeva, Marina (*continued*)
68, 262*nn*69, 77, 263*nn*78, 80, 264*nn*89, 98, 265*nn*102-3, 108-9, 270*n*24; "Nights without my beloved" ["Nochi bez liubimogo—i nochi s neliubimym . . ."], 253*n*41; "No need to call her back" ["Ne nado ee oklikat'"], 103-6; "Omens" ["Primety"], 254*n*51; "On a Red Steed" ["Na krasnom kone"], 29, 30, 37-38, 71-89, 90, 94, 110, 113, 114, 117, 137, 148, 152, 168, 171, 201-3, 214, 243*n*31, 246*nn*57, 63-65, 247*n*78, 249*n*10, 250*n*15, 266*nn*115, 1—as rape fantasy, 83-85, 89—revision of, 82-83; "Only a Girl" ["Tol'ko devochka"], 9, 13-17, 21, 22, 52, 56, 81, 98, 263*n*81; "An Otherworldly Evening" ["Nezdeshnii vecher"], 56, 243*n*36; "The Pedal" ["Pedal'"], 149, 255*n*57; "Perekop," 267*n*9; "Phaedra" ["Fedra"], 108-11, 114, 123, 182-83, 252*n*37; "Placing my hand on my heart" ["Ruku na serdtse polozha . . ."], 235*n*18; "Poem of a Mountain" ["Poema gory"], 31, 79; "Poem of a Staircase" ["Poema lestnitsy"], 243*n*31; "Poem of the Air" ["Poema vozdukha"], 132, 166-76, 188, 208, 223, 227, 243*n*37, 255*nn*105, 107-8, 266*nn*113-14; "Poem of the End" ["Poema kontsa"], 31, 82, 128, 228, 244*n*44, 251*n*22, 252*n*34, 257*n*7; "Poems to Akhmatova" ["Stikhi k Akhmatovoi"], 37-38, 56-73, 90, 130, 202, 239*n*6, 244*nn*38, 46-47—renaming of cycle, 73; "Poems to an Orphan" ["Stikhi sirote"], 181, 185-86, 192-201, 214, 227, 247*n*70, 268*n*13, 271*n*32; "Poems to Blok" ["Stikhi k Bloku"], 36-56, 57, 58, 59, 66-67, 69-71, 90, 195, 202, 240*n*8, 241*n*12, 242*nn*22, 26-27, 243*n*34, 244*nn*46-47, 263*n*81—renaming of cycle, 73; *Poems to Blok* [*Stikhi k Bloku*], 165; "Poems to My Son" ["Stikhi k synu"], 219; "Poems to Pushkin" ["Stikhi k Pushkinu"], 178; "The Poet about the Critic" ["Poet o kritike"], 247*n*67, 265*n*109, 272*n*43; "The Poet and Time" ["Poet i vremia"], 173, 252-53*n*40; "Poet-Mountaineer" ["Poet-al'pinist"], 237*n*31, 268*n*14; "Poets" ["Poety"], 260*n*46; "Poets with a History and Poets without a History" ["Poety s istoriei i poety bez istorii"], 50, 243*n*34, 248*n*3, 254*n*54, 258*n*12; "A Prayer" ["Molitva"], 9, 17-20, 21, 22, 165, 252*n*38; "Psyche" ["Psikheia"], 184; *Psyche* [*Psikheia*], 37, 73, 90-91, 218, 248*n*1, 258*n*10; "The Ratcatcher" ["Krysolov"], 251*n*27; "Roland's Horn" ["Rolandov rog"], 236*n*24; "A Savage Will" ["Dikaia volia"], 9, 20-21, 22, 24, 32, 76, 107; "Scythians" ["Skifskie"], 163, 253*n*43, 255*n*56; "Seven, seven" ["Semero, semero . . ."], 227, 261*n*55; "The Sibyl" ["Sivilla"], 267*n*8; "Sister" ["Sestra"], 254*n*51; "Son" ["Syn"], 218-19; "The Soul" ["Dusha"], 106-8, 123; "The sunset flamed" ["Zaria pylala, dogoraia . . ."], 250*n*13; "The Swain" ["Molodets"], 238*n*35, 239*n*39, 248*n*2, 250*n*15; *Swans' Encampment* [*Lebedinyi stan*], 37; "That was my life singing—howling" ["Eto zhizn' moia propela—provyla . . ."], 222; "There are lucky men and women" ["Est' schastlivtsy i schastlivitsy . . ."], 227; "These are the ashes of treasures" ["Eto peply sokrovishch . . ."], 267*n*8; "Thus they listen" ["Tak vslushivaiutsia . . ."], 255*n*55; "To Alia" ["Ale"], 216-18; "To Maiakovskii" ["Maiakovskomu"], 178, 267*n*3, 271*n*32; "To You—One Hundred Years Later" ["Tebe—cherez sto let"], 53, 100; "Trees" ["Derev'ia"], 255*n*60, 269*n*21, 271*n*33; "The Tsar-Maiden" ["Tsar'-devitsa"], 182; "The Two" ["Dvoe"], 250*n*16; "Two hands resting lightly" ["Dve ruki, legko opushchennye . . ."], 215-16, 218, 274*n*55; "Two trees want" ["Dva dereva khotiat drug k drugu . . ."], 53-54; "Whatever others don't need" ["Chto drugim ne nuzhno—nesite mne . . ."], 242*n*31; "When I gaze at the drifting leaves" ["Kogda ia gliazhu na letiashchie list'ia . . ."], 222; "Whoever has built no home" [Kto doma ne stroil . . ."], 214; "Wires" ["Provoda"], 29, 113-28, 148, 152, 227, 250*n*16, 253*n*44, 255*n*57, 256*n*62, 264*n*100; "Words and Meanings" ["Slova i smysly"], 119; "You—are stone, but I sing" ["Ty—kamennyi, a ia poiu . . ."], 245*n*53; "Your Death" ["Tvoia smert'"], 158, 263*n*78, 264*n*99

Turgeneva, Asia, 44-45

Vinogradov, Viktor, 245*n*48
Vishniak, Abram, 121, 248*n*3

Index

Vitins, Ieva, 248*n1*
Voloshin, Maksimilian, 205, 228, 237*n28*, 252*n39*, 254*n52*

wanderlust, 55, 60–61, 65, 119, 244*n44*
Weeks, Laura, 272*n44*
wings, motif of, 65, 66, 75, 86, 92, 94, 98, 106–7, 113, 130, 150, 176, 242*n22*, 252*n35*, 266*n115*. *See also* flight as metaphor for poetry
Wunderly-Volkart, Nanny, 257*n2*

Zaslavsky, Olga, 253*n44*
zhiznetvorchestvo, 33
Zholkovsky, Alexander, 59, 60, 244*n41*
Zviagintseva, Vera, 252*n39*